Gabriella Lojacono, Laura Ru Yun Pan
Resilience of Luxury Companies in Times of Change

Gabriella Lojacono, Laura Ru Yun Pan

Resilience of Luxury Companies in Times of Change

—

DE GRUYTER

ISBN (Paperback) 978-3-11-072323-6
ISBN (Hardcover) 978-3-11-076071-2
e-ISBN (PDF) 978-3-11-072351-9
e-ISBN (EPUB) 978-3-11-072354-0

Library of Congress Control Number: 2021936709

Bibliographic information published by the Deutsche Nationalbibliothek
The Deutsche Nationalbibliothek lists this publication in the Deutsche Nationalbibliografie;
detailed bibliographic data are available on the internet at http://dnb.dnb.de.

© 2021 Walter de Gruyter GmbH, Berlin/Boston
Cover image: Jezperklauzen/iStock/Getty Images Plus
Typesetting: Integra Software Services Pvt. Ltd.
Printing and binding: CPI books GmbH, Leck

www.degruyter.com

Foreword

As I write these lines, the world is still in the middle of a pandemic creating a major economic crisis. In the world emerging from this tragedy, luxury will have gone through a substantial transformation, being both the same and different. In this book, Gabriella Lojacono and Laura Pan are brightly analyzing the new luxury world taking shape in front of us. In this foreword I will share my own observations and views on this process, its fundamentals and new trends.

Luxury has existed for a long time and has overcome many types of crises, whether economic or health related, whether wars or the impact of ideologies. This one is not the first nor the last. The modern luxury sector began its expansion journey in the 1970s. Its fundamentals have not changed since. The key asset of any maison is its brand equity. Brand equity relies on heritage, *savoir-faire*, and high-quality products or services matching customers' aspirations and desires. Not what they need but what they like and dream of. Rarity and exclusivity are part of the equation. When too visible, overdistributed, and too accessible, brands lose their appeal. Exclusivity is an essential part of luxury, even if this notion has structurally changed in recent years. For these reasons, building a luxury brand from scratch is very difficult, as legitimacy increases over time. This being said, luxury is not limited to what we commonly call "the luxury sector". Every sector, from food to yachts, has a luxury sub-segment. In fast-moving sectors like technology, it is possible to create a high-tech luxury brand in a short timeframe. Apple is the most visible example, having evolved from pure tech to luxury tech.

This crisis is not the first one we have encountered, but it is probably the most severe of our generation. The way it unfolds itself, its speed, and the disruption it creates are truly unprecedented. This is what Nassim Taleb has called a "black swan". With the global interconnection of the world, black swans are likely to happen more frequently than before. We know that they will happen one day. We cannot know when, nor how they will appear.

In order to overcome future crises, luxury brands must go beyond resilience and develop their antifragility, as Taleb has brilliantly written. Many elements contribute to antifragility, depending on each sector. One key component applies to all luxury, which I call "the green zone". On a two-dimension mapping, the vertical axis goes from necessity, to comfort, aspiration, and up to transcendence. The second axis goes from alienation, to seriousness, playfulness, and decadence. The green zone starts above comfort and goes up to transcendence on the one hand, and lies between the two borders of seriousness and playfulness, on the other hand. The maisons that succeed in growing their reach and sales while expanding their green zone are the most antifragile over time.

When the center of gravity is too much on the playful side, brands can be perceived negatively in times of crisis (decadent or indecent). At the other extreme, and in periods of euphoria, too-serious brands become boring or dusty, not appealing

https://doi.org/10.1515/9783110723519-202

anymore. During crises, luxury is often criticized for what it represents, and judged on moral grounds. In such periods, luxury must be more discrete and reserved, more reassuring than playful. However, moving the center of gravity towards the quadrant necessity/seriousness (functional and value for money) is a fatal mistake. Brands in this quadrant lose their appeal and aspiration. By nature, luxury is desired, but not useful. Luxury starts where necessity stops.

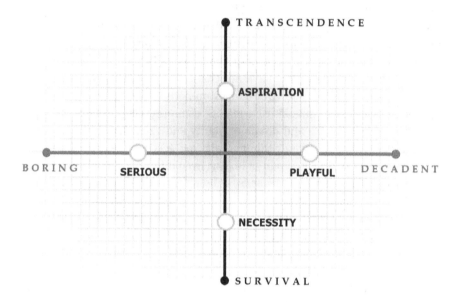

This crisis acts as a sharp revelator in many ways. It first reveals the maisons that are antifragile and manage to benefit from the crisis, or are resilient and resist the crisis, and, on the contrary, those that are fragile and weak, even if this was not visible before.

The most resilient brands all have a solid brand identity, clear and distinctive. As luxury brands cover a broad mental territory, their identity goes beyond one single product category, which is an important distinction with fast-moving consumer goods, where the link between brand and product is very tight (like Coca Cola or Nike). The larger the luxury brand territory, the more it becomes a "maison" with many rooms, and the more legitimate it is to expand its offer, even from products to hotels.

A maison's identity is forged by the vision of its founder and its country of origin. Swiss watchmakers, Italian fashion, and French luxury in general have a collective "national identity". The maison-specific style, gender, and relation to the world evolves over time, but must remain distinctive, allowing customers to distinguish a Cartier watch from a Rolex, a Hermès bag from a Dior, across the table and across the world. These resilient brands have balanced clienteles across the globe. They also have a solid human capital, staying active and creative, able to invent new ways to collaborate with each other in order to best serve their clients and connect with them.

Conversely, brands that were overdependent on Chinese travelers, relying on price differentials, are hit hard. In addition, the brands which were dependent on novelties and creating surprises also struggle. This crisis shows that distinctive, lasting beauty matters more than newness.

Creativity and creation are different things. It requires high creativity to reinterpret an iconic design while respecting it. On the contrary, a new creation can be "déjà vu", or banal, lacking creativity. Innovation is also critical, when it brings value to clients or operations. It should not be marketed for itself, for the same reasons. A new object can only be a gadget. It can bring new functions, but can also be less convenient than its predecessors. We should always bear in mind that the oldest cherry trees produce the most beautiful blossoms.

Soft luxury (fashion and accessories in particular) had recently outpaced hard luxury in the growth race; fast-fashion luxury was the growth champion of the past five years.

As the crisis has slowed time and has restricted social gatherings, fast fashion has slowed the most, and jewelry has shown higher resilience. Its desirability has remained strong despite the pandemic, and as a result sales and financial results have been positive. When you cannot travel, you need more tangible objects to express your feelings and bonds. Being anchored in long time, jewelry can bear slowness better than seasonal fashion, which evolves in quick time, becoming quickly outdated. Regarding fashion, this crisis will probably put an end to the acceleration of the number of yearly collections, encouraging more durability than fast changes. General sustainability concerns will reinforce this global trend.

Covid-19 has accelerated the transformation of distribution networks. In particular, e-commerce has experienced a phenomenal acceleration and has become a key network for the whole sector, rapidly cracking the price-point limits that were limiting its development. With the confinement, customers have gotten used to searching for information and buying online very expensive products they once only considered purchasing in a physical store.

On the other hand, travel retail, in airports or in-town, has been severely hit by the restrictions on international travel. As these restrictions impact the entire ecosystem, including airline companies, airports, hotels, and travel agencies, it will take time to resume growth. With the addition of environmental concerns, the future trajectory of this model might be very different from the previous plans. Meanwhile, with the new key role of digital, a new retail is rapidly taking shape, where customers' journeys use multiple touchpoints, forcing brands to reinvent their data management, CRM, and logistic systems.

The luxury sector was reinvented in the 1970s and has been growing rapidly since, to become a major economic sector. During this process, brands' CEOs learned that they must avoid low-hanging fruits, which can bring short-term revenues but destroy brand equity. Image control is a fundamental element. Uncontrolled licensing has destroyed several brands. Uncontrolled distribution has brought similar results, when parallel markets transship products to unauthorized networks, with low quality and discounted prices. In the end, the brand equity is diluted, and the brand appeal shrinks.

Exclusivity remains a fundamental pillar, but new factors must be considered. The common thought is that any overexposed brand would inevitably become banal, thus less desired. Desire is seen as coming from scarcity, and self-esteem from differentiation from others. But this principle has been overridden by a handful of maisons, which have broken this glass ceiling. They have reached stardom. Like in cinema, star products are a category of their own. The more they sell, the more popular they become.

What the common thinking missed, was that the luxury sector has fully embraced the star system, allowing itself to go beyond its initial limits. The sector is now embracing the social media world, which is another star system run by algorithms and star KOLs. This new star system allows star brands to reach new levels at a low marginal extra cost, becoming their own media. Indeed, the star system is so powerful that it allows an A-list celebrity to successfully launch his or her own brand, even with no legitimacy in design or even business. Star brands can also start any new product category, including high jewelry, without needing to justify their savoir-faire.

What, therefore, can we expect for the future?

With global economic growth and millions of people becoming potential customers, and thanks to the power of the star system, the future of luxury is bright. Two important trends must, however, not be overlooked. The concern about the climate implies a review of all our life habits, including consumption. Luxury must adapt to this new obligation. De-consumption and frugality will be the key words of this decade. Some think that luxury will disappear, as we will first stop consuming what we do not need, to focus on bare necessity. My view is the opposite: We mostly need to consume less of what is necessary today: water, oil, food, electricity, cars, and smartphones. If all human beings were eating the way the Japanese do, there would be no food shortage. In Tokyo, where public transport, bicycles, and local deliveries are very efficient, only 5% of people use a car, vs. 20% in Beijing or Paris. As a consequence, the air quality is much better in Tokyo than in Paris, even if greater Tokyo is three times bigger than Paris. Luxury, like art, is not in danger if we can rediscover the virtue of slowness and frugal luxury. Hard luxury consumes very little resources, is durable, repairable, reusable, and transmittable. It brings joy and happiness. We need it more than ever.

The second key trend is the growing responsibility towards the community. Especially for star brands that bear the responsibility of using their light for the benefit of the larger world. For the past 35 years, the Fondation Cartier pour l'art contemporain has been celebrating talent and the originality of creation, exploring links between art and science, independently from the art market or box office. It plays a key role on the art scene, giving visibility to talented though unknown artists (some becoming stars afterwards), and offering a window into the sensible world.

In the digitally connected world, reputation is the key currency. If insufficiently committed and generous, some maisons might get short of it. And realize that, as the Ancient Romans said, "The Tarpeian rock is close to the Capitol".

Cyrille Vigneron, President and CEO, Cartier

Introduction

The idea for this book has been around for a long time. Both Bocconi University and its School of Management have invested in the world of luxury for many years, creating a series of ad hoc education and research initiatives. Across Executive Education, MBA and Master of Science levels, we have always struggled to find a reference text that included the topics we wanted to discuss with our audience. Many books, for example, adopt a marketing-oriented perspective and focus on brand management issues that are just a piece of the puzzle and the result of many other critical processes. Thus, the first stimulus that led us to embark on this adventure was the need for a valid teaching support. A second stimulus was undoubtedly years of experience in research on the dynamics of the world of luxury built on rich relationships with its main players, in the most varied industries. These key players are not only conglomerates, but also small companies that embody the concept of *savoir-faire*. We wanted to capitalize on and "cement" this wealth of information and reflections.

Everything we report in this book is primarily the result of first-hand data, whether interviews conducted in person with senior managers and CEOs or presentations made in our classrooms to students. A source of undoubted value was the participation of the Gucci Research Lab at Bocconi University, which allowed us to personally follow a turnaround guided by authentic corporate values. The partnerships we developed with Cartier and Dorchester, which has allowed us a privileged view of the jewelry and watchmaking, and hospitality industries, further enriched our understanding, as did our collaboration with Ferrari, which led to the drafting of a case study on the concept of exclusivity.

The educational context we experience every day offers endless opportunities to improve our contribution: not only are our students a very demanding audience in terms of expectations, the pace at which luxury industries move forces us to always stay a step ahead. These pressures inspire us to always be on top of the latest developments and to develop ideas generated by the discussions we have in class. Furthermore, it is obvious that we cannot ignore the increased accessibility of both academic and non-academic publications. Specialized magazines such as *Vogue Business*, *WWD*, and *Business of Fashion* represent an important information base. We also had the pleasure of having two primary consultancy firms, Bain and BCG, on board as our partners, offering valuable opportunities for consultation.

We decided to write this book in 2020 because of the delicate historical moment that our society was experiencing. A moment that shook consciences and led various researchers on deep dives into the social phenomena that shape our world, questioning whether the contents and methods of their work were adequate to meet the challenges we're all facing. Those in our field have a great responsibility, as we "shape" people's minds and establish a foundation for their

https://doi.org/10.1515/9783110723519-203

future endeavors. If the world changes, education must also change. This prompted us to ask ourselves: "What is happening in the world of luxury and what are the key messages we want to convey and discuss in our classrooms"? We are certain that the reflections we have proposed in this text will also be of interest to entrepreneurs and managers who often look to academics for guidance: They will either find confirmation or further food for thought, and we can certainly give structure to their reflections. What we offer in this book is not "the" explanation of logics and trends in luxury; it is "our" vision of what the changing times in the world of luxury connote. We therefore do not claim to present a universal model, but to present a perspective rooted in our personal experience and the support of industry leaders.

The term "resilience" has been used excessively in recent months, often in speech and in publications to describe the capabilities of companies surviving the pandemic. The title of this book was somewhat serendipitous, as it was in the midst of writing a case study on its resilience that sprung the idea in both the writer's heads. Furthermore, at Bocconi University, the faculty of strategy and innovation has conducted extensive research into different tools and methods to measurement a company's resilience for the past 15 years. The research conducted so far has examined performance volatility and net profitability in the same indicator, over an extended period of time.

When it came to putting our ideas to paper, we wanted to review the very concept of resilience in the world of luxury, and to focus more on the determinants of the term than on its measurement. In this book, we refer to the classic measures of economic and competitive performance, and at the same time also emphasize something essential for the world of luxury, which is the ability of these companies, regardless of the context situation, to regulate and increase the intangible value of the brand. Because of this, these companies strive to remain consistent in all aspects, such as in the launch of products, in communication, in retail, and also in the management of human capital. The first thing Marco Bizzarri did when he was appointed CEO of Gucci was to leverage the quality of the people and their alignment with corporate values to reposition the brand in the market.

All the themes mentioned in this introduction will be reinforced in each of the chapters of this book, drawing examples from luxury companies across various industries, such as furniture and design, automotive, fashion and accessories, jewelry and watches, cosmetics, and more. Resilience in companies can be described by the Japanese philosophy of *kintsugi*:

> Literally meaning rejoin (tsugi) with gold (kin). The breaking of an object does not represent its end: the kintsugi, as technique and philosophy, encourages [us] to reassemble and transform it, giving it a new aspect in which the scars are not hidden but enhanced by the gold

dust. It teaches resilience, the ability to accept and embrace bad times, overcoming them through transformation and creating a new balance, a new beauty.[1]
(Annabelle Diez, Head of Client Services and CRM, Cartier South East Europe, personal communication)

Just as broken ceramics are given a new life through *kintsugi* that is more precious than their previous life, resilient companies have the ability to endure hardship and reemerge stronger than before. They have the ability to learn from past lessons and equip themselves with appropriate contingency plans to avoid repeating past mistakes.

To fully explore true resilience in times of change, we have linked this concept with the agility and ambidexterity of luxury companies. For us, all three concepts must work hand in hand. After all, rigid companies are less likely to adapt to change, and companies that are ambisinistrous are unable to juggle in times of chaos. When we speak about ambidexterity, we follow the definition coined by O'Reiley and Tushman (2004) in describing an ambidextrous organization. In the context of luxury organizations, it means preserving the past and continuing to seek opportunities to explore and new markets to conquer. Valentino is famous today because it had the courage not to remain anchored in haute couture, the legacy of its founder and its heritage to defend, but to shift focus to the world of accessories and retail expansion. Likewise, Chanel, a company that has continually reinvented itself, has moved from fragrances, apparel and accessories, and cosmetics and beauty into high jewelry and watches. Despite its constant growth as an organization, its core products, such as Chanel No.5 perfume and the Chanel Classic Flap Bag, remain the maison's most popular. This agility led us to compare luxury companies to camels Westreich (2020): They are "able to survive business downturns, changing economic conditions, and remain resilient. [. . .] If the company's a camel, with the ability to conserve losses, preserve revenue, and out-last a [financial] drought, they'll be more appealing in economic downturns".

The growth luxury companies have experienced in the past decades has led to them to seek solutions based on compromise, not to limit the extremes, but to find an optimal balance with respect to the company's skills and the expectations of its target. Distribution strategies, where today we can no longer speak of single channel, nor of double channel, nor of multichannel, offer an illustrative example. The only way to thrive is omnichannel, which carries over into communication and CRM. A second example concerns the geographic spread of assets. It is wrong to think only of China as a market for growth, as we did in the past with Europe or North America. Rather, it is crucial to be mindful of the spread of consumers globally, and we must address them all with equal attention. To put this into context, we use the concept of *triad power*, which describes a company that excels in the three regions equally, or that generates equal revenue in three major regions (e.g., Japan – or rather Asia – Europe, and the United States).

Our journey to understanding the conditions of resilience in the world of luxury is structured in eight chapters. The *first chapter* focuses on the fundamentals of luxury. We open with a discussion of some topical issues such as ownership structures, acquisition strategies, and the balance of power between creative people, managers, and shareholders. Our intent is to immediately lead the reader to understand the logic of luxury businesses and to acquire familiarity with how they are structured, using concrete examples. In this chapter, directions and methods of growth are also explained. The chapter closes with an overview of distribution models, introducing the difference between wholesale and retail, offline and online.

The *second chapter* deals with the seven paradoxes of luxury: How to balance sales growth and marginality? How to preserve and nurture historic, iconic products while also giving space to the new? How to combine exclusivity and inclusivity? How to govern marketing pressures and rarity? How to properly allocate resources between online and offline? How to be extraordinary in a context of excellence? How to expand globally and keep the global consistency?

Chapter 3 focuses on the historical beginnings of the today's largest luxury markets. Each of these dominant markets – Europe, the United States, Japan, and China – has its own origin story of how luxury was disseminated and what role history played in developing the luxury market. In Europe, we begin with the Persian Empire's influence on ancient Greece. In the United States, we show how Hollywood and its influence helped create a new luxury consumer. In Japan, we examine the democratization of luxury and the role department stores played in changing the context of luxury across Asia. And finally, China, the sleeping dragon, its cities some of the world's richest before it's social revolution, propelled by technology to become one of the largest luxury markets in the world as it reopened its borders during its social reform.

Chapter 4 explores the meaning of country of origin and how it has slowly evolved over time, not only from the perspective of a product's quality and design, but also the image projected by a country. In this chapter, we look at how countries commonly associated with poor manufacturing quality can change how they are perceived over time. As well as how consumers themselves have slowly evolved to become connoisseurs who look at country of origin from various value perspectives.

Chapter 5 is entirely dedicated to examining the international spread of brands' activities upstream and downstream, with in-depth cases from cosmetics and footwear.

Chapter 6 goes to the heart of a key process in luxury companies, namely the conception and launch of new products. This chapter is introduced by a short section on the importance of practicing scenario planning. As General Dwight D. Eisenhower famously said, "In preparing for battle, I have always found that plans are useless, but planning is indispensable".

Chapter 7 is divided into two parts. The first is a deep dive into ambidexterity and resilience, demonstrating how companies have successfully leveraged the strength of their core businesses while also investing in innovation. The second looks at new business models prompted by changes in consumer behavior and improvements in the technology available to us. As we move towards the future, the approach we take should also improve with time. This chapter aims to look at how companies could potentially fall behind if they do not prioritize innovation.

Chapter 8 discusses important topics related to environmental, social, and economic sustainability in the world of luxury. It aims to break down the fundamentals of sustainability and explain why luxury companies in particular are facing so much difficulty in turning their businesses green. This final chapter explores the different initiatives luxury companies have introduced, the complexity of their supply-chain networks, and the limitations of today's technologies.

All chapters are accompanied by concluding *takeaways*, which summarize key points and lessons.

Even though this book as a whole is the result of a common effort, the responsibility for writing of Chapters 1, 2, 5, and 6 fell to Gabriella Lojacono, while Chapters 3, 4, 7, and 8 have been written by Laura Ru Yun Pan. We believe that the book has greatly benefited from our complementarity in terms of culture, background, and age.

Note

1 All personal communications in this book come from a combination of presentations in Bocconi classes and interviews and emails with individuals and from luxury companies; they were confirmed in 2020 and 2021, just prior to publication.

Acknowledgments

It is necessary to dedicate a few pages with sincere thanks to the people who made this book possible. First of all, to our families. Writing is first of all a passion and takes time away from daily work, full of duties and urgencies, and from our affections. We were able to undertake this project with commitment and pleasure because we were supported by the people around us. A sincere thanks goes to our colleagues, Prof. Markus Venzin, who encouraged us to deal with internationalization years ago and from whom we heard about resilience applied to management for the first time; to Prof. Cinzia Parolini, who has wisely revised Chapter 5; to Prof. Nicola Misani, with whom we shared the passion for merchandising and the drafting of some cases reported in this book.

The person who connected us with De Gruyter and who encouraged us in every way to throw ourselves into this adventure was Prof. Robert Grant, an individual with extraordinary human gifts and an exceptional instructor.

At Cartier, there are many people we want to thank: President and CEO Cyrille Vigneron, François-Marc Sastre, Managing director Cartier South East Europe Art and Culture Director Viviana Caslini, Director of the Collections Fondation Cartier pour l'art contemporain Grazia Quaroni, International Marketing and Communications Director Arnaud Carrez, and International Talent Acquisition Manager Alexia Puech. Cyrille Vigneron, in addition to taking care of the foreword to our book, has generously and accurately reread the drafts of Chapters 1, 2, and 5. Inspiring leaders like Cyrille have made these companies unique.

Knowledge about the world of jewelry and watchmaking was also made possible thanks to Panerai CEO Jean-Marc Pontroué, Bulgari Italy and Turkey Retail Director Ilaria D'Arco, and Damiani Group Vice President Giorgio Damiani.

At Gucci, we owe a wealth of information to CEO Marco Bizzarri, Executive Vice President Corporate CMO Robert L. Triefus, Chief People Officer Luca Bozzo, and Global Head of Corporate Communication Claudio Monteverde. Thanks to Gucci we are also able to publish some archive images. Thanks also to our colleagues at the Gucci Research Lab – Prof. Fabrizio Castellucci, Prof. Paola Cillo, and Prof. Gaia Rubera – for three fruitful years of interaction on the Gucci case.

Our deep dive into high-end luxury furniture and design benefited from the contributions of Poltrona Frau CEO Nicola Coropulis, Molteni Group Head of Marketing and Communication Giulia Molteni, Boffi CEO Roberto Gavazzi, and Kartell's Marketing and Retail Director Lorenza Luti.

Examples from the beauty industry could not have come together without the availability of Davines and [comfort zone] Group Chairman and Owner Davide Bollati; Intercos President Dario Ferrari; Shinsegae Intercos Korea Management Board Member Anna Dato; President of Ancorotti Cosmetics Srl and President of Cosmetica Italia Renato Ancorotti; Cosmetica Italia Centro Studi Director Gianandrea Positano; Estée Lauder Companies Italia CEO and Managing Director Edoardo Bernardi; and

https://doi.org/10.1515/9783110723519-204

ICR Owner/Advisor, Accademia del Profumo President, and Co-Founder of Marvin Lab-Solue Ambra Martone.

An extended case on market selection with real methodologies and data was provided by Illy, and in particular by Coffee Culture Director and Illycaffè Board Member Daria Illy, Università del Caffè Director Moreno Faina, and Illycaffe' Deutschland General Manager Giuseppe Taccari.

We believe that one contribution of this book is the space it gives to the world of hospitality, an industry that has particularly suffered from the tragedy of the Covid-19 pandemic. The main contributors of our knowledge in this field are Bulgari Hotels and Resorts General Manager Attilio Marro; Dorchester Collection Academy at Dorchester Collection Global Director Beth Aarons, FCIPD, FIH; and Mandarin Oriental Learning and Development Manager Ella Hellowell.

As far as automotive and yachting are concerned, a special thanks goes to Dennis de Munck, Head of Employer Branding and University partnerships at Ferrari; Giovanni Perosino, Former CCO, Lamborghini; and Alberto Pastrone, Group Human Resources Director at Azimut|Benetti Group.

Revision of the distribution models included in Chapter 1 benefited from the know-how of Francesco Viana, General Manager Southern Europe presso Christian Dior Couture and a careful revision by Carlo Moltrasio, Senior Manager at Bain and Company. At Bain, we would also like to thank Senior Partner Claudia D'Arpizio and Partner Federica Levato for providing so insightful presence in all our luxury classes at Bocconi. Also, in Chapter 1, we included a detailed case on Farfetch that benefited greatly from the input of Farfetch Senior Business Development Manager Jan Radolec. In addition, we valorized the presentation of luxury companies that are included in the Deloitte Report, which is usually delivered in our campus by Patrizia Arienti, Partner at Deloitte and Touche Spa; Giovanni Faccioli, Partner at Deloitte as well as Artificial Intelligence/Cognitive, SmartCity, and Fashion and Luxury Market Leader; and Giorgio Loiodice, Director at Deloitte Consulting. This chapter also includes reference to the role of investment funds in luxury thanks to Filippo Cavalli, Director at Style Capital SGR, General Manager and Board member at forte forte Srl, and Board member at MSGM, as well as a deep comprehension of opportunities and difficulties in equity alliances thanks to Giovanni Zoppas, Former CEO at Thélios SpA; Darshan Mehta, President and Chief Executive of Reliance Brands Limited (RBL); and Meghan Whitehorn, CSR Executive at Chalhoub Group.

In Chapter 5, we provide evidence related to the international spread of the activities of Kering Eyewear thanks to Roberto Vedovotto, CEO at Kering Eyewear, and Celeste Iavarone, Project Manager, Business Development at Kering Eyewear.

Chapter 6 received relevant suggestions on merchandising and CRM from Danielle Lesage-Rochette, WW Merchandising Manager, Women's RTW and Kidswear, at Loro Piana (LVMH); Guia Ricci, Principal at Boston Consulting Group (BCG); and Ludovica Dodero, Partner and Associate Director, Fashion and Luxury at Boston Consulting Group (BCG). Next, we would like to thank Giorgio Ascheri, Made-to-

Measure Manager EMEA at Dolce & Gabbana for his wealth of knowledge on Ultra High Net Worth Individuals (UNHWI) and CRM structure, as well as, Guido Tirone, Head of Digital Analytics and Experimentation at Neiman Marcus, also provided insight on CRM and how digital transformation has changed the way luxury companies utilize customer data. For the innovation section of this chapter, we exploited the knowledge of design-thinking technique that we have gained from the challenging project we are currently undertaking with LVMH Moët Hennessy within our EMiLUX SDA Bocconi program. Our gatekeeper to the Innovation Lab of Moët Hennessy has been Andrea Pasqua di Bisceglie, Global Distribution Development Manager at Moët Hennessy.

We extend our appreciation to Maria Giovanna Sandrini, Brand and Corporate Communication Manager at Aquafil SpA, for her invaluable technical knowledge on chemical recycling and the change Aquafil is providing to the world of luxury, and to Pietro Lanza, General Manager of Intesa IBM and Blockchain Director at IBM Italia, for the ongoing support and information on IBM's involvement in sustainability related projects. Both of them provided invaluable assistance as we sought to understand the new models of luxury businesses laid out in Chapter 7.

In Chapter 8, we received the support of Geoffrey Perez, Global Head of Luxury, Snapchat, who shared with us some of the exciting projects Snapchat has worked on with luxury companies. As well as Ricky Cheung, Global Talent Attractuin & Inclusion Leader at Rosewood Hotel Group for the invaluable stories of Rosewood Hotels and their NextGen@Rosewood program.

A final thanks goes to our copy editor, Ruth Jones, for following us step by step in the editing of the different chapters and for raising useful questions for the reformulation of some sections.

Despite the invaluable contributions of all these people, many belonging to the Bocconi Alumni Community, any omissions or errors of interpretation remain with the authors, for which we apologize in advance.

Gabriella Lojacono and Laura Ru Yun Pan
Milan, March 2021

Contents

1 The Fundamentals of Luxury

Although luxury has some shared management challenges and logics, the actors have extremely varied physiognomies. In all the industries that we will deal with in this book, we find the coexistence of companies that are family owned and companies that belong to financial realities (i.e., financial holding companies, investment funds, private equity funds, etc.). These companies differ not only in governance structure, but also in their degree of industry specialization. At one extreme, there are mono-business companies and at the other large luxury conglomerates. Furthermore, large luxury conglomerates can have different profiles and exploit a wide range of different strategies. For example, LVMH and Kering have portfolios composed of different luxury companies from various industries. Concentrators such as Richemont, on the other hand, maintain a continuous flow of investments across a much narrower range of industries – in Richemont's case, watchmaking and fine jewelry.

The uniqueness of the choices made by these companies makes it inappropriate to divide them into generic groups, and we must therefore analyze their strategies case by case. In addition, the specifics of company structure in luxury makes it especially difficult to measure performance, for three reasons:

1) In luxury conglomerates made up of multiple brands, the group may choose to aggregate its portfolio, which means some brands will not be subject to independent economic-financial indicators.
2) Certain luxury groups are privately held by families or investment firms that are not listed on the stock exchange. These companies are not required to publicly release detailed information.
3) Many luxury groups are composed of both mass-market and prestige brands (e.g., L'Oréal). If their financial reports do not separate the two entities, it can be difficult to accurately measure the independent performance of the luxury business alone.

Because of this, it is more relevant to reflect on the growth path of these luxury companies rather than their financial standing. It is their evolution that has led to the uniqueness and originality of their brand identities.

The Luxury Panorama: A Rich Variety of Company Profiles

Luxury is not a sector, rather it is a culture. Because of this, it is difficult to set classifications for and make comparisons between companies. There are luxury companies that have activities in one or more of all the following industries: cosmetics, eyewear, textile and clothing, leather goods, hospitality, furniture, automotive, yachting, watchmaking, and jewelry.

https://doi.org/10.1515/9783110723519-001

For many, price point is the primary indicator of "high-end" or prestige products; if prices are relatively higher than the industry average, products are classified as luxury goods. This classification does not consider the perception of the typical customer of luxury goods who is led to make choices not merely based on price, but on the consistency between personal values and values and messages carried forward by brands. This would lead to the inclusion of various aspirational goods in the world of luxury, regardless of the price level. In some countries, luxury classification is based on a company's membership in an association such as Altagamma (Italy) or Comité Colbert (France). In today's dynamic economy, however, several phenomena are beginning to shift the way we classify luxury companies as such.

First, there is the prevalence of trading-down strategies among luxury companies and trading up strategies (premiumization) among companies in other market segments. This results in the intermixing of two worlds, creating a gray area that is not the exclusive domain of luxury brands.

Trading down means that a brand markets products in a specific category at a price point that is much more accessible than its core products but in line with the prices of the category. For example, eyewear and fragrances often lead luxury brands to compete directly with non-luxury companies in the same distribution channels (perfumeries, eyewear shops). This trend has been exasperated by the expansion of categories such as t-shirts and sneakers, which are often priced to put them within reach for younger generations. Bain and Company has reported that original and authentic entry-priced products surged during the Covid-19 pandemic, accounting for 50% of volumes of luxury personal goods in 2020 (D'Arpizio and Levato, 2020).

Premiumization is the act of elevating a product's perceived value, which makes a customer willing to spend more. It is the ability to increase the price of a product or category, creating a driver for higher margins. Premiumization can often be achieved through levers that focus on increasing product quality, beautifying the external packaging, or introducing innovation that fulfils a purpose. However, when we look closely at a few recent examples of premiumization, it seems brands have been subconsciously creating value through emotional triggers.

There are many ways to elevate a product. According to research conducted by Nielsen (2016), the five most significant attributes for premiumization are: (a) the use of high-quality materials, (b) offering superior function or performance, (c) enhanced customer experience, (d) strength or credibility of the brand, and (e) the design or packaging. Premiumization is present in almost all industries, and brands tend to utilize the same five levers as a means of elevating the brand or the product. Their goal is to justify a high profit margin. While premiumization is an interesting strategy in marketing and product development, it has also become a new way for brands to engage and develop better relationships with their consumers, especially in the midst of changing circumstances.

In recent years, a wide stream of collaborations between luxury, premium, and mass-market companies have allowed premium and mass-market companies to achieve a higher positioning for their products. Giambattista Valli is known for his haute couture gowns, which are generally destined for red carpets or other important events or to be wedding dresses for an ultra-rich audience. The brand has been considered "unreachable" for the middle class because the average price of a dress is over €2,500. H&M, meanwhile, is a mass-market retailer better known for affordability than for exquisite craftsmanship. Collaborating with Giambattista Valli allowed H&M to infuse its product presentation with glamour and catch the attention of a different segment of the market. Seen in a different way, Giambattista Valli executed a trading-down strategy, allowing it to be accessible to the average consumer, with prices ranging from US$20 to US$650. It built a household name for an exclusive brand.

Adidas is considered a premium brand, and it has frequently collaborated with celebrities. One of its most successful collaborations was Yeezy Boost by Kanye West, which was coveted by Gen Z sneaker aficionados. How did it happen? The shoes were released as a limited edition, creating scarcity. They employed an innovative technology – Adidas Boost Styrofoam soles – that set them apart. The Kardashians, fashion models, and celebrities endorsed the Yeezy Boosts, giving them cultural cachet. And the shoes were introduced at the right time, exploiting the fashion sneaker trend. If the price of the standard Adidas Boost was around US$120 to US$180, the price of the Adidas Yeezy Boost was US$220, and it was extremely difficult to purchase. Current market price can reach US$1,500 to US$2,500.

A second consideration concerns some groups, especially in cosmetics or eyewear, that include luxury, premium, and mass-consumer brands. For example, P&G has both Olay, a mass-market beauty brand, and SK-II, a well-known Japanese skincare prestige brand, in its beauty division. The same applies to L'Oréal, which carries consumer products, such as Garnier and Maybelline, but also holds the licenses to manufacture beauty products for luxury brands such as Yves Saint Laurent, Armani, and Valentino, which are grouped into its Luxe division. Estée Lauder Companies' portfolio includes luxury brands like La Mer, Joe Malone, and Tom Ford – and also Clinique, Smashbox, and Too Faced, which are sold at a different price point. Likewise, Luxottica produces a range of eyewear both through its owned brands Ray-Ban and Persol and licensed brands like Chanel and Dolce & Gabbana.

Chow Tai Fook Jewelry Group Limited is included among the top companies by sales in some luxury rankings (e.g., Deloitte's Global Power of Luxury Goods report) and is one of the most dispersed jewelry companies in Hong Kong and some parts of Mainland China. The conglomerate that owns its jewelry subsidiary is also a major shareholder in New World Development, which operates in other industries such as property development, transportation, energy, telecommunications, and casinos, among others. More recently, the family-run company's youngest generation has also acquired Rosewood Hotels and Resorts, a chain of five-star hotels across 16 countries, to extend their portfolio. As these examples show, group-level analyses of luxury groups and companies are apt to conceal important details related to the place of specific brands within a larger business structure or strategy. Therefore, if we wish to understand luxury companies, it is important to apply a rigorous analysis at the brand level.

Luxury brings together multiple entrepreneurial and managerial realities that share some basic logics (Keller et al., 2009; Kapferer, 1998; Barnier et al., 2012):

- Attention to (or obsession with) detail in all activities to ensure the highest quality
- The ability to create a timeless product that may have a secondary market price higher than the retail selling price and that can become a platform for subsequent launches
- Effective storytelling and impactful "theatricality"
- A deep connection with an audience through different touchpoints
- Strong specialization or a core business that is the origin point for the company's expansion strategy
- Authentic corporate values
- Sensitivity toward legal aspects related to the protection of the brand and intellectual property
- Powerful identifiers (i.e., signs or persons that make the brand recognizable)
- Emphasis on the importance of country of origin
- Exclusivity, which is often expressed in the limited number of pieces available (see Chapter 2)
- Controlled distribution[1]
- Aspirational and symbolic value in the eyes of consumers

All these aspects result in high-value brand equity. In particular, it will be useful to expend a few words on the meaning of "symbolic value". Symbolic value is what separates luxury from other markets. Luxury consumers appreciate purchases for more than mere functionality – they can also represent personal gratification and social affirmation. As defined by Ravasi and Rindova (2008), symbolic value is "the set social and cultural meanings associated with a product, which enable consumers to use it to communicate about their identity and social and status group membership" (p. 3).

People are willing to pay more for products and services delivered by their favorite luxury brands because they attribute to them emotional and symbolic value. This value is related to what the brand and its products mean to their customers and the society in which those customers live. It is based on customer perception; therefore, luxury is also something subjective and personal. People use these symbolic goods as key markers of class (Bourdieu, 1979) and to create social distance, similar to how companies use them as competitive weapons to generate differentiation. Emotional bonds are important across all industries, including hospitality, as the example of Dorchester Collection described below emphasizes:

> The luxury hotel market is crowded – new openings impact development, improvements take place through refurbishments, new trends are constantly emerging and global guests frequent numerous exotic locations. At Dorchester Collection, they ask their guests the reasons behind their reoccurring choice to stay at Dorchester Collection properties worldwide, when ultimately the options are endless. This question is asked in order to develop a deeper understanding their guests' loyalty.

When guests decide to stay at a hotel, they're acting on a need or a set of needs. The fixtures, fittings and décor provide the tangible benefits of choosing a certain hotel and paying a premium for those elements of luxury, such as: Egyptian cotton sheets, gold-leaf paint, state-of-the-art technology and the highest quality ingredients. These components therefore become a given expectation and without them guests would be understandably dissatisfied.

In the same way that hospitality professionals understand the functional needs of each individual, the emotional needs are a priority too. These needs reflect the essentials that make a guest's life better. By understanding and supporting these emotional needs, Dorchester Collection is able to create unforgettable guest experiences.

Emotions are the foundation of creating lasting bonds. At Dorchester Collection, it's all about how they make their guests feel and providing the right conditions for those good feelings to flourish at all of their hotels. By always paying attention to emotional needs and putting this at the heart of their brand, Dorchester Collection is able to provide a sense of belonging, which heightens the positive emotional response of their guests.

To illustrate this, consider the front desk providing a complimentary upgrade to a guest upon arrival. In view of the guest's functional needs, more space has been provided along with greater value for money. However, the real impact is the emotional benefit this has on the guest.

Following a wonderful wedding in The Dorchester's grand ballroom, a bride and groom guests were delighted to be spontaneously serenaded by musician Stevie Wonder, performing "You Are the Sunshine of My Life" on the grand piano in the hotel's promenade. This was a completely whimsical moment, extended without prior knowledge or preparation. A lifetime memory created for the couple and other guests present at the time.

A cashmere jumper was quickly rustled up by a willing employee to allow a chilly guest the opportunity to stargaze from the hotel terrace one summer evening.

All these examples share a feeling of being looked after, made to feel special and something that they will remember and share with their friends. This is how lasting connections are made.

(Dorchester Collection, personal communication)

Creating this type of value through all the elements of a brand architecture (i.e., products, values, people, organization) in a consistent way is among luxury brands' particular competencies. As Jean-Marc Pontroué, the CEO of Panerai, describes it, "Brands do a kind of emotional injection into their actions that I would call it 'brand vibration,' some kind of magic that stimulates desirability by people" (personal communication). Operating in symbol-intensive industries allows companies to make certain decisions that are motivated not by a purely economic rationale but by a strategy of creating and nurturing "symbolic capital", i.e., trust, reputation, value, prestige, honor, and attention as perceived by people (Bourdieu, 1984). This approach is also reflected in how brands fix and manage pricing strategies, which are based not so much on industrial cost as on the number of pieces made available, the existing offer on the market, and consumer perceptions and emotions. "I like to call it emotional price", says Pontroué, "something that has a logic and definition criteria that are specific to the market segment and the brand strategy" (personal communication).

In the middle of the 2020 pandemic, while many companies were struggling with decreased sales and uncertain sales campaigns, some luxury brands decided to increase the price of iconic items, such as the Chanel 2.55 and Boy and the Gucci Dionysus handbags, by up to 9%. They justified this bold choice by referring to price harmonization across countries and increasing costs of raw materials. A sure side effect was the preservation of margins in the face of revenue contraction (Sanders, 2020; Reuters, 2020b).

Because the construction of symbolic capital takes time, it finds fertile ground in family-owned companies that notoriously favor the long-term approach over short-term objectives.

Luxury brands not only struggle to compete economically; they also compete symbolically, trying to manipulate, control, and deploy symbols that have been given worth or value by the society that created them (Harrison, 1985; Bourdieu, 1984; Bourdieu, 1979). According to the French sociologist Pierre Bourdieu, the possibility of acquiring a primary position and influencing the standards of excellence depends more on cultural capital (e.g., competencies, assets, skills, etc.) than on social (e.g., relationships) and economic (e.g., financial strength, liquidity) capital. This is the reason why, when discussing luxury companies, we emphasize the importance of arts and culture as an authentic part of a company's corporate values.

Given the importance of cultural and symbolic assets for the creation of value, many brands have launched initiatives aimed at preserving their heritage and culture. These attributes are often incorporated into particular processes (so called "métiers d'art") or unique pieces. Initiatives related to brands' heritage have gone in three directions:

1) *Preserve and exhibit* objects that represent a condensation of the brand's expertise or that have marked its history. These objects often demonstrate how a company has experimented with a particular process to achieve the highest level of execution. Cartier, for instance, has collected more than 1,000 of its pieces in an art collection that allows it to stage the dedication and meticulousness of the artists and workshops behind the maison's quintessential manufacturing techniques.

2) *Start internal schools of arts and crafts* to train the new generations in the field. In 2012, Van Cleef & Arpels founded L'ÉCOLE in Paris, welcoming the general public into the world of jewelry and gemstones through courses, conferences, and exhibitions presented by passionate experts. L'ÉCOLE has opened a new permanent school in Hong Kong to satisfy the increasing demand for jewelry arts education across the Asia Pacific region.

3) *Invest in external workshops* to protect their existence, putting at their disposal the human and financial resources to carry out their business. For example, the LVMH Métiers d'Arts program is aimed at preserving and developing precious savoir-faire and access to raw materials for fashion and leather goods houses by

guaranteeing support for their suppliers. It involves the realization of common projects and exchanges between different professions, but it can also lead to the acquisition of a stake in the capital of external manufacturers, as happened in 2012 for the Roux tanneries, which specialize in the processing of calfskin, or in 2015 for the Spanish Riba Guixà, one of the leading lambskin tanneries. Similarly, in 1997, Chanel created an ad hoc subsidiary, Paraffection S.A., with the aim of preserving and promoting the heritage, originality, and productive skills of the French artisans and workshops on which couture houses depend. These can remain independent, and therefore collaborate with other brands, or they can be acquired by Paraffection. This latter option is especially important in the case of small family businesses without the human and financial resources to make their business models sustainable in the contemporary marketplace,[2] potentially jeopardizing the survival of historical skills, the loss of which would be felt by the entire system. Each of the Paraffection workshops, for example Lesage embroideries or Maison Michel hats, is a leader in its craft, despite not being known to the average consumer (Mellery-Pratt, 2015).

The relevance of cultural capital is front and center in the communication strategies of numerous luxury brands. Cartier, for example, uses its history as a through line in the product narrative. Its iconic Trinity is a legend, imagined by Louis Cartier in 1924. This emblematic piece of jewelry has three as a magic number: three bands that symbolize friendship, fidelity, and love and three types of gold (yellow, white, and rose). In its retellings of the inspiration behind the Trinity, Cartier has connected the design to other important threes: the three Cartier brothers, Louis, Pierre, and Jacques, and the legendary addresses of Cartier stores, in Paris, London, and New York.

A similar concept can be found in the idea of "soft luxury" (i.e., apparel, leather goods, accessories, cosmetics). Watching the video "Gabrielle Chanel and Literature – Inside Chanel" on the maison's website, the viewer is drawn into the world of the brand's founder through her reading habits and associations with French literary figures. It presents a portrait of Gabrielle Chanel as devoted to reading as a form of escapism and learning, a way to fuel her imagination and inner strength. By offering its audience a vision of Chanel as a supporter of the literary community, someone for whom literature helped shape a way of living, speaking, and interacting, the video extends her – and her brand's – cultural influence beyond the world of fashion.

As in the cases of Cartier and Chanel, luxury brands with long histories often draw on their heritage to increase their symbolic value. An automatic association between historicity and luxury would not leave any space for emerging brands, yet in various industries and countries, we see new, flourishing luxury companies that, despite having no history behind them, are targeting interesting niches. The relevant question is therefore: How does a new business idea make its way into this world?

To reflect on this question, let us examine four examples in different industries. **Moncler** was founded in 1952 in Monestier-de-Clermont, a ski resort near Grenoble,

France, by René Ramillon, a French mountain equipment craftsman, and André Vincent. However, Moncler only established itself as a luxury brand in 2003, when the Italian Remo Ruffini acquired the company. Moncler as we know it today is different from the Moncler of the past, both in terms of its key business processes and its presence in the market. The story of **Roger Dubuis** in 1995, making it a very young in the competitive watchmaking industry, especially in a group where it's possible to find brands like Vacheron Constantin, which dates to 1755. Even more recent is the launch of watchmaker **Richard Mille**, which launched its first model, the RM 001 Tourbillon, in 2001 as part of an initial series of 17 watches. In the luxury auto industry, **Pagani** was founded in 1992 by the Argentinian Horacio Pagani in San Cesario sul Panaro, Italy – the heart of the region where Lamborghini, Maserati, Ducati, and Ferrari are also located.[3]

How did Moncler become so famous in its second phase of life and Roger Dubuis, Richard Mille, and Pagani manage to break through in consolidated, mature industries with high barriers to entry such as cars and watches? In all four cases, there are some recurring elements: a disruptive innovative capacity (whether based on design or technology), the exploitation of a luxury feature such as craftsmanship or an engaging narrative, and the company's ability to insert itself into a very profitable market micro-niche where it could take the lead. This last consideration becomes particularly important in countries like China and India, where we see a flourishing of new brands that are breaking through the consolidated realm of luxury. The cases of Sabyasachi Mukherjee's namesake brand and of Qeelin offer insight into how new luxury companies can find their way.

Sabyasachi Mukherjee's brilliant career began in 1999, immediately after he graduated from the National Institute of Fashion Technology, Calcutta, with three major distinctions. He opened his workshop for bespoke wedding dresses, what would become Sabyasachi, with three tailors. The wedding market is particularly attractive in India (*Vogue Business* talks about a value of about US$50 billion) because Indian society attributes great religious and emotional importance to this celebration. For their wedding clothes, brides and grooms prefer to engage local designers, who are better able to understand their needs and tastes. From the beginning, Mukherjee's creative ability and great aesthetic sensitivity earned him important awards. In 2001, he won the Ritu Kumar Award for Excellence in Design and the Femina British Council 'Most Outstanding Young Designer of India' Award. In 2003 he won the Grand Winner Award at the Mercedes Benz New Asia Fashion Week in Singapore, which paved his way to a workshop in Paris hosted by Jean Paul Gaultier and Azzedine Alaïa. Later, in 2005, Mukherjee won the National Award for best costume designer for the film *BLACK* and critical acclaim from outlets such as *Women's Wear Daily* which, after his debut at India Fashion Week in 2002, declared him the future of Indian fashion. He was then stocked at influential London boutique Browns and given the distinction of being the first Indian designer to show at Milan Fashion Week.

Since then, Mukherjee's Sabyasachi brand has come a long way. The company was valued at US$35 million in 2019, and has dressed more than 50,000 brides, including celebrities such as Priyanka Chopra, Deepika Padukone, Anushka Sharma, Isha Ambani, and Shloka Mehta. He has participated in several Bollywood costume projects, including *BLACK, Guzaarish, Babul, Raavan, Laaga Chunari Mein Daag, Paa, No One Killed Jessica*, and *English Vinglish*. Prices for Sabyasachi designs range from US$10,000 to US$40,000, and more than 1,000 hours of one person's work are required to make a suit.

The brand's enormous success with younger generations has also triggered imitation by other players in the Indian wedding marketplace. Despite this growth, indigenous fabric dying and weaving techniques remain central to the atelier's designs, which incorporate these heritage crafts in a modern way. Over the years, Mukherjee has employed close to 4,500 artisans across India, in West Bengal, Bihar, Orissa, Tamil Nadu, Gujarat, and Kashmir. In his design factory in New Delhi, apart from 475 regular staff, an in-house team of 900 artisans works in a sprawling 70,000-square-foot space, with mounds of jaw-dropping vintage fabrics and antique textiles piled on the floors. Sabyasachi launched a jewelry line in 2017, and it's possible that this new venture could one day become even more lucrative than its bridal business. The brand also foresees future expansions into fragrances, footwear, and skincare.

Today, there are four Sabyasachi flagship stores in India: in Calcutta, New Delhi, Mumbai, and Hyderabad. In 2019, the brand opened its first flagship jewelry store in Mumbai. Mukherjee has also established a wholesale retail footprint for his brand in key international cities through the following retail outlets: Aashni and Co Limited, The Bollywood Closet, Piyali Ganguly, Ensemble LLC, and The Grand Trunk Clothing Pvt. Ltd. In January 2021, Aditya Birla Fashion and Retail Limited (ABFRL) signed an agreement to buy a 51% stake in Sabyasachi for ₹398 crore (US$54.53 million).

Qeelin is a contemporary fine jewelry brand founded in 2004 leveraging on the emotional resonance of Chinese mystical or superstitious symbolism. The name comes from *Qilin*, an auspicious Chinese mythical animal and icon of love. In each piece, iconic designs, carefully selected materials, and meticulous craftsmanship deliver playfulness, imagination, and Oriental beauty. The brand's iconic collection is Wulu, which features the legendary Chinese gourd, an auspicious emblem in Chinese tradition. Wulu caught the attention of the world when actress Maggie Cheung appeared at the Cannes Film Festival wearing pieces from the collection. Since then, Qeelin has been coveted among stars and luminaries all over the world. Its other famous collection, XiXi, celebrates the lion in Chinese culture.

In 2007, Qeelin opened the doors to its boutique in Paris at Jardin du Palais Royal. Today, the brand's boutiques can be found in major international capitals (Paris, Hong Kong, Beijing, and Shanghai). Since January 2013, Qeelin has been part of the Kering Group. The acquisition allowed Qeelin to accelerate its retail expansion by opening new stores (32 stores in total in 2020), to increase its international exposure by entering the US in 2015, and to launch its first high jewelry collection. The brand's profile has increased over time thanks to collaborations with Chinese actors like Gulnazar and Xiao Zhan.

In both these cases, the desire to create a blend of cultures (East meets West) while remaining faithful to traditions (Indian bridal culture, Chinese symbolism) was met by leveraging brand ambassadors who were able to affect the perception of the market and enrich storytelling. In conclusion, there is room for emerging brands to enter a niche and catch their target's attention, but what is challenging is to make this adventure sustainable over the long run.

Despite sharing the basic principles mentioned above, luxury brands are very different from each other in many aspects, including those related to their business strategy, governance mode, and historicity. It is precisely this heterogeneity of profiles that makes the world of luxury extremely interesting: operators who have different dimensions, different origins, different values, and different strategies coexist. This greatly enriches the competitive landscape and the possibilities for consumer choice and appreciation. The remaining sub-sections of this introductory chapter will reflect on the peculiarities of luxury companies, which we can group under two umbrellas: 1) ownership structure and owner identity and 2) corporate boundaries and the breadth and scope of activities. We will end by examining how companies have grown over time in terms of modalities and directions.

Ownership Structure and Luxury Companies

Ownership structure influences a luxury company's governance activities and the delegation of power among its managers. The effectiveness and speed of decision-making processes depend on how linear or complex the structure is and on the company's chain of command. To correctly set up the analysis that will help us discover a company's ownership structure, we can start by considering two dimensions (Minichilli and Quarato, 2020; Thomsen and Pedersen, 2000).

A first dimension concerns the type of owners: family members, individual investors, institutional (e.g., insurance companies or pension funds) or financial investors (e.g., investment or private equity funds), or the state.

The second dimension of analysis concerns the degree of concentration of ownership, from a single reference shareholder who holds 100% of the company's capital to public companies where ownership is fragmented in the hands of many shareholders, each with an insignificant stake.

Many luxury companies remain in the control of their founding families. According to the European Union, a company is a family business if: 1) the majority of decision-making rights are in the possession of the person(s) who established the firm, or in the possession of the person(s) who has/have acquired the share capital of the firm, or in the possession of their spouses, parents, child, or children's direct heirs;[4] 2) at least one representative of the family is formally involved in the governance of the firm.

There is no correspondence between family ownership and the size of a company's ownership structure; the variety of structures adopted by family-owned luxury companies is remarkabley broad. For example, some companies are still at the first generation, with one or more founders controlling the ownership and intimately involved in governance and management. Other companies thrive across generations, controlled by consortiums of cousins or even distant relatives who play the role of responsible owners and are well-represented in governance roles and, sometimes, still involved in management.

Family ownership has the indisputable advantage of strengthening a company's cultural capital. The conduct of the business is seen to be guided by rules, values, history, and competencies accumulated over the years by passionate family members. This narrative can be communicated in an elegant way at every meeting point, with all stakeholders, internally and externally.

The following are examples of luxury groups or companies directly controlled by families:

- Hermès: the family has reached the sixth generation and holds 66% of the capital; 10% belongs to LVMH
- Chanel: owned by brothers Alain and Gerard Wertheimer, grandsons of Pierre Wertheimer, one of Coco Chanel's first business partners
- Audemars Piguet: in the hands of the Audemars family
- Patek Philippe: the Sterns family bought the company from the Philippe family in 1932, during the Great Depression
- Azimut Benetti: founder Paolo Vitelli remains the absolute majority shareholder of the group, the largest in the world in the luxury yachting industry
- Damiani: the company was listed on the Milan Stock Exchange from 2007 to 2019, when it returned to being fully owned by the Damiani family
- LVMH: the Arnault Family holds 47.3% of the world's leading luxury group by sales value
- Compagnie Financière Richemont SA, also known as Richemont: Johann Rupert, who founded the company in 1988, is the major shareholder
- Pagani Automobili Modena: owned by Horacio Pagani, who founded the company in 1992
- Lifestyle Design (the group that includes Poltrona Frau, Cappellini, Cassina, Nemo Lighting, Ceramica Flaminia, and Fish Design): controlled by Haworth, a privately held, family-owned office furniture manufacturer headquartered in Michigan, since 2014
- Ermenegildo Zegna: privately owned and led by the third generation of the family, with Gildo Zegna as CEO and Paolo Zegna as chairman
- Giorgio Armani: the privately held company remains fully owned by its eponymous founder

- Dolce & Gabbana: Domenico Dolce and Stefano Gabbana each control 40% of privately held Dolce & Gabbana Holding SRL shares. Alfonso and Dora, Domenico's brother and sister, control 20% of the company (Binkley, 2019)

From a legal perspective, families can put in place different and highly articulated mechanisms to control the ownership of luxury groups, especially if the size of the family in question is medium to large. The following examples give an idea of the different options that can be designed and implemented:
- Kering: 41% of the company is owned by Artemis Group, the family investment vehicle founded by François Pinault in 1992
- Brunello Cucinelli: controlled (51%) by the holding company Fedone S.r.l., which is in turn owned by an irrevocable trust, "Trust Brunello Cucinelli", established in 2014 by the company's founder, Brunello Cucinelli
- Valentino S.p.A and Balmain: controlled by the Royal Family of Qatar through Mayhoola for Investments S.P.C., their sovereign investment fund, since October 2008
- Ferrari: special voting shares allow Exor N.V., a financial holding controlled by the Agnelli family through the holding company Giovanni Agnelli B.V. Exor, to control the majority voting right

There are different definitions of a family business in the literature, but they share two commonalities: family businesses can be of any size and they can be divided into listed family companies and unlisted family companies. The European Commission suggests that family-controlled companies be considered as listed when the person who established or acquired the firm (share capital) or their families or descendants possess 25% of the decision-making rights mandated by their share capital. Building on this definition, LVMH, Kering, Hermès, Richemont, Brunello Cucinelli, and Ferrari can be placed in the subset of listed family companies.

Although the luxury landscape is populated by many family companies, there are some very important examples of companies controlled by financial investors such as private equity funds. For example, in the world of Italian design, where the presence of unlisted family businesses is widespread, one of the main high-end companies, B&B Italia, is in fact part of Design Holding, a global group in the high-end design furniture industry created by the Investindustrial and Carlyle funds, which also includes Flos and Louis Poulsen. Similarly, Jimmy Choo and Versace are owned by Capri Holdings Limited (formerly Michael Kors Holdings Limited), 92.45% of the total shares of which have been purchased by institutional investors.

Who Leads a Luxury Brand? The Difficult Balance between Ownership, Management, and Creativity

Creativity is essential for luxury companies. There have been periods when the role of designers was so much to the fore that they even overshadowed company CEOs. The search for the best management configuration is a hot topic in the world of luxury, and the ideal structure varies from industry to industry, and from company to company: one model does not fit all.

Regardless of the industry, the role of the designer is not limited to do sketches, but has a strong social value: He or she must interpret what is happening in society. It is therefore necessary that the designer, whether working internally within the company or collaborating with it, captures important signals of socio-cultural changes and use them as a source of inspiration. In the world of furniture, for example, this is the reason why market research is not carried out in the classical sense. Try asking an entrepreneur in the industry if they perform competitor or consumer analysis. The common assumption in the high-end is that if you want to surprise your customers, don't ask them for their opinion – they will respond based on what they know, and you'll never get beyond the predictable. Similarly, looking at what other companies are doing will not lead to a radical departure from the mold. True innovation comes both from investments in technology (technology push) and from an interpretation of a changing world driven by a designer's sensitivities (see Chapter 6 on drivers of innovation). Competition does not take place on a purely functional level, but on an emotional and empathic one as well. An object like the Juicy Salif citrus squeezer, designed by Philippe Starck for Alessi in 1990, is not bought to have yet another citrus squeezer to use in the kitchen every morning, but for its semantics, "for how it speaks to the customer". It carries symbolic value as a design object that challenges modernist principles – which is why the customer is willing to pay €75 to have it on their counter (Verganti, 2009).

The need for symbolic value and the ability to access new perspectives push companies in the furniture industry to collaborate with external, though still experienced, designers. They are chosen on the basis of their interpretative ability to do additional research (for example on materials) and to respond to a company brief, which is usually unstructured. While outside designers act as windows on the world, bringing new and, increasingly, international perspectives to a company's corporate culture, they can also bring notoriety to little-known niche brands, especially when a collaboration involves a famous designer or architect. The paradox is that the market often ends up associating the product not so much with the company as with the designer.

In the world of clothing and accessories, an example of a designer with a broad spectrum of activities is Maria Grazia Chiuri, who was appointed the creative director of Dior in July 2016. As the designer for women's ready to wear and haute couture at Valentino with Pierpaolo Piccioli, she expressed her love for embroidery and geometric shapes in her dresses. These elements can be seen in her collections for Dior today, which include the use of chiffon, embroidery, and lace. Her passionate, rigorous, personal research on feminism shaped her debut collection for Dior in September 2016, while she delved into African culture for Cruise 2020. Apulian traditions (bobbin lace, embroidery, tarantella, illuminations, etc.) combined with the need to promote the spirit of collaboration in the middle of the pandemic and the revision of the house codes (tarot cards, gardens, and flowers) influenced her collection for Dior Cruise 2021. The same specificity of approach can be seen in the work of Hedi Slimane, who has brought modernizing, contemporary style to luxury fashion. The t-shirts, leather jackets, and Parisian street-style aesthetic that defined his work at Yves Saint Laurent have carried over to his rebranding of Celine since taking the position of the brand's creative director in 2018. Alessandro Michele, meanwhile, personifies the Gucci brand, of which he has been creative director since 2015. With his youthful language, his presence on social media, and his modern vision of the fashion world, Michele embodies the new codes of the maison and the value of inclusiveness. The extensive research activities, autonomy in the creative process, and charismatic communication essential for success make the role of designer one that transcends its professional designation to become representative of the creative vision behind a brand.

Designers can be great communicators of the history that they themselves help to create, but they don't necessarily need to have had specialized training. Giorgio Armani, for example, who has helped make Italian fashion famous around the world, entered Milan's medical university after high school, spending a few years there before joining the military, eventually finding work as a clerk at the Italian department store La Rinascente before becoming a menswear designer for Nino Cerruti in the 1960s. Famous, too, is the case of Steve Jobs, who despite not having had a design education, played a decisive role in the success of Apple's design.

A luxury designer's relevance is highly dependent on two main factors: (1) the company's attitude toward promoting radical innovation through design; (2) the industry context.

The attitude to promoting radical innovation through design. The greater the contribution expected from a designer in a brand's differentiation strategy, the more important the role of that designer as a leader in the business as a whole. A designer in this position will have a high degree of autonomy and a broad perimeter of activity. He or she will interface directly with the CEO, creating a kind of management duo at the top of the company hierarchy that must find its own balance. At the other extreme, the more conservative a company is, the less visible its creative team. Can you name those responsible for design at Hermès or Loro Piana? Individual designers at these companies traditionally take a back seat to the brands themselves. More different still are the roles that innovation and research and development play across various industries. In cosmetics, for example, it is important to invest in new formulas while relying on strategic marketing to predict market trends and consumer preferences, especially in the most advanced markets. However, there is also a decisive role for make-up artists and fashion designers in defining, even in advance of fashion, the textures and colors of products.

The industry context. In "hard luxury" industries including jewelry, watches, automotive, and yachts a "prima donna" creative figure is usually absent. Instead, the creative team applies a conservative logic respectful of the brand's traditions, emphasizing technical skills rather than novelty. In "soft luxury", apparel, leather goods, beauty, etc., there is greater receptivity to trends and willingness to experiment. The risky role of proposing new languages and artifacts is entrusted to a reference designer (or a couple of designers), assisted by the creative team (or a product or style team).[5] If we can certainly call to mind the faces and personalities of Marc Jacobs and Karl Lagerfeld, those of Flavio Manzoni (senior vice president of design at Ferrari since January 2010) or the creator of a Damiani ring or a Rolex watch are not so well known. In conclusion, where technical aspects and stability in the product portfolio prevail, product design is managed by a design team or a technical office. If there is a creative director, he or she is in charge of providing aesthetic suggestions to the product team as well as supervising visual and retail design. An example of this is Alvaro Maggini, the first-ever creative director in the history of Panerai, after having been creative director of Roger Dubuis and responsible for the creative strategy of Jaeger-LeCoultre. At Panerai, he was entrusted with the task of making the brand more contemporary while respecting its founding elements: Italian character, military DNA, and the sea. At the product level, this means providing ideas on design, colors, and straps. An exception to the minimal role typically played by creative directors in hard luxury companies is in the world of high jewelry. There, even if they may be a silent presence and not known to the general public, creative directors often exert influence over the development and design of new pieces and collections. This is the case of Lucia Silvestri at Bulgari, who became chief designer after a career in the brand's gemology department; or Jacqueline Karachi-Langane, who is responsible for all the exquisite high jewelry pieces created by Cartier, heading a team of twelve designers.

Several cases in the recent past lead us to think that consolidating the responsibilities of designer, CEO, and reference shareholder into a role held by a single individual can hardly be "the way", Take the famous case of Christopher Bailey, who has been chief creative designer at Burberry since 2009 and who was its CEO from 2014 to July 2017. Initially backed by investors, Bailey saw that support withdrawn when sales contracted in key markets. While Bailey's contributions to accelerating the company's digitalization and creating a new aesthetic for Burberry's boutiques were recognized, the role of CEO was entrusted to Marco Gobbetti, allowing the chief designer to focus on caring for the creative soul of the company. The happiest stories are always those of two perfectly timed and in-tune dancers, each with their own personality but respecting each other, and there is no better recent example of true harmony of intent between a creative and a CEO than that of Alessandro

Michele and Marco Bizzarri at Gucci. As Bizzarri has stated in many interviews: "In choosing the creative director it is important to focus on who can be comfortable in their role without an ego that wants to overlap the CEO" (personal communication). The same attitude has been frequently described by Francesca Bellettini, CEO of Yves Saint Laurent, as defining her relationship with Anthony Vaccarrello, the brand's chief designer:

> I have a very genuine relationship with him, he is my travel companion. The responsibility for the company's success lies with us. Vaccarello is the first person I call when a big decision has to be made for the brand, whether it has to do with results or not. Our relationship is 100% based on trust and respect. I'm not the type of CEO who controls (openly or not) what Vaccarello does, because it would generate fear, and this is one of the great problems of fashion.
> (speech during the Vogue Fashion Festival 2019)

There have been times when the chief designer of the brand had the highest profile; others when the CEO was the predominant proponent of the company's successes. In the past, the designer of a namesake luxury house always took charge of how their brand fit into the market and was perceived, creative decisions being paramount in the brand's positioning and identity. When Yves Saint Laurent launched his haute couture house – after Christian Dior replaced him with Marc Bohan in 1960 – French businessman and industrialist Pierre Bergé ran the business while Saint Laurent had free reign to be creative. Many luxury fashion houses have followed the same path: Marc Jacobs depended on his business partner Robert Duffy; Valentino Garavani relied on the businessman Giancarlo Giammetti. There's the famous story of businessman and racehorse owner Barry K. Schwartz, who borrowed US$10,000 to partner with his childhood friend Calvin Klein to set up what would become one of the world's most recognizable fashion brands. Neither Pierre Bergé nor Robert Duffy is synonymous with the luxury houses they helped to build, but without them the dreams of Yves Saint Laurent and Marc Jacobs would not have been possible.

The personification of a brand in its creative talent was the source of its appeal: people were proud to own an Armani suit because of the talents of Giorgio Armani. The name Brunello Cucinelli cannot be separated from the designer's cashmere and the incredible investments he has made in the well-being of workers and the creation of a school of traditional arts and crafts in Solomeo in Umbria, Italy. The inextricability of designer and brand led to the consolidation of creative and business leadership in luxury companies. "King Giorgio" became the CEO of his privately held company in 1985, when his business partner, Sergio Galeotti, died. Valentino, Gianfranco Ferrè, and Gianni Versace also took full control of their eponymous brands. It was only in 2020 that Cucinelli left the position of CEO to focus on the creative direction of his. Yet nowadays, only a handful of creative owners remain: Miuccia Prada (who invited Raf Simmons to join her in 2020), Stefano Dolce and Domenico Gabbana, Giorgio Armani, and Silvia Venturini Fendi.

The centrality and recognizability of CEOs began to gain ground when luxury fashion houses entered a new phase of fundraising in the late 1980s. Rather than seeking financing from wealthy aristocrats and millionaires, luxury fashion houses became an attractive opportunity for investment bankers. The likes of Bernard Arnault, Francois Henri-Pinault, and Nemir A. Kirdar (Investcorp) saw the potential of luxury as a way to generate value through the long-term ownership of brands. This shift also signaled the rise of conglomerates, and luxury houses were aggregated into their divisions and portfolios. Consequently, the characteristics of successful luxury executives has also had to change. It has become important for CEOs not only to manage the day-to-day, but also to do scenario planning and maintain relationships with both the financial community and the market (consumers, key opinion leaders, etc.).

Furthermore, the consumer's perception of luxury brands has changed, as well as the elements of the brand identity that resonate with society. As generational change loosened the association between a brand and the creator who gave it its name, other dimensions also became important: for example, the ability to communicate, the control of distribution, the impeccable structure of the offer, and the presence of ambassadors from different backgrounds. This is the moment when a manager's ability to actively contribute to the success of the business begins to take precedence over creative vision alone. A manager or CEO must select the right ingredients for the historical period and the life phase of the company, and creativity is just one of these ingredients. The task of investors and shareholders is to create the conditions for this to happen and publicly applaud the change to show continuous support as the structure of the company changes.

Fortunately, the cases of idyllic relationships between investors, CEOs, and creative directors are not few – though it sometimes takes a little while for a company to find the right people for each role. In 1988, Middle Eastern private equity fund Investcorp acquired 50% of the capital of Gucci; Maurizio Gucci owned the other 50%. In 1989, Maurizio became president, but under his lead results worsened. In 1993, Investcorp asked the CEO of Gucci America, Domenico De Sole, to contribute to the group's recovery. The fight between Maurizio and Investcorp ended when Maurizio capitulated and sold his 50% to the fund. De Sole was appointed COO and then CEO of Gucci. In 1994, Tom Ford joined the group as its new creative director. Thanks to the leadership of De Sole and the genius of Ford, turnaround was successfully completed by the end of 1995, and Investcorp decided to exit from its investment.

Christian Dior was originally financed and owned by French businessman Marcel Boussac (the same person who fired Yves Saint Laurent in 1960). The company went bankrupt in 1978, and Boussac sold to the French holding company Agache-Willot, which in turn went bankrupt in 1983. By the end of 1984, Bernard Arnault was able to raise the capital to take over Agache-Willot, divesting most of its assets and focusing on Dior. In 1988, when Dior indirectly acquired a 32% stake in LVMH,

Arnault gained control of the group and Dior became Christian Dior Couture, a wholly owned brand within LVMH. Gianfranco Ferrè was appointed as creative director in 1989, a position he held until 1996. In 1994, Sidney Toledano became director of the brand's leather goods division, becoming the brand CEO in 1996. When John Galliano, the brand's lead designer, was fired for making anti-semitic remarks in 2011, Toledano was the one to introduce Dior's women's RTW show at Paris Fashion Week. His speech reflected on the philosophy of the maison and its position, explicitly distancing Dior from Galliano's comments; he made sure the crisis centered on the designer rather than the brand. The show did not end in a classical way – with the designer taking a bow – but with the atelier workers dressed in their white work clothes taking the stage amid the applause of the audience. By effectively shifting focus from his designer to the team that had worked behind the scenes on the collection, and by emphasizing Dior's history, Toledano showed how the elegance and sophistication of the past could be in line with a post-economic crisis society.

The importance of the CEO today is typical not only in clothing, but also in automotive. Sergio Marchionne will forever be remembered as Ferrari's modern icon, even though he was a businessman not the creative mind behind these objects of desire; design and engineering remained in the background throughout his tenure.

If the creative soul of luxury seems to be in great ferment, experimenting with new organizational solutions that also favor a continuous dialogue with management and shareholders, the same can be said for company management. In recent years, a line has been drawn between ownership and management, leading to the appointment of CEOs with solid backgrounds in luxury (even in the same company) and in key functions (e.g., merchandising, retail, product, sales). Among the many examples are: Jacopo Venturini, CEO of Valentino, previously executive vice president of merchandising and global markets at Gucci; Riccardo Stefanelli and Luca Lisandroni, Cucinelli's co-CEOs, the former previously head of product and operations at the company for 14 years and the latter Luxottica's Brazilian general manager; Francesca Bellettini, president and CEO of Yves Saint Laurent, previously in merchandising at Gucci and Bottega Veneta; Jean-Marc Pontroué, chief executive of Officine Panerai, previously in product strategy at Montblanc; Cyrille Vigneron, CEO of Cartier, previously managing director of Cartier Japan (1997–2002), president of Richemont Japan (2002–2005), managing director of Cartier Europe (2005–2013), and president of LVMH Japan (2014–2015). Several researchers in the field of strategic leadership have highlighted the correlation between the position of CEO and previous functional experience. On the basis of a "resource dependence" approach (Pfeffer and Salancik, 1978), it seems that those who bring with them previously acquired skills that can improve corporate performance and resolve organizational criticalities are more likely to become CEOs (Hofer, 1980; Schendel, Patton, and Riggs, 1976; Starbuck and Hedberg, 1977). The choice of a "functional CEO" (i.e., a CEO with functional previous experience) is also a way to manifest externally company's priorities and strategic direction (Elsaid, Benson, and Worrell, 2015).

The type of functional background that will best serve a company depends on its business model (Chaganti and Sambharya, 1987; Gupta and Govindarajan, 1984). For example, in high-tech companies with high research and development investments, it's crucial to ensure that CEOs have technical experience (e.g., research and development, manufacturing, engineering). The goal is for companies to access experience that is consistent with the business needs of the specific historical period and life phase in which they find themselves in an immediate and productive way (Rynes, Orlitzky, and Bretz, 1997). Functional backgrounds can be clustered into three typologies: throughput functional backgrounds (e.g., product, design, operations), output functional backgrounds (e.g., sales, marketing), and peripheral functional backgrounds (e.g., legal, finance) (J. G. Michel and Hambrick, 1992). Earlier studies on executive positions in general – top manager and managing director – showed that skills considered when hiring a CEO can change over time as the organizational context (i.e., competitive strategy, performance, company size) and external conditions shift (Guthrie and Olian, 1991). However, this interest in functional background does not exclude the fact that CEOs must also have a holistic vision of the company in order to best fulfill their role (Gupta, 1984; Hambrick, Black and Fredrickson, 1992; Hitt, Ireland, and Palia, 1982; Wiersema and Bantel, 1992).

Despite this re-thinking of roles and positions, luxury remains a somewhat closed system with respect to where it looks to find professionals. It is not common to hear that a CEO or a top manager has come from a significantly different company or industry. The academic literature has repeatedly highlighted the advantages of appointing internal managers for positions of higher responsibility. These include the reduction of costs associated with induction and errors in the selection process; the ability to successfully attract and retain talent; and the enhancement of deep knowledge of the company, its products, its technologies, its markets, and its processes (Datta and Guthrie, 1994; Friedman, 1991; Gupta, 1984; Zajac, 1990). However, the same literature has also indicated that fostering an internal career deprives the company of the driving forces for innovation, which are necessary above all when a change in the status quo is required. Several studies have shown a negative correlation between tenure and strategic change as well as the necessity to include an outsider in the event of a corporate crisis (Helmich, 1977; K. B. Schwartz and Menon, 1985; Wiersema and Bantel, 1992). An organizational crisis can in fact lead to a questioning of internal and firm-specific knowledge. The choice of outsiders also has an important signaling power inside and outside (Friedman and Singh, 1989).

This situation can also be analyzed from another point of view: Why do the executives of luxury companies prefer to stay in the same organization rather than go looking for new stimuli elsewhere? Research done by Shipilov and Godart in 2015 found that around two thirds of open positions in LVMH brands were occupied by high-potential managers already in the group. This long-term employment is particularly true in large luxury groups where the ability to move to different brands allows individuals to benefit from further learning opportunities and face new challenges. Indeed, brands belonging to a conglomerate such as Kering are quite autonomous from a management point of view and evaluated on the basis of their own profit and loss. A manager switching from Kering eyewear or Bottega Veneta to Gucci is therefore making a significant change, despite remaining within a single group of companies. Intra-group mobility also allows for the identification of best practices and their transfer to different businesses (i.e., products, channel, geographic market).

What today can favor a transition into luxury from someone outside this world is having a strong specialization in an area in which these companies still have a lot to learn: for example, digital or corporate social responsibility, as well as previous experience in industries related to entertainment, content providing, and technology. Not surprisingly, those of us in luxury industries often find ourselves in company meetings where Google, Netflix, and Apple are cited as exemplary, inspirational cases. While we have yet to see a significant influx of talent from outside luxury industries, there is widespread movement between industries that may be industrially different but that adopt the same logic of luxury: from clothing to watchmaking, from eyewear to clothing, and vice versa. What makes the difference when evaluating talents is having internalized a special sensitivity for this world which, as we will see in this text, has very peculiar rules of the game.

From Single-Industry Businesses to Conglomerates

The previous sections have been dedicated to understanding the variety of ownership and management models of luxury companies, highlighting topical issues such as the relevance of the creative soul of brands in different historical periods. This last section aims to analyze the differences between companies from another angle, considering the effects on company size that follow choices relating to two factors:

a) *The type of approach that animates a company's growth strategy*, which can be based on the pursuit of *operational synergies* between various businesses (identified in terms of products, market, technology, channel, etc.) that share a set of resources and skills or of *financial synergies* in which individual businesses are quite independent from each other

b) *The three classic dimensions of corporate scope*: 1) vertical scope, i.e., the degree of vertical integration upstream and downstream; 2) product scope, i.e., the range of industry segments or industries in which a company operates; and 3) geographic scope, i.e., the geographical expansion of procurement, production, and sales activities

These choices can be implemented using different modalities: organic growth or external growth (mergers, acquisitions, equity or non-equity alliances). However, before entering into a discussion of the merits of different directions and modalities of growth, let us consider the six examples of Audemars Piguet, Damiani, Ermenegildo

Zegna, Shiseido, Cassina, and LVMH to understand and highlight some different approaches to growth as well as corporate scopes.

Audemars Piguet. In 1875, Jules-Louis Audemars and Edward-Auguste Piguet put their watchmaking passion to good use and created the "Grande Complication", their first watch, a pocket watch, which gained immediate notoriety. Since then, Audemars Piguet has remained true to its origins both in terms of type of product and location of production. The brand handcrafts 40,000 pieces a year in Switzerland (a volume that is 40% less than Patek Philippe and five times less than Rolex), in three iconic models: Royal Oak, Royal Oak Offshore, and Millenary. The Royal Oak, launched in 1972, remains the brand's best-selling model ever, especially in the US, UK, and Germany.

Damiani. In 1924, Enrico Grassi Damiani started designing and producing diamond jewelry in Valenza, one the most important places for hand-crafted luxury jewels in Italy. Damiani's legacy of jewelry making has been passed down through three generations. Damiani has a highly talented team of jewelry manufacturers, master jewelers who have contributed to the company's success over many years. In addition to its own pieces, Damiani offers its design, conception, and production expertise to third parties. In 1986, Damiani began the process of transforming itself into a group, acquiring the following companies over a period of 30 years: Salvini (1986), Bliss Gioielli (2000), Rocca 1974 (2008), and Venini (2016). In terms of geographic expansion, the company's internationalization process dates to 1998. Today, Damiani is present in twenty countries with 62 boutiques and 150 dealers.

Zegna. The history of Ermenegildo Zegna begins in 1910, with a passion for its place of origin – Trivero, Piedmont – and wool weaving of the best possible quality. This passion has been successfully passed down through four generations, the last of which recently joined the company. Textile processing is carried out entirely in-house, including procuring the best raw materials (cashmere, merino, and mohair) and carefully selecting suppliers, i.e., breeders and sheep farmers, from different countries around the world including South Africa, Australia, and Mongolia. Splendid Zegna fabrics, in addition to being sold to other manufacturing companies, have been used, since 1960, for the creation of men's suits. In the twentieth century, the vertically integrated Italian group expanded from its textile production division to ready-to-wear, casual, and sportswear lines under three brands: Ermenegildo Zegna, Z Zegna, and Ermenegildo Zegna XXX Collection. With the aim of overseeing all textile processes, Zegna bought the silk-weaving company Tessitura di Novara in 2009, the textile manufacturer Bonotto in 2016, and jersey producer Dondi in 2019. At the same time, the company has developed a growing international orientation, which today represents more than 80% of turnover. Zegna has also internationalized from a production point of view, opening factories outside Italy in Spain and Switzerland, and through its retail and wholesale expansion. Today, Zegna is present in around 500 stores, 50% or which are directly operated, in 80 countries.

Shiseido. Shiseido was founded in Tokyo in 1872 by the pharmacist Arinobu Fukuhara. Despite its pharmaceutical roots, the company soon established itself as a source for cosmetic products with unique characteristics. Its first were Eudermine (an extremely effective moisturizing lotion), seven colors of face powder, and a cold cream. Shiseido's Hanatsubaki (camellia), the first perfume created in Japan (the best perfumes were previously imported from France), debuted 1917, followed by two other floral fragrances: Ume (plum) and Fuji (wisteria). In 1957, Shiseido began exporting its products to Taiwan.

The internationalization of the company began in the 1960s with the creation of foreign branches in Hawaii (1962), the US mainland (1965), and Italy (1968), continuing in later decades with Singapore (1970), New Zealand (1971), Thailand (1972), France and Germany (1980), the UK (1986), Canada (1993), Brazil (2001), Russia (2007), Vietnam (2008, with construction of a factory completed in 2009), and Greece and Switzerland (2010). In 1991, Shiseido established its first manufacturing base in Europe.

The company began its market penetration strategy in the 1980s with the introduction of an anti-aging line and solar products, followed by the large-scale launch of fragrances in the late 1990s, targeting international markets (see Chapter 5). The company's first men's line dates to 2004. Shiseido has also undertaken several brand acquisitions, from Helene Curtis (1997) to Nars (2000) to Bare Escentuals (2010), as well as joint ventures including a licensing agreement with Dolce & Gabbana beginning in 2016. While it has for the most part limited its activities to cosmetics and fragrance, in 1973 Shiseido opened L'Osier, a French restaurant in the Tokyo neighborhood of Ginza that received three Michelin stars for the first time in 2008. The company is publicly traded and has been listed on the Tokyo Stock Exchange since 1949.

Cassina S.p.A. was founded in 1927 in Meda, Lombardy, in the center of the Brianza furniture district, by the brothers Cesare and Umberto Cassina. The company is known for its artisanal production of high-quality chairs, tables, sofas, and armchairs. Since the Second World War, Cassina has expanded its product range and market outlets, becoming active in large hotel, restaurant, and cruise ship projects. Collaborations with renowned designers and architects, from Andrea Branzi to Angelo Mangiarotti to Afra and Tobia Scarpa, is one of the founding elements of Cassina's success on an international level. Indeed, it was a collaboration with the Italian architect and designer Gio Ponti that led to one of Cassina's most iconic products, the "superlight" chair, which first appeared on the market in 1957 and is still in the catalog today. The company has also sought to expand its offer through acquisitions. Two important milestones in its history are the acquisition of the design rights of Le Corbusier, Pierre Jeanneret, and Charlotte Perriand in 1965 and the acquisition of the production rights of models by Gerrit Rietveld, Frank Lloyd Wright, and Charles Rennie Mackintosh in 1972. In 2005, Cassina was acquired by Poltrona Frau, and in 2014, the entire Poltrona Frau Group, now renamed Lifestyle Design Group, was taken over by the American Haworth. Today, Lifestyle Design includes Luxury Living (Fendi Casa,

Bentley Casa, Trussardi Casa, Bugatti Home), Poltrona Frau, Cappellini, Cassina, Janus, Ceccotti Collezioni, Luminaire, Karakter, and Dzine.

LVMH. In October 2020, major business journals announced the closing of the deal of the year: the acquisition of Tiffany & Co. by LVMH group for $131.50 a share, less than the original negotiation price. The deal benefits both sides: acquiring Tiffany allows the group to reinforce its presence in "hard luxury", where it already operates with Bulgari and Tag Heuer; becoming part of LVMH means that Tiffany now has an entity behind it capable of making substantial investments in product and retail. This acquisition has therefore created a new threat for the Richemont group, the undisputed leader in the hard luxury world. According to Euromonitor data, LVMH can now expect to achieve a 17.3% market share in hard luxury, approaching the 19% held by Richemont in the same market (Sherman, 2020).

Tiffany is the most recent brand to be acquired by LVMH, but it will not be the last. The group has pursued its existing diversification strategy since it was created in 1987 (Table 1.1), acquiring existing brands in order to hold them and let them grow. This strategy, implemented by LVMH chair Bernard Arnault, prioritizes long- over short-term objectives; its horizon is typical of an entrepreneurial mindset rather than a financial one (Friedman and Paton, 2020).

Table 1.1: Creating a Conglomerate Year by Year.

	1980s	1990s	2000s
Brands incorporated (year of establishment)	1987: Creation of LVMH with the initial incorporation of Louis Vuitton (1854), Moët & Chandon (1743), Hennessy (1765) 1988: Givenchy (1952)	1993: Berluti (1895), Kenzo (1970) 1994: Guerlain (1828) 1996: Céline (1945), Loewe (1846) 1997: Marc Jacobs (1984), Sephora (1969) 1999: Thomas Pink (1984), Tag Heuer (1860)	2000: Emilio Pucci (1947) 2000: Rossimoda (1977) 2001: La Samaritaine (1870), Fendi (1925), DKNY (1984) 2010: Moynat 2011: Bulgari (1884) 2013: Loro Piana (1924), Nicholas Kirkwood (2004), J.W. Anderson (2008, minority stake) 2015: Repossi (1920) 2016: Rimowa (1989) 2017: Christian Dior (1946) 2018: Jean Patou (1912) 2019: Fenty (organic growth, JV with Rihanna), Stella McCartney (2001, JV, Stella McCartney owns the majority stake) 2020: Tiffany & Co. (1837)

Table 1.1 (continued)

	1980s	1990s	2000s
Industries added	Leather goods, wine and spirits, couture and RTW	Men's shoes, leather goods, and RTW; perfume, cosmetics, and skincare; retail; watches	Jewelry, fragrances

Source: Prepared by authors from available public data.[6]

What we immediately ascertain from these examples is that luxury companies have since the mid-twentieth century pursued international expansion such that today the geographical spectrum of sales is very broad. Cassina, for example, is considered the first true Italian international company, having approached foreign markets as early as the 1960s; by the 1980s, its exports had already exceeded 70% of turnover. Established luxury brands from developed markets have been able to expand in this way because they have leveraged both advantageous positions in their respective domestic markets and a positive image associated with their countries of origin as specialists in particular industries to seek growth opportunities in other countries, especially in times of crisis in domestic consumption. This internationalization took place according to the classic model of the international enterprise: export-based, keeping all value-generating activities in the country of origin.

Although brands with overseas sales of over 50% are now the rule, each has different key foreign markets in its portfolio. Among the most difficult markets is Brazil, where duties and tariffs at prohibitive levels create challenging conditions for any foreign company. There are also very few companies that can be said to have "Triad Power", i.e., an equal distribution of sales in the three main markets of Japan, Europe, and the United States – markets where the most important battle for companies operating on a global scale is taking place (Ohmae, 1986).

However, this high degree of international exposure does not characterize brands from all countries. Let's take India as an example: the country is home to artisans renowned for their skills in textiles, embroidery, jewelry, and cosmetics. Yet almost all Indian luxury companies have maintained a local scale over time. The reasons for this low international exposure cannot be limited to the small size of these companies, often workshops with just a few artisans. Many have developed a specialization – such as embroidery – much appreciated by international clients; therefore, they operate in a B2B market with very concentrated foreign customers. Other companies, especially in the world of jewelry or clothing, have developed a business model and an offer to satisfy the specific tastes of the local consumer and therefore do not lend themselves to being parachuted into markets with different tastes. In any case,

India is a market with such high growth potential that companies that "stay local" can expect an adequate return in the long term.

Still, there are exceptions. Forest Essentials, a pioneer in ayurvedic skincare, was founded in Delhi in 2000 by Mira Kulkharni. The brand, which is proud of its production in India, sells in 80 stores in the country. It has also managed to spread rapidly in hospitality, supplying around 190 hotels with candles and soaps. The brand has attracted the interest of Estée Lauder Companies, which has held a 40% stake in Forest Essentials since 2008. Thanks also to its connection with this important group, Forest Essentials has boosted sales in 120 markets through e-commerce. A similar case of a company expanding beyond a traditionally closed domestic market is that of Natura, a personal care company from Brazil, one of the largest markets for hair products in the world. Even before sustainability became imperative, 70% of Natura's hair products were "green", yet until 2016, its presence abroad was limited to 10% of turnover. Today, this share has risen to 45% thanks in part to its acquisition of Aesop and The Body Shop, which together represent 37% of turnover. In 2020, Natura acquired Avon Cosmetics, becoming one of the top five beauty groups worldwide.

We can differentiate between companies by looking at the industries in which they operate, the activities that are carried out within company boundaries, the type of connection between businesses within a company, and the type of business model they follow. From the examples described above, we can identify *single-industry* companies that have maintained a strong specialization, be it watches, textiles, clothing, or furnishings. These companies have grown by modifying the level of vertical integration (above all internalizing distribution activities with the opening of directly operated stores), entering new geographic markets, and covering other roles in the value system to approach new customer targets. This is the case of Zegna, where the core business of textiles provided the base of skills and activities that allowed it to expand into tailored clothing. Or the case of Damiani, which capitalized on its core competency in high jewelry to expand into retail (with Rocca) and more accessible items (Salvini and Bliss).

Then there are *multi-industry* companies that operate in different related industries, such as Shiseido, whose brands range from skin care to make-up to fragrances. These companies have pursued a marketing-driven program of diversification in which corporate advantage depends on marketing skills (i.e., management of sales channels, brands, communication), an area in which important operational synergies between businesses are created. However, these companies can also invest heavily in research and development to generate technology and innovation resources that can be effectively shared across businesses (e.g., Shiseido's different cosmetics areas) (Corbetta, 2020).

Finally, we find the *conglomerates*, such as LVMH, Kering, and Richemont, which, like multi-industry companies, are present in many industries but are not correlated with each other. The intent of diversification for conglomerates is to implement *financial synergies* and ensure that the holding transfers support activities such as HR, finance, and legal between businesses or favors the sharing of best practices that can refer, in this historical period, to digital, sustainability, and omnichannel strategy above all.

In luxury, conglomerates have the characteristic of always having a core business, a division that is the most important in terms of weight on turnover and/or margins.[7] This is not necessarily one of the company's historical or original businesses. In the specific case of LVMH, we can see in Table 1.2 that Moët Hennessy, despite being one of the first businesses in which the group invested, has a weight of 10% on total revenues, but ensures a very high profitability on sales.

Table 1.2: LVMH: Turnover and Profit by Business.

(In million euros)	2017	2018	2019
Selective Retailing			
Revenue	13,311	13,646	14,791
% on total group revenues	31%	29%	27%
% France	12%	12%	11%
% Rest of Europe	8%	9%	9%
% USA	39%	38%	37%
% Japan	1%	2%	2%
% Rest of Asia	28%	27%	27%
% Other Markets	12%	12%	14%
Profit from recurring operations	1,075	1,382	1,395
Profit/revenue	8%	10%	9%
Operating investments	570	537	659
Number of stores	1,880	1,940	2,011
Watches and Jewelry			
Revenue	3,805	4,123	4,405
% on total group revenues	9%	9%	8%
% France	6%	6%	5%
% Rest of Europe	25%	23%	23%
% USA	9%	9%	8%
% Japan	13%	12%	12%
% Rest of Asia	31%	35%	38%

Table 1.2 (continued)

(In million euros)	2017	2018	2019
% Other Markets	16%	15%	14%
Profit from recurring operations	512	703	736
Profit/revenue	13%	17%	17%
Operating investments	269	303	296
Number of stores	405	428	457
Perfumes and Cosmetics			
Revenue	5,560	6,092	6,835
% on total group revenues	13%	13%	13%
% France	11%	11%	10%
% Rest of Europe	24%	22%	20%
% USA	17%	16%	15%
% Japan	5%	5%	5%
% Rest of Asia	30%	35%	40%
% Other Markets	13%	11%	10%
Profit from recurring operations	600	676	683
Profit/revenue	11%	11%	10%
Operating investments	286	330	378
Fashion and Leather goods			
Revenue	15,472	18,455	22,237
% on total group revenues	36%	39%	41%
% France	9%	9%	8%
% Rest of Europe	23%	23%	23%
% USA	18%	18%	18%
% Japan	11%	11%	11%
% Rest of Asia	31%	31%	31%
% Other Markets	8%	8%	9%
Profit from recurring operations	4,905	5,943	7,344
Profit/revenue	32%	32%	33%
Operating investments	563	827	1,199
Number of stores	2,002	1,852	1,769

Table 1.2 (continued)

(In million euros)	2017	2018	2019
Wines and Spirits			
Revenue	5,084	5,143	5,576
% on total group revenues	12%	11%	10%
% France	6%	6%	5%
% Rest of Europe	18%	19%	18%
% USA	32%	32%	33%
% Japan	6%	6%	7%
% Rest of Asia	22%	23%	24%
% Other Markets	16%	14%	13%
Profit from recurring operations	1,558	1,629	1,729
Profit/revenue	31%	32%	31%
Operating investments	292	298	325
TOTAL GROUP REVENUES	43,232	47,459	53,844

Source: Compiled by authors from available public data.[8]

In LVMH, the most important division is fashion and leather goods, which represents 36% of revenues with a profitability of 32%, making it the group's most profitable division. This data could change in the future, as the acquisition of Tiffany & Co. will surely add weight to LVMH's watches and jewelry division, as well as giving the group a greater market share in that industry. Meanwhile, Richemont's jewelry houses (Buccellati, Cartier, Van Cleef & Arpels) can rightly be considered the group's core business, responsible for 51% of its total sales in 2020. The group's specialist watchmakers (A. Lange & Söhne, Baume & Mercier, IWC Schaffhausen, Jaeger-LeCoultre, Panerai, Piaget, Roger Dubuis, Vacheron Constantin) account for 20% of sales. Additional business areas online distributors (Watchfinder & Co., Yoox-Net-a-Porter Group) and "other" (Alaïa, Chloé, Dunhill, Montblanc, Peter Millar, Purdey, Serapian) follow.

Richemont's online distributors deserve a separate mention. Despite representing 17% of the group's turnover, these entities represent enormous growth potential for the entire group. They make core competency in digital available to all the group's brands and allow for expansion both in geographic markets inclined toward online purchases and in hard luxury categories more generally (Prahalad and Hamel, 1990). It is thanks to its familiarity in this area that Richemont entered a new alliance with Alibaba and Farfetch in November 2020, following joint ventures already in place between Richemont and Alibaba and between Farfetch, JD, and Tencent. This has resulted in an interesting consolidation in the largest luxury and online sales markets. The new partnership is aimed at facilitating the expansion of international luxury brands in the Chinese market as well as accelerating the digitization of luxury. Despite this aggregation with common purpose, Yoox-Net-a-Porter and Farfetch will maintain their business models based on wholesale and marketplace, respectively.[9]

If conglomerates make portfolio choices by deciding which businesses to invest in or disinvest from, the brands that they are composed of are, like all luxury companies, also authors of growth strategies aimed at broadening their scope and increasing their size. In general, we see a particular agility in luxury companies, which are able to promptly absorb changes in the social and competitive context, evolving their presence in the market and internal organization to suit an altered environment. In our opinion, there is no better example of ambidexterity than luxury brands. They show commitment to preserving a core business while also being careful to seize opportunities for the development of new skills and growth at the perimeter of their activities. In identifying new opportunities, they are perfectly aware that a brand's expertise can be strong somewhere but not everywhere: "In order not to fail in the growth path, a brand must always ask itself if it is providing a good reason to the market to join a new proposal" (Jean-Marc Pontroué, CEO, Panerai, personal communication).

Following the concepts of ambidexterity as described by O'Reilly and Tushman (2004, 2008) and Gilbert, Eyring, and Foster (2012), luxury companies have especially shown a core ability to:

1) *Exploit the present*, adapting the business model across different geographies (e.g., Asia vs. Europe vs. North America) and market segments (e.g., Generation X, Generation Z, Millennials)
2) *Explore the various trajectories of future growth* and adopt multiple business models

Ambidexterity is the central factor in allowing luxury companies to be resilient. In our research, we found these companies to have a unique ability to diversify their revenue generation by being ambidextrous from the point of inception. An example is Chanel, a company that is built on two separate business entities: (a) apparel and accessories – a high price point, targeted toward a more sophisticated client base; and (b) cosmetics and beauty – a more accessible product range, targeting a more aspirational client base. Despite its success with this structure, Chanel has not failed to explore other trajectories of growth, like the introduction of high jewelry and watches in 2013 and 1999, respectively. The reasons behind these growth strategies are highly varied and range from the increase in market power, to control along the supply chain of activities with greater added value, to the achievement of first-mover advantages by launching products and services or by structuring processes that exploit trends.

Growth Strategies of Luxury Companies: Directions and Modalities

The previous section was dedicated to the presentation of the main types of companies by industry specialization, highlighting the difference between an approach to growth aimed at pursuing operational synergies compared to one where financial synergies are dominant. As we have seen, all companies present in the market over a number of years have progressively changed their scope and size. Companies make decisions targeted both at strengthening their presence in existing businesses – defined as a combination of product offered and market served, which we can also consider from a geographical point of view – and at entering new businesses, whether related or unrelated. Companies execute these choices using various modalities: organic growth, non-equity alliances, equity alliances, and mergers and acquisitions.

Organic growth allows companies to enhance internal resources and skills as well as to encourage internal creativity. Internal growth can take place, for example, by expanding on foreign markets through exports or by creating commercial and production branches. Likewise, an increase in the number of directly operated stores (DOS) is a matter of internal growth. A brand like Brunello Cucinelli has significantly increased revenues by relying on progressively investing in its DOS network (from 61 stores in 2013 to 107 in 2020) and building its brand identity. Upstream, companies invest in proprietary production facilities: for example, Fendi, which in 2020 started the construction of a new factory in Tuscany, to open in 2022.

Another frequent form of internal growth is product and process innovation resulting from a company's research and development or design departments. To boost the generation of innovation internally, several companies have created incubators disconnected from the business so that their activity can take place outside of daily operations. By opening up to external influences through various forms of collaboration, these incubators can access new stimuli and information about trends. This is how LVHM's beauty incubator, Kendo, was born, from which brands such as Fenty Beauty and Kat Von D originated. In the same spirit, the Moët Hennessy Innovation Lab explores opportunities for innovation in the world of spirits.

Non-equity alliances are partnerships based on the signing of a contract stipulating that the parties will undertake to collaborate on a specific area of activity. The actors involved therefore remain independent and continue to carry out their primary activities autonomously. The reciprocal commitment ends when the contract expires, unless it is renewed (automatically or upon further negotiation). Luxury alliances include recurring forms such as:

– *Licensing*: the licensor grants the licensee the right to use the brand to carry out production and marketing activities in exchange for a royalty

- *Franchising*: the franchisor grants a franchisee the right to run a business selling a product or service using the franchisor's business system under its brand
- *Strategic supplier agreement*: the brand creates a long-term collaborative relationship with the supplier to involve it in a process of continuous improvement

Licensing has been used a lot in the past by luxury brands, especially for expansion into the cosmetics and eyewear industries. If you look at beauty groups like Coty, Shiseido, and L'Oréal, you can see how in their portfolios licensing for fragrances and make-up is still a recurring modality. In the case of Coty, this dependency on licensing is even greater following its acquisition of the prestige part of P&G Specialty Beauty Business in 2016. The use of licenses in this industry is understandable if we think of the investments in research and development and assets that are necessary to develop a new beauty product, investments different from those required in the worlds of clothing and leather goods.

However, the ongoing trend is to increase brand control as much as possible and limit licensing to a minimum. This is the path followed by brands such as Ferrari, which announced in 2019 that it wanted to reduce licensing agreements by 50%, and Dior, which under the leadership of CEO Sidney Toledano cut license agreements from 300 to only a few (The Fashion Law, 2019). Luxury conglomerates have embarked on the path of cutting licenses specifically in the world of eyewear, opting for more direct forms of presence. This is a sign of change in the competitive logics of B2B relations in the eyewear industry. Globalization and the desire for tighter control of the elements of brand identity have encouraged luxury companies to internalize business as they adapt their business models to meet growing demand. In addition, they have brought both design and production in-house and assumed direct control of the supply chain in cases where they do still work with external suppliers. Kering chairman and CEO François-Henri Pinault chose internal growth as an alternative to licenses for the group's eyewear brands, leading to the creation of Kering Eyewear in 2014 and the group assuming direct control of the entire value chain. As a consequence of this strategic decision, Safilo, for example, lost the Gucci license two years before it expired. Furthermore, in March 2017, Kering and Richemont announced a partnership agreement for the development, manufacturing, and worldwide distribution of the eyewear categories of Cartier and other brands. Richemont also became a shareholder of Kering Eyewear. Today, Kering Eyewear designs, develops, and distributes eyewear for a portfolio of fifteen brands: Gucci, Cartier, Saint Laurent, Balenciaga, Bottega Veneta, Alexander McQueen, Stella McCartney, Alaïa, Courrèges, Montblanc, Brioni, Boucheron, Pomellato, McQ, and Puma. The design of the glasses is carried out by brand-dedicated designers working full time at the brands' offices, ensuring consistency with all the other elements of the offer (Lojacono, 2018). Around 70% of production needs are met by over 20 suppliers across the two most important Italian industrial clusters for eyewear (Valdobbiadene and Cadore, Veneto), providing unique craftsmanship skills and competencies, proven manufacturing expertise, quality and innovation, an unparalleled ability to immediately react to market needs, and high flexibility in product allocation. The other 30% of production is carried out by around 40 suppliers in China, Japan, France, and Italy (regions other than Veneto). In 2020, Kering Eyewear achieved around €500 million in revenues, with 1,550 employees (60% women, 55% global). This example from the world of eyewear allows us to highlight an important message: the choices made by ambidextrous luxury companies are not static but dynamic. A set-up resulting from past decisions can naturally evolve in another direction due to a changed context or new internal needs. Companies that have decided to abandon licenses have moved on to various forms of greater integration with direct investments or hybrid methods such as joint ventures.

Non-equity alliances also include *brand collaborations*, i.e., partnerships that involve a multiplicity of players, such as brands, artists, celebrities, retailers, cultural and sports organizations, to achieve a common purpose (e.g., product launch, event creation, sharing the same store network, or creating a social or employee initiative) (G. Michel and Willing, 2020). These collaborations are extremely varied, bringing together haute couture designers like Alexander Wang and Giambattista Valli and fashion retailers like H&M as well as brands and online retailers (e.g., Off White for Luisaviaroma and Mr. Porter; Dolce & Gabbana for Mytheresa), luxury brands from different industries (e.g., Bugatti and Jacob & Co., Porsche and Embraer),[10] or brands and artists (e.g., Louis Vuitton and Jeff Koon for the "Masters" handbags line, Lady Dior Art Bags in collaboration with various artists) or brands belonging to very different worlds (e.g., Dior with Vespa and Air Jordan, Stella McCartney with Adidas, or Gucci with North Face). Co-branding has also been undertaken between fashion brands and sports teams and associations for the launch of capsule collections (LV X NBA, Gucci X New York Yankees). The purpose of these partnerships is for luxury brands to legitimize themselves in a context far from their usual one, such as streetwear, sportwear, or high-tech (as in the case of Hermès and Apple), with a wider audience, achieving even higher volumes than usual, and for their partners to improve the perception of their own brand and reposition themselves toward the premium market segment (i.e., trading up). These collaborations are both critical and risky for luxury brands, which, in order to preserve their symbolic and aspirational content, must make careful choices relating to partners and the content and communication of a common offer, as well as the volume to be poured onto the market.

Collaboration is not just about signing products or collections: it extends to communication and social and humanitarian initiatives. Rolex and National Geographic have signed "Perpetual Planet", a joint initiative to generate knowledge and raise awareness about the wonders of the planet (particularly oceans, poles, and mountains) as well as the challenges it faces. This goal will be pursued by support expeditions that allow scientific knowledge in order to fuel research and invention.

The project will develop new exploration technologies as well as organize public initiatives that raise public awareness.

Equity alliances. The world of equity alliances includes minority equity stakes, cross equity stakes, and joint ventures. The latter can be equal, majority, or minority. In the process of closing licenses in eyewear, LVMH entered a 51%-stake joint venture with the eyewear manufacturer Marcolin called Thélios to get access to crucial Italian technology and product development expertise. This decision left traditional manufacturing partners with fewer licensed brands in their portfolios.

Joint ventures are widespread in international expansion strategies when entering markets characterized by high cultural, administrative, and economic specificities. Having a local partner can make it possible to overcome the "liability of foreignness" – the disadvantages that a foreign player faces when entering an unfamiliar context – faster and better (Mezias, 2002; Zaheer, 1995). Having an ally in the host country undoubtedly facilitates the understanding of consumer habits and preferences, allowing the new entrant to adapt its presence in the country, identify valid suppliers and intermediaries on site, and access constant support in territorial expansion, including suggestions of the best locations and facilitated negotiations with landlords. In short, local partners provide essential market knowledge of what is in most cases a highly diverse country. In the Middle East, for example, a very difficult market from a regulatory and distribution point of view, Chaloub is the key partner for expanding companies. It boasts a consolidated alliance with brands such as Louis Vuitton, Christian Dior, Sephora, Fendi, Chaumet, Christian Louboutin, and Berluti (Snell and Bigelow, 2019).

Reliance Brands Limited (RBL) India performs a similar role in India, a market where organized distribution represents less than 10% of retail value and luxury channels mainly refer to malls, airports and hotels, multi-brand stores, and e-commerce. However, luxury is moving increasingly to street locations, like Kala Ghoda in Mumbai. Reliance is catching the trend and has started experimenting with a new format. At The Tank in Ballard Estate, customers can shop last season's luxury-brand clothes, with price tags reduced by 30 to 50% (Vogue, 2013). The space was originally open to Reliance employees only, but was later made accessible to the public.

RBL is part of Reliance Industries Limited (RIL), a US$173 billion market-cap conglomerate, the number one company by profit in the Fortune Global 500 rankings, and the 96th largest company in the world. It began operations in 2007 with a mandate to launch and build international and domestic brand equity in the premium to luxury segment across fashion and lifestyle spaces. Its current portfolio of brand partnerships comprises, among others, Bally, Bottega Veneta, Burberry, Ermenegildo Zegna, Giorgio Armani, Hugo Boss, Jimmy Choo, Kate Spade New York, Kurt Geiger, Paul Smith, Pottery Barn, Salvatore Ferragamo, Steve Madden, Tiffany & Co., Tumi, and Villeroy and Boch. Today, RBL operates 438 mono-brand stores and 346 shop-in-shops in India. In May 2019, it marked its first international foray by acquiring the British toy retailer Hamleys, which owns 187 stores spread across 16 countries.

It is surprising to note that the aforementioned partners provide high value to the joint venture both from a strategic and operational point of view. They themselves operate in luxury retail with formats of their own conception, both traditional and innovative, like The White Crow by Reliance Brands and Level Shoes by Chaloub in Dubai Mall.

Mergers and acquisitions (M&As). From the perspective of the acquirer, the rationales behind M&As can be grouped into the following strategic goals: to increase the market share in a specific industry segment; to get access to new product or service categories, as well as untapped foreign markets; to acquire know-how in specific business areas (e.g., digital, sustainability, DTC); to create value for the acquired brand by valorizing the capabilities and assets of the acquirer.

In December 2020, Remo Ruffini, CEO of Moncler, a brand with a turnover of approximately €1.63 billion, announced that it had closed an agreement for the acquisition of 100% of Stone Island. Moncler's shares immediately jumped 6.5%. What reasons could have led Moncler to take over a brand with a turnover of €240 million, rooted in Italy and with 75% of sales through wholesale? On the one hand, Moncler has the ability to broaden its customer base to a younger segment and increase exposure to men's RTW. On the other hand, there is a great opportunity to grow Stone Island in international markets and the retail channel (80% of Moncler's turnover), taking advantage of the buyer's knowledge, especially in important locations such as Korea, Japan, and the United States.

Acquisition opportunities increase after a crisis, as fragile companies become available. These waves of M&As have an immediate impact on industry consolidation.[11] In some industries characterized by entrepreneurial ferment and high start-up rates, it is possible that new companies with insufficient managerial and financial resources to cope with growth may prefer to enter the mainstream of large companies. This is common in cosmetics, where groups such as Estée Lauder and L'Oréal have in the past acquired emerging and independent brands (so-called *indie brands*). The barriers to entry to operate in this industry have therefore been reduced, thanks to the possibility of communicating and selling online and of finding a dense network of specialized suppliers to whom to transfer the production. However, growth is not sustainable for these small businesses.

The changing business portfolios of conglomerates show how the acquisition of existing international brands has led to external growth. Conglomerates have been able to accelerate their growth process, finding well-known brands with strong roots in their respective industries. The acquired companies have often benefited from joining these groups, which have put in place human and financial resources and skills to enable development, sometimes at a critical moment in their lifecycle. Acquisitions have therefore been the preferred mode of expansion for "serial buyers" such as Richemont (Table 1.3), which has used simultaneous acquisitions to buy many watch component manufacturers.

Table 1.3: M&A: Richemont's Major Luxury Brand Acquisitions.

Year	Brand
1988	Richemont is formed, owning Cartier, Montblanc, and Chloé (among others)
1994	Acquisition of Purdey (high-end rifles)
1996	Acquisition of Vacheron Constantin
1997	Acquisition of Officine Panerai and Lancel
1999	Acquisition of Van Cleef & Arpels
2000	Acquisition of Jaeger-LeCoultre, IWC, and A. Lange & Söhne
2007	Acquisition of Alaïa
2008	Acquisition of Roger Dubuis
2010	Acquisition of Net-a-porter.com
2015	Richemont merges The Net-A-Porter Group with YOOX Group
2021	Richemont acquires Delvaux

Source: Compiled by authors from available public data.

It is interesting to note how the two main luxury groups – LVMH and Kering – are owned by French entrepreneurs, but many of their manufacturing facilities, especially in clothing and leather goods, are centered in Italy. The dynamic between the two countries contributes to a perfect harmony between the brand-centric French and the product-centric Italians. This is quite clear in eyewear and cosmetics, where international brands rely on the superior quality of Italian manufacturers: eyewear under the LVMH and Kering brands is produced in the eyewear industrial cluster in North-East Italy (Veneto); the majority of luxury make-up products are produced in a "Cosmetic Valley" close to Milan by around 500 contract manufacturers.

This mode of growth is not limited to luxury groups; there are independent brands that have used acquisitions to fuel external growth, acquiring suppliers from different upstream stages of the supply chain (e.g., Chanel buying a majority stake in Richard Tannery, the supplier of the lambskins used to manufacture small leather goods), as well as brands specialized in other product categories or market segments (e.g., Chanel buying men's swimwear brand Orlebar Brown or Moncler's acquisition of Stone Island).

Acquisitions are the method par excellence for investment funds creating their portfolio of assets. The difference with respect to the acquisitions mentioned above is the time horizon of the investment.[12] If luxury brands and conglomerates make an acquisition with a long-term objective, in the case of funds, the aim is to increase the value of the investment in a few years and then sell it off at the right time. The funds actively contribute to increasing the value of the acquired company by introducing managerial skills in critical areas.[13] A recent case is that of Style Capital, which in 2020 acquired the Australian brand Zimmermann, which joined Forte Forte, MSGM and Re/Done in its portfolio.[14]

In the growth path, the modes described above are used to expand in three different directions; the combination of directions and modes shapes a company's growth strategy. Table 1.4 presents the three growth dimensions in detail.

Table 1.4: Directions of Growth.

Directions of Growth	Typologies	Definition	Examples in Luxury
Operational Reinforcement: Growth in existing businesses	Product Adjacency	Launch of new goods or services to customers already served	Chanel Boy (2011/2012) Virtual customer service
	Customer Adjacency	Entry into new customer segments	Zegna moving from B2B to manufacture men's suits sold in retail stores to consumers (1960) Bulgari from high jewelry to lifestyle and affordable lines under the same brand umbrella Tod's from casual and formal shoes to elegant luxury women's shoes (with the acquisition of Roger Vivier in 2015) Armani from haute couture to Emporio Armani (1981)
	Channel Adjacency	Use of new distribution channels to reach customers already served	Cartier joining Tmall Luxury Pavilion (2020)
	Coverage Adjacency	New openings of stores or locations in a given country	Mandarin Oriental opening a new hotel in Como (Italy) in 2020, following the existent one in Milan
Related Expansion: Growth in a new business in an industry in which the firm already competes	Segment Adjacency	Enter into a new segment in an industry in which the firm already competes	In 2018, Lamborghini launches the URUS, a luxury SUV
	Geographic Adjacency	Entry into a new geography	Boffi kitchens entering India in 2013

Table 1.4 (continued)

Directions of Growth	Typologies	Definition	Examples in Luxury
Related Exploration: Growth by adding new businesses to the portfolio through entering a new related industry	Industry Adjacency	Entry into a new industry through horizontal, related diversification	Cosmetics companies adding skincare to make-up
	Vertical Adjacency	Expand along the industry's value chain through vertical integration	In 2013 Chanel acquires Bodin-Joyeux, a lambskin tannery in central France that produces the leather Chanel uses for quilted handbags In 2015, Hermès buys Melaleuca Crocodile Farm in Mareeba (Australia) In 2013, Louis Vuitton buys Johnstone River Crocodile Farm in the north of Queensland (Australia) In 2019, Chanel acquires a 20% stake in Kenissi, an industrial arm of Tudor specializing in Swiss automatic movements Chanel, through Paraffection, buys Roveda (1999) and Gensi (2015), footwear producers in Italy, with which the French brand was already collaborating
Unrelated Exploration: Growth by adding new businesses to the portfolio through entering a new unrelated industry			In 2000, a licensing deal with L'Oréal Group creates Armani Beauty, and in 2005, Giorgio Armani SpA enters an agreement with Emaar Properties to establish Armani Hotels & Resorts

Source: Compiled by authors from Morosetti, 2020.

Unrelated exploration is usually more consistent with a financial approach than an operational approach. However, what ultimately matters are a company's strategic priorities. What drives entry into unrelated territories at the group level (e.g., LVMH), might not be a driver at the brand level (e.g., Bulgari). Entering the hospitality, the beauty, or the eyewear industry for a brand specialized in jewels, apparel, and leather goods offers the opportunity to create multiple touchpoints with its clientele, expanding its reach and the market for its core products. The further a company moves away from its existing businesses, the more effort it has to invest to accumulate new resources and competencies. This means that among a company's operational reinforcement options, widening the product line is probably the simplest and most natural because it can be dictated by the existing rules of the business. Often, long-standing, iconic products give birth to new generations of products that respect brand heritage but enrich the offer.

Upstream vertical integration has been increasingly pursued to achieve tighter control of suppliers and to allow luxury companies to preserve intrinsic product quality. Furthermore, this strategy allows a luxury brand to enhance production knowledge that can be used in other businesses. One of the challenges of internationalization is the difficulty of finding the right quality and quantity of raw materials to expand geographically. For example, Hermès controlled the tanning and manufacturing of the crocodile skins used in some of its products, but relied on independent farms for the skins themselves until acquiring Melaleuca Crocodile Farm in 2015. In other cases, upstream vertical integration provides continuity, allowing the savoir-faire of artisans in heritage industries to be fully incorporated into the business. This has been Chanel's motivation: it has ensured outstanding production capacities, strengthening its connections with different territories through its Paraffection program. Acquired artisans' workshops can continue to work for other brands, with confidentiality on all projects, without interference from Paraffection or the broader Chanel Group. They have the unique opportunity to expand their know-how working with different clients and to attract new talent.

Vertical integration can also mean internalizing distribution activities that would otherwise be carried out by independent intermediaries. As we have seen, the increase in the weight of direct distribution in recent years – through directly operated stores (DOS) or proprietary e-commerce (Brand.com) – has reached unstoppable proportions. To better understand this choice, the next section will present the main distribution models, focusing for simplicity on the world of personal goods (jewelry, watches, clothing, leather goods, shoes, cosmetics). As we shall see, descriptions of the business models that dictate the distribution of luxury products also include the growth modes described above, such as franchising.

Growth Directions and Modalities in Hospitality: The Case of Dorchester Collection

Dorchester Collection was founded as a hotel management company in 2006, creating an intimate portfolio of stunning hotels – it manages nine of the world's foremost luxury hotels in Europe and North America. At the time of its founding in 2006, Dorchester Collection consisted of five hotels: The Dorchester (London), The

Beverly Hills Hotel (Beverly Hills), Le Meurice (Paris), Hôtel Plaza Athénée (Paris), and Hotel Principe di Savoia (Milan). Since then, the company has added four more hotels to its portfolio with Hotel Bel-Air (Los Angeles), Coworth Park (Ascot), 45 Park Lane (London), and Hotel Eden (Rome). Each hotel is legendary in its own right, with a rich heritage and worldwide reputation for offering the best and most sought-after experiences of good living, charm, elegance, and unparalleled standards of service. Dorchester Collection has made a deliberate decision to remain small and intimate in order to protect the core proposition: To be treasured by guests, cherished by employees, and celebrated worldwide.

One of Dorchester Collection's aims is to build on the brand loyalty that it has maintained since the portfolio was created through a selective expansion strategy focused on key gateway cities worldwide. With Dorchester Collection's continuous investment in taking the luxury experience to new levels, major restorations have recently taken place in many of the hotels including The Beverly Hills Hotel, The Dorchester, Le Meurice, Hôtel Plaza Athénée, and, most recently, Hotel Eden, which reopened in April 2017. In 2018, Dorchester Collection announced its first hotel and residences in Dubai, opening at the end of 2022.

With the exception of Coworth Park and 45 Park Lane, which are more recent developments, the other hotels within Dorchester Collection enjoy a rich heritage and presence in their cities, pre-dating the creation of Dorchester Collection as a brand. For example, The Beverly Hills Hotel was built two years before the city of Beverly Hills was founded, and Hôtel Plaza Athénée was the reason Christian Dior chose to open his first boutique on avenue Montaigne in 1946. At Le Meurice, also in Paris, Salvador Dalí would stay for months at a time, leading to the hotel's distinctive surrealistic design. The Dorchester's Oliver Messel Suite was created by the eponymous theatre designer and remains one of the most celebrated hotel suites in London. Today, Dorchester Collection treasures the events and memories of the past and invites their guests to become part of the rich heritage through their own experiences.

CEO Christopher Cowdray united the hotels under the umbrella of Dorchester Collection, creating a shared vision and company values that link the behaviors it upholds as a business, financial goals, and sales and marketing strategies to harness the legendary reputation of each hotel into a single, ultra-luxury global hotel brand. Despite numerous proposals, Dorchester Collection has not been tempted to diversify away from its core proposition of offering ultra-luxury accommodation. In 2020, Dorchester Collection opened Mayfair Park Residence – a strategic plan to offer ultra-luxury residential apartments in London's prestigious Mayfair neighborhood. These apartments adjoin the celebrated 45 Park Lane hotel and, as such, the residents of Mayfair Park Residences can be assured of the exceptional care and service that being part of Dorchester Collection provides. Looking ahead, in 2022 Dorchester Collection will open its first hotel and residences in Dubai. Again, this is a strategic move into a new location for the company, with the opportunity to engage with an existing loyal and local audience and to build new relationships and presence within the Gulf Corporation Council (GCC) region.[15]

Dorchester Collection not only considers innovative design and architecture, it continuously seeks out new locations based on it's guests' preferred destinations. In recognizing the contribution of key markets, Dorchester Collection has been agile in operating satellite sales teams in gateway cities where they doesn't have hotels (Dubai, Moscow, Beijing, Sydney, Atlanta, Chicago, New York, Peru, Shanghai), in addition to offices in Los Angeles and its UK and Europe headquarters in London. Having Dorchester Collection–trained employees positioned in such cities ensures a genuine and informed sales interaction, one that is representative of the brand and encourages strong relationships to form with its clientele, building both loyalty and longevity. Dorchester Collection continually reviews the need to strategically position a global sales force to ensure it is building upon its global reputation for having a discerning international guest list.

Dorchester Collection now operates primarily as an owner of a collection of hotels. But it has also diversified into management contracts by invitation. Unlike many hotel companies, Dorchester Collection owns and operates its hotels. Within the industry, there are several other business models in addition to the way Dorchester Collection operates. For example, a hotel property could be owned by an individual or by a corporation. The hotel owner may, however, choose a hotel management company to run the day-to-day business. In some cases, a company may own a diverse portfolio of properties and may choose several different operators to run its properties. This is often in order to make the most of the strengths of an operator located in a particular geographical region. Franchising is an effective way for a hotel owner to buy into the strengths of a readymade brand, with the further benefit of access to its sales networks and databases including loyalty platforms. Dorchester Collection constantly reviews its global market for new opportunities to purchase and/or manage hotels. Heritage, location, and compatibility with their guests' refined tastes and lifestyles are the ultimate deciding factors these decisions. A management contract can only be formalized when the partnership is aligned on common values and is respectful of Dorchester Collection's core principles.[16]

Regardless of the business models, from franchising to managed hotels, each company has its own strategy that it seeks to leverage in ways that work best for its market and growth plans. However, what's important in the ultra-luxury market is the degree to which each of these models provides a close connection with the guest.

Growing Downstream: What Distribution Model Fits Better?

Distribution has historically represented the main point of contact between brand and customer, the place where a brand could not only display and sell a product but also convey a series of communication messages about the brand in general.

The store had the important role of transferring essential information through a series of services designed to accompany moments of interaction with the customer
before, during, and after a purchase. The selection of the offer and the methods of
interaction themselves vary according to the specific distribution format. According
to a hierarchical model, at the first level of choice, companies find themselves opting for one of two business models that differ in terms of investment level, risk, and
business control: retail or wholesale (Figure 1.1). Both models at the top of the decision-making hierarchy can then provide for a cohesive physical and online presence.
There are brands that decide to adopt a single-channel strategy and focus on a single
distribution channel (usually retail) and brands that pursue a multi-channel strategy,
with a different weight of retail and wholesale.[17]

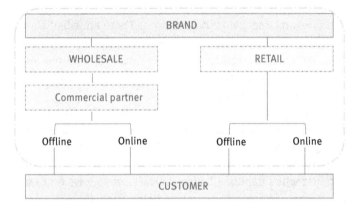

Figure 1.1: Business Models in Distribution.
Source: Compiled by authors.

Retail today represents a weight on the value of sales between 80% and 100% for
brands like Louis Vuitton and Dior. The wholesale channel is still extremely relevant for other companies. Considering bags, shoes, clothing, hard luxury, and cosmetics, in 2019 the wholesale channel was 59% of the 281B of the market (D'Arpizio
and Levato, 2020).

Organizing a retail channel means articulating a direct presence in a given territory, with its own staff and direct investments in the structures to support it. This is
the reason why all the retail models, both online and offline, are defined as "direct
to consumer" (DTC): obviously they allow a high level of control over interactions
with the customer. While online DTC represents a great opportunity for small brands,
especially start-ups, to have a direct connection with consumers, they generally lack
the resources to invest in physical locations; large brands can better orchestrate the
full range of DTC options, from offline to online.[18]

The retail channel includes the following forms of directly operated stores (DOS), as illustrated in Figure 1.2:

- *Free-standing stores* (FSS), some of which represent flagships, that is, stores that are the pinnacle of the brand, offering all product lines and located in the main shopping streets of international capitals. These stores welcome customers who want to have a 360-degree experience of the brand.
- *Shop-in-shop* (SIS), spaces inside department stores managed directly by brands with their own employees but that take the form of concessions whereby the brand pays the department store rent and/or a percentage of the sales generated. Department store traffic can generate sales opportunities for the brand, and the SIS model retains some advantages of the FSS (store atmosphere and display, control over product pricing, dedicated and trained sales associates, etc.).
- *Pop-up stores* in luxury resorts and tourist destinations. These are small shops that have an ad hoc communication style and collection, offering customers something they would not find in a flagship. Brands try to deliver the same message, but a different experience. For example, Dior launches the Riviera collection specifically for pop-ups in summer destinations.
- *Travel retail*, i.e., transit shops in major international airports. The offer is usually very limited, often to accessories and easily available items. At an airport, travelers waiting for flights can visit the shops as a diversion; however, the time available to see, choose, try on, and pay is usually limited compared to that taken by an FSS customer who intentionally goes to the store to have a relaxed shopping experience. A part of travel retail is also wholesale, as there is almost always (with some exceptions) a partner who manages the store on behalf of the brand.
- *Outlet*, where brands can sell items from past seasons with a relevant discount on the full price, but also some ad hoc lines and styles not available in the retail stores. Outlet is a new retail classification for luxury brands.

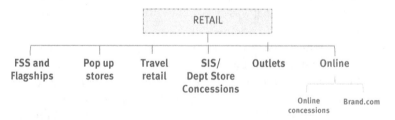

Figure 1.2: Multiple Formats in Retail.
Source: Compiled by authors.

The wholesale channel, on the other hand, envisages the intervention of a business partner that mediates the relationship with the customer. This implies a lower level of control and does not allow companies to gather information about the customer or from the customer. It is also difficult to govern pricing policies. However, this does not mean that it is impossible to adequately monitor the relational methods at the place of purchase, as brands are attentive to the partner selection process and try to set up collaborations inspired by the retail model. For example, it is not uncommon for partners to agree to share periodic reports with a brand that summarize important information relating to its sales performance and comments provided by customers, even with respect to competitors. Wholesale is the most recurrent distribution choice taken by small brands.

Figure 1.3 presents the main models in wholesale:

- *Franchising*, although in the eyes of a customer a franchise may look like a DOS, the management of the store is entrusted to an independent entrepreneur (the franchisee). This form is very effective in difficult markets, where duties and tariffs or permits may create impediments, or small markets, as well as in cases where brands may wish to accelerate the time to market. Franchising is now on the verge of extinction due to brands' need for greater control over interactions with the customer.
- *Department stores* that organize and manage a space dedicated to the brand. Sometimes, the partner will recreate the world of the brand in a small way in the space allocated to it, creating something that it is personalized and not generic. This makes it possible to adopt a retail philosophy in the wholesale sector and convey a message consistent with the overall distribution and communication strategy. This approach is reinforced by the appropriate location with respect to the overall layout of the floor, for example putting a brand close to certain competitors and not to others. Department stores, which have multiple categories, from cosmetics, to catering, to jewelry, have the enormous advantage of being traffic generators. They also differ from each other in terms of strategy and target – in London for example, Harrods has a different setting and is aimed at a different market than Selfridges.
- *Multi-brand stores* or boutiques, which represent the hard core of wholesale distribution. Here, independent commercial entrepreneurs select an assortment of brands and offers based on their reference market and create a package of services. The historical role of boutiques in the industry was that of curators presenting a selection of brands to customers, which could include small and independent brands that introduced innovation and new styles. Some are themselves well-known brands with loyal customers, and luxury brands compete for a relationship with them that can also result in exclusive collaborations. Even in this form of distribution, it is possible for the commercial partner to organize customized spaces for the brand.

Covid-19 has boosted the performance of Brand.com platforms, leading to advanced virtual modes of interaction through augmented reality (AR), gaming, live-streaming, apps, and social media of all kinds. AR solutions can not only convince uncertain customers to buy, they also help in reducing returns, especially for some categories like footwear. AR and gaming together also help to increase and innovate in customer engagement strategies.

In addition to the Brand.com websites, brands increasingly control online concessions. The customer may use a multi-brand ecommerce site as an interface, but he/she buys directly from the brand, which also records the execution of the economic transaction. Today, luxury companies from all industries are well aware that websites are not only a communication channel but also a platform to increase sales revenues and customer loyalty. Distribution strategy requires a holistic approach to all channels, both online and offline.

Figure 1.3: Multiple Formats in Wholesale.
Source: Compiled by authors.

Although conceptually it is useful to keep the two business models distinct, brands must necessarily adopt an integrated approach to deliver a clear and consistent, but not necessarily identical, message to the customer both online and offline. This need extends to all aspects of the business right down to how products are displayed, matched, and presented.

Since the early 2000s, the world of luxury has changed on the distribution front, adding further elements of complexity. Online sales are developing, primarily on the wholesale front, with purely online distributors or *e-tailers*, like Yoox Luisaviaroma, Mytheresa, Matchesfashion, or combinations of online platforms and brick-and-mortar (e.g., Harrods, Selfridges, etc.), usually physical stores that started up an equally relevant (or even more relevant) e-commerce business.[19] We should also mention 24 Sèvres, the platform launched in 2017 by Le Bon Marché with a curated selection of over 150 luxury womenswear brands.

Last but not least, there are the marketplaces that mediate the relation between brands, stores, and customers, usually without owning any inventory. Well-established examples include Tmall Luxury Pavilion, JD Luxury, and Farfetch.[20] When Farfetch launched in 2008, it adopted a new business model for the world of personal goods (at that time essentially clothing and footwear), namely that of a marketplace that connected consumers to a global network of fashion boutiques and brands. In 2015, Farfetch decided to pursue a multi-channel strategy, combining a strong online presence with a foothold in brick-and-mortar and acquired Browns, which operates two iconic fashion stores in London.

Today, Farfetch is one of the world's largest luxury e-commerce players. Different from most rivals, its business model involves making third-party sellers, from tiny boutiques to department stores to global brands and retailers, list products on its site (Lojacono and Misani, 2019). Farfetch processes sales and handles logistics, but it does not hold any inventory. When a customer buys a product on the platform, the order is directed to the boutique or brand that holds it in stock, which wraps the order in Farfetch packaging and books pick-up by a logistic partner managed by Farfetch. Payment is processed by Farfetch, which earns a commission on the value of the order – negotiated on a case-by-case basis, usually around 30% – and passes the rest on to the seller.

Farfetch provides its customers with a consistent experience on the website and on mobile devices. In-house content creation allows the platform to achieve a luxury product presentation with a consistent look and feel, with short lead times and low cost. The content creation process includes styling, photographing (in Farfetch's own studios), photo-editing, and content management. Farfetch has also developed tailored merchandise descriptions, size and fit information, and detailed measurements information to help customers and minimize returns. Production centers located in Guimarães (Portugal), Los Angeles, São Paulo, and Hong Kong processed over 465,000 products and produced approximately 2.4 million unique luxury images in 2017.

Farfetch has also invested in developing a fully integrated logistics network. Effective fulfilment to over 190 countries of over 8,000 parcels per day requires an extensive knowledge of how to manage and optimize the complexities of each country combination, including duties and bureaucracies. To maximize service, Farfetch depends on correct execution by sellers, and it will quickly remove under-performing stores from the platform after a frustrating customer experience. Finally, the platform offers customers a free return service.

Farfetch's business model is attractive to both luxury customers and luxury sellers. To customers, Farfetch's marketplace model provides global access to a very comprehensive range and depth of luxury products online, from over 3,400 brands. Not only can customers count on finding their favorite luxury brands on the platform, they can also discover new brands and unconventional items selected by independent boutiques and not stocked by traditional inventory-bearing e-tailers. To luxury sellers (boutiques and brands), Farfetch offers wide distribution and access, allowing them to make their inventory available to a global audience with no need to increase their physical footprint.

Since its inception, Farfetch has had big ambitions. Some saw it as the future Amazon for luxury. "What makes us different is that everyone else is operating on a retail model, but we are a platform, not a shop, an enabler not a competitor, and we are reaping all the advantages that such a position entails", notes José Neves, Far-fetch's founder, chairman, and CEO. "We believe we are the only global luxury plat-form at scale" (Paton, 2018). Neves made clear early on that he wanted to pursue more business in emerging economies, such as China and the Middle East, as well as sign on additional retailers and brands in mature markets. In June 2017, Farfetch started an equity partnership with JD.com, China's second-largest e-commerce plat-form, which invested around US$397 million to help the company grow its Chinese business. It has also partnered with Chaloub in Dubai to expand in the Middle East. When Alibaba and Richemont announced their partnership to accelerate the digita-lization of the luxury industry in 2020, they also declared their intention to invest a total of US$1.15 billion in Farfetch Limited and a new Farfetch China joint venture.

In its years of operation, Farfetch has also expanded by acquiring similar busi-nesses in new industries. On December 12, 2018, the company announced its pur-chase of sneaker and streetwear marketplace Stadium Goods for US$250 million, its first major move since going public on the New York Stock Exchange in September of that year.[21] Part of a new wave of peer-to-peer e-commerce platforms, Stadium Goods allows sneaker aficionados to buy and sell directly from each other. Stadium Goods continues to operate as a subsidiary of Farfetch, with its entire product selec-tion available on the Farfetch platform. In August 2019, Farfetch acquired Italian contemporary fashion group New Guards Group (NGG) for US$675 million in cash and shares. The group, founded in 2015 by Claudio Antonioli, Davide De Giglio, and Marcelo Burlon, has a portfolio that includes Off-White, Palm Angels, Marcelo Burlon County of Milan, Heron Preston, Alanui, Unravel Project, and Kirin Peggy Gou. In 2019, NGG recorded a turnover of US$345 million, 95% of which was made in the wholesale sector, and a pre-tax profit of US$95 million. The aim of the acquisition, as stated by Farfetch, was to strengthen development potential in direct sales, particularly through new concessions on its marketplace for NGG's brands. News of the deal was not welcomed by the stock market, with a drop of about 40% in the value of Farfetch's shares, which reached a minimum value of US$10.10 per share.

Today, Farfetch's additional businesses include Farfetch Platform Solutions, which services enterprise clients with e-commerce and technology capabilities, and Browns (acquired in 2015), which offers luxury products to consumers online and offline (with three boutiques in London). Farfetch also continues to invest in busi-ness solutions and advanced technologies, such as its "Store of the Future" aug-mented retail solution. In the third quarter of the 2020 fiscal year, the company reported revenue of US$438 million, a 71% year-over-year increase. Its gross mer-chandise value (GMV) and digital platform GMV growth rates are accelerating – they are up 62% and 60% year-over-year, respectively, reaching record highs of US$798 million GMV and US$674 million digital platform GMV, with Adjusted EBITDA improved to US$(10) million from US$(36) million in the third quarter of 2019. Farfetch handled transactions worth US$1,021,037 for the full year 2019, with US$459,846 gross profit and a net loss (after tax) of US$(373,688). It operates in 190 countries with items from more than 50 countries and over 1,300 of the world's best brands, boutiques, and department stores.

In 2020, Neves described his company's success in terms of an overall shift to online channels:

> What we are seeing is the acceleration of the secular trend of online adoption in luxury – an industry that is still very underpenetrated. The capabilities developed across the Farfetch platform over the past thirteen years in anticipation of the eventual digitization of the luxury industry uniquely position Farfetch to capture this opportunity today. And our recently announced partnership with Alibaba and Richemont further positions us to seize the opportunity to bring the luxury industry into the next generation and drive sustained growth and market share for many years to come. (Rigby, 2020)

Online is rapidly evolving and is subject to changing technology and consumer preferences as well as the introduction of new services. The competitive landscape is becoming increasingly crowded, with new entrants from technology enablement companies like Shopify and luxury sellers, i.e., larger and more established companies such as luxury department stores, luxury brand stores or online retailers, and independent, multichannel players operating brick-and-mortar stores with an online presence.

Pure online players are also changing their physiognomy following growth strategies that see them as protagonists of IPO (Mytheresa), unprecedented alliances (Farfetch, Alibaba, Richemont), acquisitions of other players (Farfetch and NGG and Stadium Goods), expansions of their range of services and products (Farfetch with its "second life" program and "90minute delivery" service, Mytheresa with its launch of a men's section, or Yoox Net-a-Porter ramping up its offer of watches from Chopard and Piaget). In the beginning, online took the luxury world by surprise; brands lacked strategic vision and orientation in digital spaces, believing that e-commerce was an unsuitable channel to market high-unit-value products associated with a pleasurable in-store buying experience. It therefore took more than a decade for luxury brands to shift their online presence from the mere presentation of products and events such as fashion shows to a site also organized for sale – a real business. In the meantime, Luisaviaroma.com grew to become a €100 million business and most independent stores decided to integrate their offline presence and online channels.

As we have seen, different distribution models attract specific clusters of customers But there is also overlap between customers and channels: a customer decides to access a specific format based on location, emotion, time available, and specific product and service needs. For this reason, the design of the distribution business model must start with the customer's needs. Luxury brands should be present in all channels and models – and succeed in all of them, too.

Implementing a valid distribution policy that leads to satisfactory economic results implies the management of multiple levers. For example, if you do not want to grow your business perimeter, but rather increase sales per square meter, you need to make investments in training sales associates, the renovation of existing stores to attract more customers and increase the conversion of purchases/visits, and the value of the average receipt. On the other hand, a company may want to increase its perimeter in terms of the number of stores to steal market share from competitors, expanding the presence of FSS in second-tier cities. Or a company could decide to progressively move from wholesale to retail, while also increasing concessions, in the face of modest results from independent stores. In this case, we can see the advantages of an immediate connection with the customer that extends to customer care activities and repair and maintenance services. Finally, distribution strategy must be adapted to the geographic market. Brands now operate in multiple countries and must avoid a generic and aseptic presence as much as possible. They need to make sure that standardizing across markets doesn't make for a bland experience. This theme will be studied in depth in Chapter 2.

Takeaways
- Symbolic value rather than functional value is a key factor that helps define the concept of luxury.
- A variety of profiles can be adopted in terms of ownership structure and identity as well as breadth and scope of activities (single-industry vs. multi-industry company).
- One of the key challenges presented in this chapter is to find the right balance between attention to creativity and following basic economic rules and requirements.
- While preserving their heritage, companies have grown over time by expanding within their core business, exploring new territories, or through different modalities (e.g., mergers, acquisitions, alliances, organic growth).
- Growth has led to increases in company size, but also mature new competencies.
- In pursuing growth, luxury brands have been ambidextrous, i.e., strengthening their core business, while finding new business opportunities. Ambidexterity has been identified as a main source of resilience of luxury brands.
- Wholesale requires less financial investment and risk but simultaneously allows less control of the relationship with the customer. Brands must leverage their wholesale partners to ensure effective communication.
- Retail requires a lot of investment in terms of capital expenditure and people, but is characterized by full control. The high risks related to the retail channel come from the need to own stock and achieve high sales per square meter to be profitable. Furthermore, freestanding stores (FFS) involve a high associated economic outlay due to high main-street rents.
- When planning a brand's strategy, it's necessary to adopt a customer's perspective and understand their different needs and purchasing behaviors across channels, online and offline. Clients should not perceive that they can get different products, prices, or services online. This is the reason why an omnichannel perspective – rather than multichannel – must be followed.

Notes

1 It is no coincidence that all the main conglomerates have significantly increased the weight of their direct channels, including their e-commerce. Gucci is a perfect example in this regard: since 2015 it has tried to significantly reduce wholesale in favor of direct-channel sales, which today represent almost 85% of the company's revenues.

2 In this book, the business model is intended as the concrete representation of the company's competitive strategy, i.e., its offer, aimed at a well-identified target of the market; the ways in which it competes with other players (pursuing a sustainable competitive advantage); its way of distributing and communicating the offer; and the organization of key processes (expressing key competencies in some areas of management). It is this synthesis of elements that defines the structure of costs and revenues and therefore company profitability. For a complete examination of definitions of business model definitions used over time by management authors, see Ovans (2015).

3 According to the Deloitte Global Powers of Luxury Goods Report (2020), Richard Mille is the fastest growing luxury company based on 2016–2019 sales CAGR, equal to 58,7%.

4 Privately held universal control is usually defined as having a greater than 50% voting stake. The majority of decision-making rights are indirect or direct.

5 Sometimes companies entrust the creative direction of different product categories to specific designers. Consider the case of Dior, where the women's line is headed by Maria Grazia Chiuri and the men's line by Kim Jones. In 2020, Silvia Venturini Fendi handed over her role as creative director of women's ready to wear (RTW) to Kim Jones as well, meaning he now holds two positions at two different brands, like Karl Lagerfeld, who was Fendi's creative director for 55 years and at the same time signed the Chanel collections. According to WWD, design duos are proliferating and represent 7% of the brands listed in the official calendars for New York, London, Milan, and Paris. Having two people at the helm can benefit the collection development process because it allows a fruitful reconciliation of visions from the early stages, especially if the designers have different social, cultural, and geographical origins (Socha and Esch, 2020).

6 See LVMH Corporate Website and LVMH: A Timeline Behind the Building of the World's Most Valuable Luxury Goods Conglomerate, October 30, 2020, by The Fashion Law, https://www.thefashionlaw.com/lvmh-a-timeline-behind-the-building-of-a-conglomerate/.

7 For the identification of the core business according to historical, quantitative and qualitative method, see Morosetti (2020), Zook and Allen (2001), and Zook (2007).

8 See LVMH Corporate Website.

9 The highlights of the agreement, as stated in the official press release, include provisions that Alibaba launches Farfetch luxury shopping channels on Tmall Luxury Pavilion and Luxury Soho and invests in the newly formed Farfetch China Joint Venture and in Farfetch Limited; that Richemont invests in the newly formed Farfetch China Joint Venture and in Farfetch Limited and explores additional opportunities to work closely with Farfetch and Alibaba to leverage their platforms and augmented retail technologies, also forming a steering group to be joined by influential luxury leaders Johann Rupert and François-Henri Pinault; and that Artemis increases existing ownership in Farfetch with additional investment (E. Clark, 2020; Hall, 2020).

10 Porsche and Embraer partnered to sell a matching limited-edition "Duet" including private jet Embraer Phenom 300E and a Porsche 911 Turbo S for $11million.

11 According to McKinsey's State of Fashion report (2020), listed fashion companies representing around US$50 billion of revenue are loss-making or have high level of debt. See also: BOF Team and McKinsey and Company (2020).

12 According to the Deloitte Fashion and Luxury Private Equity and Investors Survey 2020, 65% of investors usually hold their fashion and luxury investments for less than five years, with a 77% average majority stake. The drivers that influence exit are equally distributed among market trend mismatches, closing investment period, high returns opportunity, and change in the general investment strategy.

13 Deloitte Fashion and Luxury Private Equity and Investors Survey 2020 revealed that internationalization and digital strategy were the levers widely adopted by investors to increase the brand value.

14 Style Capital is a specialized fund with over €125 million of committed capital that invests in small and medium companies (with sales of €10 to €100 million), supporting their growth.

15 The region is comprised of six countries: Saudi Arabia, Kuwait, United Arab Emirates, Qatar, Bahrain, and Oman.

16 A management contract is an agreement whereby two or more parties, who are usually experts in their fields, come together, utilizing their unique strengths to create a partnership that maximizes revenues and minimizes risks.

17 Explanations of business models in distribution greatly benefited from interviews by the authors with Francesco Viana, general manager Southern Europe Christian Dior Couture, in 2019 and 2020.

18 On this subject, see also Sherman, L., Can Young Luxury Brands Bypass Wholesale?, Business of Fashion, February 24, 2016. https://www.businessoffashion.com/articles/retail/can-young-luxury-brands-bypass-wholesale

19 All these websites (e.g., Matchefashion, Mytheresa) have been included in the e-tailers category because their physical presence is very limited in terms of number of stores and weight of offline sales on total sales.

20 Cross-border e-commerce platforms, known as Haitao, offer a further opportunity for luxury brands to reach Chinese online consumers. This model allows expansion in Asia without establishing a local legal entity and warehouse. For details, see Casey (2021).

21 In September 2018, Farfetch went public on the New York Stock Exchange at a price of US $28.45 per share, corresponding to a corporate valuation of US$5.8 billion. After the IPO, José Neves owned 14.8% of the company's shares and the majority of votes.

2 Key Strategic Paradoxes in the World of Luxury

Many people associate luxury with specific brands and their iconic products. The fact that these brands have a long history – more than a hundred years in many cases – should lead us to a static view on luxury. This is a misconception: investment in innovation and well-orchestrated growth strategies have allowed luxury companies to prosper in difficult times as well as in prosperous ones (see Chapter 1). The tension between the preservation of heritage and a continuous push to innovate is only one of several key issues that guide the strategic agendas of luxury companies. In a challenging environment, these issues represent paradoxes managers must manage to maintain their relevance and continue to succeed.

This chapter will discuss some of these paradoxes as depicted in Figure 2.1. Successful brands do not actually see them as dilemmas and do not choose between two sides of the equation (e.g., exclusivity and inclusivity, local relevance and global consistency); they manage to crack the paradox by finding balance.

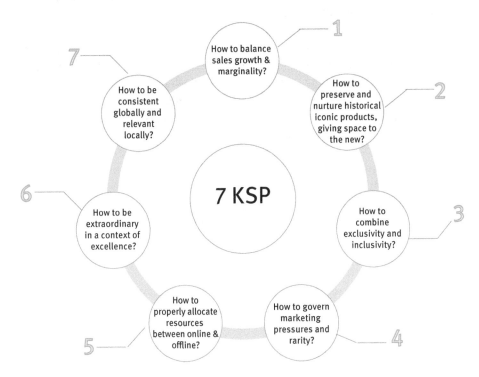

Figure 2.1: Key Strategic Paradoxes, KSP.
Source: Compiled by authors.

https://doi.org/10.1515/9783110723519-002

The basic hypothesis of this book is that the most resilient companies, i.e., those that are able to maintain satisfactory performance over time despite external turbulence, have been agile in managing these questions in a consistent way with respect to time and space.

Paradox 1: How to Balance Sales Growth and Marginality?

Growth strategies have led luxury companies to explore new related or unrelated businesses as well as new geographies and market segments (Corbetta and Morosetti, 2020). By exploiting valuable competencies (e.g., in brand management or retail) in the management of symbol-intensive goods, successful luxury companies have been able to increase turnover and company size. Unfortunately, profitability has not always followed a similar growth path. Luxury is highly sensitive to changes in customers' tastes and habits and to the evolution of international markets. This peculiarity requires a special ability to detect trends in the macro context and develop an attitude toward innovation.

We can trace the resilience of luxury brands to their ability to be agile and immediately tune in to the constantly shifting needs of a consumer beset with uncertainty. Following the financial crisis of 2008, Hermès was able to increase revenues, keeping the same profitability as before the global downturn (see Figure 2.2). Its success through this period allows us to reflect on the brand value of these companies with respect to turnover, generally a very high ratio. Hermès has a ratio that is three times the value of a company such as Zara (Inditex group). Because of this, it has proved to be a resilient brand even in the most recent economic recession of 2020, holding its position as 28th in the annual Interbrand Best Global Brands Report, without any loss of brand value. Louis Vuitton has shared Hermès's happy fate, maintaining 17th place in the ranking and recording only a 2% reduction in brand value.

Like certain materials, some companies have shown an ability to transform without breaking, absorbing the impact of an external crisis only to return the blow with greater vigor. These entities emerge strengthened from the crisis, regenerated, ready to make a rapid leap forward, reaching performances far superior to those of the pre-crisis situation. The stock market has incorporated these signals and expectations into share prices: those of luxury companies like Hermès and LVMH (the group, all brands and divisions included) have proven to be very resilient to the Covid-19 pandemic, as shown in Figure 2.3.

The ability of luxury brands such as Hermès and Louis Vuitton to preserve or improve margins manifests without radical changes in their business modes. This comes as no surprise to those who are familiar with these companies' ambidexterity:[1] they maintain their commitment to their core business while simultaneously exploring opportunities in other areas where they can realize the value of their competencies.[2]

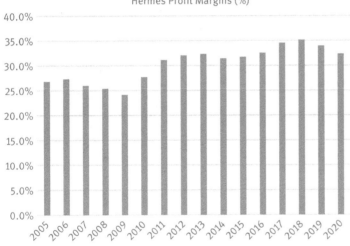

Figure 2.2: Sales and Profit Margins of Hermès 2005–2020.
Source: Compiled by authors based on corporate data.

Consider, for example, Gucci. When the brand's parent company, Kering Group, appointed Marco Bizzarri as Gucci's CEO in 2015, he promoted a new corporate vision based on self-expression and inclusivity, leading to increased turnover and return on sales. No other Kering-owned brand performed as well in the period 2012–2018 (Figure 2.4).

In 2017, Gucci ranked 51st among global brands in all industries in the Interbrand report. Just three years later, in 2020, it has jumped nineteen places, landing at 32nd overall: Gucci is now the highest ranked Italian brand in the report. The growing strength can be attributed to Gucci's coherent experience across its touch-points and

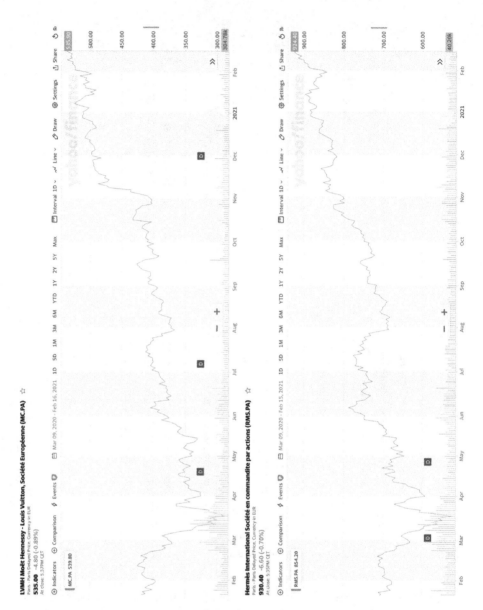

Figure 2.3: Share Price Changes of LVMH and Hermès Since February 2020.
Source: Screenshots based on Yahoo! Finance.

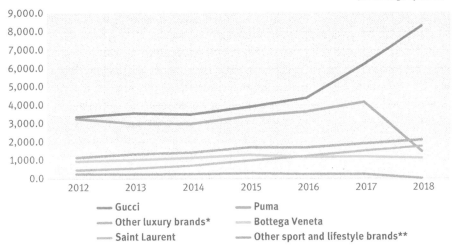

Figure 2.4: Gucci's Sales and Return on Sales for 2011–2018 and Global Revenue of the Kering Group 2012–2018, by Brand (in Million Euros).
Source: Compiled by authors based on corporate data.

its engagement with a new generation thanks to the authentic narrative vision of the brand's creative director, Alessandro Michele.

Gucci has not substantially modified the geography of its distribution, confirming a well-balanced split of sales among Europe, Asia, and North America. Leather goods is the predominant category (57% of sales); ready to wear (RTW) is an important line in terms of positioning and communication, but accounts for only 18% of total sales (€1.5 billion).

The Gucci case allows us to introduce another important consideration. In 2021, journalists and commentators published many articles about the reduction of the brand's turnover by 22% in 2020 compared to 2019, to reach a value of €7.4 billion. In this regard, we can first note that sharp ups and downs are now part of the economic system and, on a micro level, of all companies' lives. It was impossible for Gucci to maintain the very high growth rates recorded since 2017, and a readjustment of results was inevitable. Secondly, only a superficial reading of the data would attribute this decline to Gucci's poor ability to react to the pandemic. The reasons could also be reasonably sought not externally, but internally, and traced back to merchandising policies, to the search for consensus in market segments other than those the brand has traditionally pursued, to lower spending power, and to the decision to progressively abandon the wholesale channel and focus on retail stores (currently, they number 483, representing 87% of sales). As reported on the Kering web site, in the first quarter of 2021, Gucci realized revenues of €2,167.7 million, up 20.2% thanks to collaborations, appreciated product launches and local clienteling activities.

It should be noted that, even given the pronounced instability of economic systems, companies' resilience must be appreciated over a long period, not a limited one. Luxury companies in particular have business trends that cannot be fully assessed in the short term. Those like Chanel, for example, are characterized by low but continuous growth, while brands like Gucci or Dior have historically had cycles of very strong growth and moments of decline. This is coherent with the evolution of the volume of queries provided by Google Trends related to Chanel and Gucci since 2004 (Figure 2.5). As Hyunyoung Choi and Hal Varian assumed in 2009, these query data are correlated with the level of economic activity in given companies and can also be helpful in predicting the subsequent releases of economic highlights.

Another extraordinary example of combined sales and margins growth is Ferrari (Figure 2.6), a brand with higher multiples than many luxury firms in 2019 (Figure 2.7).

Ferrari has kept a strong focus on cars, which represent around 77% of sales, although it operates in other businesses, from engines, to merchandising, to licensing, to F1-related sponsorship. According to the Brand Finance Luxury and Premium 50 2020 Report, Ferrari is the brand with the highest Brand Strength Index (BSI) score. BSI is a driver of brand value and is based on factors such as marketing investment, staff satisfaction, and corporate reputation. Ferrari's brand value grew to US$9.1 billion (+9%) in 2020 (Brand Finance, 2020).

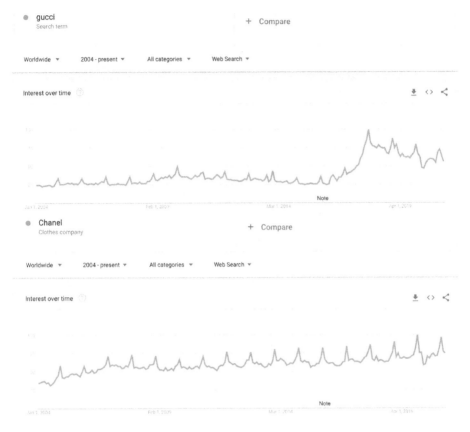

Figure 2.5: Volume of Queries Related to and Chanel Gucci, 2004–2021.
Source: Screenshots based on Google!Trends.

Undoubtedly, in 2020 luxury companies, like those in other industries, faced important challenges due to Covid-19. Together with uncertainty on the demand side, the closure of retail stores and production facilities created significant challenges. Forty percent of luxury goods are produced in their country of origin: this is the reason why Italy and France were particularly affected (Achille and Zipser, 2020).

Still, the resiliency of the industry is apparent. Estimates coming from major consultancy companies report a 30% reduction in luxury sales compared to 2019, a decrease that is less significant than other industries. Furthermore, there is a general consensus that the pandemic's effect on sales will be a V-shaped curve, with a negative peak followed by an immediate return of interest by luxury consumers. According to Bain and Company, personal luxury goods will not return to pre-pandemic levels before 2022–2023 (D'Arpizio and Levato, 2020). However, there are brands that achieved double-digit growth in the last quarter of 2020 (e.g., Bottega Veneta, Dior, LV). Let us also consider that during the pandemic, a situation of general uncertainty led people to save, rather than spend, money. When this period of

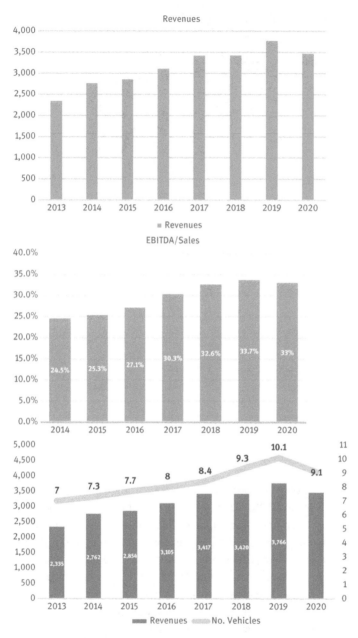

Figure 2.6: Net Revenues of Ferrari (Million Euros, Except Percentages), EBITDA/Sales, Revenues and No. of Vehicles, 2013–2020.
Source: Ferrari corporate profile.

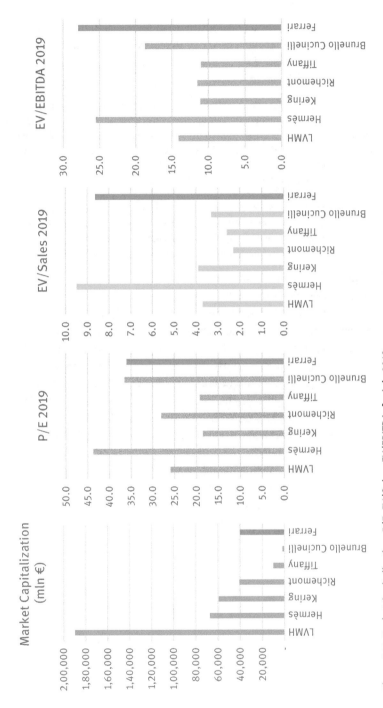

Figure 2.7: Market Capitalization, P/E, EV/Sales, EV/EBITDA, for July 2019.
Source: Compiled by authors based on corporate data.

uncertainty ends, they will "click and buy", causing cash to flow into the market in a surge of hysteric demand. The offer must be ready to match the expectations of an especially eager customer base, and time to market and post-sales service will be key strategic elements in brands' response:

> Time to market can be reduced if you are faster in decision making and execution, nevertheless incorporating at the latest possible [moment] in the process the feedback from the market. But today we have the possibility to rely on 3D printing to speed up prototyping of eyewear and to go faster to industrialization (e.g., selecting materials, set[ing] machinery to drill materials). Prototyping by hands (sic) typically requires three days that can be lowered to three hours using 3D printing. Another way to decrease time to market is reducing the product offering – that means the number of styles and SKUs for each single brand (at Thélios we did it by 40%). In this case, we managed it smartly combining a push approach, i.e., launches driven by us, and a pull process, i.e., products asked by the market. It could be a mix 60%–40% or 70%–30%, whatever it is, this allows [us] to reduce complexity, granting at the same time, an even more consistent image of the brand in the market. (Giovanni Zoppas) (Former CEO, Thélios, personal communication)

The pandemic did not invent something new; it accelerated existing trends (like digitalization and orientation toward sustainability) and instigated a profound structural revision of key processes, from product development, to communication, to commercialization. This immediate reaction could help shelter luxury brands from the ongoing shocks to health and socio-economic systems as the pandemic continues and in its aftermath. To be resilient, companies must develop special abilities in scenario planning to implement adequate short- and long-term action plans (see Chapter 6). For luxury companies in 2020, another drama has been turned into an opportunity, stimulating them to challenge the status quo. This is a secret to resilience.

In 2020, luxury companies were the protagonists of an unprecedented revolution, embarking on a digital adventure. They strengthened their presence online and on social media, experimented with games and gaming, engaged local customers, and provided clients with new forms of interaction based on personalized experiences – while implementing a real omnichannel strategy for the first time. Never before have values such as social responsibility guided the review of a company's main business processes, from operations, to product development, to human resource management.

Paradox 2: How to Preserve and Nurture Iconic, Historical Products while still Giving Space to the New?

Over the years, luxury companies have faced the dilemma of deciding how much space and what role to give to the products of the past and how much to invest in innovation. Another way to frame the paradox would be: "How to keep the heritage alive, source of inspiration for the new?"

There are companies that deliberately choose to see the "new" as an accessory to historical products; others that use the past solely as a source of inspiration for new launches; others still that gradually give more and more space to novelties, leaving only a residual role for history. In this section we will outline all these different approaches.

The idea for Flos, a leader in high-end lighting, was born in 1960, and officially founded in 1962; the company's flagship product, the Arco Lamp, designed by Achille and Piergiacomo Castiglioni, launched that same year. This splendid artifact of Italian design, repeatedly imitated, is still in the catalog today and represents one of Flos's best-selling products. Despite this exceptional result – to have created a product that remains perfectly in line with consumer tastes over a period of nearly 60 years – every year Flos invests in research and development and presents new products at the Milan Furniture Fair. The Arco Lamp demonstrates that timeless does not mean belonging to the past and aging well; it means that design has no age and cannot be dated. A piece designed in the mid-twentieth century can still feel contemporary. Of course, even timeless designs must be nurtured, in the same way that 500-year-old Japanese gardens require daily care.

Poltrona Frau, a luxury design brand founded in Turin in 1912, presents a different case. Its iconic products, including the Chester (1912) and Vanity Fair (originally produced as Model 904 in 1930, revised in 1984), represent powerful brand identifiers that have continued to prepare the field for successful launches. Over the last ten years – and with greater strength and strategic awareness, over the last five – Poltrona Frau has undertaken a vigorous rethinking of its collection, maintaining a solid link with tradition in terms of construction techniques, taste, and upholstery materials while becoming more contemporary (the Americans would define the style as "transitional") and international, less linked to a single iconic product and more interested in global furnishing solutions that provide answers to the varied needs of the modern luxury consumer.

As a result of this process, which is still underway, the products developed by Poltrona Frau during its first 100 years of life (1912–2012) represented just under 32% of total sales in 2020, with the remaining 68% consisting of products developed over the last eight years, and 44% products from the last five years alone.

Poltrona Frau still sells classic products, but it has chosen to integrate them into its collection alongside contemporary products, emphasizing the thread that binds the Chester to designs like the Archibald armchair (number three model in sales) by Jean Marie Massaud, which debuted in 2009, or the Let It Be sofa (Poltrona Frau's best-selling model) by Palomba Serafini Associati, which debuted in 2017.

Cartier revolutionized the watch industry at its founding in 1847, and its best-known watches (Santos and Tank) date to the early 1900s; they continue to be among the maison's most-sold items. However, the success of its iconic models has never prevented the company from launching other well-performing pieces like Ballon Bleu, Pasha (relaunched in 2020), and Panthère. At the same time, aesthetic variations on products have always been important for Cartier. Usually, especially in jewelry, the company offers a full suite of pieces (bracelet, ring, necklace, etc.). Then, it introduces variations with different materials (yellow, pink, white, platinum gold) and precious versions that include gems and other embellishments. Cartier's history has been defined by its pioneering attitude both in terms of design and materials: first to launch a wristwatch, first to use platinum, first to introduce the guirlande style, first to mix green, blue, and red in jewelry (in the Tutti Frutti collection). For Cartier, novelty is fundamental and deeply rooted in the values of the maison.

Cartier's efforts focus on supporting its iconic lines (Love, Juste un Clou, Trinity), with launches aimed at enriching the collections with new price points (e.g., the Juste un Clou flex bracelet) and extending these lines with new offers in terms of materials. This goes hand in hand with investments aimed at stimulating creativity and newness (e.g., Clash) and creating "simple animations", i.e., exclusivities/limited editions tied to specific events such as Chinese New Year. A separate case is that of high jewelry, where new thematic collections with several hundred pieces are presented every year, such as the brand's 2020 [Sur]Naturel collection, which employed flora and fauna themes.

The world of luxury is filled with similar examples. Hublot has offered its loyal customers watches made in the Swiss precision tradition since 1980, yet continues to pursue innovation. Today, its product line includes watches made with high-tech materials such as "Magic Gold", obtained from the combination of 18K cast gold and ceramic and priced at over €20,000. In 2018, Hublot launched the Big Bang Meca-10 P2P, a watch that can only be purchased using Bitcoin. Chanel's 2.55 flap bag first appeared in 1955. Repeatedly reimagined in new colors and variations, it remains the company's iconic product. This has not, however, stopped Chanel from launching other best sellers, such as the Boy in 2011.

It seems that, over time, these companies have been able to activate a virtuous circle between the past, the present, and the future. Historical products represent the brand and its roots, but they continue to attract attention because companies invest in innovation, drawing new audiences to their collections; new products find fertile ground when they come from a brand that has a well-represented heritage. This is perhaps one of the most complex and debated tensions within luxury companies. How does care for the past influence and balance decisions about how much and in what direction to innovate?

Ferrari, for example, has chosen to incorporate the past into the future in its development of new cars, starting from historical models but experimenting with futuristic technologies. The Ferrari Monza SP1 and SP2 draw on the company's history, specifically Ferrari's groundbreaking designs from the 1950s. They also incorporate new material technologies and innovative aerodynamic design features.[3]

Moving to the world of high-end clothing (and partly also leather goods), the seasonality of collections coexists with carry-overs (permanent items). Dior, for example, combines the typical two haute couture collections and four RTW (spring, winter, cruise, fall) with the 30 Montaigne Wardrobe, which includes the famous Bar jacket with its 73 years of history. Gucci has also sought continuity with its past in recent years, recovering the brand's original identifying signs from its Florentine archives, from hardware like the horse bit or the lion's head, to codes such as its 1966 floral print, GG signature, or the web (i.e., the company's famous red and green stripes), to materials such as bamboo or iconic products such as the ACE sneaker (Figure 2.8).

Gucci Women's Spring Summer 2016   Gucci Cruise 2019   Gucci Men's Fall Winter 2016   Gucci Women's Fall Winter 2015

Figure 2.8: Valorizing Gucci's Archives: Bamboo and Lion Head, Flowers, Web, and Horse Bit. Source: Courtesy of Gucci.

An extreme expression of this concept is found in Sergio Rossi, the Italian footwear company bought by the Chinese Fosun in 2021, for which 100% of turnover comes from shoes designed using models collected in the archive – one third from the famous Sr1 line. Another exemplary case of a brand capitalizing on established codes is Bottega Veneta. There, designer Daniel Lee was able to creatively sublimate the classic, logo-free *intrecciato* (basket weave) and softness typical of Bottega's bags into new forms and scales (like in the Cassette, with its big, chunky weave), attracting a new audience of younger customers and widening the brand's offer to include shoes and RTW. Customers under 40 years old represented around 60% of sales in 2020 vs. 45% in 2019 (Guilbault, 2020).

Valorizing the archive is key to keeping a brand's heritage alive; it is a source of inspiration for the new. Picking elements from the archive is not merely a way to blend past and present; archives define a specific aesthetic vocabulary and grammar which participates to the brand specific style and makes it recognizable through time: "Our Clash collection took explicit elements of design from the 1930s to make a very new creation. It is like Ludovico Einaudi reinterpreting Domenico Scarlatti to compose movies sound tracks" (Cyrille Vigneron, President and CEO, Cartier, personal communication).

The structure of the product portfolio and the weight of new products compared to historical ones is the subject of a brand's merchandising choices, which will be discussed more fully in Chapter 6. This process of selecting and managing the mix of items in a product line was called into question in 2020, especially during the lockdown in Europe, and will certainly lead to new "rules of the game". Store closures, a more casual style of professional clothing, the uncertain economic situation, reduced disposable income, the difficulties of coordinating design teams remotely, the interruption of production activities in the middle of a sales campaign, and the impossibility of staging live shows to debut their collections forced companies to rethink their consolidated activities. One outcome of this rethinking was an explosion of new presentation formats for collections: the show behind closed doors, live streaming, the multi-faceted digital experience. For example, in 2020, Balenciaga organized a VR runway to launch its fall/winter 2021 collection, delivering Oculus glasses to 330 people worldwide, and released a video game, *Afterworld: The Age of Tomorrow*, which was available on the brand's website (Madsen, 2020).

From launch to presentation and marketing, a move toward more "sustainable" business practices has found support with prominent personalities such as Giorgio Armani and Alessandro Michele. It is not unthinkable that new business models will emerge from the crisis, altering the industry's organization and disrupting its equilibrium. During the lockdown, for example, some brands facing store closures and the cancellation of retail orders started experimenting with pre-ordering: the collection is presented, but production takes place only on the basis of orders for which the customer has already paid. Adopting this new business model would allow companies to avoid waste by producing only what their customers purchase. This is a "demand pull" logic that combines the benefits of advanced planning with tailor-made features. This method of product distribution is already in use among non-luxury companies such as Pangaia, which uses newsletters to introduce special products in its activewear line, giving its community of consumers a few hours to book and pay upfront for the pieces they desire. Once the orders have been collected, a production process is activated which, respecting the criteria of eco-sustainability, is particularly long and complex: "We produced these items based on demand to create limited quantities and reduce unnecessary waste" (Pangaia, n.d.).

The pre-order model is not totally new to the world of luxury fashion. Trunk shows, for example, have long functioned as a way for customers to essentially pre-order items from a new collection, and some websites have integrated the practice into their operations. Moda Operandi, for example, posts editorial photos of pieces straight off the catwalk, offering the items for purchase within a limited period – usually three to seven days. The user pays a deposit of 50% of the price to hold their selections, and Moda Operandi undertakes to deliver the goods before the retail launch of a given collection – whether or not the selected pieces make it to stores at all. The production process is rationalized because it's based on the request from the final customer.[4]

Implementing a pre-order model is not without difficulties, as it requires decisions made in concert with other players in the supply chain that require high margins of flexibility in purchasing and production decisions. In the meantime, as they lay the groundwork for new ordering and production models, several brands have devised an intermediate solution. To rationalize their collections, they are producing small quantities of product during the season, adjusting the stock promptly with respect to changes in demand and using Artificial Intelligence (AI) tools to support the process. This model is not without its problems, first of all the management of complaints related to possible delays or cancellation of production and possible returns of products bought based on photographs alone.

Paradox 3: How to Combine Exclusivity and Inclusivity?

In the collective imagination, luxury is often associated with high prices, waiting lists, and limited quantities; in a word: exclusivity, or access for a few. "Luxury is finite and limited in its very essence. It is limited because of the precious materials it uses, or the rare know-how it requires. Luxury is exclusive by nature. We love luxury because it is limited. We desire it because it is exclusive, and because we want to be part of it, now, or someday" (Cyrille Vigneron, President and CEO of Cartier, personal communication). Ferrari perfectly embodies this concept of exclusivity in its attitude toward its products. "We sell one car less than the market demands and limited series are like a reward for our loyal customers", says Dennis De Munck, Ferrari's head of employer branding and university partnerships (personal communication). Nurturing exclusivity is part of Ferrari's DNA. Company founder Enzo Ferrari never dreamed of creating road cars and only did so to fund his racing team. Even then he never planned on ramping up production to turn a quick profit. His goal was to make what was necessary to ensure his racing team could participate in the most important races. For example, when the Ferrari 250 GTO debuted in 1962, FIA regulations required a minimum production run of 100 cars to be built in order for the model to be approved for participation in Group 3 GT car races. Originally, Ferrari only built 36 250 GTOs – 33 in the initial production and an additional three later on. There were rumors that he got away with it by numbering the chassis out of sequence, making it look like 100 vehicles were actually made; when inspectors from the FIA visited the factory in Maranello, Enzo and his team would suggest that other cars were located in rooms or garages in other towns and cities. The truth involves significantly less intrigue: homologation papers were issued for the Ferrari 250 GTO based on the features it shared with the 1960 Berlinetta SWB, of which 100 were actually produced.

Over the years, Ferrari's competitors have adapted to demand, producing hundreds and thousands of cars a year. Yet Ferrari has consistently sought to minimize, rather than maximize, its production numbers. The company continues to produce just the cars it needs to maintain its aura of exclusivity. Not that Ferrari has never experimented with increasing production to satisfy demand. In the early 1990s, Ferrari came out with the Ferrari F40 (Type F120). Originally, production was planned for 600 vehicles, but due to the model's popularity, Ferrari produced a further 800, which were released the following year, many of them destined for Japanese clients who, at the time, were aggressively buying Ferraris and other luxury goods due to Japan's booming economy. Then, in late 1991 and early 1992, the Japanese stock market collapsed and the Ferrari F40 lost three quarters of its value overnight. Although Ferrari as a company survived the recession, the oversaturation of the F40 had gone against Ferrari's core values of rarity and exclusivity, and the experiment offered a clear lesson for the company. In the years since, Ferrari has only produced the limited numbers of vehicles planned for in their initial proposals, deciding never to repeat the mistake of the 1990 F40.

Ferrari's historical commitment to exclusivity today shapes a purchasing process that is highly dependent on the relationship between the company and its consumers and collectors. The first step to owning a limited-edition Ferrari is to build a relationship with your local dealer. Ferrari works closely with its network of dealerships to determine which of their most loyal clients deserve a special edition car. In other words, they act as the gatekeepers. While a good relationship with your local dealership can put you on the shortlist, it is Ferrari's CRM team that compiles candidate profiles to decide who on their long list of clients is most suitable for the limited-edition releases.

The selection process for limited-edition Ferraris is not based on the number of cars a person already possesses, nor their loyalty to the brand. There have been occasions where celebrities and athletes have been offered the opportunity to enter the Ferrari ecosystem without having to build up a collection, with the expectation they will return after their first limited edition to purchase a second or third Ferrari in the future. Likewise, Ferrari does not select the top 500 clients on their list. Rather, the CRM department within Ferrari looks at varied criteria, including but not limited to individuals' purchase history of first-hand range models, their usage of each of their Ferraris over time, their re-sale of certain models, and their purchasing behavior. Over the years, Ferrari has produced limited editions of both road cars and track cars. As such, it is rare for the team at Ferrari to offer track cars to clients who prefer luxury comfort road cars, or vice versa. While there are many stories of disgruntled collectors who feel they have been snubbed because they were not given the chance to buy one of Ferrari's limited-edition models, it is important to note that the CRM department takes an intimate, personal approach in their selections, taking the time to discover exactly what their clientele are like, their interests and preferences, so as to best determine the select few who will truly appreciate a car for what it is.

In September 2018, Ferrari released The Monza SP1 and SP2 highly limited-edition roadsters, aimed exclusively at its most loyal customers and collectors. The cars are part of the Ferrari Icona series (by definition limited-edition vehicles) and combine high performance (a V12 engine, making them Ferrari's highest performance road cars ever at the time of their release), innovation (a virtual wind shield, among other new features), and a "fun to drive" experience with design elements borrowed from Ferrari's late 1940s/early 1950s "barchetta" GT race cars. Only 499 of the SP1 and SP2 combined are planned for production, to be delivered to clients between 2019 and 2021.

The Monza SP2 was the 1st car off the production line when Ferrari re-started production following a seven-week long Covid-19-imposed pitstop in April and May 2020.

Ferrari nurtures exclusivity, the pinnacle of luxury experiences. This management of "rarity" was well understood by Enzo Ferrari, who applied it to his business thinking: that Ferrari should offer one car less than the market demands. The customer who does not gain access to a Ferrari today will be the first to request a car next time.

Enzo's motto, "The Ferrari is yet to be built" (Ferrari, corporate presentation), is a clear reference to the continuous development and innovation that continue to guide Ferrari's designs. Seen in relation to this position of never being fully satisfied, the company's limited editions and tightly controlled distribution model make sense as strategies to uphold central values. Ferrari is always seeking to go further from an engineering, manufacturing, design, and customer satisfaction point of view; it is more concerned with the next new thing than the familiarity of the status quo. The success of Ferrari's limited editions confirms the desirability and value-retention of its business model: a 2013 LaFerrari that sold for over €1.3 million at the time of its release is today worth several times that amount.

Exclusivity can be connected not only to a deliberate choice to release limited quantities of product (i.e., *rarity of output*), but to different types of "rarity":

- *Rarity of input*: the materials necessary to create the product are themselves limited, necessitating a low level of production. Think of the wines of Franciacorta, which, since they must be made of grapes grown only within a territory of a certain number of acres, can be produced only in limited quantities. The same scarcity applies to yellow and pink diamonds. In this case, the critical choice for companies is to understand where and through which channels and geographies to direct their product to best enhance its value.
- *Rarity of distribution*: a product is only available through limited channels and is not widely distributed, either online or geographically. Ferrari, for example, relies exclusively on its network of trusted dealers around the world to sell its cars. Critical issues are related to location choices and proper empowerment and education of local networks.
- *Rarity of information*: only certain facts about a product and the brand are made available to the public, and access may be limited to a select community of experts and clients. For example, there are brands within Richemont Group nobody has heard of because they only cater to bespoke clients. The reason why we never hear of them is that they do not advertise. It's necessary to belong to the world of high jewelry to gain access to information about these brands; custom pieces are made only for a narrow clientele. Ferrari pursues a similar philosophy, giving very few people the chance to experience the company's One-Off service.

The concept of exclusivity brings us back to the reasons why people buy luxury. Among the motivations mentioned in Chapter 1 are aspiration, scarcity, and the desire to differentiate ourselves from others. As a consequence, if an item is easily accessible, people might question the price: they may not see it as rare enough to warrant the expense. People desire more what they lack and what is hard to get; they feel good when they are able to acquire what others cannot.

This association between luxury and rarity has sometimes been perceived negatively, as a limiting factor on elements of production and consumption. The idea of a "glass ceiling" preventing some groups of people from enjoying luxury goods seems to be in conflict with current social trends toward inclusivity, making too much exclusivity something that could dilute brand equity. However, exclusivity and inclusivity are not in fact in contradiction:

> We love luxury to celebrate our successes, our achievements, as a reward of (sic) our efforts. As this aspiration to overcome our limits is a universal dream, luxury is truly inclusive. This is why luxury retail stores must be inviting and welcoming, even if the products are exclusive. [. . .] True luxury is to cultivate the art of being exclusive but not excluding, inviting but not expected.
> (Cyrille Vigneron, President and CEO of Cartier, personal communication)

The concept of "inclusivity" is complicated and much debated. It has various dimensions: social equality regardless of income level, gender equity, aversion to any form of racial discrimination, etc. Topics very important to Gen Z and Y – which, according to Bain and Company (2017), will represent more than half of the world's luxury market by 2025. Star brands have successfully cracked this paradox: the more they sell, the more desirable they become. A dilemma exists therefore only for "mid-size" brands: Should they stay exclusive to stay aspirational, risking being outpaced by others? Or should they become more inclusive to expand their reach but risk losing their exclusive cachet? How can they break the glass ceiling?

Some considerations emerge from an in-depth look at some practical cases. First, the desire to look different and unique is very present in Europe and the US, where luxury has historically been a marker of social class. However, the dominant markets are now China, Japan, and Korea, which have stronger drivers for *assimilation* rather than *differentiation*: looking like others is reassuring. Luxury becomes, paradoxically, equally a sign of differentiation (depending on personal wealth) and assimilation (belonging to a group). This of course allows for an easier combination of exclusivity and inclusivity.

A second important note is that embracing the value of inclusivity does not represent a structural modification of a company's modus operandi, which can continue to be based on exclusive logics. It means a new organizational culture based on the acceptance of multiple forms of diversity and multiple possibilities of self-expression. Each brand has chosen its own perspective on the topic, disseminating its guiding principles inside and outside the organization.

In beauty, the progenitor of a new generation of "inclusive" brands is Fenty, created in 2017 within Kendo, LVMH's beauty incubator. The brand, which has Rihanna as its ambassador, has become famous for its "foundation for everyone": Pro Filt'r, which is available in more than 40 different colors (Wingard, 2019).

However, the brand that fully embodies the concept of inclusiveness in the eyes of the new generation is undoubtedly Gucci. CEO Marco Bizzarri has redefined the key values of the organization by placing all aspects of inclusiveness at the center of its relations with the internal and external community. This also led to a review of the organization chart, with the appointment of a Global Head of Diversity, Equity and Inclusion. Does this mean that Gucci has given up on the luxury world's classic canon? Absolutely not: It has only "democratized" luxury, allowing everyone to access the offer, then using customer relationship management (CRM) (see Chapter 6) to segment customers based on their brand loyalty. The most loyal ones, in terms of the budget they allocate to the brand and their frequency of buying, have exclusive access to personalized services.

Paradox 4: How to Govern Marketing Pressures and Rarity?

Luxury is not exempt from marketing strategies that aim at optimizing communication by exposing the consumer to a large number of messages on different channels and in different ways. The motive behind this intense activity is not so much an immediate return on sales, as a desire to communicate to a wide audience beyond the target market. These marketing pressures are amplified in the digital environment. Social media and e-mail notifications allow brands to further expose their customers to messages about their policies (commercial, promotional, etc.) and their services as well as their products. As we will see in Paradox 6, communication is moving toward greater customization, both in response to CRM strategies and through the use of analytics. However, many communication campaigns still have a deliberately large and indiscriminate audience. Widespread and prominent communication campaigns reiterate essential elements of brand architecture. They emphasize a company's mission and its unique selling proposition, using tangible brand elements such as colors, iconic products, architectures, or brand ambassadors. Another case in which communication becomes omnipresent is the launch of a particular service, product, or special event, or a collaboration between brands. It is here that paradoxical situations are most frequently encountered, above all in personal goods (i.e., cosmetics, watches, jewels, apparel, leather goods, etc.).

Take the clothing and leather goods business. Within companies, there are now roles dedicated to managing the world of influencers and social media. These figures create lists of influencers that are consistent with the brand identity, going beyond determining the activity or brand portfolio on which to collaborate with a particular influencer. Brands select the social media that can best convey certain messages with respect to the target they want to hit. When a new collection debuts with a fashion show, news of the event appears on various channels and is communicated by brand ambassadors. In the case of product launches, items are physically sent to influencers, who are expected to feature the product on the same designated launch day. PR gifting programs have become recurrent and generous.

It therefore happens that consumers are exposed to the same object repeatedly, especially if they are connected to multiple influencers selected by the brand. This creates a paradox. Although they may seem to be everywhere, these new objects of desire are often rare and difficult to find for those not connected to the brand. Customers who go looking for them may find that they are already sold out and not destined to be restocked, or customers may be required to sign up for grueling waiting lists in order to obtain them. And by the time the desired product arrives, the urge to possess it has already passed.

An extreme example of this situation is the case of Dior's famous collaboration with Jordan Brand on the Air Jordan 1 OG Dior sneakers, which ran from the end of 2019 through the spring of 2020. The sneakers, which were created in both high- and low-top versions, have appeared on various blogs, Instagram accounts, and YouTube channels, and have been worn by international celebrities. The dream of having them has become collective. Too bad that the same sneakers were never available to the brand's customers other than those at the very top of the CRM pyramid. The shoes were reserved exclusively for celebrities, very, very important customers (VVICs), and a few lucky individuals who participated in a lottery – the prize being the opportunity to buy one of the few remaining pairs, available for the sticker price of €1,900.

In the same line, we may remember the media rumor that accompanied the debut of LV's collaboration with Supreme in 2017. Despite the worldwide anticipation that followed the news, the brands' coveted items (from RTW to a skateboard) were announced to be only available in eight pop-up stores in London, LA, Sydney, Tokyo, Seoul, Beijing, Miami, and Paris, which remained open for about two weeks. Early access was provided to VIPs and VVICs, who could buy directly from LV, wherever they were, without visiting the pop-ups. Unfortunately, LV and Supreme cancelled the release of the collection in the two US pop-ups a few days before the launch. On opening day, people queued for hours to purchase the pieces of this very limited edition. Many of them remained without; not to mention the discontent of those who weren't in those eight lucky cities.

In general, the imbalance between marketing pressures and rarity can have a boomerang effect for companies. Aggressively promoting an exclusive product can nurture brand notoriety, but it can also frustrate a brand's community of loyal customers.

Paradox 5: How to Properly Allocate Resources between Offline and Online?

A brand's online presence includes not only e-commerce, but all the digital strategies a company can put in place to communicate with and engage its customers. Through websites, social media, and other types of applications, a brand can connect with clients as it does in the store and even access opportunities not available in a traditional retail environment. Yet despite the advantages offered by online channels, luxury brands were slow to adapt to the virtual marketplace. Until recently, they neglected online spaces under the assumption that they did not allow customers to have first-hand interactions with a brand. For a long time, this paradox did not register with luxury companies, and was not part of their decision making; all efforts were concentrated on brick-and-mortar.

When the world was forced into lockdown in 2020, luxury companies were no longer able to ignore online spaces. In the subsequent months, they have engineered a kind of revolution in how they communicate with and engage their customers. The transformation of their approach included three key decisions. First, luxury companies recognized the importance of organizing their digital presence and took full control of the channels they were already active on (previously they had often relied on service providers). Second, in anticipation of a limited re-opening, they reconsidered the role of their retail stores, focusing on entertainment and experience. Third, brands sought to coordinate their efforts online and offline, creating a cohesive strategy of consumer engagement.

These three key decisions are part of a wider question about the allocation of resources to offline and online and the management of a complex omnichannel strategy. When everyone has one or more digital devices, used constantly for many purposes, the problem is not to find a way to replicate online the same experience the consumer can have offline. The real questions are: What to offer online, what to offer offline? What should the experience be online and offline? The side question for physical retail becomes therefore: If many things which used to be possible only in-store are now more easily available online, how should the store experience evolve? Apple has been a pilot in this field, allocating only 50% of its stores' selling space to transactions and reserving the rest for non-transactional experiences like the Genius Bar. Luxury stores are also becoming more experiential and social and less transactional.

To the consumer, online and offline channels must be perfectly coordinated, appearing as part of a unified brand image. Instead of seeing digital as a parallel world, companies now understand that it is integrated with the physical experience. An omnichannel strategy must therefore adopt the customer's perspective; this is what drives brands' retail and communication strategies. All actions must be coherent; the message the brand delivers in multi-brand stores, department stores, retail stores, and online should be consistent and face the same audience. Communication and CRM strategy, as a set of principles and messages, act as an umbrella under which specific initiatives can be planned for different tiers of customers. Fashion shows or dedicated fairs are marquee events that convey the main concept and key values of the brand offer through staggered access to different clients. VVICs are physically invited to the show; VICs have a private presentation in the store (i.e., a trunk show) in advance of the rest of the market. Later, the boutique presents the collection to a wider pool of clients.

Simultaneously, the brand can use its online channels to deliver the same message, mirroring the coherent visual presentation of the fashion show. For example, a newsletter announcing the new collection can be sent to clients, and introductory YouTube videos can be uploaded on the brand's channel. In both streams – online and offline – different actions can be planned for different tiers of the CRM pyramid. CRM is not only a database, it is a set of retail marketing activities that should be in line with product development and merchandising strategy. The relationship with the clients is the final aim, and all touchpoints must be organized around a perfect understanding of their tastes and preferences.

A perfect allocation of resources and integration of online and offline comes from understanding the similarities and differences between the two channels. Integrating online and offline starts with recognizing that online key performance indicators (KPIs) have some peculiarities. In general, sales value depends on the traffic generated, the conversion rate of traffic to purchase, and the average order value.

Sales Value = Traffic x Conversion Rate x Average Order Value

Online, traffic is related to the following actions:
- *Traffic sources* that can generate high-quality traffic on web sites – traffic that leads to transactions. The most important of these is paid search (SEM, i.e., search engine marketing, and SEO, i.e., search engine optimization)
- *Newsletters* that companies can send to a database of clients
- *Organic Search* and a direct link to the website that customers can use to access the brand without passing through a third party
- *Social media* (e.g., Instagram, Facebook, Tik Tok), which is increasingly important

Another dimension influencing traffic is geography. There are numerous implications when companies decide to add a country to their website, from languages to custom duties, differences in customer interaction, transportation requirements, fiscal regulations, and many more. This is the reason why European companies began exploring online by targeting mature markets where they already had retail stores. In the last five years, companies have started to recognize that it is possible to reach a wider pool of customers online than offline, and are expanding the scope of their websites and other digital channels accordingly. As in the physical world, conversion online is influenced by the services and the assortment of products the company offers. Omnichannel services include things like the ability to check availability in-store, reserve in-store, return in-store, click-and-collect, pre-order products, and set up private, in-store appointments. They give customers the perception that the website is like another boutique, providing the same services the client would get in store. The level of service and experience the brand delivers through different touchpoints online and in store should be the same.

This coherence and integration between online and offline extend beyond services to include visual merchandising and CRM. Visual merchandising online should follow the same guidelines applied to boutiques and window displays. If a new collection is launched in the boutique, the website launch should include the same image. Customer databases and segmentation online and offline must be integrated in an overall platform, with coordinated initiatives. Brands should have a single, master database containing all information about their clients, those who shop in-store as well as those who make purchases through the website. In the recent past, there were different systems for collecting data about the client online vs. offline. Now, however, brands are starting to expand their reach to cities and regions where they do not have a physical presence, necessitating a more holistic understanding of their customer base. Online is not only a way to attract new clients; it is a way to keep in touch with existing clients. Personalizing connections to online clients can be a way to bring them into a brand's offline activities. Francesco Viana, general manager Southern Europe of Christian Dior Couture, describes this process as part of a cohesive effort by the brand's sales team: "At Dior, we monitor the purchases online of all clients. If a client buys a dress, she/he receives a call from a sales associate in the country establishing a more human approach and getting a personal and intimate feeling" (personal communication).

A brand's assortment of products is key to conversion because the wider the product range and availability, the higher the possibility of transforming traffic into sales. However, increasing assortment (i.e., having more SKUs and/or a larger quantity per item) has the financial impact of having too much backstock. A true omni-channel approach improves the way companies manage assortment because it is based on the integration of different stocks. The company is able to offer to the client more products without of the risk of overstocking because both store and website inventory are available on the same platform. According to Viana:

> Stock does not belong to any boutique, it belongs to the brand. Whoever comes first is served, independently from where the item is physically located. If a client enters a boutique in Rome to buy a pair of shoes and that are not available at that time, it is still possible to obtain that same pair from online inventory or from another store anywhere in the world, with a delivery to the store the client went to originally or to the client's home.   (personal communication)

Unfortunately, few luxury brands have implemented this type of integration, and many are therefore missing out on the opportunities it affords. It may be effective, for instance, to occasionally direct clients' attention to online or offline only, tailoring events and product launches to make purchasing only available through the website, or increasing footfall by making some products, experiences, or facets of the brand only available in-store. Depth and breadth of assortment online depends on the business goals a company pursues in the digital environment, which may not be the same for all offers. Many luxury brands, like Hermès, see their online presence as an important communication platform rather than a sales generator. Although they have increased their online SKUs over time, they continue to exclude iconic, hard-to-get products, especially those that are very expensive (e.g., Birkin bags) from their online sales platforms.

Lastly, the *average order value* depends on the product mix and decisions about whether to apply a mark down or keep items at full price. Online and offline pricing strategies must follow the same logic, both in terms of the set price for a particular item and in terms of timing. The issue of pricing is extremely critical in the case of multi-brand independent websites, a topic already present in the wholesale channel. However, the aggravating circumstance of controlling online pricing is that price differences are visible on a global scale, leading the client to arbitrage. The fact that many of these multi-brand sites are now shifting their business to apps makes monitoring by companies more challenging.

Paradox 6: How to be Extraordinary in a Context of Excellence?

Going beyond expectations may seem difficult, especially with experienced, sophisticated customers who are "spoiled" by their favorite brands. It takes real care, consideration, and passion. How can you pleasantly surprise a customer who is already used to high standards of service? Here, thinking outside the box and focusing on innovation produces the most gratifying results, as it often leads to multiplying points of contact with the target audience. Factory visits and events, for instance, can be spectacular platforms for storytelling and represent a kind of reward for a brand's acolytes.

Many actions can be pursued to create a special experience for the customer, and they can be variously combined together. Below, we mention just a few:
1) Designing unforgettable locations
2) Proposing services that allow an intimate experience with the brand
3) Expanding the points and opportunities for contact with the customer

1) Designing an unforgettable location
Given the advancement of online channels (their weight on market value will grow from 12% in 2020 to 30% in 2025, according to D'Arpizio and Levato's 2020 report for Bain and Company), stores are being rethought as entertainment spaces, places where the customer intentionally goes to have fun, to see something new, participate in a limited-admission event, admire the architecture, or see an artistic exhibition. Gentle Monster, a Korean eyewear brand launched in 2011, was immediately

successful thanks to the original set-ups of its stores.[5] Each one is conceived as an exhibition space that must convey the brand image and not just contribute to the sale of products. Every Gentle Monster store, from Los Angeles to Shanghai, is different from the others, each one inspired by a precise concept that changes periodically like a series of exhibitions, with the inclusion of design objects and sculptures.

Another example is the famous Louis Vuitton Island Maison in Singapore. Occupying one of two island pavilions designed by Israeli-Canadian architect Moshe Safdie to compliment his Marina Bay Sands waterfront development project, visitors can get to the Maison by crossing an open bridge, taking a tunnel connected to the nearby mall, or by boat. The interior spaces were designed by Peter Marino, and there is an exhibition area dedicated to the world of travel as interpreted by LV since the early twentieth century; a library with a selection of books on travel, design, art, and culture; and a series of sculptural installations. The men's area is characterized by the use of shipbuilding timber and nautical details; the women's has sailing masts suspended in the air. The mezzanine is dedicated to travel with a breathtaking view of the Singapore skyline and a private lounge that looks like the deck of a luxury yacht. Also, in Marina Bay, Apple's first floating store, designed by the British architecture firm Foster + Partners, opened in September 2020.

Pushing the boundaries of what a physical space can be, Burberry's collaboration with Tencent on the British brand's immersive retail experience in the MixC Shenzhen Bay development strives to create something unexpected for digitally savvy Chinese luxury customers. Burberry's website describes the concept as:

> . . . a space of exploration, designed to inspire and entertain luxury customers, where they can interact with our brand and product in new and exciting ways, in person and on social media. [. . .] Through a dedicated WeChat mini program, customers can unlock exclusive content and personalised experiences and share them with their communities. The store is made up of a series of spaces for customers to explore. Each has its own concept and personality and offers a unique interactive experience. (*Burberry Shenzhen China*, n.d., paragraphs 2–4)

In addition to large-scale concept stores, pop-ups certainly deserve a place in a discussion of branded spaces. They have been an important trend in recent years (see also Chapter 1). The idea is to create a temporary, themed space with an exclusive and limited product offer, creating a customer experience different from the one offered in store. Initially, the pop-up was merely a communication tool, but it has become a very effective way for marketing, CRM, and merchandising to expand how customers understand the brand. Customers are used to visiting boutiques in major cities, but they spend their holidays elsewhere, in resorts and smaller towns. Their moods also change, meaning a destination pop-up needs to provide a different declination of the brand identity than an urban boutique. A new strategy must be defined in terms of communication and even product (capsules sold only in pop-ups, even if some items are present online). The aim is to provide a difference in the shopping experience, since it makes little sense for a customer to buy something on vacation that they can find at home. Pop-ups can be in resorts, department stores, custom-built structures in public areas, or any other available spaces. The only necessary feature is that they are temporary, open for less than a season – sometimes for only a month. This new retail approach is promoted by the brand on all its channels and is a way to find new clients and try new locations without investing a huge amount in terms of CAPEX. Luxury brands have also discovered that pop-ups can be highly profitable. They are an important element of Dior's strategy, which in 2019 activated about 25 pop-up stores worldwide, from Tulum to Cortina.

2) Propose services that allow an intimate and personal experience with the brand
Being one of the "Ferraristi" means not only having strong feelings about driving, but also being a part of a world of events where Ferrari owners can race in a real circuit. And the most loyal ones earn an invitation to pick up their limited-edition car in Maranello. When a client buys a Ferrari, he or she downloads an app to follow its assembly in Maranello step by step in real time. The relationship with a community of driver-owners is so important that Ferrari's dealer incentive plan is based less on revenues generated and more on how relationships with customers are managed. This is in line with Ferrari's key values, which put the emotions of fans, dealers, customers, and even children who dream of owning a Ferrari ahead of everything else.

Designing experiences connected with the emotional needs of clients is also at the heart of Dorchester Collection's strategy. The luxury hotel market is crowded – new openings impact development, improvements take place through refurbishments, new trends are constantly emerging, and global guests frequent numerous exotic locations. At Dorchester Collection, guests are asked the reasons behind their recurring choice to stay at Dorchester Collection properties worldwide, when ultimately the options are endless. Their answers are based on their emotional values and what they really enjoy when visiting the hotels, rather than how a property has taken care of their functional needs. It is the emotional component of a guest's stay that ultimately fuels loyalty, something Dorchester Collection has taken to heart in developing the services it's offer to guests.

All Dorchester Collection hotel teams are committed to finding genuine and meaningful ways to engage with guests, in order to create lasting memories. It is essential that team members build real and lasting emotional connections. Evidence of the power of these connections can be found in real-life stories that play out across the company on a daily basis. All team members are therefore empowered to make decisions to ensure complete guest satisfaction. They are encouraged to think creatively and to be generous with their time and in their actions. Rather than extravagant gestures, it is more about considering what matters most to their guests. Often, they find it's the simplest things that have the most lasting emotional effect.

Employees are also encouraged to host guests, extending invitations to dine or simply enjoy a cup of tea and a slice of cake with them. Spending time together allows them to share stories, gain a greater understanding of one another, and create special bonds. Over time, this transforms into genuine and lasting relationships: "I love to be surprised, it's a special way to show kindness", exclaims one guest testimonial (Dorchester Collection, personal communication).

A wonderful demonstration of these relationships is the way Dorchester Collection guests often come to team members for advice. They have been asked everything from ideas for children's names to advice on purchasing houses, yachts, and cars. So comfortable is a Dorchester Collection guest in the hotel, that it is not unusual for employees to be invited into his or her life. For example, hotel employees describe being invited to celebrate a special occasion such as a family wedding or a birthday. Guests also show a genuine interest in the wellbeing and career progression of team members. It is perhaps no surprise that another benefit of these strong relationships is that Dorchester Collection has high employee retention rates.

As both Ferrari and Dorchester Collection show, the opportunities to create a unique relationship between customer and brand are endless and involve a wide range of services.

Some are illustrated below in examples of companies that have implemented one-of-a-kind experiences, personalization, trunk shows, consignment, concierge, and technology-based experiences such as AR, VR, and gamification.

One-of-a-kind experiences. In 2019, Panerai became the first brand to launch a watch that could not be bought in a store. Instead, the watches were delivered to clients upon their arrival at one of a series of exclusive events. Panerai combined limited-edition watches in a bundle that included a priceless, once-in-a-lifetime experience. For example, in 2019, Panerai organized a special launch for its Submersible Marina Militare Carbotech watch. The 33 lucky individuals who were able to snap up the offer were invited to the Italian Navy base in La Spezia for 48 hours to experience training activities with the Italian Navy, each day culminating in a night of festivities. This is a highly unique experience, as the naval base is off-limits to civilians.

Other limited-edition Panerai watches include singular experiences as optional add-ons, only available upon purchase of the watch in question. For example, clients who bought one of 36 limited-edition Luminor Tourbillon GMTs could pay a €20,000 premium to be flown to Auckland, New Zealand to attend the final race and other events leading up to the America's Cup along with challenger *Luna Rossa* in March 2021. Clients received their watches upon their arrival in Auckland and had the once-in-a-lifetime experience of boarding the *Luna Rossa*.

When this spectacular event was presented in spring 2019, Panerai was still working on the prototype for the watch, which launched in November 2020. Even then, collectors had started securing their watches. This entire package created a lot of buzz in the industry, and all pieces were sold months before the event, despite the hefty price of €190,000, including the America's Cup perk.

Following the success of previous endeavors, Panerai has also offered 24 selected clients the possibility of accompanying Mike Horn on an expedition to the North Pole in 2021, an experience focused on the importance of preserving the Arctic and saving the oceans. For this project, Panerai will release nineteen Mike Horn limited-edition Submersible EcoTitanium watches, which cost €39,000 each, and five Submersible Tourbillon EcoPangaea. This model, which costs €190,000, is made from repurposed pieces of Horn's boat, and sold out within minutes of it being made available at private events.

The same philosophy has been adopted by Cartier, which entrusts to its stores the role of excelling in services (based on a sophisticated personal relationship management system), explaining the brand, creating museum-like displays to show off the best of the maison's creations, and entertaining and thrilling customers with events for special occasions and concerts. The role assigned to Cartier's stores is part of an omnichannel strategy that requires a perfect integration between offline and online, facilitated by the coordinated management of logistics and CRM systems. This integration is further strengthened by the use of social media and new "clienteling" strategies in which sales associates are empowered to take on key roles in virtual customer engagement. On this front, China is an important leader; having been the first country to enter lockdown due to Covid-19, it was able to experiment with innovative and very effective forms of customer engagement that have since come to serve as a source of inspiration for brands all over the world.

Personalization, individualization, and customization have become quite common in luxury marketing strategies. Although interchangeable in common usage, in the marketing context the meaning of each of these three terms is not the same. Personalization involves the ideation of an individual marketing mix based on previously collected customer data (Arora et al., 2008; Franke, Keinz, and Steger, 2009). Individualization is even finer, identifying the characteristics, motivations, and preferences of every "me" in the audience. This satisfies luxury consumers' need to be recognized individually, beyond the historical and superficial data included in databases. This is important for CRM activities, which can evolve from simple personalization to more sophisticated individualization techniques based on data and artificial intelligence (AI) and a cross-functional cooperation on customer data among service, sales, marketing, and IT. A customer's individual journey is tracked in real time, allowing "white-glove" service and a consistent experience across all touchpoints that is tailored to the customer's unique needs. Those needs can be categorized according to three main archetypes: preventing issues before they occur, solving problems before customers raise them, and personalizing responses when customers reach out (Agrawal et al., 2018 and 2021). Knowing clients intimately can help companies avoid exposing them to communications related to services or products already bought – and should incentivize a return to store and more spending.

In customization, the client proactively specifies one or more elements of his or her marketing mix. This means the luxury brand lets the customer participate in the design of the product. Customization provides an experience that is not normally accessible to everyone. Chaumet and the British sartorial brand Turnbull and Asser have become famous for creating bespoke items for their clients; Roja Dove, meanwhile, creates special perfumes for his.

This last mode is very common in the automobile and yacht industries. For instance, Lamborghini offers a "Customization Program" in four steps, each offering a higher level of customization than the last:

1) *Ad Personam*, the option to tailor the car to the client's needs, allowing them to choose among a vast array of options including more than 300 colors and thousands of possible combinations. In 2019, 61% of all delivered cars had at least one bespoke element. The client also has the option to create his or her own, eponymous color.

2) *Special series*, meaning limited editions of existing cars without the option of changing their structure.

3) *Few Off*, rare cars like the Sian, presented at the Frankfurt auto-show in September 2019 with a price tag of €2 million+VAT. Lamborghini pre-sold all 63 cars based on a technical description and a scale model. The first car was delivered to the client in December 2020.

4) *One Off*, the chance to design a car from scratch. This program can be initiated every two years for the price of around €8 million per car. An example of such a model is the Aventador J.

Lamborghini's Past Chief Commercial Officer Giovani Perosino described the company's strategy as the intersection between a culture of individualism and savvy business decisions:

> We are living in the age of you, each of us want to be a protagonist, to be "the one". We would love to sell 8,000 different Lamborghini. Our customization strategy allows us to be a customer-centric company but also to increase profitability. In individualization, the contribution margin was about 60%; in 2019. It's a win-win situation where all stakeholders along the journey earn, from the customer, to the sales people, to the dealer, to the HQs.　　　(personal communication, May 2020)

Similarly, every car in Ferrari's portfolio is made to order, and clients have the freedom to customize their vehicles (Lojacono and Pan, 2020). However, the level of customization depends on an individual customer's relationship with Ferrari and the amount of money they are willing to spend. To explain its system, Ferrari has created the customization pyramid that is exhibited in Figure 2.9.

Starting at the bottom of the pyramid is the "Carrozzeria Scaglietti" personalization program, in which each client may choose their paint color, upholstery, wheels, rims, etc. Just like purchasing a car from your regular auto dealer, a variety of options is available to the client at their local dealership. The next level up allows the client to select special equipment, such as a specific type of breaks, performance tires, or satellite alarm system. If these options are not satisfactory for the client, they may choose to go to Maranello, Italy, where many more options for the interior, exterior

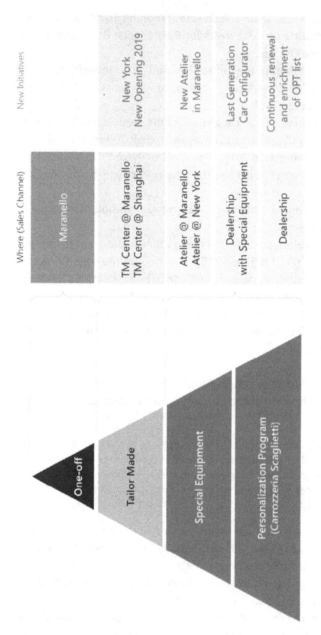

Figure 2.9: Ferrari Personalization Offer.
Source: Ferrari company presentation, p. 14, investor meeting, December 4, 2019.

(color, materials, fixtures, and accessories), and additional equipment can be made available.

Moving up one level higher, the Tailor Made service allows clients the maximum freedom of choice: to combine any of Ferrari's three collections – Scuderia, Classica, and Inedita – to reflect the company's sporting soul, heritage, and innovation. A client may also take inspiration from other sources and adapt the car's various elements according to their taste. For example, a Riva yacht owner who is customizing his (or her) Ferrari may choose to use the same kind of wood finish for the interiors of his Ferrari 812 Superfast or specify the use of only Poltrona Frau leather seats with a certain type of stitching. Since this service goes above and beyond what would typically be offered by any car maker, it should not come as a surprise that it is only available to special clients who have an existing relationship with Ferrari. Finally, at the top of the pyramid is the special-project program "One-Off". Launched in the late 2000s, it is the ultimate bespoke service, allowing clients to create a one-of-a-kind Ferrari inspired by modern or classic Ferrari models. Only very few of these one-off models, developed together with the client and the Ferrari Design team, are produced – one is the unique P80/C (Borgomero, 2020). The one-of-a-kind design also comes with ultimate secrecy; neither the price of the car nor the identity of its owner is ever revealed.

In clothing, there are different forms of customization ranging from made to order (MtO) to made to measure (MtM) to bespoke, with an increasing degree of autonomy of choice on the part of the customer, as well as different types of service. There are many reasons why a customer might be interested in made to measure or bespoke clothing: the difficulty of finding well-fitting or interesting garments in ready to wear; the need to have something exclusive, not worn by others; the habit of having only tailored garments; the desire to enjoy a private experience with dedicated staff; or participation in a special occasion, for example, a red carpet or a wedding.

Christian Louboutin, famous for his red soles and painfully high-heeled shoes, offers bespoke services to some of his most loyal clients. These services are only known to a very few and are never advertised. The bespoke service, unlike made-to-order, which is an activity that is sometimes offered in-store, allows a client to create the shoes of their dreams. The process starts with the client submitting a request for the bespoke service to their local headquarters: if you are located in Asia Pacific, this would mean Christian Louboutin's headquarters in Hong Kong. A client representative will review the client's purchase history and profile before responding to the request. If the client's profile matches their expectations, they will connect the client with the bespoke project manager in Paris to set up their first appointment. This service is highly exclusive, and requires the client to travel to the brand's Paris headquarters at 19 rue Jean-Jacques Rousseau for their first appointment and the four to five subsequent fittings. The first meeting involves a brain storming session to discuss the various shoes and designs the client most prefers from Christian Louboutin's existing collection, and then further deduce various heights, supports, and materials. A mold of the client's foot is taken and measured by a master cobbler, who will hand carve the custom foot last that will be used to create the shoe. The idea is to create a "Cinderella fit", unique to the client's foot. This service is often offered to clients who either have oddly shaped feet, or feet too large or too small to fit standard shoe sizes. However, the service is of course open to any who can afford it – a rarified group, as the consulting fee starts at €3000, with additional charges for fabric and materials.

Trunk Shows are exclusive presentations in stores or other locations for a small number of customers. They offer the possibility of buying before products are presented to the market. This is similar to the pre-order model described in this chapter and which will be discussed again in Chapter 7 on new business models. Trunk shows are organized as "personalization" services: they are always by invitation, and the latest season's materials, fabrics, and models are presented together with non-seasonal carryovers, archives, etc. This allows clients to select from a wider range of items than what is typically available in stores. Some companies are now taking the trunk show to the customer, providing an intimate, in-home experience.

Consignment is a form of shopping widely used in the Middle East where, for cultural reasons, women prefer to try on and select clothing in the intimacy and tranquility of their homes. A stylist, an agent, or a personal shopper chooses items from one or more brands based on the needs and tastes of the customer and brings them to their clients' homes, supporting them in their choices. In the event of a purchase, the intermediary receives a commission.

Concierge services involve the brand organizing a private presentation of the collection at the client's home or in a selected location (for example, a hotel suite). Concierge services appeal to ultra-wealthy clients who care for privacy and exclusivity; this purchasing mode is also very common in the Middle East. The package of services can include experiences beyond selecting clothes: bespoke travel, private visits or tours (e.g., museums, wineries), a tailor or designer visiting a client's house for appointments, or the private viewing of a fashion collection in the client's home. Unlike consignment, with concierge, the brand maintains direct and privileged contact with the customer.

In the digital environment, concierge becomes a technology-driven business model in which consumers using the website to place an order can request a specialist assistant (a concierge), an option that is also available by phone. Services offered by the concierge include advice, rapid delivery, and trial of a variety of sizes. Payment is required if the client buys something, and the concierge gets a commission. The way the business model is structured allows the brand to reduce returns and related costs.

Companies like Quintessentially, which provides bespoke access and day-to-day assistance to manage requests coming from members related to travel, education, personal shopping, weddings, and art, specialize in concierge services.

Technology-based experiences increasingly play a role in customization services, and consumers appreciate the use of augmented and virtual reality (AR, VR).
Several studies have shown that retailers and brands can benefit from the adoption
of these new technologies to achieve a higher conversion of visits into purchases
and a lower percentage of returns (Ossola, 2020). It is for this reason that more and
more brands are introducing AR and VR to allow 3D modeling or virtual garment
try-on. Gucci has created a section in its app, Sneaker Garage, with Gucci Virtual 25,
the first virtual sneaker. It is also possible to create a personalized sneaker using all
the elements of the various models in the collection, share it with friends, and vote
for the favorite among those shared by users. Gucci has also teamed up with Snapchat to create an app that allows sneaker enthusiasts to virtually see a selection of
styles being worn before finalizing their purchases. In addition, some brands are
seeking to maintain a continuous and exciting relationship with their audience
through gaming, with Louis Vuitton and Prada among the pioneers.

3) Expand the points and opportunities for contact with the customer
Luxury companies try to offer multiple opportunities to communicate brand values,
both to their loyal customers and to a wider audience. With this aim, for example,
exhibitions have been organized such as Dior's *Designer of Dreams*, which traces
the history of the maison from 1947 to the present day and which has made stops in
Paris, London, and Shanghai. The Fondation Cartier pour l'art contemporain presented a program of exhibitions and live performances starting in 2020 at the Milan
Triennale. This collaboration was inaugurated with a presentation of the Fondation's collection curated by the Argentine artist Guillermo Kuitca, followed by the
exhibition *The Yanomami Struggle* by Claudia Andujar, a Brazilian artist who has
dedicated her life to photography and the defense of the human rights of the Yanomami people in Brazil. Similarly, the Fondation Louis Vuitton, a museum and cultural center inaugurated in 2006 and sponsored by the LVMH Group, serves to
promote art and culture through a non-profit foundation and, since 2014, a permanent art gallery in Paris.

In Milan, a similar initiative by Prada led to the founding of the Fondazione
Prada, a cultural institution dedicated to the realization of contemporary art, cinema, photography, and architecture projects, in 1993.

Other brands – from Armani and Bulgari to Versace and Audemars Piguet –
have sought opportunities for contact with their customers outside of shops or the
virtual world by entering the hospitality industry. This mode of growth responds to
the desire of the new generation to spend their money on memorable experiences
rather than physical goods.

How has Bulgari moved from jewels for celebrities to hotels? Early in 2000, the
company, which was founded in Rome in 1884, had the idea that hotels could enhance the brand's visibility around the world. However, this idea would need to be

sublimely executed for the brand to achieve its desired impact. To preserve prestige, Bulgari brought the concept of rarity into its hotel strategy: selecting only a few cities around the world and keeping the hotels small to allow for more personalization and support an intimate relationship with customers. The Italian craftsmanship that is essential to Bulgari's DNA as a jewelry maker carries over into its hotels, from design to services. Italian architect Antonio Citterio designed the furniture, taking the same approach as Bulgari does with jewelry: attention to detail, Italian style, timeless design, comfort, and beautiful materials. The residential style of the project underlined the brand's Roman origins and draws inspiration from the mosaics of the Roman Baths of Caracalla, which also inspired Bulgari's The Diva jewelry collection. The first hotel opened in Milan in 2001; as of 2020, Bulgari had added five more (London, Shanghai, Dubai, Bali, Beijing); another four will open by 2022 (Rome, Tokyo, Paris, Moscow).

When Bulgari opened its first hotel in Milan, it did not want to put the focus on its jewels or the history of the brand because it did not want to give visitors the impression that the hotel was a form of commercial promotion. In recent years, clients have loved seeing the connection between the brand, its heritage, and the hotels, and Bulgari's hospitality business is quite mature. Today, the brand has a much stronger presence, as does its archive, and pictures of products. The hotels can become iconic if positioned in the right locations; Bulgari wants them to be walking distance from its stores or high-end shopping areas. They cater to metropolitan and sophisticated travelers and collectors, as well as the local community, especially for food and beverages.

Bulgari's hospitality project has created an incredible number of synergies, with the hotels benefiting from their association with jewelry and fashion's glamour and visibility. Celebrating the Dolce Vita and their association with icons in the film and fashion world has been an incredible boost for both businesses. At the same time, all important brand events – during fashion weeks, for example, or for presentations of high jewelry collections – take place at Bulgari hotels, where the brand can host customers, celebrities, and other important people. The art of entertainment, already part of the brand identity, became the art of hospitality.

When it started its hospitality project, Bulgari was not part of LVMH – it was an independent company controlled by the family. It therefore partnered with Ritz Carlton, acquired by Marriott International, borrowing the hotel group's specialized knowledge in the luxury hospitality field. Choosing a single strong partner has a more meaningful impact, especially if both partners have a long history in their fields. Ritz Carlton's training and service models complemented Bulgari's expertise. A 50/50 joint venture was created between two family-owned businesses, leaders in their domains. Each had distinct responsibilities. Bulgari realized that it was not possible to curate everything alone, especially for the hotel restaurants, and explored additional collaborations. It partnered with Niko Romito, a three-star Michelin chef and specialist in Italian cuisine. He created a simple menu to be replicated around the world, including typical dishes like risotto and Milanese *cotoletta*. *This* is authenticity.

Initially, Bulgari's idea to expand into hospitality was criticized. It was thought that entering into a new business where it did not have a reputation or expertise could contaminate its prestige in jewelry. The journey has been successful because Bulgari has maintained control over operations and is fully involved and dedicated to the project; it has a marketing and communication department dedicated to hotels alone. Bulgari is now also exploring collaborations with Berluti, Technogym, Maserati, Gymnasium, and La Mer.

Collaborations are also a path hospitality is exploring to create new frontier services for clients. In 2020, Mandarin Oriental entered a partnership with Harrods to offer "Penthouse to Penthouse", a bespoke retail experience exclusive to guests of Mandarin Oriental Hyde Park in London who book a penthouse or a premier suite. This experience includes private tours of Harrods and of its safe-deposit department, the most historic area of the building, before and after opening hours; a personal shopping experience; and styling services provided by the store's private shopping team. Mandarin Oriental also offers other experiences to special clients such as wine- and spirit-sampling masterclasses, gifting services and gift wrapping, and food experiences with specialists that include Blending with a Tea Tailor, Coffee Roast Master Class, Chocolate and Pastry Tasting, and Art Lifestyle Advisory (Mandarin Oriental, 2020).

Paradox 7: How to be Consistent Globally and Relevant Locally?

This paradox offers a variation on exclusive-inclusive. Global expansion, after all, involves making something exclusive, universal. Brands that operate internationally need to be consistent in their identity but also relevant to local tastes, cultures, and preferences. The risk is that, in developing a unique approach that can be deployed globally, they may become irrelevant locally.

For long time, Burberry sold the same trench coats worldwide, until it realized that in Japan its clientele was predominantly female. Women are often petite, and in Japan, it rains in summer when the weather is hot. Burberry started to design light raincoats for Japanese ladies to wear in summer, which became best sellers throughout Asia. Burberry's gamble was successful, but the opposite risk, if a brand adapts too much to local tastes, is a loss of global consistency. So, how can a luxury brand become global? How can it adapt positively to local contexts while keeping its universal appeal?

The country-of-origin effect contributes greatly to this issue because it represents a core element of the brand identity and affects perceptions and purchasing decisions overseas. Luxury is traditionally linked to well-identified geographies associated with specific skills and reference industries. Without going into the technical definition of the country of origin (COO) that is presented in Chapter 4, France and Italy are undisputed leaders in the production of luxury goods because a high value is attributed to French and Italian savoir-faire. Attributes typically associated with Made-in-Italy products are excellent design, high quality, uniqueness, authenticity, and status (Statista, 2019). International brands relocate their production to Italy because the country is known for its production abilities. It is no coincidence that the best-known brands in women's shoes (from Louboutin to Manolo Blahnik, Jimmy Choo, Dior, and many others) are made in Italy.

In the past, brands from countries with established luxury industries leveraged this undisputed advantage to enter new geographic markets by replicating the business model used in their home countries. The basic idea was that in order to respect the brand identity, no changes could be made in the offer, in communication, or in marketing. This thinking has been strongly disavowed in recent years for at least two reasons:

(1) Several cases of bankruptcy and subsequent exit from the foreign market involving international brands have revealed the risks of clashing with the cultural, economic, and administrative specificities of the local context. Among these cases, we can mention La Perla (Atwal and Bryson, 2017), a well-known brand of women's underwear, which entered India in 2007 by opening a shop in the Oberoi Galley in Mumbai with the Murjani Group, a franchise that was also in partnership with Gucci and Jimmy Choo. In 2012, the company decided to exit the Indian market: the super-premium segment represented 1% of the market and the liberalization of the brand's conservative Indian partner had been overestimated. La Perla returned to Delhi in 2015 with a new partner (DLF Emporio) and an Indian CEO who defined an expansion strategy based on e-commerce and men's underwear. A similar case is that of Bulgari, which closed its stores in India in 2011 due to the competitive situation (high fragmentation of the industry, with customer loyalty to small trusted jewelers) and local tastes. It returned three years later, opening a shop with Luxco India Retail at the DFL Emporio in New Delhi with 20% local, traditional products and personal and discreet service in private rooms. In other cases, it was not so much the competitive strategy toward the market that was poorly formulated, as the way of entry. This was the case of Maserati, which exited the Indian market in 2013 after two years with ten cars sold and numerous complaints about the negligent behavior of the local partner in after-sales service. Maserati returned in 2016 with three new showrooms.

(2) The main market for luxury personal goods is China, which in 2019 was worth about 35% of the world value of sales and, according to estimates by Bain and Company reported by D'Arpizio and Levato (2020), should reach 47% to 49% on a total value of €330 billion by 2025. In the past, 55% of these purchases were made outside of China; at least 50% of this 55% will unfortunately be repatriated as an autonomous internal market develops (Boston Consulting Group and

Altagamma, 2020). It is impossible to predict whether this phenomenon will become structural or will only concern the next two to three years. This new trend will particularly damage the sales of brands dependent on tourists. Jean-Marc Pontroué, Panerai's CEO, describes what this means for his company:

> We see significant growth in China as it was in the past, but there is an issue that is different: the Chinese are staying in China. Chinese people used to travel a lot and spend 2/3 of what they were spending on Panerai when travelling abroad. Limitations in travelling diminish tourism also in Hong Kong from mainland China and we do not see positive estimates. Panerai has six boutiques in Hong Kong and four in Macau; 82 boutique stores in Asia Pacific (out of 139 globally). Our new stores will open in China.
>
> (personal communication)

Corporate strategies should therefore not aim to attract Asian tourists to the Montenapoleone stores in Milan or rue Saint-Honoré in Paris, but must think how to develop an ad hoc strategy for Asian markets increasingly characterized by "local pride" and interesting start-ups in the world of luxury. Considering the cosmetic world, there are Chinese brands like Perfect Diary which are far preferred over foreign ones by local consumers.

The aforementioned reasons have now made it mandatory for all luxury brands that have international expansion ambitions to adopt localization strategies; that is, adaptation to local specificities that represent barriers to entry (Vishwanath and Rigby, 2006). If the business model of the company is too far removed from the local environment, making the adaptation effort too massive and inconsistent with the brand DNA, it is better to exclude that country from the portfolio in the market selection process. This decision is known in the international business literature as "the paradox of being consistent" (Alcácer, 2015).

Localization could cause companies to set up new formulas specifically invented for new host environments that valorize local endowments of tangible and intangible assets.[6] This is what Moët Hennessy did in China and India. In 2014, Chandon India became the first sparkling wine produced in the country, in the Nashik region, with the finest local grapes according to a centuries-old standard. It is now available across 22 cities in India in three variants (Brut, Rosé, and Délice). Chandon China was founded in 2013 in the heart of the Ningxia Hui Autonomous Region, one of the country's largest winegrowing areas and ideal for chardonnay and pinot noir, two varieties that are essential for creating sparkling wines using the traditional method. The same approach has been followed by Louis Vuitton, which launched its Suhali range of bags (Le Fabuleux Noir Black and Le Talentueux White) in 2003, all of them made in India with natural-grained goatskins from the local tradition.

Localization strategy can involve different dimensions, including:
- *Locations.* For example, Cartier boutiques around the world feature materials, decorative elements, and colors typical of each area. Bulgari hotels have similar

designs, but different looks and feels. The hotel in London in Knightsbridge, which opened in 2012, has a façade similar to that of the Milan hotel. However, the bedrooms in London emphasize silver, connecting silver use in Bulgari's jewelry with the silversmith tradition in the UK. The silver pattern of the hotel's headboards dates to the late nineteenth century. Silver coupled with mahogany recalls a Riva yacht – the classic Italian speedboat – and the period of "La Dolce Vita". This is quite different from the hotel in Milan, which uses oak and dark colors. Only the lobbies are the same, with the same furniture, colors, accessories and pictures of Italian models and actors.

– *Services*. For example, Bulgari's private rooms in its jewelry shops in India or concierge and consignment services in the Middle East.
– *Merchandise*. For example, Gucci dedicated a 2020 collection to Micky Mouse to celebrate the year of the mouse according to the Chinese calendar. Also, in 2020, Dior launched is first capsule exclusively for the online shopping event Singles' Day in China. All major brands have launched fragrances with oud, an oil derived from a resin produced by trees belonging of the Aquilaria genus of the Thymelaeceae family, which has a distinctive scent and is one of the most expensive natural resources in the world, exclusively for Arabian customers, both men and women. Luxottica invented the "Asian fit", Oakley or Ray-Ban sunglasses (like the Wayfarer) that feature the classic style but have been modified to fit higher cheekbones and wider nose bridges.
– *Communication* using influencers, product names, and messages adapted to the local culture.
– *Marketing* that considers, for example, the importance of digital channels.

All these actions are not painless for companies and incur the so called "Liability of Foreignness" (Hymer, 1960; Hymer, 1976; Mezias, 2002; Zaheer, 1995), i.e., the disadvantages of foreign players when entering a new context (see also Chapter 5). Problems arise from the unfamiliarity companies have with local culture and administrative procedures; the necessity to establish valuable relations with clients and suppliers and, internally, with employees; and the impossibility of taking advantage of benefits available for local companies. Foreign brands therefore require time to acquire adequate knowledge of local markets. They also need to launch ad hoc actions which, at least in the first stage, significantly increase the costs of expansion into the market, thus reducing profitability. Sacrifices must be made if a long-term vision is adopted in which international growth is a priority on the strategic agenda.

Respecting local cultures and doing the proper fine-tuning can equally be a source of economic satisfaction. This is the case of Tiffany & Co., which followed a successful strategy in Japan, a market that represents 17% of stores and 15% of total sales, the American brand's most profitable market. Earnings from operations in Japan as a percentage of net sales was 35% in 2019, while in the Americas it was 20% and in Europe 17%.

Takeaways
- The luxury business is facing some important strategic challenges: increasing size and improving profitability; managing a commercial offer in which timeless and new products coexist; the compresence of exclusivity and inclusivity; the compromise between marketing pressures and rarity; the integration of online and offline channels and communication; the difficulty of exceeding expectations when standards are already very high; the necessity of being globally consistent and locally relevant at the same time.
- Successful luxury companies do not privilege one side of a paradox; they manage to crack the paradox. This has led to creative solutions that are transforming luxury brands.
- An emphasis on contact with the customer outside of stores, driven by experiences in the virtual world, has prompted some brands to invest into non-industry-related activities. This includes entering the hospitality industry as well as exploring new technologies for augmenting customers' experience. New strategies respond to the desire of younger generations to spend their money on memorable experiences rather than physical goods.
- Still, challenges remain. All luxury brands with international expansion ambitions must adopt localization strategies, i.e., adaptation to local specificities, which often represent strong barriers to entry into new markets.

Notes

1 See the explanation of ambidexterity in Chapter 1.

2 In this book, we assume that a company's core business is the main source of corporate profitability. Core business is based on a company's unique capabilities and is represented by a set of products and services identifying the company in the marketplace.

3 See https://www.ferrari.com/en-PS/auto/monza-sp1.

4 General trunk shows are a re-show of the catwalk pieces, which are kind of like "master garments". The ordering process of the materials may already be in progress and orders might have already been forecasted, but usually not yet manufactured. Usually, for wedding dresses, they have the pieces of the collection and they set up trunk shows around the world. People try on the "sample" before deciding to put down a deposit and have the items made. These sales events were traditionally called trunk shows, as the sales person would travel with a trunk of clothing samples.

5 In 2017, L Capital Asia, LVMH's investment arm, decided to invest into Gentle Monster, allowing the brand to further grow internationally and increase its notoriety.

6 For levers and sub-levers of adaptation, see Ghemawat (2007).

3 Old Worlds and New Worlds

This book focuses on luxury from a European perspective – in Chapter 4, we will look at country of origin and how European countries, predominantly Italy, Switzerland, and France, retain their expertise and credibility in the manufacture of luxury goods. Still, as the following pages will show, the ways that different regions interact with today's Euro-centric luxury business depend on their own histories of luxury. The term luxury comes from the Latin "luxus" and indicates an overabundance or excess, something unnecessary in everyday life. As we shall see in this chapter, the idea of luxury has evolved over time, going through different stages and adapting to changing cultural norms in all of today's major luxury markets: Europe, the United States, Japan, and China.

Europe: The Epicenter of Luxury

Luxury at the Time of the Greeks and Romans

The origin of luxury in Western civilization can be traced back to the time of the ancient Greeks, in particular the expansion of the Macedonian empire under the leadership of Alexander the Great. However, luxury was not valued in the early city states of classical Greece. The city of Sparta is a clear example: Citizens of Sparta led a frugal life (we still use the adjective "spartan" to describe to describe an environment free of luxury or even comfort), priding themselves on their military discipline and prowess. According to philosophers and scholars, the idea of luxury was born not in Greece but in the East, where the Persian Empire was rich in luxury and pomp long before the Greek city states. The contrast between the two civilizations, frequently at war with one another, became part of narratives that are still with us today. The difference between the austere simplicity of the Spartans and the opulence of Persian army when they met at the Battle of Thermopylae is as crucial to the message of Zack Snyder's 2006 film *300* as it was to Greeks who first told tales of Leonidas's last stand.

While Alexander's victories in Persia and the expansion of Greek civilization after his death integrated luxury into the culture of the Greek city states, values of austerity and simplicity remained important. Luxury was viewed negatively by the philosophers of the time, from Plato to Aristotle, who condemned glitz and luxury as private ostentation, but at the same time accepted its use, for example, in public works. This tension regarding the use and value of luxury continued in the Roman Empire. Although luxury was widespread in ancient Rome and especially among Roman matrons – women who possessed Roman citizenship and were married to men from noble families or otherwise high ranking in the society – philosophers

https://doi.org/10.1515/9783110723519-003

and writers condemned its nature, which was in stark contrast to Roman values of frugality and simplicity. The jewels, shows, banquets, and ceremonies that enlivened life for wealthy Romans were seen by many as signs of decadence and weakness, so much so that some Roman emperors such as Marcus Aurelius, tried to block the spread of these excesses within the aristocracy, but in vain. Early Christianity, which drew on the disdain for the pomp of the Egyptian Pharaohs that was widespread in Jewish thought at the time, placing value instead on the frugal lifestyle of the people of Israel, picked up this distrust of luxury as it spread throughout the Roman Empire.

Luxury in the Middle Ages and Early Modern Age

The concept of luxury as it developed in antiquity began to evolve during the late Middle Ages and the early modern age, as European cities grew. Ostentatious clothes and accessories helped to define a person's social class, and as people beyond the aristocracy acquired the means to purchase luxurious materials for themselves, new sumptuary laws sought to regulate how that wealth could be displayed. In this period, those condemning luxury did so not because it went against their moral values, but because its democratization represented a weakening of the class boundaries on which medieval society depended. In other words, the regulation of luxury became a way to control and manage power.

Indeed, European sumptuary laws, which controlled who was allowed to wear certain materials, helped to create fashion in the thirteenth century. Regulations dictating the proportions of clothes for different social classes (e.g., the width of sleeves, the length of a dress train, or even the size of buttons) created standards that needed to be followed – and invited clever subversions, with new styles being invented to get around the rules. In addition, the first workshops of artisans, tailors, and shoemakers began to appear.

Luxury thus became not only a way to show social class and power, but a source of income for the cities that created laws to regulate it. Failure to comply with the regulations resulted in an economic sanction that ended up in the city coffers. Even the artisans could be sanctioned, if they were found guilty of having produced garments not in line with the parameters of the social class to which their client belonged. While most laws regulated the dress of women, fines were directed against their husbands and families. This was not just because men were the primary property owners of the time. Wealth was held by families, and the dress of the women in those families – the styles, fabrics, and accessories they wore – was one way that these families broadcast that wealth. As a family gained financial power, sumptuary laws regulated how that power could be publicly presented. This helped preserve the social order (by making clear who had *social* power, i.e., a high official rank or aristocratic status) and attempted to prevent excessive spending on clothing (depleting finances to gain an appearance of wealth in a gamble that this would lead to social success). However, since the very existence of the laws was effectively proof that dress mattered, there were many incentives to dress as sumptuously as one could – and thus also frequent fines to be collected.

The use of luxury to concentrate and display power may have arisen in the Italian courts of the Renaissance, but it reached its fullest expression at Versailles, in the court of Louis XIV in the seventeenth century. The French king wanted to weaken the aristocracy in pursuit of an absolutist policy that would centralize power. The incredible pomp displayed by the sovereign at court increased over the course of his reign, becoming more and more difficult for aristocrats to emulate due to the very high costs of emulating the sovereign, thus increasing the distance between the King and even the wealthiest of his subjects. Meanwhile, the court's need for luxury products and materials contributed to the rise of the urban bourgeoisie, the class of merchants and artisans that supplied these products, and that was gradually integrated into the social circles of the aristocracy as its wealth increased, creating a new social class.

Luxury in the Eighteenth Century

The eighteenth century was an interesting turning point for the European luxury world. Sumptuary laws were gradually abolished in the seventeenth century, as they were not very effective, and the eighteenth century saw cultural upheaval regarding the concept of luxury. Luxury became an integral aspect of European cities, which were being transformed by the Industrial Revolution. While traditionalists maintained that luxury was best confined to certain social classes, the idea that the strength of a country could be measured by the spread of luxury and well-being among its subjects began to gather strength in Europe's increasingly prosperous, and populous, cities.

Where public opulence had been a way for previous generations to solidify social hierarchy, luxury in the eighteenth century became a form of private expression for individuals eager to enjoy their new-found affluence. This is a fundamental step in the historical evolution of luxury, because the negative connotations ascribed to luxury in early eras by moral authorities like the Catholic Church began to give way to a secular school of thought that saw it as adding value to society. No longer a danger to the lower social classes, luxury could be an effective tool for creating jobs and a useful stimulus for industry and commerce. Coupled with emerging ideas of social progress, luxury became something *good*.

The eighteenth century was a period of great ferment and cultural debate on the theme of luxury. It was a rhetorical theme of the French Revolution, and a subject of concern for monarchies in England and Holland. It was the focus of commercial and cultural exchanges throughout Europe and along trade routes that included

European colonies in the Americas and elsewhere, as well as a defining feature of the new urban society born of the Industrial Revolution. Constant comparisons between sophisticated Paris and provincial Geneva even recalled comparisons between urban, educated Athens and rural, disciplined Sparta in antiquity. This is when the modern concept of luxury emerged, and the point where the world of luxury as we know it began to take shape.

Luxury between the Nineteenth and Twentieth Centuries

Between the nineteenth and twentieth centuries the discussions on the topic of luxury gradually disappeared from European intellectual discourse. The Industrial Revolution and the birth of the concept of capitalism shaped the modern conception of luxury. Although it remained "superfluous" – having to do with wants rather than needs – luxury began to be conceived of as "necessary" for the capitalist economic system. The regulations and restrictions of previous centuries were simply replaced by taxes on luxury goods, an important source of income for the state. The more affluent classes used their purchasing power to dictate the tones and tastes of society, while the ambitious middle classes began to cultivate the desire for consumerism and luxury in a modern key as signs of aspiration.

Throughout the nineteenth century, luxury became more and more a means of personal expression. Expensive taste, exhibited in public, was a way to show off one's spending power and announced a break with the less well-off social classes in a society with increasing social mobility. As luxury became more widespread, the production of luxury objects also shifted. If in the nineteenth century luxury was still linked to the workshops of artisans, the twentieth century saw the birth of today's best-known luxury brands. From Chanel to Dior, Prada to Valentino, the emergence of luxury brands – as opposed to materials, styles, or products linked to individual craftspeople – marks the turning point of the modern consumerist era. Mass production and the expansion of markets meant that luxury became an integral part of modern society, with mechanisms that continue to evolve.

European luxury brands – yacht makers, furniture, fine wines, jewelry, and apparel, among others – remain top of mind for contemporary luxury consumers. While many brands such as Cartier, Dom Perignon, and Louis Vuitton have years of heritage behind them, younger European brands have built on this heritage and craftmanship to leap forwards in the world of luxury. Other countries and regions play key roles in today's luxury market, yet Europe is still the leader, with the largest luxury market and the majority of the world's top luxury brands.

The United States: Luxury Consumption's Big Bang

The United States has been the leader in global luxury consumption since 1996; in 2019, the value of personal luxury goods in the United States was worth somewhere around €75 billion. The same year, Bain and Company predicted that this value would continue to climb, as the country was experiencing exponential wealth growth coming from new industries such as tech, new media (social media and creative media), and direct-to-consumer brands: there were 407 IPO filings in the US in 2020, the highest in 20 years. In addition, the United States is home to the world's largest volume of ultra-high net worth individuals (UHNWI); according to Statista, there are around 80,500 people with net assets exceeding US$50 million in the country. This is over four times the number of UHNWIs in Mainland China (excluding Hong Kong and Taiwan), which has a population of 1.44 billion compared to 332.3 million for the US, as of 2020 (Worldometer, n.d.).

The size of its market makes the United States a very important country for many luxury companies. This is especially true for luxury cars, yachts, and private jets. In 2019, Lamborghini delivered close to 2,400 vehicles to the United States alone, over three times what it delivered to Greater China and the United Kingdom, which were their second and third largest markets, respectively. Similarly, Ferrari delivers somewhere between 2,800 and 3,000 cars to the Americas annually, with the United States accounting for the majority of final orders. The United States is not only an important country for luxury brands in terms of luxury consumers, but also in terms of financial investors. Since the US possesses a third of the world's wealth, as well as being the No.1 country in terms of foreign direct investments, it is an attractive source of funding for many companies, especially luxury companies that seek further opportunities to grow. The United States is without a doubt the most important market for luxury brands, and this trend will continue to rise in the coming future, as new wealth is created every day.

The New World

As compared to Europe, China, or Japan, the United States is considered part of the "New World", lands that only came into regular contact with the "Old World" civilizations of Europe, Asia, and Africa following the Renaissance expansion of the European empires. While this book will not delve into the complicated history of European colonization, acknowledging the links between this process and the emergence of our modern idea of luxury can help us understand links between Old and New worlds that are important for luxury industries today.

For the Europeans of the fifteenth, sixteenth, seventeenth, and eighteenth centuries, the New World offered unprecedented opportunities for new trade routes, enterprises, and unchartered land mass. Between Christopher Columbus's arrival in the Bahamas in 1492 and the beginning of the Seven Years' War between France and England in 1754, Spain, The Netherlands, France, and England all tried to colonize parts of the United States. Today, the remnants of this early European influence can still be seen in various regions, from Creole French influence in along the Mississippi River to British customs in New England and the East, the legacy of the Dutch in New York and still vibrant Spanish culture in Texas, California, and throughout the Southwest (Alchin, 2017).

The First Signs of Wealth

Between the mid-1700s and late-1800s, the United States underwent a massive transformation. The American Revolution laid the foundations of democratic government and kickstarted Western expansion. Conflicts with Indigenous peoples escalated as settlement pushed beyond the Mississippi River. Successive waves of immigration altered the demographics of the former British colonies, as well as those of the former Spanish and French colonial territories that the US acquired through war (Spanish) and purchase (French). The Civil War tore the country apart – and emancipated 2.9 million enslaved Black Americans. All the while, the Industrial Revolution brought manufacturing, rail lines, and other important advances to the United States, connecting what had previously been isolated colonial outposts. Just as the general population in Great Britain saw an elevation in wealth during its industrial revolution in the eighteenth century, the United States experienced a similar period of rapid economic growth in the late nineteenth century, a period the American writer Mark Twain called the Gilded Age. The construction of the railroad connected different regions, facilitating trade, and the average annual salary was said to have increased by 48%. The possibility of earning significantly higher wages than they would at home led to an influx of skilled migrant workers from Europe who would further transform American society in the coming decades.

Despite the increase in overall social welfare during this period, much of the wealth in the United States was concentrated in a handful of families, such as the Rockefellers, the Vanderbilts, and the Du Ponts. Their lavish lifestyles did not become part of the American lifestyle until after the First World War, when the "Roaring Twenties" brought a version of the luxuries of the Gilded Age to the masses.

Lavishness After Periods of Depression

History presents an interesting cycle: When we look at the growth of luxury and lavish indulgence in the modern era, much of it is driven by a period of temporary subjugation or depression. The spread of luxury depicted in Figure 3.1 shows the consistent growth of a country's economy at the inception of new era – the Industrial Revolution, for example. The United States, more so than any other country in the world, has gone through bursts of industrialization that injected new wealth into the society. The first of these occurred in the 1920s with the implementation of mass production, and later again in the 1950s after the Second World War.

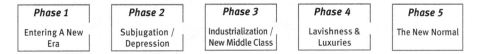

Figure 3.1: The Phases of Social Development and Adoption of Luxury over Time.
Source: Compiled by authors.

While the United States was not significantly involved in the First World War, it still experienced some of its upheavals, as the country was unprepared for the disruptions the war caused to global systems. Like Japan, which also remained peripheral to much of the conflict, the United States rationed food and materials to become more efficient and introduced women into the labor force. When the war finally ended in 1918, the United States was faced with crippling debt and high unemployment rates for returning veterans. However, as Europe recovered in the 1920s, the US also prospered, with the "Roaring Twenties" bringing prosperity to the middle class.

The 1920s was an exciting time in the United States, as many businesses that started before the First World War benefitted both from wartime increases in efficiency and the introduction of women to the labor force. Henry Ford's assembly line allowed automobiles to be manufactured economically, making them affordable for middle-class households. In California, the production of American war propaganda paved the way for the Golden Age of Hollywood as post-war audiences flocked to cinemas. When the stock market crashed in 1929, movies became an important form of escape for ordinary Americans, an oasis in the Great Depression.

In the 1950s, Hollywood studios, reeling from the cumulative effects of the Depression and the aftermath of the Second World War, began to look for alternative filming locations. Production moved offshore, to exotic locales such as Italy and France. While Hollywood was no longer the film-world epicenter it had been in the 1920s and 1930s, the opulent lifestyles of the movie stars and other celebrities who still called it home meant that it remained a beacon of luxury. These stars became conduits for the European luxury brands that were starting to make inroads in the American market. Bulgari, a Roman jewelry brand famous for its colored gems, gained popularity in the United States in the 1950s with the help of Elizabeth Taylor, who had encountered the brand when she was filming in Rome. When she set her eyes on the beautifully colored gems and Italian craftsmanship, it was love at first sight. As her then-husband Richard Burton noted, "I introduced Liz to beer, and she introduced me to Bulgari" (Fasel, 2018).

Luxury brands flourished in the United States in the 1950s, both thanks to wider exposure to Europe and to rampant economic growth. American sweetheart Grace Kelly married Prince Rainier III of Monaco in 1956, capturing the imagination of a country eager to prove its sophistication. Many wealthy Americans were looking to stylish icons and celebrities like Kelly as models who would show them how to solidify their social status. They were also beginning to travel overseas, commissioning custom dresses from famous designers – specifically haute couture from houses such as Christian Dior, Chanel, and Valentino.

The New Luxury

While for the American elite, this surge of interest in European luxury goods was merely an extension of their already extravagant lifestyles, the social paradigm separating them from the new upper middle class was shifting. European brands that were struggling in their home markets reached out to American businessmen as financial backers for their emerging young designers. One of these rising stars was Yves Saint Laurent, who left Christian Dior to start his namesake brand. Saint Laurent and his brand, with its focus on fashion and ready-to-wear rather than laborious and highly crafted haute couture, were pivotal in the democratization of luxury. His clothes were designed for everyday life and were made for comfort at a more affordable price (Cabigiosu, 2020). By the late 1960s, these European imports would be joined by rising American-owned brands such as Ralph Lauren (1967) and Calvin Klein (1968).

The "New Luxury", which in this book we will consider as premium goods, became the identity for most American brands. From the late 1960s to the early 2000s, American brands – Coach, Michael Kors, Tommy Hilfiger, Guess, and Stuart Weismann, among others – catered to the masses. Even Tiffany & Co., which was established in 1837 as a stationary and fancy-goods emporium, is known for affordable luxury. Although many iconic stones that have passed through Tiffany's ownership – including the Tiffany Diamond, a perfect yellow diamond acquired in 1879 – the "palace of jewels" has been, throughout its history, best known for its silver collection and affordable diamond engagement ring. It wasn't until the late 1990s and early 2000s that Tiffany & Co. restructured its branding to elevate itself as a luxury brand ("History of Tiffany & Co"., n.d.).

The United States' Insatiable Appetite for Luxury

The United States, throughout its history, has pinballed between extreme highs and extreme lows. Yet despite its periods of depression, the US is one of the most resilient luxury consumer markets in the world. Unlike Japan, which has struggled to find its way back as a major power both politically and economically since suffering a great financial downturn in the 1990s, the United States has consistently showed a v-curve recovery shortly after a crisis. Today, the United States remains the world's largest luxury market, both for personal goods and overall (Statista, 2021a).

This insatiable appetite for luxury is driven by the cultural influence of aspirational lifestyles like those of celebrities and influencers. The Kardashian-Jenner family, who have accumulated a massive amount of wealth by broadcasting their lavish lifestyle, has become a pinnacle of the American dream of the early twenty-first century. Just as high-society women in the 1950s looked to icons such as Elizabeth Taylor, Jackie Kennedy, and Princess Grace of Monaco as beacons of style, today's moneyed classes look to the Kardashian-Jenners as a reference point for how newfound wealth can be enjoyed. According to a 2020 report by Credit Suisse (Shorrocks, Davis, Lluberas, 2020), the average wealth of Americans in the United States rose from approximately US$220,000 to US$470,000 between 2000 and 2019.

Despite the economic downturn brought on by the Covid-19 pandemic, the United States is still the single largest market for luxury goods. LVMH's 2020 first quarter financial reports show the United States contributing 24% of their overall revenue, coming second to the entire continent of Asia (excluding Japan), which is responsible for 34%. While forecasters predict that China will overtake the United States, this has yet to be realized, and for now, financial reporting methodologies make it difficult to compare the consumption volumes of the United States and Greater China. Regardless, an insatiable appetite for luxury goods will continue to drive US consumption volumes for the foreseeable future, and the United States is more than likely to return to normalcy in one to two years.

Japan: Democratization of Luxury and the Maturing Consumer

Up until 2016, Japan was the world's largest individual consumer market of luxury goods. Even after the financial crisis in 2011, Japan bounced back to briefly retake its position as the world's second largest market for luxury goods, right behind the United States, before being overtaken by China. Yet the downturn was significant; a 2017 Luxury Report by McKinsey and Company reported that Japan faced a downturn in the market between 2007 to 2012 at a rate of −6% per annum. Following the Tōhoku earthquake and the subsequent Fukushima catastrophe, the Japanese luxury market shrank by over 1 trillion yen. Before diving into Japan's recovery, it is important to understand what fueled the exponential growth of the country's luxury appetite and how Japan changed the world of luxury.

Luxury Entering Japan

The Meiji Restoration, also known as the Meiji Reform, played a key role in Japan's emergence as the industrial capital of Asia in the early twentieth century. When the Japanese Emperor Meiji restored practical imperial rule to the country in 1868, after over two hundred years of feudal military rule during the Edo period, he sought to modernize the country, opening its borders, encouraging industrialization, and introducing Western ideals. However, it wasn't until the late 1950s, as Japan rebuilt after the Second World War, undergoing a second industrial revolution, that the "Japan Postwar Miracle" radically increased personal wealth in the country. During the post-war recovery period from 1945 to 1956, Japan's per capita GDP grew at an average annual rate of 7.1%. According to Carl Mosk (n.d.), Japan's exponential growth was mainly due to its heavy investment in industry and infrastructure, with a focus on achieving more output per unit of input and prioritizing speed. Japan became the factory of the world, dominating through economies of scale. At the same time, the Japanese government was adamant on improving the social welfare of its people, investing heavily in education and social capabilities and internalizing labor markets. This led to a larger workforce and subsequently higher incomes per household.

The first luxury brands entered Japan in the early 1900s, with French brand Louis Vuitton being one of the first to set up a retail store in Tokyo, in 1918 (LVHM, 2020). However, when the Second World War hit, many luxury brands retreated from the Japanese market, going into "hibernation" and suspending all business in the country until conditions were right for them to return. The sharp rise in Japan's GDP from the mid-1950s to late-1960s allowed it to catch up to booming economies in Britain and the United States, and there was pent up desire for foreign goods and luxury brands. At the time, "Made in Japan" was associated with fast, cheap, and low-quality goods, which led the majority of Japanese to believe foreign-made products were superior in both quality and durability. This belief slowly turned into conviction, and the idea of owning a foreign-made luxury good became a symbol of economic success and social acceptance among the Japanese (Atsmon, Salsberg, and Yamanashi 2009).

The Democratization of Luxury

Post-war westernization brought increased opportunities for foreign trade. The Japanese embraced this new lifestyle as a symbol of democracy and an expression of their desire to catch up with richer economies in the West. Throughout the country, people abandoned traditional kimonos for t-shirts, jeans, and other forms of Western dress, and their first introduction to this new style and behavior was through their local department stores. These became destinations for discovery – in 1956, the Tokyo department stores Takashimaya and Mitsukoshi organized an Italian and a Parisian Fair, respectively – and they played a critical role in exposing the Japanese to Western culture. In turn, Japan's newfound love for Western goods pushed its department stores to constantly transform and upgrade their offers in order to keep up with demand. As early as 1952, Takashimaya dedicated a floor in its Osaka location – "Salon le Chic" – to European luxury accessories.

The increase of both household disposable income and exposure to imported goods in the post-war era started a chain reaction that led to Japan to embrace conspicuous consumption. Yet while the Japanese luxury market was lucrative, a lack of exposure hindered the entrance of many foreign brands – Chanel and Cartier did not enter Japan independently until the early 1990s. In order to meet the growing demand for luxury goods, entrepreneurial Japanese began to purchase products in bulk in Europe, reselling them in Japan for triple the price and creating a parallel market. At the height of Japan's post-war luxury boom, many businesses emerged to cater to the demand for luxury in creative ways. European luxury tours would take Japanese tourists to famous shopping streets such as the Champs-Élysées in Paris, Montenapoleone in Milan, and Bond Street in London to purchase goods they could not find at home. The surge of Japanese tourists visiting European luxury stores and fear of a parallel market over which it had no control prompted Louis Vuitton to initiate a research project on Japanese luxury consumption in the late 1950s. Soon, other luxury brands followed suit, investing heavily in establishing their footprints in Japan. By the late 1970s, some of the world's most renowned luxury brands had established themselves in Japan, and by the early 1990s the Tokyo neighborhood of Ginza had a luxury strip to rival those that had drawn Japanese consumers to Europe in previous decades.

The Japanese Become Luxury Connoisseurs

The "stages of luxe evolution" introduced by Chadha and Husband (2006) show the maturity of a nation with respect to behavior toward luxury spending. In Japan's rise and fall from the 1900s to the mid-1970s, we can see a shift in luxury consumerism from Stage 1: Subjugation (poverty and deprivation) and Stage 2: Start of Money (burst of economic growth and start of luxury consumption), to Stage 3: Show Off (display of economic status). Between the late 1990s and early 2000s, Japanese luxury consumers moved from Stage 4: Fit In (large-scale adoption of luxury) to Stage 5: Way of Life (confident, discerning consumers). As luxury brands have spread throughout Japan, Japanese consumers have matured in their relationship to the world of luxury. At this stage, they have developed strong relationships, trust, and loyalty with brands, as well as a deeper understanding of their own style and confidence in their luxury purchases. Luxury is no longer a status symbol or a means to stand out, rather it has become part of their lifestyle. They are discerning toward what they wear, where they eat, what they drive, and where they holiday. The Japanese do not buy into luxury for its brand equity, but they seek to understand each and every detail that goes into the product. So much so, that Ferrari considers the Japanese market as one of the most difficult to please.

Japan as an Independent Market

When luxury brands such as Tiffany & Co. and Hermès entered the Japanese market in the 1970s, they had little experience with the needs and preferences of the country's luxury consumers. To expand their knowledge, many brands relied on department stores. By using externalities such as licensing, franchising, and wholesale models as a lever, department stores including Mitsukoshi, Takashimaya, Sogo, and Seibu were able to share their clientele lists with brands, while also spreading their footprint to various cities across Japan. This allowed luxury brands to disseminate, conquering the Japanese market without investing too much on analyzing its customer base.

The democratization of luxury through affordable, branded goods such as accessories has been key to the success of the Japanese market. Luxury brands such as Yves Saint Laurent, Gucci, and even Chanel have at various points agreed to launch locally made collections under brand licenses for the Japanese market at a much lower price compared to those in their home countries.

By the late 1980s, luxury brands were top of mind for Japanese consumers. Department stores shifted from franchisees to distributors and retailers as brands became less dependent on them for access to customers. This liberation of the market made it easier for brands to branch out on their own, but this was no easy feat. Foreign companies were not allowed to open bank accounts in Japan, nor obtain official documentation to establish independent entities. This meant that luxury brands were a liability and posed huge risks for Japanese landlords. Their previous arrangements with department stores had shielded brands from these barriers, but as they attempted to enter the market independently they encountered hurdle after hurdle. Many brands had to depend on trading companies and wholesalers to open Japanese boutiques and to facilitate transactions between the brand headquarters and Japanese consumers. For this reason, even after foreign luxury brands became well-established in Japan, department stores continued to play an important role, becoming partners in expanding enterprises.

The relationship between brands and department stores began to flourish, with each side negotiating to ensure its needs were met. Relationships with local department stores gave brands more autonomy over the offer and its distribution; as essential middle men in a complex regulatory environment, department stores were able to secure exclusivity. As Takashimaya, Isetan, and Daimaru looked to expand their footprints internationally, entering emerging markets such as Singapore,

Malaysia, Australia, and Taiwan, they brought with them international luxury brands, developing the luxury shopping malls that are part of the luxury culture in South East Asia today.

The appetite for luxury goods in Japan leading up to the crash of the stock market in 1990 saw an exponential rise in luxury consumption, so much so that the market had to be managed as a single entity. Indeed, from the 1980s to the financial crisis of the early 1990s, Japan was one of the largest single luxury markets in the world after the United States. Today, many luxury houses still isolate Japan as a single market in their financial reports. Despite being a relatively small country, it is responsible for approximately 10% of global luxury consumption. In 2020, Japan reported a contribution of 8% of Richemont's total revenue generation, 7% of LVMH's total revenue, and 7% of Kering's total revenues.

China: The Re-emergence of the Sleeping Dragon

China's appetite for luxury has been a key topic since the 2010s. In 2018, China was responsible for one third of total global luxury consumption, a proportion of researchers have predicted that this will continue to grow at a CAGR of 3% to 6%, with the potential to contribute to over half of the world's luxury consumption by 2025. While the Covid-19 pandemic, which saw one of China's largest manufacturing hubs, Wuhan, placed in complete lockdown in January 2020, has cast doubt on this forecast, China has been quick to bounce back. As the government started to ease restrictions across China in May 2020, more and more consumers found themselves lined up outside luxury stores, namely Chanel, Louis Vuitton, and Hermès, waiting to perform what journalists have called "revenge shopping". Whether or not this surge in consumption was a psychological side effect of the lockdown, it was a saving grace for luxury companies, with China fueling their recovery throughout 2020. Despite the shift in consumer behavior brought on by the pandemic, it seems that China's appetite for luxury is not slowing down.

Yet it would be wrong to assume that Chinese luxury consumerism is a new phenomenon, arising only in the last two decades. Chinese luxury spending was merely put on hold during the decades leading up to the country's Social Reform. Delving into China's history can help us understand its relationship with luxury.

The Forgotten History of Chinese Luxury

China has had a long history of opulence and luxury, which we can trace as far back as its first dynasty (2070–1600 BCE). Geographically isolated, the Chinese, like their counterparts in Greece, developed a sophisticated society. At the same time when Greek philosophers such as Aristotle, Plato, and Socrates were developing their ideas, in China, philosophers and strategists such Lao-Tzu, Confucius, and Sun-Tzu were laying the foundations of their own schools of thought. In parallel to this thirst for knowledge existed a thirst for power, the need to be constantly placed above others. Emperor Qin Shi, founder of the short-lived Qin Dynasty (221–207 BCE), was obsessed with the concept of immortality and would spare no expense in the search for the "elixir of life". He went as far as sending thousands of men to scour the Earth for remedies to extend his longevity. Unfortunately for Qin Shi, his fear caught up with him, and he died just 15 years after becoming emperor. Nonetheless, he ensured that upon his death, he would be entombed in Xi An with more than 8,000 life-sized terracotta warriors, 130 chariots, 520 horses, and 150 cavalry, among other grave goods, a symbol of his endless opulence.

The Han Dynasty, which followed the Qin, brought peace and prosperity for a little more than 400 years, a period also known as Ancient China's "golden age". China developed the foundations of its culture and became a global powerhouse, expanding its borders and fostering science, invention, and exploration. It saw the invention of paper and record keeping, as well as iron casting and acupuncture, and there were significant advances in Chinese medicine, mathematics, construction, agriculture, engineering, and astronomy. Populous villages grew into cities, and many people lived comfortably. The rich lived in big houses decorated with exotic carpets and art, wore silk robes, and were generally well educated. This is not to say that there were not wealth disparities. Wealthy people relied on enslaved *gu li* for manual labor, and the poor lived in crowded houses and struggled to feed their families. Peasants in rural China were better off as they owned farmland and were able to work hard to make a living, but they did not participate in the opulence that defined the most privileged spheres of Chinese society at this time. Still, overall standards of living improved during the Han Dynasty, and art and culture flourished.

The empire's expansion fueled much of this wealth, especially as it established the Silk Road, trade routes that extended beyond its borders all the way to the Mediterranean. The second century BCE was an interesting time in history, as the Romans were gaining control over Europe. The opening of the Silk Road established a connection between two great powers: with Rome controlling the west and China the east, they were able to trade safely across thousands of kilometers. Silk became one of China's most lucrative trades with the Romans. When it arrived in Rome, the Romans had never seen such fine material. Silk garments grew in popularity among the aristocracy and soon the raw material was worth its weight in gold. Meanwhile, trade between the two empires brought gold and other luxuries to China, and merchant families in particular to experienced more luxury as their wealth grew.

The Ming Dynasty (1368–1644 CE), brought another wave of economic growth to China. During this era, the Chinese population doubled and both the Great Wall of China and the opulent Forbidden City were completed. Fine art and luxuries, including the blue and white porcelain vases more commonly known as Ming Vases, jade, and ivory, flowed along trade routes that now included the New World. Prosperity encouraged the appreciation of exceptional craftmanship and decorative arts such as cloisonné enamel, bronze, lacquerwork, and finely carved furniture as evidence of a person's wealth and culture (Britannica, 2020).

The last imperial Chinese dynasty, the Qing, was not as fortunate. The fifth largest global power, China faced attack from Britain, France, Germany, Russia, and Japan. Opium, smuggled by the British from India into southern China, spread throughout the country, resulting in widespread addiction and social disruption. China's growing opium habit weakened the country and its military, leading eventually to its defeat, and the handing of Hong Kong island over to the British Army. The last emperor of China was PuYi, whose incapability of ruling his country, combined with the deterioration of unity among China's people, precipitated the end of the Qing Dynasty. His life and death were romantically depicted in Bernardo Bertolucci's 1987 film *The Last Emperor*. Sun Yet-Sen, leader of the Kuomintang (KMT) Party, asked the then 6-year-old emperor to abdicate in 1912, and China began a period of republican and socialist rule.

The Roaring Twenties: Shanghai

The end of the Imperial Era was a turbulent time. While the Manchu tribe, to which the last emperor belonged, sought to reinstate an imperial form of government, the rural parts of China were witnessing a surging anti-imperialist movement that sought to keep China a republic. Meanwhile, major Chinese cities were experiencing the "New Cultural Movement", which took place in the 1910s and 1920s. Urban populations discarded classical Chinese ideals in favor of Western ones such as democracy and science. Shanghai was an epicenter of the movement, thanks to the French and British who frequently travelled through the port city, bringing with them their culture and love for Western luxuries. So great was their influence, they transformed Shanghai into one of the least Chinese cities in China. An American living in the city at the time suggested:

> When a traveller arrives in Shanghai to-day he is struck by the fact that to all intents and purposes he might be in a large European city, tall buildings, the well paved streets, the large hotels and clubs, the parks and bridges, the stream of automobiles, the trams and buses, the numerous foreign shops, and, at night, the brilliant electric lighting – all are things he is accustomed to.
> (Pott, 1928, p. 1)

Western culture began to seep into Shanghai as early as the 1840s, when foreign settlers were allowed to take up residence. The tree-lined streets and cafes of the French Concession – conceded to the French in 1849 – the private jazz clubs with British flair, and entertainment centers modeled on those of New York's Broadway made Shanghai a distinctly cosmopolitan city. Most Shanghainese residents were foreign educated and spoke English fluently, and since the port city was filled with merchants, it was considerably wealthier than its neighbors. Shanghainese families used their immense spending power to import Lagonda cars directly from Britain and sought the best gems from Indian and Jewish jewelers.

Yet a racial divide was also emerging, as the all-white, British, municipal government imposed a separation that made Shanghai's Chinese residents – with some exceptions for the English-speaking elite – second-class citizens. When the Chinese Communist Party, led by Mao Zedong, took full control of the country in 1949, the city's Western residents fled, and Shanghai's Chinese elite were exiled. Many escaped to the Republic of China, more commonly known as Taiwan, which had been divided between the Kuomintang (KMT) and the Communist Party of China (CPC) in 1927, at the start of the Chinese Civil War. Others, along with many wealthy residents of Guangdong, found safe passage to Hong Kong and Macau, which at the time were under British and Portuguese rule, respectively. Only those who had existing business relations in their countries of exile managed to escape with parts of their wealth intact.

Hong Kong and Taiwan's Disparity with China

While China closed its borders from 1949 to 1976, wealthy Chinese who escaped to Taiwan and Hong Kong continued to live their expensive lifestyles in exile and remained part of the international luxury market. China is often viewed as a new world for luxury spending, but this is untrue. Chinese luxury consumers, which include those living in Hong Kong and Taiwan, are in fact very mature. Today, Hong Kong and Taiwan possess some of the highest numbers of luxury stores per capita, compared to neighboring countries in Asia. Hong Kong, which is 0.9% the size of New York in terms of land area, has 13 Chanel boutiques. New York has six.

When China finally reopened its boarders after Mao's death, Hong Kong was one of the first destinations Chinese citizens were able to travel to. It became their gateway to the outside world, and their first experience of modern-day luxury consumerism. As China started to trade internationally and its economic strength grew, the new wealth of those in Mainland China began to challenge that of those who had left China at the end of 1949 to set up their empires in Hong Kong, Taiwan, and beyond. Today, tensions between "old" and "new" money, and debate as to the class implications of both, continue.

China's Cultural Reform and Technological Transformation

The Chinese Social Reform of the late 1970s involved the country reopening its doors to the world, initiating an economic reform that resulted in new economic opportunities and an elevated standard of living. The almost 30 years of the Cultural Revolution resulted in deep and debilitating poverty, an experience China did not want to relive. Many believe that this is the drive behind China's unstoppable growth; once the country opened up, there was no desire to go back. In 2000, China's government decided to become a member of the World Trade Organization, and China's wealth started to grow exponentially.

China in the 2000s was a force to be reckoned with, as Chinese companies were now able to send representatives around world and work with foreign businesses. The country saw an explosion in passport applications; after 30 years inside closed borders, Chinese tourists were ready to experience what the world had to offer. China was considered a young country, still playing catch up with modern technologies and new governmental policies. This turned out to be an advantage, as it enabled China to adopt the latest technology without the legacy issues associated with phasing out older, established systems. Jack Ma, the founder of Alibaba, an online marketplace that connects vendors to buyers, was thought to be out of his mind for introducing something so complex to a country that was only beginning to understand the internet. Little did China know that the launch of Alibaba and the SARS pandemic in 2002 would begin its journey to become a technological giant in less than two decades.

How China Leads the Luxury Market

It was not until the early 2000s that China's cultural reform led to a greater exposure to foreign luxury. Throughout the 1950s to 1990s official limits on the number of wealthy Chinese prevented prosperity from translating into wide-spread personal wealth. Factory owners, who were still under strict communist hierarchy, were restricted to producing standard goods: mass-manufactured clothing, tires, paper, toys, etc. Still, brands such as Ermenegildo Zegna and Pierre Cardin tried to make inroads. Louis Vuitton and Cartier relied on connections with China that went as far back as the 1910s to help them move into the country. Both brands set up their first post-cultural reform stores in 1992, in Beijing and Shanghai, respectively. By 1999, other luxury brands were following suit, and China was considered more international. However, it wasn't until 2002 that Shanghai constructed its first luxury mall, Plaza 66.

The establishment of luxury shopping malls, and a new appetite for luxury goods, encouraged many brands to enter China in the 2000s. They lined Nanjing Road in Shanghai and filled up luxury malls such as Plaza 66 and SKP Beijing. However, these brands failed to account for the exorbitant government tax on luxury goods, which was over 50% of the retail price, resulting in final prices that were a far cry from those in the tax-free region of Hong Kong. Chinese consumers continued to look elsewhere for luxury goods, searching for better price points for the same product. Hong Kong luxury stores were beset with long lines and empty shelves as Chinese luxury consumers arbitraged on the tax difference. This phenomenon caused havoc and imbalance for luxury brands, which had invested heavily in entering China, only to see that most sales were coming from Hong Kong.

Furthermore, adventure- and experience-seeking Chinese travelers embraced visa-free travel to Japan and Europe. Following in the footsteps of the Japanese tourists of the 1980s, they crisscrossed Europe in tour busses, visiting luxury shopping destinations in multiple countries. According to a report by Goldman Sachs in 2015, only 4% of China's population owned passports (Kawano et al., 2015), so these Chinese tourists were not only buying for themselves, but for their friends and family. The volume of sales was so high that luxury stores in Europe had to begin limiting groups shopping together, to one luxury item per group for fear of not being able to cater to their local clientele.

Much of this changed in 2015, when luxury brands decided to restructure their pricing strategies. In Chapter 8, we discuss the challenges brands faced during the period known as the "Chinese Bulimia", when the price disparity between Asia and Europe came close to exceeding 80%. Luxury brands reduced the price gap between Europe and Asia in the hope of bringing Chinese luxury consumers back home and increasing their ROI on the retail networks they had established in Mainland China. Some brands even went as far as lowering their margins to match price points between Hong Kong and China, reducing price arbitration.

In the background of this reshuffling, a technological revolution was happening. Alibaba and Tencent's messaging app WeChat had become essential tools of everyday life in China. WeChat, which allows users to create forums and group chats and perform monetary transactions in addition to messaging one another, allowed Chinese luxury consumers to become even more connected. Users within its forums were exchanging information on price differences between countries, availability of luxury products in specific stores, and what special editions were available where. Personal shoppers or "dai gou" located in specific countries or locations would source luxury goods for communities of luxury consumers they interacted with on WeChat. While *dai gou* are critical players in China's luxury consumption, it was the ability of Chinese consumers to connect through technology that changed China's luxury market. While it took Japanese luxury consumers almost 40 years to mature in their tastes and behaviors, in China this process took only 10 to 15 years.

Today, China leads the world in overall e-commerce transactions. Chinese and foreign brands (not exclusively luxury) on Alibaba generated US$74.1 billion in one day, on Singles Day (November 11) in 2020, as compared to Amazon's US $4.9 billion on Prime Day in 2019. The purchasing power of Chinese consumers is proving to be far more resilient than that of those in the West. Not only this, but Chinese consumers are also comfortable making untraditional purchases online, including buying cars through Alibaba's Tmall. In 2016, models by Volvo, Mercedes-Benz, Jaguar, and Range Rover made up the top 10 cars sold through the site (Rapp,

2017). The same year, Italian luxury car maker Maserati appeared on Tmall for the first time, selling out 100 Maserati Levante 350hp SUVs in just 18 seconds – a new record! (MarketingtoChina, 2016)

China will remain one of the most interesting markets for the world of luxury in the coming years, as it does not seem to be slowing down. In 2021, Plaza 66 overtook Harrods as the world's highest grossing shopping mall, a position Harrods had not relinquished in decades. While most of this is due to regular lockdowns in the UK, it should not come as a surprise, as China's appetite for luxury is, for the time being, insatiable.

Takeaways
- Luxury has a rich history in all of today's major markets.
- European luxury began with Greek and Roman debates about the moral value of decadence and austerity. In the medieval period and the Renaissance, the lavish wardrobes of the upper classes existed alongside sumptuary laws designed to enforce class distinctions and Christian moral philosophy that saw luxury as a moral ill.
- Our modern conception of luxury emerged in Europe around the turn of the twentieth century, as luxury artisans gave way to boutiques, some of which would become the brands we know today. Consumption also changed, as people began to use luxury as a means of personal expression.
- The history of luxury in the United States parallels what happened in Europe, except that while Europe was always a producer of luxury, the US was primarily a consumer until the mid- to late twentieth century. Today, the US is the world's largest luxury market, as well as being an important source of funding for luxury companies.
- Luxury consumption in the United States is trend driven, with people looking to celebrities as models of how to live a luxurious life. It was movie stars like Elizabeth Taylor who introduced luxury to American consumers in the post-Second World War era.
- Japan emerged as a luxury market when it opened its borders during the Meiji Restoration. After going into a period of dormancy during the Second World War, it became a major market in the post-war period, eventually becoming the second largest market in the world.
- High barriers to entry mean that even today, local intermediaries (i.e., department stores) remain key players in Japan, helping foreign luxury companies enter the market. In turn, Japanese department stores have used their connections with luxury brands to establish the luxury malls that characterize twenty-first-century luxury shopping in Asia.
- China has a long, overlooked, history of luxury, going back 4,000 years. Tracing this history through the Han and Ming Dynasties to Shanghai of the 1920s, we can see how China, rather than being a new luxury market, is in fact an old and very established one.
- The Cultural Revolution cut Mainland China off from the world luxury market, but Chinese consumers in Hong Kong, Macau, Taiwan, and elsewhere remained important luxury clients.
- After Social Reform, luxury stores in Hong Kong were a point of entry for consumers from Mainland China eager to spend newly acquired wealth. In the late twentieth century, luxury brands that tried to establish stores in Mainland cities like Beijing and Shanghai were challenged both by local regulations and by customers willing to arbitrage in other markets to avoid high taxes at home.
- Thanks to China's rapid technological development, Chinese luxury consumers are the most tech-savvy in the world, adding a dynamic to the Chinese market with important lessons for luxury companies.

4 The Value of Country of Origin

Country of origin (COO) has played an important role across luxury industries, especially in conveying a message about the quality, heritage, and craftmanship of a company's products. This has been particularly important for luxury brands with origins in countries that have a rich history associated with specific areas of expertise, such as Italy for leather goods, Switzerland for watchmaking, Germany for luxury cars, and Great Britain for textiles. However, as the supply chain become more globalized, the true meaning of COO becomes more difficult to discern. Research on country of origin has tried to subdivide the meaning, considering a product or brand's various sources or points of origin including country of manufacture (COM), country of design (COD), country of assembly (COA), country of brand (COB), and country of parts/raw materials (COP). These designations often overlap. In this chapter, we will explore the challenges luxury companies may face when trying to balance their global footprint, their heritage, and the customer's perception of both a brand and its products.

Challenging the traditional meaning of country of origin will allow us to gain a more contemporary perspective on this aspect of brand identity, including how globalization has changed the way consumers see value in country of origin. In the past, when luxury goods industries were centered around a handful of brands, COO was an easy indicator of what was authentic and of high quality: Made in Italy designations had more cache than Made in China. These associations influenced the consumer's product decision journey based on the three types of beliefs: descriptive, informative, and inferential (Martin and Eroglu, 1993). Nowadays, luxury goods are more accessible, and this has created a proliferation of products and brands. As a result, COO no longer provides the consumer with a compass to navigate varying but consistent levels of quality among products from different countries. Instead, it has evolved into a value-added proposition. As consumers become mature in their luxury consumption, their expectations based on intrinsic and extrinsic cues become more astute. While this creates both opportunities and threats for heritage countries such as Italy, Switzerland, France, and the United Kingdom, it also levels the playing field for evergreen brands coming from countries with lesser heritage, such as Japan, China, and South Korea. What are these brands expected to do in order to adapt? Will moving part of their manufacturing to non-heritage countries affect the consumer's perception of a brand?

As luxury consumers shift their purchasing decisions from premeditated to impulsive, the demand for and volume of luxury goods rises. In the pages that follow, we will analyze the different strategic decisions made by luxury companies to meet these demands and their motivations to move parts of their manufacturing, assembly, or supply chain away from heritage countries, and vice versa. Through their subsequent success and failures, we can better understand whether or not COO has any significant effects on these decisions.

https://doi.org/10.1515/9783110723519-004

The Definition of Country of Origin

There are many ways to define country of origin: it could be the birthplace of a company's founder, the location where the company was founded, or even where the craft began. In the context of luxury, there are five definitions commonly used by companies:

(1) Birthplace. Country of origin is defined by the birthplace of the founder, rather than a location associated with expertise in a relevant craft or industry, or one connected to the subsequent growth of the brand.

– *Ferrari:* Enzo Ferrari, an avid race car driver and builder, was born in the Province of Modena. Prior to the creation of his namesake car company, he worked extensively with Alfa Romeo, including managing its racing division. Due to a conflict with the management team, he left Alfa Romeo to establish his own automotive company but was not allowed to manufacture racing cars. The headquarters of this new company was initially established in Modena, subsequently moving 30 minutes south to Maranello in 1943, after the original building burned down. It wasn't until after the Second World War, when the Italian government required his support to restart automotive manufacturing in the country, that Ferrari regained his status as a race-car builder. In March 1947, the 125S, his very first super car manufactured under his own name, rolled out of Ferrari's Maranello factory, forever linking what would become a world-renowned auto company with the region in which both it and its founder were born.
– *Panerai:* Giovanni Panerai opened a watchmaker's workshop and watch shop on Ponte alle Grazie in Florence in 1860, moving to Palazzo Arcivescovile around the beginning of the twentieth century; he started making and selling his own designs when he received a commission from the Royal Italian Navy. In 1916, Officine Panerai filed its first patent – for the Radiomir, a radium-based powder that gave its watches luminous dials. Today, Panerai's historic store still stands in Palazzo Arcivescovile in Florence's Piazza San Giovanni. Although the watches are made at the company's headquarters in Geneva, Switzerland, Panerai remains a Florentine brand.

(2) Manufacturing and Assembly. Country of origin is defined and always associated with the place of manufacturing and assembly. The company prides itself on where its products are made.

– *Rolex:* Rolex was founded by the German watchmaker Hans Wilsdoft. His career in the watch trade brought him to Switzerland and subsequently the United Kingdom, where he started the company. After the Second World War, he moved Rolex closer to his suppliers, and has since remained in Switzerland. In 1930, Rolex adopted the term Swiss Made on all its watches.
– *Lamborghini:* Lamborghini started as a tractor manufacturer founded by industrialist Ferruccio Lamborghini. It was not until 1963 that it entered the luxury car

market to compete with Ferrari. Between 1978 and 1998, Lamborghini changed owner multiple times, eventually landing at the Volkswagen Group under the Audi division. Despite its foreign ownership, the majority of Lamborghini's manufacturing and assembly, including upholstery, takes place in Sant'Agata Bolognese, Italy, and the company remains an Italian brand in terms of COO.

(3) Growth. Companies that seek investment and new talent may adopt a country of origin that differs from the birthplace of its founder or that of the brand.

– *Moncler:* Moncler was founded by two Frenchmen in the Alpine town of Monestier-de-Clermont in 1952. After significant financial issues, Italian businessman Remo Ruffini acquired the company in 2003 and listed it on the Milan Stock Exchange in 2013 under the new name Moncler SpA. Ruffini has managed to turn the business around to create one of the most profitable luxury apparel companies to date, and Moncler is now considered an Italian company.

– *Farfetch:* Farfetch is a marketplace ecommerce platform founded by Portuguese entrepreneur Jose Neves in June 2007. As a tech-luxury company, Neves sought to maximize Farfetch's capabilities and therefore registered the business in the United Kingdom. In 2018, when Farfetch was listed in the NYSE, it proudly hung both the Portuguese and British flags to symbolize its dual identity.

(4) Appellation. In the food and beverage industry, appellation of origin is preserved and protected by regulatory bodies. Depending on the region, location, and country, each regulatory body has its own specific requirements to claim country or appellation of origin.

– *Champagne:* In the nineteenth century, the insect pest phylloxera wiped out the extensive vineyards of France's Champagne region. Wine growers faced imminent catastrophe, leading to the formation of the Association Viticole Champenoise in 1898. To protect the region, the Champagne houses filed various lawsuits to claim exclusivity for wines harvested and produced in Champagne, and in 1904 the Fédération de syndicats called for the demarcation of the vineyards entitled to the appellation. In 1936, Champagne won the battle for official recognition, becoming one of the few regions to not require the AOC label to guarantee the origin of its products.

In 1993, Yves Saint Laurent launched the new fragrance "Champagne", intended "for light, happy and bubbly women". However, a lawsuit filed by the Comité interprofessional du vin de Champagne soon forced the fashion house to change the name in France. The fragrance, packaged in a bottle shaped like a caged champagne cork, was renamed Yvresse in 1996.

(5) Craftmanship. To emphasize the authenticity of a product through its craftmanship, culture, and traditions, a brand may choose to highlight a country of origin associated with a craft or technique essential to that product.

- *Loro Piana:* Loro Piana is an Italian brand that is proud to label its products "100% Made in Italy". There are, however, three exceptions: (1) the panama hat, which is woven and made by artisans in Panama; (2) the brand's espadrilles, which uses a shoe-making technique indigenous to Spain and are labelled "Made in Spain"; and (3) Lotus Flower fabric, one of Loro Piana's "Excellences", which is produced using traditional methods unique to South East Asia. Loro Piana works with artisans in Myanmar to produce its Lotus Flower fabrics, and the country is credited as the COO of the material.
- *Murano Blown Glass:* Glassblowing was invented by Syrian craftsman as early as the first century BCE. The craft migrated from the Middle East to Egypt and eventually to the Venetian island of Murano, where artisans perfected *cristallo*, an especially clear glass made using mold-blowing techniques (*Glass Blowing History*, n.d.). Even though glassblowing is now practiced around the world, particularly in countries such as China, Japan, and the United States, the most exquisite blown glass is still recognized as that which comes from Murano.

Globalization and the Perception of COO

Globalization is defined as the process by which businesses develop international influence or operate on an international scale. As such, the globalization of luxury goods has its beginnings as far back as the 1300s, when bespoke clockmakers and dressmakers would travel across Europe and other continents to cater to the needs of royalty and aristocrats. At that time, COO played a very important role, whereby the country of origin of the designer and crafter of said bespoke pieces brought a sense of prestige to their work due to its association with expertise and craftmanship. Each and every craftsman's know-how, or *savoir-faire*, was their unique value positioning. It not only provided them with a stream of loyal clients but also the reputation that came with catering to an exclusive list of clients. By the nineteenth century, individual artisans had begun to expand their influence, founding boutiques that would become the templates for the first luxury houses.

It was not until the twentieth century that modern luxury brands began to emerge, usually bearing the family name of their founders and made famous by their star-studded client lists. This was the moment when luxury houses truly became globalized. In 1953, Guccio Gucci decided to bring his namesake brand to the United States, starting a revolution in the world of fashion and luxury by instilling in American consumers the concept that being designed and made in Italy was the quintessential sign of distinction for luxury goods (Silver, 2019). Unlike other luxury houses founded in the early 1900s, Gucci was not associated with aristocrats or noble families; rather, it appealed to celebrities and socialites who were known as jetsetters and tastemakers, setting the trends that defined luxury living. The timing was also opportune as the United States had just recovered from the Second World

War and was entering an era characterized by a new type of wealth and spending. The popularity of Gucci allowed Made in Italy to flourish as a marker of quality and craftmanship.

While at the time of its American expansion, Gucci was known for its innovative use of alternative materials such as canvas and bamboo, it was its Florentine-made leather goods that changed the game. The history of tanning and leather goods in Italy can be traced to the Roman empire. Techniques were perfected in the height of the Medieval period. The establishment of *Arte dei Cuoiai e Galigai*, the Florentine leather guild, in 1282 protected each family's secret techniques for producing quality leathers (Confraternita dei Legnaioli, n.d.). The guild consolidated expertise to foster a level of mastery that was unrivalled by anyone else in the world (Made in Italy Accessories, 2014). Even today these techniques remain closely protected family secrets, and they continue to be handed down through the generations. According to the International Council of Tanners (2019), statistics from 2015 show that Italy accounts for 6.3% of the world's leather production and is the only European country in the top ten.

Gucci's entrance into the American market introduced a fresh audience to Italian craftmanship. Reinforced by similar expansions by likeminded Italian luxury houses such as Bulgari and Prada, which entered the US in the 1970s. it allowed a new group of consumers to familiarize themselves with Made in Italy as a signifier of quality. When the popularity of Made in Italy grew in the 1980s, COO branding became a significant contributor to Italy's economic growth, as well as the advancement of the world of luxury goods. This was because the label was associated with quality, high specialization, differentiation, elegance, and experience. The association with such positive values eventually created a sense of trustworthiness and a proxy for assessment. This new audience started to develop a new "consumer attitude" toward luxury goods, which can be explained by the following three types of beliefs, which were established by Martin and Eroglu (1993):

1) **Descriptive:** direct experience with the product
2) **Informative:** information derived from outside sources such as advertisements, word of mouth, or social media
3) **Inferential:** beliefs formed by making an assumption (correct or incorrect) based on reputation, association with another product, or an image of country in the consumer's mind

Audiences who make decisions based on "descriptive beliefs" are considered to be mature consumers, who have previously had direct experience with the product and make their decisions based on this experience. Those who make "informative" decisions rely on information derived from external sources, such as advertisements, recommendations from friends and family, or research. Finally, audiences who make "inferential" decisions are those who have had the least exposure to the product and therefore make decisions based on secondary information or positive associations with more general categories. An example of this is when an inexperienced person goes to a wine shop to buy wine for the first time. This person is unlikely to know the difference between new-world and old-world wines, or understand the differences between grape varieties. However, he or she does have a larger set of beliefs and associations to call on to make a decision. Someone who believes that the best cuisine comes from Tuscany may decide to purchase a Tuscan wine, believing that the wine should be just as good as the food. Or he or she may prefer a New Zealand wine due to the general belief that the country's air is fresher and its soil more enriched than that of a European country, therefore believing that New Zealand will produce a much cleaner wine than France or Germany. While these beliefs may not always be accurate, they still act as indicators of perceived quality and trustworthiness.

In addition to the three types of belief, consumers utilize intrinsic and extrinsic cues when evaluating new products. Intrinsic cues are not based on product characteristics but are related to intangible values such as emotions (how do you feel during or after making a purchase) and beliefs, while extrinsic cues are based on parameters that help a person make logical deductions, such as price, value, and country of origin (Veale and Quester, 2009). Luxury consumers who are less mature or less familiar with the products on offer tend to make purchases by weighing intrinsic and extrinsic cues (Aaker, 2010), and they are more likely to use COO as an extrinsic cue rather than focusing on the intrinsic attributes of the country in question. COO therefore acts as an indicator of value, particularly for new and/or inexperienced luxury consumers, who are likely to be drawn to luxury items made in a country that has been historically associated with a particular product type, for example, leather goods from Italy, perfume from France, or a watch from Switzerland (Rezvani, et al., 2012).

A study by Bourne (1957), related to product conspicuousness, investigated the impact of product and brand values based on the two functions (1) exclusivity and (2) visibility (to others). Exclusivity refers to products accessible or possessed by a few, while visibility relates to the obviousness of luxury to others rather than to one's self. Immature luxury consumers may tend to favor products with more visibility as a way to "show off" their social standing. However, the same study found that while a product's country of origin was a weak determinant in most purchasing decisions, it had significantly more influence for purchases of luxury goods. Bourne concluded that products bearing "Made in" labels from countries with positive COO were likely to be favored over those from countries with less positive COO.

Limitation of Country-of-origin in the Globalized World

As European brands established themselves in North America in the 1960s, 1970s, and 1980s, the positive connotations of Made in Italy and similar COO markers were able to successfully play on all three types of belief: descriptive (as customers gained exposure to European luxury brands), informative (as brands became part of celebrity and pop culture), and inferential (as the association between luxury and famous brands' countries of origin evolved into a cultural trope). While this success benefited Italy greatly, with a surge in other countries outsourcing manufacturing to take advantage of the Made in Italy label, the value of Italian craftmanship and quality was also abused by other brands. Those emerging from lesser known countries were slowly adopting other methods of enhancing quality without bearing the cost of actually manufacturing their goods in Italy. At the same time, they applied various unregulated COO strategies to suggest that at least some aspect of their products had an Italian connection. Table 4.1, which is borrowed from Aichner (2014), outlines some of these strategies.

Table 4.1: Regulated and Unregulated COO strategies.

Strategy Name	Strategy Type	Regulated by Law
1) "Made in . . ."	Explicit	Yes
2) Quality and Origin labels	Explicit	Yes
3) COO embedded in company name	Implicit	No
4) Typical COO words	Implicit	No
5) Use of COO language	Implicit	No
6) Use of famous or stereotypical people from COO	Implicit	No
7) Use of COO flags and symbols	Explicit/Implicit	No
8) Use of typical landscapes or famous buildings in COO	Implicit	No

Source: Compiled by authors from Aichner, 2014.

Many luxury brands use both regulated and unregulated COO strategies to signal and strengthen their origins and brand identity. A few examples include Bulgari, with its logo typeface that uses the classical Latin letter "v" instead of the modern "u", symbolizing its historical ties to the city of Rome. Another is Acqua di Parma, a cologne maker proud of its origins: appropriately named "Water of Parma", both its name and choice of language encapsulate a sense of place. Even recognizable brands such a Ferrari are not ashamed of utilizing these kinds symbols to promote their origins. Much like how Valentino Garavani is known for his dresses in "*rosso* Valentino", a red Ferrari is not only a symbolic choice for recognition, but also an homage to Italy's racing colors: *rosso corsa* (Rees, 2018). These examples are indicative of how important unregulated COO markers are in broadcasting a brand's identity to its consumers. Many companies use similar strategies to create connections to a particular country of origin – even when in reality, the suggested connection is quite far from the truth.

When unregulated COO is used simultaneously with informative and/or inferential beliefs, emergent brands can leverage partial information consumers may possess to quickly establish their luxury status. A very interesting case of such an application is Shiseido's prestige cosmetics brand Clé de Peau Beauté, "key to skin beauty" in French. Shiseido is a Japanese beauty and cosmetics corporation, and its tenure in the industry far exceeds most. Its namesake brand has gained success in Asia and around the world, yet when Shiseido decided to enhance its offer by introducing an ultra-exclusive brand, it decided on a French-sounding name as a way to symbolize foreignness and stand out from its Japanese counterparts. Clé de Peau Beauté was even marketed to omit the Shiseido name, separating it from its Japanese parent company (*Shiseido Repositions*, 2010).

Shiseido chose a specifically French-sounding name because France has been synonymous with the beauty and perfume industry since the twelfth century. Going back as far as the 1900s, France has given birth to some of the world's most renowned beauty brands, namely Guerlain, Lancôme, and L'Oréal (Jones, 2010). Shiseido's predominantly Asian consumers had always seen France as the birthplace of beauty, so creating an association between the country and its new product line was exactly the type premiumization strategy Shiseido was aiming to achieve. Although the Clé de Peau name is misleading, it proves that the association with a particular country of origin plays an important role in developing a consumer's perception of know-how and quality.

Shiseido's Clé de Peau Beauté launched in 1982 (Clé de Peau, n.d.), a time when foreign luxury beauty brands in Japan were few and far between. Many were already household names, such as Elizabeth Arden, Lancôme, and La Prairie. When Clé de Peau Beauté entered the market, consumers didn't question the brand's origins, believing instead that since high-priced European beauty brands held such prestige, so would this new French-sounding beauty brand (Slater and Umemura, 2017). However, by the early 2000s, this type of strategy was no longer feasible. Back in the 1980's, globalization was limited to hugely successful companies catering to a handful of wealthy individuals who had travelled internationally, by the turn of the twenty-first century the internet and search engines had dramatically altered the consumer landscape. Consumers today are highly informed, and the details of a product or a brand's country of origin are just a click away. Brands looking to replicate the success of Clé de Peau Beauté in utilizing unregulated COO will find it extremely difficult to convince twenty-first-century consumers to take association and origin as interchangeable qualities.

Today we are at the height of globalization, and the concept of country of origin has begun to blur (Urbonavičius and Gineikienė, 2009). Emergent and established brands can no longer depend on inferential beliefs to sway the purchasing decisions of their customers, and consumers are becoming more and more immune to marketing tactics that attempt to leverage their informative beliefs (Collins, 2015). Consumers themselves or those in their inner circles are extremely likely to have experienced the product at some point, and thus to make better decisions about what to believe. Does this mean the end of brand strategies that play on unregulated COO? Are consumers educated enough to differentiate between leather goods made in Tuscany and those made in Morocco, or watches made in Switzerland vs. those made in Japan? The short answer is, no. In the globalized world, country of origin has taken on a new connotation, evolving in the mind of the consumer to symbolize different aspects of a luxury product. No longer simply a proxy for quality and trustworthiness, country of origin has become a value proposition in more ways than one.

The Evolution of Country of Origin

To understand the evolution of country of origin, we can take a two-pronged view: first, observing how a country with a negative COO perception eventually matures into a country with a positive COO perception; second, noticing how, in the world of luxury specifically, a customer who becomes more mature in their consumption behavior will put their trust in a brand rather than relying on country of origin as a signal of quality and excellence.

Evolution from Negative to Positive Perception

The story of Rolex's rise to become one of the world's most loved luxury watch brands offers an example of how country of origin can evolve over time. When asked, people are quick to identify Rolex as a Swiss-made watch, and while this is true today, Rolex's beginnings were in England. Long before Switzerland became synonymous with precision and accurate time keeping, the watchmaking industry flourished in other parts of Europe, namely Italy, Germany, France, and England. Watchmaking only arrived in Switzerland in the middle of the sixteenth century, when French refugees persecuted for their protestant faith arrived in the country, bringing with them their skills in the construction of clocks, jewelry boxes, and mechanical toys. The migration of skilled workers into the French-speaking region of Switzerland, especially into Geneva and Neuchâtel, introduced a method of producing elegant and complicated timepieces with "a greater than ordinary division of labor [and] prices that defied [their] competition" (Landes, 2000).

Even then, the capital of the world's watch industry was Britain, and Swiss watchmakers competed by copying British styles and design. They went as far as putting Britain as the place of manufacture on the finished pieces and exporting them as "English watches". At the time, there were no laws in place to regulate country of origin, and Switzerland, a country with no heritage in watch making, was not exactly top of mind for consumers. Local watchmakers depended on exports due to the small size of their home market, and their "Made in . . ." strategy was a way to change the end consumer's perception, and begin to make space for Swiss watches elsewhere in Europe. It was not until the 1840s that the Swiss watchmaking industry gained a technological edge through the invention of machine production and the introduction interchangeable parts which, combined, led to higher yields and efficiency. While this allowed the Swiss to catch up to the British in terms of manufacturing volumes, it wasn't until the watchmakers across Geneva and Neuchâtel came together and learned from each other's failures that they truly gained an advantage. The unique positioning of Switzerland, surrounded by countries with strong clockmaking traditions, and its experience in the trade allowed for its new reputation as the epicenter of timepieces to emerge.

Nowadays, we associate precision and accurate time keeping with Switzerland, and most, if not all, of the world's top luxury watchmakers have either relocated manufacturing to Switzerland or are owned by Swiss watchmaker conglomerates. Two that come to mind are Panerai – a Florentine watchmaker owned by the Swiss-based Richemont Group and manufactured in Neuchâtel – and Glashütte – a German watchmaker, still manufactured in the small town of Glashütte but owned by Swatch Group. In addition, luxury brands traditionally known for apparel and accessories have extended their collections into watchmaking. They too have sought out Swiss manufacturers. Chanel's watch brand, which launched in 1987, was originally produced under contract by Swiss manufacturers. In 1993, the French fashion house's owners, Gerard and Alan Wertheimer, acquired their supplier, G&F Châtelain of Le Chaux-de-Fonds in the canton of Neuchâtel (*Chanel*, 2019). Chanel continued to invest into their watch business, eventually acquiring Kenissi (Corder, 2018), a Swiss automatic movement manufacturer in 2019, the same year Chanel was awarded the Grand Prix d'Horlogerie de Genéve in the ladies' category for the Chanel J12 12.1.

The evolution of Swiss watchmaking – from a country of copycats to one of high prestige – can be understood if we consider the following hypothesis: that if a country with a negative COO perception allocates investment and innovation toward improving its expertise and reputation, it has the ability to change the consumer's perception. This concept can be seen in many industries outside luxury. One of the most prominent of all is the automotive industry in Japan.

Using the evolution in the watchmaking industry as a case study, we can observe that there is a strong correlation between investments and innovation and a shift in consumer perception from negative to positive, as shown in Figure 4.1. Countries are expected not only to invest time and money, but also to provide education and opportunities to further develop the work force in the target industry. This will lead to strides forward in innovation, such as technological advances, increases in manufacturing capacity, and improvements in efficiency.

Figure 4.1: Drivers of Change in COO.
Source: Compiled by authors.

In the world of luxury, this phenomenon has also been observed in the manufacture of luxury sneakers. While traditionally sneakers were not part of the luxury goods repertoire, the "athleisure" trend of the late 2000s introduced designer sneakers as an essential luxury item (Gosselin, 2019). In 2017, Balenciaga, a historic French fashion house owned by Kering Group, released the much-coveted Triple S. The statement sneakers were initially produced in Italy but due to its increased demand, Balenciaga quietly moved their production to China. When news broke of the change in manufacturing countries, many were left to question whether this offshoring stunt was really a way to cut down on costs (Silbert, 2018); historically, China has been associated with cheap labor and poor quality. Despite the move, Balenciaga did not change the US$795 price point for the Triple S (Danforth, 2017). Instead, it hedged its risk by predicting that its customers would continue to buy into the hype despite the change. Surprisingly, a 2018 article in *Footwear News* reported the positive news Balenciaga had hoped for, with a headline that claimed, "Balenciaga's Dad Shoes Could Help the Brand hit the Billion-Dollar Sales Mark" (George-Parkin, 2018).

In sneaker-related forums and comments on Hypebeast.com, there are ongoing arguments about whether or not Balenciaga's offshoring to China was not a way to cut costs, but a way to exploit the expertise and experience of Chinese sneaker manufacturers. The stigma of China being a place for cheap manufacturing has led to negative perceptions of it as a COO. However, many neglect the fact that just like car companies in Japan or watchmakers in Switzerland, the "copycat" has the added advantage of learning from other countries' mistakes to improve and innovate. In this case, China possessed a skill that was not as well recognized in the Italian shoe industry. According to data by Statista (2020b), between 2013 and 2019, China led the world in sneaker manufacturing with an average of 14 billion pairs produced a year, as compared to Italy, where they produce less that 200 million pairs a year. It would be safe to assume that its production volume and dominance over the market gives China the upper hand in the field of sneaker manufacture (Velasquez and Donaldson, 2018).

Evolution Through Maturity of the Customer

According to Bain and Company's Worldwide Luxury Monitor, the democratization of luxury occurred somewhere around 2001 (D'Arpizio and Levato, 2020). This refers to a period in which luxury goods, traditionally out of reach from the middle class, became more accessible (Plażyk, 2014). During this shift in consumer behavior, luxury brands dealt with a surge of new luxury consumers with appetites for flaunting their newfound access to luxury goods. This phenomenon is very much linked to the idea of the nouveau riche, and to ideas of conspicuous consumption as following a recent increase in wealth or status. The world of luxury saw these types of luxury consumers as possessing a lower level of sophistication than more established customers, buying into luxury as a way to project their identity to others. They are often drawn to obvious logos, popular luxury brands, and luxury goods with COOs that are synonymous with high quality or prestige (e.g., Made in Italy or Made in France).

Almost 20 years after the democratization of luxury, these consumers have familiarized themselves with individual luxury brands and their values (Aaker, 2010). They no longer depend on extrinsic cues to make decisions on whether or not to make a purchase from a particular brand, nor do they depend on informative or inferential beliefs. Rather, their direct experience with different brands over a long period of time has established their familiarity with and maturity toward these brands and their products. This shift has had a significant impact on the importance of extrinsic cues in luxury branding, especially when it comes to country of origin. What once acted as a proxy for good quality, as indicated by the "Made in" identifier, has become significantly less important, while intrinsic cues such as emotions and impulsiveness have increased in importance. Therefore, when a brand with a strong sense of value attached to it such as Louis Vuitton decides to open a new factory in Texas, its customers do not question its decision to offshore (Adams, 2019). Consumers trust that a company as prominent as Louis Vuitton will make the right decision – not only to move closer to its customers, but also to bring jobs into the United States.

Country of Origin in the Eyes of the Connoisseur Luxury Consumer

As discussed previously, in the evolution of COO, consumers who are less familiar with luxury tend to depend on "Made in" labels and other extrinsic cues to identify quality and prestige. Based on this theory, we can assume that once consumers become mature and familiar with a brand, and their dependency on extrinsic cues decreases, their reliance on COO to define a product's quality will also diminish. Similarly, as these consumers become more mature, so does their knowledge of the brand and its heritage (Khan and Bamber, 2008). In reference to Figure 4.2, as consumers move further toward the right on the x-axis, they shift from mature consumers to connoisseurs, becoming discerning and even demanding in their luxury consumption. They are informed and knowledgeable from a product standpoint, aware of where the best cashmere and silks come from, or the mine sites for pink and yellow diamonds (Flora, 2016). They cannot be easily fooled by unregulated COO, nor do they put much emphasis on regulated COO strategies. They expect to have the best raw materials from countries where a particular raw material originates, and well-crafted products with connections to countries with strong craft traditions. For example, cashmere from Mongolia, silk from China, pink diamonds from Australia, etc.

To demonstrate this, we can take the example of a Hugo Boss suit. Examining the garment, we can see that it was manufactured in Turkey using fabrics from Loro Piana. This one product therefore has three countries of origin: that of the brand (Hugo Boss is from Germany), the suit's manufacturing and assembly (carried out in

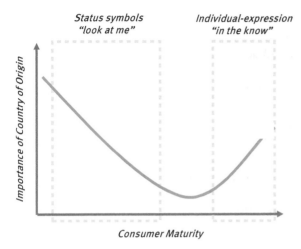

Status symbols
"look at me"

Individual-expression
"in the know"

Importance of Country of Origin

Consumer Maturity

Figure 4.2: The Importance of Country of Origin Based on the Maturity of the Luxury Consumer.
Source: Compiled by authors.

Turkey), and the fabric (woven in Italy). This begs the question: Which of these COOs plays the most important role in creating value for the consumer? Based on the characteristics reviewed, consumer perceptions should fall into three categories:

1) **Unsophisticated consumer:** They focus on where the suit is manufactured. If we consider Hugo Boss as a brand, it does not stand out from competitors such as Ermenegildo Zegna, Canali, or Tom Ford: they all have a similar level of prestige. Therefore, the unsophisticated consumer will turn to other markers, comparing this suit's "Made in Turkey" tag to the country of manufacture of another brand. Value, for this type of consumer, lies in the country of manufacture.

2) **Matured consumer:** The assumption is that this type of consumer has developed a long-term relationship with the brand. He has purchased from Hugo Boss and loves its style, design, and fit. He trusts that Hugo Boss would use the best materials and manufacturing and therefore puts less emphasis on the country of manufacture and the source of raw materials.

3) **Connoisseur consumer:** This type of consumer has long-term relationships with multiple brands in this category. He chooses this suit based on the fabric by Loro Piana. This consumer is looking for a "Super 150" or higher designation, which denotes how pure the wool is and the thickness of the wool fibers (Chow, 2014). He understands the differences in quality based on a grading system only a connoisseur would be familiar with.

The concepts described above suggest that heritage brands, those with deep history and expertise, tend to have the upper hand. Since they have established both credibility among their loyal customers and brand equity throughout the years, their reliance on COO is rarely ever questioned. Neither the unsophisticated consumer nor the connoisseur consumer has reason to cast doubt – heritage brands have a reputation for always sourcing the best materials and utilizing the world's best artisans.

How brands are leveraging COO to entice the connoisseur? Examples of evolution observed in the modern-day luxury apparel industry indicate that the connoisseur consumer is on the rise. Luxury brands are taking advantage of artisans from around the world who specialize in unique handiwork and sourcing unique foreign materials to elevate their products, as well as cater to this new breed of discerning customers. One example is Dior's 2020 cruise collection. Maria Grazia Chiuri, the brand's creative director for womenswear, explored the use of African wax cotton in a modern silhouette. She worked with local artisans and designers to come up with meaningful prints that aligned with both African culture and Dior's DNA. Chiuri believed that these fabrics had to be made in Africa by local artisans, which led to a collaboration between Dior and Uniwax, a textile company based in the Ivory Coast (Deeny, 2019). In addition to this, she worked closely with African designer and "Made in Africa" pioneer Pathé Ouédraogo (Salter, 2019). The result of this collaboration was positive, and involving artisans from across the African continent transformed the collection, as Chiuri's collaborator, the anthropologist Anne Grosfilley, described in an interview published in *Fashion Natwork*: "From Marrakech, to West African printing; to beading with references to its role in the cultures of the Aruba in Nigeria; Masai in Tanzania and Zulus in South Africa. The whole of the Africa Continent is celebrated!" (Deeny, 2019).

In addition to this, brands that have long been associated with "Made in Italy" have begun to seek unique know-how from abroad to cater to their most elite consumers. Ermenegildo Zegna was one of the first luxury suiting brands to highlight Japanese workmanship. In 2015, it launched a capsule collection of suits from their couture line. These garments, manufactured in Japan, were an homage to Japanese cultural heritage and sartorial know-how. The exclusive collection was limited and only accessible to a handful of clients (Ferrante, 2015).

Likewise, an article by written by Ferrarini (2010) explains that Mario Prada, grandfather to Muccia Prada and current co-owner of the namesake brand, loved to travel. He often sought after precious materials, exotic leathers, and fabrics to be used in his products, as well as discovering sophisticated craftmen and manufacturers to bring his designs to life. The first Prada accessories were said to have been made by Alsatian and Austrian leather artisans, Bohemian crystal-makers, and English silversmiths. The brand used the best skills and materials from across Europe to cater to the curious connoisseur. In 2011, Miuccia Prada embodied her grandfather's approach to products by launching the "Made in . . ." project. Prada collaborated with a number of artisans to manufacture specific goods highlighting each artisan's unique traditional know-how, materials, and manufacturing techniques. This collection included tartan wool kilts labelled with "Prada Made in Scotland", Chikan embrioded garments labelled "Prada Made in India", Denim produced by the Japanese company DOVA using Japanese denim labelled "Prada Made in Japan", and Alpaca Wool sweaters labelled "Prada Made in Peru" (Davis, 2010). Just like Ermenegildo

Zegna Couture's Made in Japan collection, this collection was also released in limited pieces at much higher price points, in hopes of attracting the connoisseur consumer (Blanchard, 2010).

While country of origin still plays a very important role in positioning luxury products, luxury companies also understand that their loyal customers have grown tired of "Made in Italy" or "Made in France" labels. They trust their favorite brands wholeheartedly and seek alternative experiences. In recent years, luxury brands have experimented with capsule collections highlighting the craftmanship and quality of foreign countries, as discussed in the examples above. As luxury consumers continue to shift from unsophisticated to sophisticated, they too will seek different ways to experience the craftsmanship and materials that luxury brands have to offer, redefining the relationship between COO and quality.

Takeaways
- Country of origin has long been perceived to affect consumer choice. However, it is clear that as time passes, consumer behavior changes. In the past, the application of unregulated country of origin marketing was a way to win consumers, but as the world has become more globalized and digitally connected, consumers are more agile and in tune with the luxury brands they buy into.
- The "Made in Italy" label is no longer a proxy for quality and authenticity, and consumers have become more open minded, trusting brands when they seek alternative countries in which to manufacture their products. Similarly, countries that have traditionally been frowned upon due to associations with cheap or bad quality products have risen in customers' esteem. By investing in industry development and innovation, countries that were once derided as copycats have persevered, improving on the failures of incumbents to become, in some cases, new leaders in their areas of expertise.
- Country of origin touches on other aspects of "origin", including the origin of a raw material or even the origin of knowledge. With the changing times, consumers are becoming more informed about where their luxury goods come from. As they become more sophisticated and knowledgeable, they seek the best in materials (e.g., silks, wool, fibers, exotic leathers, etc.) and artisans, always on the lookout for something unique and meaningful. Luxury brands should therefore not be bound by their connection to a heritage country (UK, Germany, Italy, or France); rather, they should embrace the best sources of materials or the most skilled artisans, incorporating them into their products to deliver a meaningful experience to their connoisseur consumers.

5 The International Spread of Luxury

We can use different indicators to evaluate a company's international exposure, depending on the point of view we adopt and the objectives of the analysis. Indeed, a company's degree of internationalization can be measured both by looking at its *upstream activities*, i.e., supply and production markets, and its *downstream activities*, i.e., sales. Focusing upstream in a company's supply chain means analyzing where the product is designed and produced. In this case, indicators of internationalization include the weight of the value of foreign purchases or processes compared to the total and investments in research and development made abroad on total investments in research and development, as well as structural measures such as the number of suppliers or controlled factories (with variable equity participation) abroad and the number of employees engaged in operations or research abroad. Considering downstream activities, the more traditional operative indicator is the percentage of sales made abroad or with international clients (e.g., in the case of hospitality). Downstream structural measures include the number of shops, dealers, and branches in other markets, the number of employees in commercial activities (e.g., store managers, sales associates) and service activities (e.g., customer care) abroad compared to the total number of employees in the same activities. However, measuring internationalization is one thing – assessing what it means for company performance is another.

Both academics and managers have raised the question of the existence of a positive relationship between international exposure and business profitability. However, studies that have attempted to answer this question have highlighted curves of different shapes, thus not giving a univocal answer. One reason for this may be that these studies frequently use only easily available indicators such as return on equity (ROE) or return on assets (ROA) as a dependent variable. These indicators fail to isolate economic performance in international markets. It would be preferable to calculate the return on foreign assets (ROFA) or return on foreign sales (ROFS). Moreover, economic performance depends not only on international exposure, but on the "quality" of a company or brand's presence abroad – its foreign market commitment (FMC) (Lojacono and Venzin, 2008).

Selling abroad does not automatically mean that a company has a strategic approach to internationalization – it may not be a strategic agenda priority. Being involved in international operations does not mean being committed to them. To assess a company's level of commitment, we need to know more about its knowledge and control of the local context, as well as its (verified) corporate organizational structure: Who holds the reins of international expansion? In addition, there is no coincidence between a company's commitment to internationalization and the methods it uses to establish an international presence; many companies have a strong international vocation and achieve brilliant results while adopting a model based on exports, without

https://doi.org/10.1515/9783110723519-005

direct investments abroad. Typically, a good understanding of a company's level of FMC includes analysis along the following three levels:

- **Commitment of resources**, which is the extent to which a firm invests in its international activities financial or knowledge resources that are difficult to bring back home
- **Previous experience**, which consists in managers' or founders' and CEOs' personal and work experience abroad – useful for the internationalization of the firm
- **Local networks**, which consist in having relationships with local partners or direct knowledge of a country prior to entry

We should remember that the world of luxury does not consist solely of large, hyper-structured groups used to sailing in international waters. There are many small and even micro companies for which the choice to move abroad creates great structural tension and increases the level of corporate risk. As an example, consider that in Italy the average size of a furniture company is six employees, seventeen for a footwear company. For small companies, the best results in competitive and economic terms often come when the CEO is personally involved in the internationalization process, traveling abroad both to monitor the evolution of markets and to activate and manage valuable relationships with local actors. The more closely a company follows a foreign territory, and the more timely first-hand information it has access to, the more it can optimize its decisions. The goal is to create second-home markets – i.e., markets in which the company moves as if it were "at home" – in the country where its HQs is located.

Finally, recent research suggests that, for companies of all sizes, a strong commitment to foreign markets must be reflected in the management structure, which should include foreigners or at least individuals with solid experience abroad (minimum five years of stay in other countries). An international organizational structure can help a company seize opportunities on a global scale and address the difficulties of crossing national borders or reviewing its presence abroad.

However, it is important to recognize that simultaneous entry or presence in as many markets as possible (*market-spreading strategy*) without consolidating a presence in some of them does not denote careful planning and allocation of resources and therefore high commitment. Instead it indicates an opportunistic, "hit-and-run" attitude. It means seizing opportunities to increase sales, even momentarily, without evaluating the strategic attractiveness of the market, which would require a different kind of commitment. The market-spreading strategy does not adapt to business models based on differentiation, the importance of services and proximity to the customer, or the adaptation of the offer system. In these cases, concentration is desirable, especially in the early stages of the internationalization process. According to the literature, concentrators and spreaders can be rigorously identified:

- **The concentrator** operates in less than ten markets, and at least 50% of sales are made in the three largest ones
- **The spreader** is present in more than ten markets, and less than 50% of sales are made in the three largest ones

Managers and entrepreneurs are undoubtedly interested in knowing if there is a proven correlation between the number of markets in a portfolio and profitability abroad. Yet one strategy is not necessarily better than the other; the best results are obtained by choosing the approach that is most consistent with the business model that a company wants to internationalize. Concentration will most likely be the best choice in the following scenarios (Katsikeas and Leonidou, 1996):

- *If fixed costs* are incremental for every export market and increase with the number of markets served (e.g., adaptation to technical norms, set of a marketing organization with reps, offices, and equipment)
- *If products compete on non-price factors*, need personal selling, and require after-sales service
- *If the company is risk-adverse* and in the early stages of internationalization
- *In case of large, stable, and mature markets* with high competition that require active marketing (advertisement, additional sales personnel, etc.)

However, research carried out by Bocconi University in collaboration with Confindustria Lombardia (with a sample of around 1,500 companies) has shown that the best operating profitability is achieved not at the two extremes (spreading and concentration) but through a mixed or "ambidextrous" approach: companies operating in more than ten markets *and* with at least 50% of sales being made in the three largest. Boffi, for example, exports 85% of its turnover abroad to around 96 markets, yet 55% of its turnover is achieved in its four main markets, the United States being the first, with a 23% weight on total sales.

Market selection is a critical choice in international business, precisely because a selection must be made. If there is no fit between a market and the company's business model, it is better not to include that market in the portfolio. The difficulty could far outweigh the benefits and the required adaptation could be so extreme as to distort the company's competitive strategy. It is one thing to adapt, quite another to revolutionize an existing model in an effort to be appreciated.

The evaluation of a company's commitment to internationalization, like other forms of analysis, must be dynamic. Companies can start with a limited commitment and then increase it over time as they acquire greater familiarity with foreign markets and develop a more articulated organization and methodology. This is consistent with what is theorized in the Uppsala Model, where companies' international growth is represented according to sequential steps both in terms of markets (the closest markets, both culturally and geographically, are approached first) and of entry methods (the initial engagement in indirect internationalization and occasional export can, over a period of years, result in the creation of production and commercial branches) (Johanson and Vahlne, 1977; Johanson and Wiedersheim-Paul, 1975). However, this model finds an exception in some cases where companies have immediately launched into distant markets while attempting to acquire direct control of them, setting up commercial branches and direct stores.

Traditionally, this discussion about the spread of activities abroad would quickly turn to celebrating the successes of luxury companies in international end markets. The recent health, social, and economic crisis has brought everyone's attention to the issue of the international deployment of supply chains and above all of the correlation between production choices and proximity to outlet markets. Here, industries other than textiles-clothing, as well as examples from the mass and premium markets, provide many useful insights into the deployment of international activities in the light of strategic motivations guided by changed contexts and renewed competitive methods. This chapter, without pretending to enter into the merits of legal aspects of internationalization, proposes a series of qualitative reflections on the theme of the international expansion choices of luxury companies. These will complement what has already been proposed in Chapter 4 on the themes of localization strategies and country of origin.

Valorizing a Competitive Edge Overseas

The international vocation of Western luxury companies is undisputed. International customers have long had an appetite for luxury from regions with historical expertise in certain kinds of production. Specialization created a virtuous circle between artisans' knowledge and a sophisticated market; a rich offer of goods encourages consumption, which in turn encourages production to continually surpass itself in order to keep up with market demands. Sophisticated markets are the ones that push supply to continuously improve standards.

These companies have therefore achieved a competitive advantage in domestic (or even regional) competitive arenas before expatriating to markets where the sources of this advantage can be exploited.

Countries that lack local producers capable of competing with new arrivals from abroad – i.e., those where a difference in the quality and diversity of the offer would be immediately apparent – are especially attractive to companies that are expanding out of sophisticated local markets and creating value for international customers. However, two factors can hinder the creation of value abroad (Alcácer, 2014):

1) *Lack of consistency between business model and market characteristics.* In the literature, this is known as the **"paradox of being consistent"**. The market is unable to understand and recognize the value associated with a business as is, necessitating the creation, from scratch, of an ad hoc formula. Better, then, to exclude a country that presents this paradox, unless a company can find a suitable niche.

2) *Vulnerability in general of companies that cross national borders* without any familiarity with the relational, cultural, social, and/or administrative context of the host country (the so called **"liability of foreignness"**). This leads companies to incur extra analysis and adaptation costs or to invest directly to fill the gaps (e.g., lack of qualified intermediaries). This is in addition to the costs of managerial coordination, which increase as structures become larger and more dispersed.

Even if it is possible to contain adaptation needs and consequent costs, companies can still run into difficulties in capturing the value generated by internationalization. For example, it could be difficult or expensive to protect intellectual property, since patents and trademarks must be filed for each country in which a company operates. The possibility of fully capturing the value generated on international markets can also be limited by an incorrect choice of local partner. This can lead to an unstable alliance that is not aligned in terms of mission, strategy, governance, culture, and/or organization (processes, structures, skills).

Kenichi Ohmae (1989) argues that for an international alliance to work, ten golden rules must be respected:
1) Alliance is a personal commitment; it is made by people
2) It will take management time; if you don't have it, don't start it
3) Mutual respect and trust are essential
4) Both partners must get something out of it; mutual benefit is essential
5) Make sure the company draws up a good legal contract and verify the potential involvement, formal or informal, of other stakeholders (state, distributors, etc.)
6) Markets, circumstances, and partners' priorities change; be flexible
7) Be aware of partners' interests, expectations, and time scale; one unhappy partner is a road to failure
8) Socialize with your partner; partnerships with friends are more stable
9) Appreciate different cultures
10) Take steps to make sure that headquarters is committed

If on the one hand relying on a local partner can help a company overcome the *liability of foreignness*, on the other hand the wrong choice of ally can result in an entry market failure. As we saw in Chapter 2, several brands have been forced to leave the Indian market and re-enter with a different partner before establishing a presence in the country. Tiffany & Co., for example, seems to have finally managed to find the right strategy for India by partnering with Reliance Group in 2019.

A thorough market selection process should not focus on chasing promising markets for growth rates or following adventurous competitors. Neglecting the difficulties of value creation and value capture can lead to poor results from the point of view of revenues and margins, and can even force a company to exit a market. Setting up a correct assessment of foreign markets means asking two important questions: Why is this market attractive? And is it within my reach, or are there internal or external factors limiting what I can achieve?

Assessing Market Attractiveness

Market attractiveness refers to concrete benefits offered by a foreign market. Evaluating market attractiveness involves exploring the opportunities open to a company that is moving across boundaries. The analysis can be set up to evaluate a single market taken on its own without any comparison, or it can put several markets under observation simultaneously. Both formats involve the systematic collection of quantitative and qualitative information, skimming to identify a short list of interesting markets for the company.

As a first step, it is a good idea to establish an outlook on the cultural (e.g., consumer attitudes, core values of the society, religious affiliation), demographic (e.g., urbanization, age structure, sociodemographic trends, education), political (e.g., political system, political stability, government efficiency, corruption), legal (e.g., openness to foreign investment, IP protection), economic (e.g., GDP and GDP per capita, income structure, inflation rate, exchange rate, capital markets), and infrastructural conditions (e.g., logistics, internet access, retail landscape) of the target country. A rich source of macro data for all countries in the world is the International Futures (IFs) forecasts, which are produced in cooperation with the Strategic Foresight Project of the Atlantic Council and the US National Intelligence Council. IFs forecasts are accessible via Google's Public Data Explorer and include forecasts for agriculture, domestic government, economy, education, energy, environment, health, infrastructure, international politics, population, social/human needs, and transportation. Detailed country reports are also available from The Economist Intelligence Unit and Passport Euromonitor International.

A valid aid in understanding the business and institutional environment of a target country, especially in case of foreign direct investments (FDIs) is the analysis carried out every year by the World Bank, which leads 190 world economies to package a well-known indicator, the Ease of Doing Business (EoDB) rankings. The EoDB captures ten important dimensions (each consisting of several indicators) of the regulatory environment affecting firms, giving equal weight to each topic. It provides quantitative indicators on regulations for starting a business, dealing with construction permits, getting electricity, registering property, getting credit, protecting minority investors, paying taxes, trading across borders, enforcing contracts, and resolving insolvency. All 190 economies are ranked based on their EoDB: a high ranking means the regulatory environment is more conducive to starting and operating a local firm. The most recent rankings, benchmarked to May 1, 2019 (issued in 2020), reported New Zealand, Singapore, Hong Kong, Denmark, and Republic of Korea as the top five economies in terms of EoDB. France is positioned 32nd and Italy 58th.

The Hofstede Insights, meanwhile, is an important source of information regarding the cultural specificities of the target country and the degree of dissimilarity with respect to the country of origin. Geert Hofstede was an authoritative researcher in the field of cultural differences between countries and developed a rigorous methodology to measure them in collaboration with IBM between 1967 and 1973. This included a large database of IBM employee value scores covering more than 70 countries. The original framework of Hofstede's research was based on four key dimensions: power distance, individualism vs. collectivism, masculinity vs. femininity, and an uncertainty avoidance index. Subsequently, two further dimensions related to long-term vs. short-term orientation and indulgence vs. restraint were added. By accessing the Hofstede Insights website, it is possible to study the culture of a country through the lens of Hofstede's "6-D Model", which provides a comparative overview of the cultural drivers for the countries in the database.

Hofstede believed that the culture of a country could not be transformed, and that it was necessary to understand and respect it; no thought is more relevant in the delicate historical moment that the world of luxury is experiencing. International expansion strategies must therefore pass through a profound analysis of the cultural and social specificities of the host country, even if the elites who buy luxury products are westernized and follow the local orientation less in this type of purchase. This is the first step in crafting adequate adaptation strategies. As mentioned on several occasions in this book, companies' ability to be agile in adapting to the space-time context by enhancing their skills is a primary source of resilience.

This agility is also expressed in the search for the best compromise between global consistency and local relevance. Making continuous adjustments to account for the polarized and divergent needs of the market can be counter-productive when brand identity must be both ubiquitous and consistent. In recent years, jewelry brands have managed this tension between global and local by tailoring store interiors to account for local context or by launching capsules for special events (e.g., the exclusive Bulgari Serpenti Forever capsule collection for Ramadan).

Cartier has proven to be exemplary in achieving a good balance between the opposing needs to preserve brand specificity and satisfy the increasingly pressing demands of international boutiques. This has required a great deal of organizational effort, with the goal of empowering individual markets. Launch plans, even sketches of novelties, are shared in advance to collect feedback and identify needs relevant to specific contexts. There are regular product variants for the Middle East, for Chinese New Year (like the Ballon Bleu watch with a red dial), and special sizes and execution for Japan (like a mini Tank Américaine). Furthermore, Cartier ensures local exclusivity for limited-edition launches designed by aggregating boutiques on the basis of a criterion of "distribution relevance" with respect to the product and the client targets. In 2019, Cartier launched Les Galaxies in less than ten boutiques around the globe, achieving an incredible success.

The sources mentioned above are useful for the multi-dimensional perspective they provide on the current and prospective situation of a given country. However, they remain general tools, without the focus that would allow them to account for the objectives of a company's growth strategy abroad on the one hand and its industry and business model on the other. A thorough evaluation of market attractiveness must therefore build on these general indicators by assessing factors relevant to the industry, company, and specific goals of international expansion. Figure 5.1 depicts this logic flow of valuation, moving from a broad country level to the industry level of analysis to understand the fit between the host market (or markets) and the firm's business model. The company's strategic goals for its international foray drive the selection of data and information for evaluation and dictate the evaluation criteria.

1. Strategic Goals   2. Country-level Analysis

MARKET ATTRACTIVENESS EVALUATION

4. Firm Fit   3. Industry Fit

Figure 5.1: Market Selection: The Four Levels of Market Attractiveness Evaluation.
Source: Compiled by authors.

A correct approach to the analysis of the attractiveness of the target market must be based on a deep understanding of the reasons why a company is considering entering the foreign market and international expansion in general. First, the assessment depends on the company's objectives in going abroad, both upstream and downstream. Indeed, a company may need to reduce production costs in order to be more competitive in international markets. In this case, foreign markets are valued on the basis of localization advantages which have to do, for example, with the cost of labor. In the past, this has prompted some companies to implement arbitrage policies (i.e., shifting a country's comparative advantage to other markets) based on aggressive choices to relocate production to low-cost countries (e.g., Philippines, China, Vietnam, Cambodia, Bangladesh). However, as we will see, while this motivation has certainly been dominant in markets characterized by price-based competition, it does not characterize the upstream internationalization choices of luxury companies.

Another important motivation, typical of the B2B world, is the desire to follow the expansion of a company's customers into a new market. In this case, the decision to expand internationally is a necessary condition for survival: clients that are companies with a global presence want to have suppliers with the same market scope. The supplier that remains on a local scale risks being replaced by other suppliers not only abroad, but also in the domestic market. Here, therefore, the choice of market is almost obligatory, leaving the company only to consider logistical and cost factors in its evaluation of the city or specific area in which it will locate its activities (production or commercial). For example, the leading Italian B2B cosmetics company Intercos took its first steps outside Italy to be closer to its most important customer – American Estée Lauder Companies (ELC). Dario Ferrari, the founder of Intercos, and Leonard Lauder, ELC chairman emeritus since 1999, believed that geographical proximity would be a source of continuous innovation and a shorter time to market, a benefit to both companies and justification for Intercos to set up its first factory in the United States. The joint venture between Intercos and ELC was dissolved in 1991, but the company still has some factories in operation in the US to better serve its American clients. Today, Intercos has net sales of €750 million (66% make-up, 19% hair and body, 15% skincare) and more than 550 international customers (50% established brands, 31% emerging brands, 19% retailers). The split of turnover is 50% Europe, Middle East, and Africa (collectively EMEA); 33% Americas; and 17% Asia.

The last two strategic objectives are certainly more important for luxury companies and therefore deserve an in-depth study: 1) the search for opportunities for growth in turnover, the so-called "market-seeking" approach; 2) the identification of knowledge platforms at an international level that can fill a need for valuable resources and skills, i.e., a "resource-seeking" attitude.[1]

Market-Seeking Imperative

When pursuing a market-seeking approach, a company will look for growth opportunities in markets that are interesting because of their current size or the growth rate of purchases of identified luxury categories. Table 5.1, for example, shows the ranking of the top 30 countries by value of sales of luxury goods (Passport, Euromonitor International 2020). China's importance in the global scenario immediately emerges, both in terms of the current size of the Chinese market and in terms of consistent growth, even in 2020, a year of many contractions, some of them significant.

Another important dimension for assessing the importance of a specific market for a luxury company is the number of high-net-worth individuals (UHNWIs) in the country, here defined as persons with assets of at least US$1 million in current

Table 5.1: Retail Value (RV) of Luxury Goods from 2015 to 2020, Growth Rate and CAGR, Number of Billionaires, Number of High Net Worth Individuals (HNWI), Population and Retail Value (RV) per Capita in 30 Countries.

Countries	RV 2015	RV 2016	RV 2017	RV 2018	RV 2019	Δ19vs15	RV 2020	Δ20vs15	CAGR 2015–20	No. HNWI .000	No. Billionaires .000	Population .000	RV per capita .000
China	1,69,737	1,93,722	2,22,581	2,52,963	2,86,597	69%	2,84,213	67%	9%	1,717	142	13,95,380	0.204
USA	1,79,948	1,83,470	1,86,075	1,98,773	2,04,270	14%	1,68,862	-6%	-1%	21,580	358	3,28,240	0.514
Germany	59,159	63,009	63,848	61,632	68,693	16%	59,318	0%	0%	2,241	66	83,019	0.715
United Kingdom	48,375	56,874	60,228	58,693	62,566	29%	54,248	12%	2%	2,641	24	66,647	0.814
Japan	45,919	45,589	47,300	48,979	50,298	10%	41,468	-10%	-2%	3,738	15	1,26,167	0.329
France	40,757	41,090	41,683	41,199	44,172	8%	35,346	-13%	-2%	2,788	28	64,822	0.545
Italy	29,478	31,895	32,685	32,589	34,039	15%	27,279	-7%	-1%	1,500	15	60,360	0.452
South Korea	20,300	21,318	22,475	23,339	24,475	21%	24,313	20%	3%	963	9	51,709	0.470
Canada	15,372	16,867	18,069	18,856	19,598	27%	16,061	4%	1%	1,634	21	37,589	0.427
Spain	16,617	18,548	19,711	20,324	20,953	26%	15,300	-8%	-1%	570	24	46,937	0.326
Taiwan	10,722	11,484	11,774	12,590	13,300	24%	12,923	21%	3%	450	13	23,589	0.548
Russia	11,953	12,695	11,524	13,181	14,405	21%	12,098	1%	0%	84	43	1,44,426	0.084
Switzerland	14,154	13,949	14,415	14,260	15,186	7%	11,907	-16%	-3%	762	19	8,545	1.394

Australia	10,975	12,190	12,027	12,106	12,980	18%	11,674	6%	1%	1,526	12	25,358	0.460
Netherlands	8,506	8,351	8,708	9,843	11,318	33%	10,540	24%	4%	625	9	17,282	0.610
United Arab Emirates	15,644	13,565	12,556	12,264	12,525	-20%	8,706	-44%	-9%	61	4	9,437	0.923
Hong Kong, China	14,658	13,621	14,053	14,919	12,421	-15%	7,333	-50%	-11%	348	39	7,507	0.977
Thailand	7,094	7,554	7,903	8,506	8,745	23%	6,932	-2%	0%	63	10	69,626	0.100
Singapore	8,254	8,326	9,007	8,931	9,271	12%	6,781	-18%	-3%	229	12	5,704	1.189
Sweden	4,540	5,145	5,299	5,327	6,414	41%	6,371	40%	6%	359	13	10,230	0.623
India	5,658	5,756	6,582	7,436	7,507	33%	6,110	8%	1%	228	39	13,26,619	0.005
Mexico	5,385	6,570	7,243	7,785	8,191	52%	6,040	12%	2%	158	9	1,25,929	0.048
Turkey	5,196	5,823	5,994	5,757	5,617	8%	5,789	11%	2%	127	9	82,004	0.071
Philippines	4,594	4,929	5,402	5,753	6,327	38%	5,485	19%	3%	58	9	1,08,117	0.051
Poland	3,112	3,949	4,553	5,096	5,770	85%	5,072	63%	8%	41	6	38,411	0.132
Brazil	5,890	5,004	4,635	5,219	5,649	-4%	5,006	-15%	-3%	174	11	2,11,070	0.024
Malaysia	3,794	4,387	4,774	5,147	4,486	18%	4,052	7%	1%	43	9	32,523	0.125
South Africa	3,938	4,103	3,583	3,452	3,565	-9%	3,229	-18%	-3%	61	4	58,558	0.055
Indonesia	2,494	2,731	3,009	3,346	3,503	40%	1,773	-29%	-6%	116	9	2,70,626	0.007
Romania	1,084	1,265	1,312	1,352	1,527	41%	1,224	13%	2%	19	2	19,415	0.063

Source: Compiled by authors based on Passport, Euromonitor International and Forbes 2020 World's Billionaires List.

exchange rate terms. Along this dimension, the undisputed importance of the United States emerges, followed at a great distance by Japan. The value of per capita sales of luxury goods can also be included in the analysis of a country's UHNWIs, and here Switzerland and Singapore share the first position.

Considering a market's attitude to luxury in general can be a first step in the evaluation process, before entering into the merits of the specific categories of interest. From there, a detailed analysis can reveal important distinctions between countries. As an example, restricting the field to beauty, it is interesting to note that in Italy and France, the weight of luxury beauty on the total sales of beauty and personal care reaches 20%, a percentage weight higher than US/China, even though the latter countries' markets have higher retail.

It is not easy to find good and ready data on all luxury products and services. We therefore need to start with the world of luxury in general and then find proxies that allow the international business developer to understand if there are elements of strategic importance in the target market. Consider eyewear, where through Passport it's possible to obtain a global retail estimate. The data reveals that the United States excels in this industry, but is losing ground, while China (second in the ranking), Mexico, Netherlands, and Turkey are the markets that record the most interesting growth rates. Further important dimensions in this area (which includes not only sunglasses, but also glasses and contact lenses), such as the spread of eye-related diseases (e.g., myopia) and the trends of the fashion industry (sunglasses are considered an accessory that follows the rhythms and trends of fashion), can also be deduced. However, this tells us nothing about high-end eyewear. To understand this segment, we need to integrate the quantitative overview with other information such as an accurate mapping of competitors onto the market, their strategies, and their economic and competitive performances. For example, even a superficial survey shows how the eyewear industry is fragmented and local, with different companies moving from one country to another. The only brand that is found in almost all markets is Ray-Ban.

The best way to understand the attractiveness of a new market to a company in an industry, like eyewear, where many factors are in play, is through qualitative observation. A prolonged presence as an observer in a target market allows a company to understand its habits, lifestyles, and commercial methods. The aim is to collect valuable, qualitative information that allows a company not only to decide whether to enter the market, but also how this entry must be realized (entry mode and adaptation strategy).

When retail value data is not available or further quantitative elements are required to support a company's valuation of a target market, commercial flows can be analyzed to provide a better idea of its attractiveness. The import trends for a good into a country is a valid proxy for growing interest in a specific category, but above all for the opening of the market toward foreign production. In this case, UN Comtrade, a free-access database of detailed global trade data, is very helpful. UN

Comtrade is a repository of official international trade statistics and relevant analytical tables. Using the customs code (HS classification) for a product or product type, it is possible to download the data of interest, namely its trade value and quantity. Furthermore, it is possible to trace a country's partners. Table 5.2 illustrates a possible structure for analyzing import flows, starting from 2002, for the furniture industry. The table shows the twenty main furniture-importing countries alongside the weight on world imports and the CAGR (i.e., the average annual growth in the reference period) for each in three different time intervals. Analyzing the average CAGR for a particular industry allows a company to immediately detect those countries that are above the average and therefore the most interesting, at least at first glance.

Still, this quantitative information is not sufficient to give us a full understanding of the market's potential for a luxury company. It must be accompanied by a sophisticated interpretation based on a deep knowledge of the industry. What the table shows us are overall values that do not discriminate, for example, by price range. A first step toward greater awareness of the market's competitive logic would involve:

1) The identification of the main partner countries that export to a specific market in a product category
2) The weight of competing companies' exports to that country

Information related to the latter point is the most difficult to obtain; even listed companies typically publish the split of turnover by macro-area and not by individual countries.

As an example of what is involved in such a detailed analysis, let us examine the place of Italian furniture companies in the US market. Half of the top twenty countries from which the United States imports furniture products are characterized by competitive cost approaches, with China, Mexico, and Vietnam in first place. Vietnam saw an average annual increase of 30% from 2002 to 2019 and of 50% for the period of 2002 to 2009 alone. Italy is in fifth place, immediately after Canada, but registers average annual decreases of 1% in the American market, which grows by 6% every year. Suffice it to say that the weight of the import of upholstered furniture (sofas and armchairs) to the United States from Italy went from 47% in 2002 to 6% in 15 years. From this we can infer that economies like Italy's are not made for today's price competition because they are unable to achieve cost advantages similar to those of other world economies.

In the past, large Italian furniture companies managed to achieve high volumes in the United States by leveraging consolidated relationships with large retailers. Today this market has been invaded by low-cost competitors; furniture products allow for standardization, which means that the industry is open to the advantages of economies of scale. This is why a country like Italy must preserve the ability to leverage the advantage of differentiation and not compete on volume, where the game is now definitively lost.

Table 5.2: Import of furniture of top 20 Countries by Trade Value, Market Share, and CAGR (2002, 2009, 2017, 2018, 2019).

Country	Trade Value 2002	Market Share	Trade Value 2009	Market Share	Trade Value 2017	Market Share	Trade Value 2018	Market Share	Trade Value 2019	Market Share	CAGR 2002–2009	CAGR 2009–2019	CAGR 2002–2019
USA	28,36,82,54,757	33%	31,68,22,72,213	23%	65,69,81,51,241	30%	70,69,01,69,326	30%	65,66,17,55,658	29%	1%	7%	5%
Germany	8,07,02,39,000	9%	13,87,70,25,253	10%	18,61,50,57,132	9%	19,54,85,70,943	8%	19,01,15,35,297	8%	7%	3%	5%
United Kingdom	5,68,17,27,998	7%	8,25,85,44,341	6%	11,17,74,69,550	5%	11,27,23,57,572	5%	11,43,61,98,248	5%	5%	3%	4%
France	4,64,33,25,945	5%	9,03,26,21,601	7%	10,56,16,93,823	5%	11,51,12,12,222	5%	11,41,78,83,351	5%	9%	2%	5%
Canada	3,62,14,53,882	4%	5,75,61,02,746	4%	7,65,84,23,370	4%	8,82,80,44,298	4%	8,71,17,03,553	4%	6%	4%	5%
Japan	4,12,35,85,516	5%	5,37,93,82,073	4%	8,77,85,71,977	4%	7,98,77,09,056	3%	8,17,73,11,466	4%	3%	4%	4%
Netherlands	2,20,93,74,154	3%	3,73,99,73,294	3%	6,08,42,00,727	3%	6,84,23,00,873	3%	7,05,07,71,084	3%	7%	6%	7%
Australia	1,00,93,27,742	1%	2,70,31,00,410	2%	4,39,15,76,665	2%	4,90,71,56,631	2%	4,61,35,19,123	2%	13%	5%	9%
Spain	1,49,18,70,312	2%	3,55,03,79,561	3%	4,29,77,30,218	2%	4,67,74,14,799	2%	4,50,65,29,960	2%	11%	2%	7%
Switzerland	1,92,63,92,449	2%	3,32,21,69,589	2%	4,04,01,19,514	2%	4,26,19,29,122	2%	4,10,73,81,062	2%	7%	2%	5%
Poland	54,65,43,000	1%	1,60,58,39,839	1%	3,11,35,90,599	1%	3,69,53,19,892	2%	3,91,31,83,554	2%	14%	8%	12%
Belgium	2,37,10,61,322	3%	3,89,67,02,025	3%	3,57,20,53,293	2%	3,72,14,84,781	2%	3,80,11,02,391	2%	6%	0%	3%
Italy	1,39,05,40,601	2%	3,03,89,49,337	2%	3,67,55,19,350	2%	3,98,64,60,584	2%	3,74,45,76,987	2%	10%	2%	6%
Austria	1,79,50,11,065	2%	3,03,57,16,209	2%	3,22,41,88,869	1%	3,49,34,59,778	1%	3,56,39,69,226	2%	7%	1%	4%
Mexico	1,37,88,39,017	2%	1,53,87,53,465	1%	3,58,25,88,661	2%	3,75,05,52,259	2%	3,54,62,24,864	2%	1%	8%	6%
Czechia	51,23,23,864	1%	1,47,06,74,037	1%	3,32,06,05,499	2%	3,56,52,13,111	2%	3,49,90,50,220	2%	14%	8%	12%

Rep. of Korea	52,54,06,995	1%	1,33,16,03,426	1%	2,99,84,91,274	1%	3,17,42,82,640	1%	3,31,49,79,234	1%	12%	9%	11%
China	36,93,50,293	0%	1,73,80,89,612	1%	3,49,76,56,978	2%	3,75,01,99,994	2%	3,30,36,69,656	2%	21%	6%	14%
Sweden	1,34,49,62,779	2%	2,19,02,30,200	2%	3,09,11,76,808	1%	3,25,14,81,150	1%	3,12,56,31,166	1%	6%	3%	5%
Norway	97,95,05,174	1%	1,98,03,75,176	1%	2,51,89,53,296	1%	2,51,52,15,179	1%	2,45,96,01,183	1%	9%	2%	6%
Slovakia	23,88,32,570	0%	80,04,25,635	1%	1,84,52,77,586	1%	2,21,90,47,414	1%	2,34,96,63,657	1%	16%	10%	14%
World	**85,05,55,49,268**	**100%**	**1,36,44,85,20,334**	**100%**	**2,18,02,85,20,873**	**100%**	**2,31,96,36,94,429**	**100%**	**2,23,78,20,09,445**	**100%**	**6%**	**5%**	**6%**

Source: Compiled by authors based on UN Comtrade Database, HS Classification, Codes: 9401; 9403; 9404; 9405 – http://comtrade.un.org/db.

However, even after an Italian furniture company has identified a strategy that will allow it to compete in today's American market, successfully expanding into this market requires adequate knowledge of its structural characteristics. In the United States, architects and interior designers have significant influence on the purchasing process for furniture products, selecting standard items (wardrobes, kitchens, bathrooms) in the context of large turnkey projects. A furniture company therefore interfaces not with shops, but with multiple interlocutors, from the developer, to the general contractor, to the large international architecture firm, to the procurement company. Poltrona Frau, for example, started as a residential business for home furnishings and has consolidated in this way on the Italian market. But it has two business units dedicated to turnkey projects: Custom Interiors and Interiors in Motion were born in the 1980s. These businesses, though small at first, were the driving force for the company's expansion into the United States and later Asia, with the opening of the business units' first commercial branches between the 1990s and the beginning of the new millennium (Lojacono and Carcano, 2018).

Similar considerations are evident in other typical made-in-Italy industries such as footwear. By analyzing the export flows of the footwear industry, we can see that low-cost countries are the world leaders in terms of the value of sales abroad. However, Italy ranks first among European countries, an excellent signal of the Italian competitive advantage.[2] Looking at the CAGR, China appears to have grown a lot in the past, but recently a substitution effect is emerging within Asian countries, and Vietnam is growing more than China.

At the same time, within the European Union, Italy is undergoing strong pressure in terms of competition from certain countries such as Germany, France, Spain, and Portugal. The rules of the game are therefore changing. When interviewed, entrepreneurs and managers mention, on the one hand, strong Asian competition for volume productions and, on the other, increased competitive pressures within Europe itself. Italian footwear companies are particularly worried about this latter issue, as it concerns product types and price ranges that are more directly competitive with their own. For Italian companies pursuing internationalization – both upstream and downstream – the logic of cost savings is weak in a new competitive scenario where there are countries that have a comparative advantage. In other words, the challenge for Italy is no longer to compete in terms of volume, but to develop and maintain quality, niche strategy, differentiation, and uniqueness: these are the strengths that Italy can leverage in the new global panorama. Meeting this challenge involves identifying places where the competitive advantage afforded by this strategy will be significant; Italian companies have become market seeking in their approach to expansions abroad.

Figure 5.2 shows further evidence of Italy's progress in terms of moving closer to a strategy based on quality and not on volume. The average price of footwear rose significantly from 2000 to 2019, especially in exports. The best way forward for Italian footwear companies, which are often small, is to operate within a strategic cluster linked to differentiation and uniqueness, growing via expansion into new markets. This is a phenomenon that can also be observed in other Italian luxury-related industries.

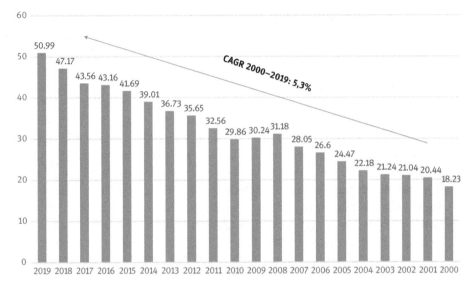

Figure 5.2: Trend of the Average Price Related to the Export of Italian Footwear (in Euros). Source: Compiled by authors based on ISTAT; Confindustria Moda for Assocalzaturifici.

Moving from the macro-economic to the corporate level allows us to draw attention to the other two elements of the scheme proposed in Figure 5.1. The detailed analysis of the target country must consider evaluation criteria inherent to:
1) The structural characteristics and typical dynamics of the industry to which a company belongs
2) The specific business model of the company

A brand like Poltrona Frau is not only interested in knowing how many sofas are sold in the United States or China, just as a brand like Boffi, a specialist in high-end kitchen design, cannot base its expansion decisions, for example, in India, on the number of kitchens sold in the country. In addition to using data on the economic stratification of the population (such as those reported in Table 5.1), it is necessary to have qualitative information about the local design culture, among other qualities that affect local tastes and preferences. A customer is unlikely to recognize the value of a kitchen priced at a minimum of €30,000 if he or she does not see the appeal of its design beyond the manufacturing quality. Other important information for furniture companies could concern real estate development in the country, trends in the hospitality industry and the expansion plans of luxury hotel chains, and the status of turnkey projects. Likewise, the existence of an adequate distribution structure or valid commercial partners are essential if a company is to establish a recognizable presence in a new market.

Consider the Italian beauty brand Davines, which grounds its identity in quality, Italian heritage, scientific innovation, and environmental friendliness. The company, today present in 90 countries, began its international expansion in 1994. Its portfolio includes professional hair-coloring products, hair and scalp care, styling products, and skin care under the Comfort Zone brand. Created in Parma in 1983, Davines achieved total sales of €163 million (around €350 million in retail value) in 2019 and obtained B-Corp certification in 2016. A company like Davines is not simply interested in cosmetic market trends, but in very specific dimensions within its business models: the relevance of the professional niche in the haircare world, attitudes toward the values inherent in all aspects of corporate social responsibility (not only the environmental sphere), and the propensity of local customers to buy foreign products, especially in markets that boast a cosmetic tradition and strong national brands (Lojacono and Misani, 2017).

Once a company has collected all the data that it considers important, it must develop a methodology or analysis criteria to enhance them effectively. As an example, we can look at the Italian coffee company Illy,[3] which has for years carried out some interesting analyses to evaluate its current positioning abroad and growth opportunities along two tracks: assessment maps and scoring.

Elaboration of two-dimensional synthesis maps. A first matrix (Figure 5.3) relates the economic trend (real GDP CAGR over a certain period of time) with the dummy of the Illy share (weight of Illy's exports on the total Italian export of coffee for a specific country). In the four quadrants, Illy then measures the presence bubble in the country in relation to the tons of coffee sold as a portion of the company total. This type of map allows us to verify what kind of presence the company has in mature and stagnant economies vs. more dynamic or emerging economies, as well as gauging where new markets might be discovered.

A second map (Figure 5.4) maintains the Illy share, but replaces economic trends with the weight of Italian professional coffee-machine imports on a country's total coffee and machines imports.

This map shows that there are countries with a different level of maturity: 1) consolidated markets (high import and high Illy share), 2) learning markets (low import and variable Illy share, indicating that there are still market opportunities to explore), and 3) new focus countries (high imports from Italy but low Illy share). Illy needs a different strategic approach for each of these markets. Cluster 2, for example, requires substantial investments to move those countries' culture and experience of coffee toward the Italian model on which Illy's products are based; China is included in this cluster.

Scoring System. To process the information collected in a company's initial analyses, it is possible to assign a score, for example from one to five, to some variables of attractiveness. This score is then weighted based on the strategic relevance of each variable to the target market. The final average of these weighted scores is the score for the

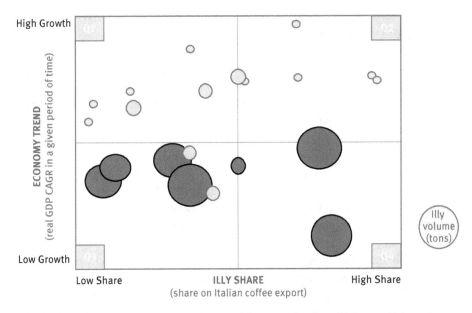

Figure 5.3: Economic Trend and Share on Total Italian Export of Coffee with Dummy Values.
Source: Compiled by authors.

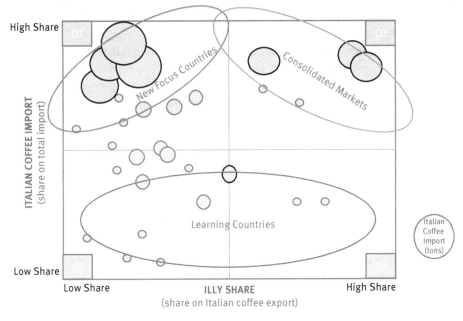

Figure 5.4: Italian Coffee Import and Illy Share on Italian Coffee Export with Dummy Values.
Source: Compiled by authors.

market. Illy, for example, considers market size (size of the retail market for roasted and ground coffee in volume in tons, weight 25%), market growth (roasted and ground coffee market CAGR in volume over the past three years, weight 25%), market profitability (average retail market price of roasted and ground coffee in euro/kg, weight 30%), and coffee consumption (average retail market for roasted and ground coffee in kg/inhabitant, weight 20%). For each of the four dimensions, Illy assigns a score from 1 to 5. When weighted, combined, and averaged, these scores provide an overall evaluation of the target market.

This scoring system can become even more sophisticated by employing methodologies such as analytical hierarchic process (AHP), a technique for making complex decisions based on the explicit weighting of criteria and the pair-wise comparison of alternatives (Saaty, 2013). AHP provides a framework for structuring a decision problem, representing and quantifying its elements, relating those elements to overall goals, and evaluating alternative solutions. It decomposes a problem into a hierarchy of more easily understood sub-problems. The elements of the hierarchy can relate to any aspect of the problem – tangible or intangible, carefully measured or roughly estimated, well or poorly understood. The decision makers evaluate its various elements by comparing them to each other two at a time (pairwise comparisons). In making the comparisons, the decision makers can use concrete data about the elements, but they typically rely on their judgments about the elements' relative meaning and importance. The AHP converts these evaluations to numerical values that can be processed and compared over the entire range of a problem. Finally, numerical priorities are calculated for each of the alternatives.

The AHP allows companies facing complex decision-making processes to deconstruct a problem into different hierarchical levels. The input of several stakeholders, who actively contribute to identify and weigh the selection criteria and analyze the data collected, make it possible to come to a consolidated decision. As a result, all the actors involved share the final choice and commit to the execution phase.

As we can see, the evaluation process is anything but random; it requires the development of a rigorous methodology, the criteria of which change from company to company. An important part of the process is the collection of qualitative and quantitative information, which are integrated into an overall picture, assigning great importance to knowledge that can be acquired directly in the field. Spending time in a prospective market area to understand its dynamics is the best investment that a company can make, allowing it to evaluate entry opportunities as well as design the most appropriate mode of presence.

Resource-Seeking Imperative

Let's now shift our perspective and consider a company with a primary goal of filling a skills gap to feed the innovation processes. In addition to geographical expansion, meeting this goal could lead to entering a new business (new product and/or new customer segment). In this case, assessing a market's attractiveness does not mean looking for indicators of its size and growth, but rather identifying important learning sources. These can be research centers of international reputation and/or an ecosystem that supports success in a particular industry. Depending on a company's needs and interests, useful information might have to do with the education system, the quality of human capital, the presence of production districts, investments in research and development, the number of start-ups, and the ability of the country system to dictate macro-trends at an international level in certain industries, among other factors.

To better understand how this goal might affect a company's decision to expand internationally, we can take the example of Shiseido. Founded in 1872, as of 2019, this Japanese beauty multinational had an annual turnover of ¥1,131.5 billion (year-over-year growth in 2019 was 3.4%). In 1980, Shiseido's strategic plan envisaged the expansion of the offer to perfumes, an industry in which Japan had neither production history nor a developed market (at the time, fragrances in the country accounted for less than 1% of the total value of cosmetics sales). Shiseido therefore looked to France, a country with a long perfume history and sophisticated market, to develop a line of perfumes adapted to international standards. After an initial attempt to gain expertise that could be transferred to production centers in Japan, Shiseido changed tactics. Instead of looking for a joint venture with a local company, it made direct investments in France, opening a branch in Paris and a factory in Gien (a town in Loiret, south of Paris), in the heart of the industrial perfume district. This factory which was then also used for the production of perfumes for the Japanese market, after adequate adaptation. To have daily contact with the sophisticated French consumer, a key source of learning, Shiseido acquired two Parisian beauty salons, Carita and Alexandre Zouari, and in 1992 it opened Les Salons du Palais Royal.[4] The weight of the perfume business, developed in collaboration with famous designers, is now equal to 10% of the group's total turnover.

Another example of internationalization driven by the search for learning opportunities is that of Intercos, a company that today boasts 15 global industrial operations production sites (7 in Europe, 5 in Asia, 3 in the United States); 15 commercial offices (7 in Europe, 4 in Asia, 4 in the United States), which are also responsible for strategic marketing activities; and 11 research and development centers (5 in Europe, 3 in Asia, 3 in the United States). The idea of having production and research in other countries was first of all a consequence of the evolution of the company's business model. CEO Dario Ferrari's intuition was to abandon the role of original equipment manufacturer (OEM) before the advance of low-cost countries could change the purchasing logic of Intercos's international customers. Instead, the company has focused on investing heavily in research and development to develop innovative formulations. Its offer includes not only powders (blushes, face powders, and other cosmetics, and the first product category for which cosmetic multinationals outsourced production) or creams, but a service that keeps its clients on the cutting edge of innovation. Today, 17% of Intercos's workforce is employed in research-related activities, and the company invests 8% of turnover every year in this function. This effort has made it possible to create more than new 1,300 formulations. While these are passed on to its customers, Intercos holds the patents. There are also exceptions, where innovation originates from a joint effort with the customer, who is then willing to pay a fee to acquire exclusivity. The fact that Intercos maintains ownership of its formulas means that it can use them in multiple projects.

By becoming an engine of innovation, Intercos has begun to displace not only production, but also the "thinking heart" of the company in key markets, from France to China and Korea. This is possible because the company has included presence in these markets, at all levels of activity, in its expansion. Figure 5.5 describes the geographical and category expansion of Intercos since its foundation in 1972.

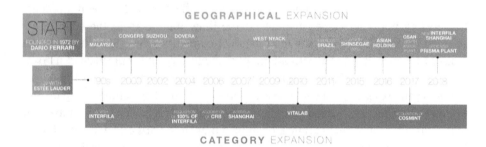

Figure 5.5: Geographical and Category Expansion of Intercos.
Source: Intercos Corporate Presentation.

Thanks to this path of internationalization, Intercos is today an insider in local markets, able to acquire the first-hand knowledge it needs to fulfill real beauty needs and to support international clients (brands) in their international expansion strategies. Essential to its status as an innovator, it is well positioned to scout, anticipate, and even drive trends in fashion and cosmetics (especially with reference to the influential Asian market).

Identifying Factors that Can Reduce Market Attractiveness

To conduct a complete assessment of the attractiveness of foreign markets, it is not enough to acquire information and develop a methodology to identify the potential for dimensional development and learning opportunities in the target market. Limitations must also be considered – obstacles that may prevent a company from fully grasping international opportunities. These obstacles may be internal or external. Internal barriers include factors like a lack of adequate skills necessary to move internationally, time constraints on top management, a lack of financial resources, or other hurdles to planning for and adapting to entry in the target market. External barriers might include differences in payment systems, regulations, exchange rates, customs policies, geographical distance (which causes increased logistical costs as well as long delivery times and the risk of a stock outage), issues with the distribution structure, or customs and traditions in force in the target country.

In many countries, import duties and other regulations (non-tariff barriers) aim at protecting local industries. As a consequence, they become difficult to enter or to develop a profitable business in. India or Brazil, despite their large populations and large bases of HNWIs, have high import duties and remain "small" markets for international luxury brands. History has shown that the global trend is to gradually reduce these barriers and expand free zones, with occasional exceptions such as the recent trade war between the US and China.

Regulation and non-tariff barriers mostly exist for cosmetics, food, and alcohols, but they also affect other categories, including precious metals and endangered species. New regulations on materials can change the rules of the game for entire categories – for example, the State of California's decision to ban all exotic skins. In some countries, there are also relevant commercial regulations (e.g., on licenses) and limitations that force foreign companies to find local partners in order to operate. Conversely, countries that do not have strong regulations (defined in the academic literature as "*institutional voids*") linked to intellectual property or distribution are dangerous because a brand can be quickly counterfeited, creating confusion for consumers who desire to buy genuine products.

In luxury, specificities related to wealth and culture might represent an insurmountable obstacle for international brands. For "wearable luxury", there are key cultural differences between nations and cultures. In Europe, Latin countries value fashion and "what you wear"; Scandinavians are more interested in luxury "at home". Depending on the product category, the potential of different countries can vary significantly, even with the same wealth per capita. This doesn't mean that the situation is static:

Things can change. In 1970, [a] Moët Hennessy market survey in Japan concluded: "yes for Brandy, no for Champagne". Fifty years later, Brandy has become very small and Champagne second worldwide. The reason is the emancipation of working women, who became financially independent, and prefer to drink Champagne with their friends than sake or whisky. Reversely, the new tax scheme on corporate expenses discouraged businessmen to invite their partners in bars and treat them with Brandy or whisky.

(Cyrille Vigneron, President and CEO of Cartier, personal communication)

Australia is another interesting case. It was for a long time a remote market where people cared little for luxury. The arrival of new migrants from Asia changed the dynamics, making this market one of the most vibrant in Asia Pacific.

Pankaj Ghemawat (2001) has summarized all these barriers using the acronym CAGE, which stands for cultural, administrative, geographic, economical. The greater the CAGE distance between the country of origin and the target country – the more different they are along those four dimensions – the greater the difficulties of entry and expansion. Low export levels and higher internationalization costs reflect large CAGE differences. Customs duties, intermediation margins (which are connected to the presence of multiple players in the distribution chain), transport, and adaptation costs with respect to the local culture can all lead to substantial increases in the cost of the product and modify the positioning of the company in the host market.

Sephora, for example, exited the Japanese market in 2002, three years after opening its Ginza store. The selective beauty retailer, which is owned by LVMH, had presented itself as a classic French perfumery, downplaying other aspects of its assortment, in a market not very interested in this category, as we saw in the Shiseido case. Sephora also underestimated the power of Japanese department stores, which closed the market and prevented key brands from joining Sephora. As a consequence, Sephora had low assortment and attractiveness, as well as high rents to pay in a luxury area. Established distribution networks can actually block new entrants in a country. Similarly, Sephora opened in Hong Kong in 2010, but closed after a month due to competition with local multi-label cosmetic retailer SaSa. When Sephora recently re-launched in Hong Kong, it chose a different strategy, offering more exclusive brands, "cult-beauty" brands from the US, and bespoke beauty services (Lim, 2019).

Differences in culture have also generated problems for Dolce & Gabbana. In 2018, the Italian fashion house's advertising campaign #DGLovesChina, promotional material for a planned fashion show in Shanghai, caused controversy for showing a Chinese model struggling to eat pizza and spaghetti with chopsticks. The campaign, condemned as racist by both Chinese and Western commentators, can best be described as disastrous. Stefano Gabbana and Domenico Dolce asked for "forgiveness" in a video posted on Weibo (Christoferi, 2019), but the impact of the campaign was far reaching. The brand's revenues from Asian markets suffered a steep decline, it was forced to cancel its planned show in Shanghai, and some Chinese e-commerce sites declared a boycott, further damaging Dolce & Gabbana's access to its customers. On the internet, there was no shortage of videos of consumers and influencers burning or destroying the brand's products in protest of Dolce & Gabbana's perceived assault on China's dignity. Although the controversy surrounding #DGLovesChina was not the only reason for the decline in the brand's revenues from Asia, and China in particular, in 2018 and 2019 – tensions around global trade and the protests in Hong Kong also played a role – the backlash was both swift and significant, with consequences for the brand's reputation in a powerful target market.

Dolce & Gabbana is not the only brand to have made headlines in recent years for a lack of sensitivity to local culture. In 2019, Bulgari introduced a special edition of jewels and watches to celebrate the year of the pig. The tagline chosen for the campaign translated to "Be my bright JEW in the palm (做我的掌上明 JEW)". In Mandarin, the word "pig" is pronounced "zhu (猪)", which is similar to the pronunciation of Jew in English. The transliteration the brand chose created an association that deeply offended the Jewish community, whose traditions do not allow the consumption of pigs and their derivatives (Y. Pan, 2019).

In August 2019, images of a Versace t-shirt featuring the names of cities and their respective nations on the back made the rounds on social media, showing a list that began Milan-Italy and went on to include lines for, among others, London-UK and Chicago-USA – but also Hong Kong-Hong Kong and Macau-Macau. The brand apologized for this "design error" on its official Weibo account, explaining that it had withdrawn the shirts from the market in July. Commentators, however, saw the text as evidence of Versace's support for the independence of Hong Kong and Macau (Koetse, 2019).

Dior has also stumbled, apologizing in October 2019 when an image circulated in the media of a maison employee showing a map of China that excluded Taiwan during a presentation at a Chinese university (BBC, 2019). Self-ruled since the 1950s, Taiwan officially remains a Chinese province.

German designer Philipp Plein faced a boycott campaign in 2015, just as his company was expanding into Asian markets. Organized on Weibo, the campaign focused on a t-shirt designed by Plein in 2007 featuring the words "FUCK You China". The designer responded to accusations of racism by citing the brand's most recent advertising campaigns – which featured models of color almost exclusively – and by making a statement in which he claimed that the "FUCK" in the controversial message was actually an acronym for the "Fascinating and Urban Collection: Kiss" making the shirt's message, rather, "Kiss you China" (Il Messaggero, 2015; China Daily, 2015). These examples confirm the validity of Geert Hofstede's directive to "understand and respect" national cultures. At the same time, they demonstrate the power of social media to circulate any type of information quickly and uncontrollably. Any missteps a brand makes have the potential to be seen by a global audience.

Because of the difficulties outlined above, companies are not, as a rule, equally present and equally profitable in all major regions of the world. A careful analysis of the split of luxury companies' revenues by geographic area shows that sales abroad exceed 50% of the total. The internationalization of sales is therefore in a mature phase, especially in key markets, which for European companies are the countries of Europe itself, Japan, and the United States. However, some Asian and South American markets remain little explored. Nicola Coropulis, CEO of the historic Italian design company Poltrona Frau, confirms this, noting:

India is a very complex market. We are present there with our direct branch that manages the direct store in Mumbai, coordinates the activity of dealers in the area (including Pakistan) and also carries out business development activities on turnkey projects. South America is still a market to be explored with the sporadic presence of retailers and a very high business volatility. We have a dealer in Brazil, one in Chile, one in Panama, one in Paraguay, we are negotiating a new space in Colombia. In South America, we do occasional business, only residential, in purely export mode, without any involvement in large projects.   (personal communication)

It is not easy to find timely and updated data on luxury brands' distribution of sales by country. The composition of the small sample included in Table 5.3 can, however, provide some insight. As we can see, the classic aggregation strategy allows us to identify three important regions – EMEA, Asia Pacific, and the Americas – plus Japan. Some companies are well balanced worldwide, meaning they are strong in all important markets (China, Hong Kong, Korea, Japan, MEA, US, and Europe). This is true for LVMH group, Chanel, Hermès, Rolex, Cartier, and Gucci, but not necessarily for all others.

Table 5.3: Revenues by Region of a Sample of Luxury Companies in 2019.

	EMEA	Americas	Japan	APAC	RoW*
Azimut Benetti	62%	3%	N/A	4%	31%
Brunello Cucinelli	45%	33%	N/A	10%	12%
Chanel	37%	18%	N/A	44%	1%
Damiani	76%	N/A	10%	9%	5%
Dolce & Gabbana	51%	16%	5%	22%	6%
Ferragamo	25%	29%	9%	37%	–
Hermès	30%	18%	13%	38%	1%
Kering Group	33%	19%	8%	34%	6%
Gucci	28%	20%	8%	38%	6%
LVMH Group	28%	24%	7%	30%	11%
Ferrari	48%	29%	N/A	23%	–
Potrona Frau	55%	12%	3%	30%	–
Richemont SA	30%	18%	8%	38%	6%
Tiffany	11%	44%	15%	28%	2%

Note: *Rest of world
Source: Compiled by authors based on publicly available data; Ferrari data refer to car shipments.[5]

We can confirm the importance of Asia and Japan for many companies (or groups), while Damiani, the historic jeweler founded in the Valenza gold district in 1924 by Enrico Grassi Damiani, and the yacht-building group Azimut Benetti show a strong rootedness in the European context. Azimut opened a direct sales office in Shanghai in 2008 after receiving its first orders for mega-yachts from Mainland China. However, sales of smaller yachts in China never took off, due to the lack of a Chinese boating tradition and government restrictions on luxury expenses. After a few years, the Shanghai office closed and the business moved to a partner in Hong Kong. Azimut Benetti's remaining offices are in London, Dubai, and Fort Lauderdale (US).

As we can see, limiting factors lead to different choices/challenges for large and small companies. It seems like the table suggests that smaller companies tend to stay closer to home in their expansion strategies, focusing on markets that offer few hurdles. Large companies, meanwhile, look to global markets, but may still (as the examples show) encounter challenges related to CAGE differences (especially cultural ones) as they attempt to become "local" in new target markets.

In conclusion, we see how there are companies that have managed to find the "good compromise" or balance mentioned above, and then implement strategies that have led the brand to be experienced as "local". This has resulted in effective control of all the main luxury markets, from east to west. On the other hand, there are brands that because of their very small size or the difficulty in recognizing and managing local specificities have remained anchored in their region of origin. Still others make a conscious decision to concentrate in certain areas of the planet was an intentional choice. The companies in this last group focus their attention on countries that are consistent with their business models and able, without making particular efforts, to appreciate the value created by the brand.

Combining Learning and Market Opportunities with Obstacles in the Same Assessment Framework

We can only assess the real attractiveness of the market when considering both of the competing forces discussed in the previous sub-sections: opportunities and limitations, the latter preventing companies from fully exploiting the former. While it is conceptually useful to separate these two forces into two levels of analysis – especially when a company is preparing to carry out an initial assessment of a target market – score-based methodologies like those discussed earlier in this chapter in the section on market attractiveness consider both simultaneously as a single measurement object.

In 2000, Gupta and Govindarajan provided a very effective model that can be applied to understanding past and future internationalization decisions. The model, depicted in Figure 5.6, deals with which markets are more or less strategic for an internationalizing company. This matrix has the advantage of facilitating an understanding of both opportunities and obstacles.

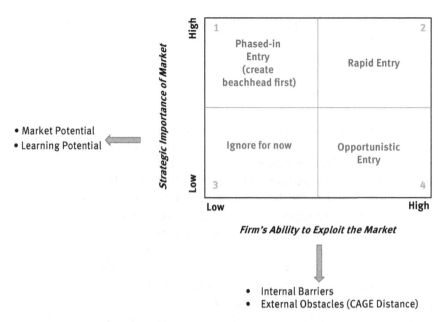

Figure 5.6: The Attractiveness Matrix.
Source: Compiled by authors based on Gupta and Govindarajan, 2000.

Internationalization is usually not the result of a carefully planned process, but rather involves catching opportunities and using ad hoc solutions to respond to problems related to mode and speed of entry. However, firms need a broad framework to direct their expansion toward markets in which the chances for success are higher. The crucial dimensions of the model are:

1) *The strategic importance of the market*, which depends on expected rates of growth and profit opportunities in the firm's product categories and/or on the learning potential offered by the target market. This is what has been detailed in previous paragraphs.

2) *The firm's ability to exploit the market*, depending on available resources and capabilities as well as external obstacles. For this latter dimension, the CAGE distance model has been suggested in the previous sub-section.

The two extreme quadrants, numbers 2 and 3 (bottom left and top right), are easy to understand. However, the other two sections of the matrix require an explanation:

- *Phased-in Entry* (quadrant 1, top left). The appraisal of market attractiveness is particularly positive, but at present there are factors that can reduce the probability of success in the case of entry. The firm should therefore wait for the right moment, while trying to adopt an incremental approach. That is, time can be invested to better understand the dynamics of the target market by being present as an observer or by entering a market similar in culture and economic characteristics, but less complicated from a competitive and regulatory point of view. An example would be that of Canada vs. the United States. The two countries are similar in terms of culture, but Canada is less challenging to enter because of the competitive landscape. If entry difficulties depend on internal barriers, the company can explore ways to bridge a skills gap or find adequate financial resources to support market entry. These difficulties are often quickly circumvented by entering into an alliance with a valid and reliable local partner.

- *Opportunistic Entry* (quadrant 4, bottom right). The market itself does not express great potential for learning or growth in turnover, but allows, for example, the company to satisfy sporadic and non-binding orders that help saturate production capacity.

An evaluation that derives from the attractiveness matrix must be understood as dynamic and not static: a foreign market in quadrant 1 can pass to quadrant 2 once internal and/or external difficulties have been resolved; a market in quadrant 2 can fall into quadrant 4 once its strategic opportunities have been exhausted.

As an example, we can use this framework to conduct a brief qualitative evaluation of four potential markets – United States, France, China, and Vietnam – using as our test case the Italian hair and body care company Davines. While there is room for debate and interpretation, Vietnam likely qualifies as an opportunistic entry. The country's strategic importance seems to rate poorly, given its small economic size and the fact that its share of affluent consumers interested in high-end Western brands is much less significant than those of other countries in the same region. The match between Vietnam and Davines's resources and capabilities is also low, because Davines has to depend heavily on local partners to distribute its products in the country.

France and the United States are both strategically important, but for different reasons. The US professional market is the largest in the world and will probably remain so in the coming years, at least for hair care. Moreover, a large and wealthy segment of US customers are interested in the typical blend of quality, science, and sustainability values associated with Davines. Indeed, coherent with the model's suggestion for rapid entry, the United States was the first country where Davines established a subsidiary. The strategic importance of France rests more on opportunities for raising brand awareness than on profit and learning potential. A significant presence in France lends credibility to Davines in the eyes of customers and allows it to track market trends and evolving customer tastes. Looking at how Davines entered the French market, where it developed its presence relatively late (phased-in entry) and was cautious in its investment, suggests fit with Davines' resources and capabilities could be lower in France than in the US.

China is already the largest market in the world for skin care and, while coming third to the US and Brazil, will be the fastest growing market for hair care in coming years, together with India. So, its strategic importance is obvious. The focus must be on the second dimension of Gupta and Govindarajan's (2000) model, the firm's ability to exploit the market. Is Davines endowed with the resources and capabilities needed to successfully expand in China? Table 5.4 illustrates the major pros and cons of expansion in China, based on the characteristics of the market and Davines.

Table 5.4: Davines's Expansion in China: Pros and Cons.

PROS	CONS
Affluent local customers interested in high-end Western brands	Significant presence could require large investment
The experience of the founder, Mr.Davide Bollati, with launching and staffing local subsidiaries	Relatively low brand awareness of Davines compared to other Western companies
"Going natural" movement in the industry could help Davines and make Chinese customers receptive	Special local needs could require product adaptation (local R&D center and factory)
	Limited current local interest in product sustainability
	Barriers to entry (e.g., in China, exemption from animal testing is possible only for local producers)

Source: Compiled by authors based on corporate data, 2020 and Lojacono & Misani, 2017.*
* Lojacono G., Misani N Davines: Internationalizing a Niche, The case centre, 2017

The table suggests that the firm's ability to exploit the Chinese market is at best moderate. This is coherent with the fact that Davines started to consider entry into China only in 2015, more than 20 years after its first steps toward internationalization (phased-in entry). The model also indicates that Davines may want to wait before creating a subsidiary in China. However, the choice could be less about *whether* to enter China than *how* to do it. Previous experience in the US, France, and Vietnam suggests that, in terms of entry modes, Davines could choose among three options:

1) *A large subsidiary with a research and development center*, a factory, and responsibility for all local marketing activities; this solution would be expensive and Davines might want to involve local partners to share costs. The main benefits consist of overcoming entry barriers and adapting to local needs.

2) *A small subsidiary without research and development or factories*, in charge of market development and distribution of Davines's products. This solution is more consistent with the resources available to the company and allows for a gradual expansion, without distracting Davines from mature markets that still offer opportunities for growing market share.

3) *A partnership with local distributors*, replicating the approach used in Vietnam. While minimizing investment, this solution might have the lowest probability of effectively developing the brand in China and growing sales.

Using the matrix to examine test-cases like Davines allows us to put ourselves in the shoes of managers and make choices, first relying on secondary data and then drafting in-depth checklists aimed at collecting information in the field through interviews. But remember, positioning markets in the matrix and determining a possible entry mode in this type of test-case scenario should aim not to identify the "best solution", but to simply list the available options and evaluate the costs and benefits of each one.

Internationalization on the Supply Side

Considering the possibility of organizing a production footprint without geographical limits makes the decision-making process related to the supply chain even more complex. For each ingredient of the production mix and for each production phase, a company not only has to understand whether to pursue the option of internalization, but also where to carry out these activities. Therefore, for each phase/material/component, a company has 2 (internalization or outsourcing) * 196 (countries in the world) options for carrying out these activities. Obviously, not all countries are going to provide advantages to a company interested in moving some of its activities offshore, so the list of countries will be quickly narrowed down to those that are. But the decision to internationalize production is still complicated, becoming even more so as the degree of diversification of the company increases, with multiple categories of products and services.

From a decision-making point of view, therefore, the choices upstream of the value chain, i.e., research and development and production, take place at three levels that are often considered simultaneously:
1) *What*: identification of activities in which the entire value chain can be decomposed
2) *How*: identification of which activities are suitable to be outsourced and which ones must be held within the company boundaries
3) *Where:* identification of all possible locations where internalized or outsourced activities are to be carried out

Figure 5.7 shows how, in a first level of analysis, a company has to make choices of vertical integration and location – abroad or in the country of origin – for each activity. Between the two extremes of total integration and outsourcing, there are the intermediate forms: strategic alliances that can be equity-based (joint venture) or non-equity (as in the case of collaboration agreements between companies aimed at co-development).

GEOGRAPHICAL LOCATION →

MAKE OR BUY DECISIONS ↑

Location / Make or Buy	Domestic	International
In	Inhouse	Foreign Subsidiaries (captive offshoring)
Hybrid configurations (Strategic Alliances)	Strategic Alliance with a domestic partner	Strategic Alliance with a foreign partner
Out	Domestic Suppliers (outsourcing)	Foreign Suppliers (offshore outsourcing)

Figure 5.7: The Two Dimensions of Reconfiguration of the Value Chain.
Source: Compiled by authors based on Contractor, Kumar, Kundu, and Pedersen, 2011.

The first two levels in the figure refer to the typical make-or-buy dilemma. That is, companies individually take all the activities that generate value for the end customer and ask themselves which ones it makes sense to retain internally (thus increasing the level of integration downstream) and which ones can be usefully outsourced and entrusted to companies outside the company perimeter. The basic criterion in economics suggests basing this analysis on the contribution that the business makes to the uniqueness of the company's positioning in the competitive arena. Activities with higher "added value" are internally withheld. In the world of luxury, there are multiple configurations that depend on industry specificities. As we have seen in the previous chapters, in the world of leather goods and textile-clothing, many cases confirm a general tendency toward internalization (in a total or partial way) aimed at controlling the sources of critical materials (leather and fine yarns); increasing a brand's differentiation, credibility, and legitimacy in the competitive arena; stabilizing procurement costs in volatile markets; creating barriers for competitors; extending corporate social responsibility policies to all activities in the supply chain; and providing various types of support to suppliers. Among many examples, we can mention the following:

- Zegna acquired a 60% stake in a 2500-hectare property in New South Wales, New Zealand, that specializes in rearing merino sheep, a crucial material for the brand, in 2014.

- Gucci bought 70% of the Pigini shoe factory in Recanati (Macerata), a Gucci sub-contractor for 20 years, for the production of classic and sports women's shoes in 2003.
- Kering acquired a farm in Thailand, allowing it to ethically raise pythons to supply skins to all leather goods of brands under the Kering umbrella, in 2017 (Management Decisions, 2019). In 2013, Kering took over France Croco, a company specializing in the processing of exotic leathers that joined the Italian Conceria Caravel (owned by Kering since 2008) in guaranteeing the supply of precious leathers to group brands.
- LVMH entered into partnership with the historic Tannerie Masure, a specialist in vegetable tanning, in 2009 to found the Tanneries de la Comète SA. In 2011, the French giant acquired 51% of Heng Long International Ltd, one of the world's most important suppliers of crocodile skins, and in 2012 the group acquired control of Tannerie Roux.
- Hermès acquired Tanneries d'Annonay in 2013, making it part of HCP (Hermès Cuirs Precieux), the division of Hermès that controls six tanneries, dedicated to the supply, dyeing, and finishing of high-quality leathers for other brands.
- Chanel became major shareholder of Richard Tannery, a specialist in soft leather, specifically quality lambskins originating from a few select places such as Aveyron (South of France) and Entrefinos (Spain), in 2016. This integration follows several acquisitions made over time such as that of Guasse, a glove manufacturer, in 2012 and of Bodin Joyeux, a historic supplier of calfskin leather used mainly for bags, in 2013.

These companies internalized activities and expanded production capacity not only by acquiring existing entities, but also by creating new ones. This is the case for Fendi Factory, a new, 13,000-square-meter bag factory in Bagno a Ripoli (Florence), operational as of 2022, as well as the new Yves Saint Laurent factories in Scandicci (Florence) and Balenciaga's in Cerreto Guidi (Florence). These brands are investing in Italian excellence, gaining important skills. Their presence also benefits the district because working with established brands repetition sharpens local skills (Pieraccini, 2020). According to McKinsey, more than 40% of global luxury goods production happens in Italy (Achille and Zipser, 2020).

Internalization can also be a viable strategy for activities beyond those relating to a company's core business. Chanel, for instance, decided to buy jasmine plantations in Grasse necessary for the production of its famous Chanel No. 5 perfume. There is also the case of luxury-brand eyewear, which has recently been affected by internalization strategies. There, luxury conglomerates are seeking to better control the creative process of design as well as commercial policies (adopting the same criterion of selectivity) and pricing (avoiding discounts that are not in line with the brand approach). In the luxury furniture industry, we usually have a medium-high level of integration, especially for the core categories of a company. This integration has been facilitated by the use of new technologies such as 3D printing or laser cutting leather and fabrics. In Italy, we can cite the examples of companies such as B&B Italia, Poltrona Frau, Molteni, Cassina, and Boffi that have all pursued these strategies.

The advantage of internalization depends on the type of technology (which is connected to the base material) involved in a particular production activity and to the production volumes. Processes that involve rare materials and high levels of skill are often brought or kept in-house. Those that involve industrial processes and newer technologies are often outsourced. The Italian company Kartell, a leader in the production of furniture in plastic materials, has based its competitive and economic success on extreme outsourcing. The brand "edits" projects by international designers, developing, prototyping, and industrializing them. It entrusts production to world leaders in plastic molding in dimensions similar to those of its products. Kartell has therefore maintained a structure of variable costs, benefiting from the specialization and structure of suppliers with whom it has exclusive contracts. Outsourcing is common in the case of furniture production for the world of turnkey orders, which is characterized by different rhythms and volumes from those of the residential and retail market. Outsourcing also has clear advantages in the cosmetics world, where all brands at an international level benefit from the existence of a rich panorama of independent producers.

On a slightly smaller scale, in the case of luxury, there are activities that are crucial for the generation of value that a company will outsource in recognition of extraordinary – and difficult to replicate – external skills. This is the case in the jewelry and watch industries, where very integrated companies coexist with companies that carry out only the prototyping phase internally and rely on external laboratories for the realization of their pieces. Even companies with a high level of vertical integration, like Cartier, outsource when they need additional production capacity or specialists in delicate processes. As with companies' internalization strategies, internationalizing to access outsourcing opportunities can allow a company to develop new processes or expand production by relying on a more diverse range of suppliers.

The second level of analysis when assessing the attractiveness of upstream internationalization involves determining *where* a company should carry out research and production activities, as well as where to procure raw materials. When a company is expanding into new markets, the chance to link that downstream expansion to local research activities can be invaluable. This has been a recurrent strategy in clothing and accessories in China, where numerous international companies have set up research and development centers to adapt their product lines to local requirements.

Kering Eyewear and Cartier, partners in a joint eyewear venture, have since the beginning of their collaboration developed numerous Asian-fit models for Cartier. In the current collection there are around 40 of those models, representing 20% of the entire collection. For spring/summer 2021, Kering Eyewear released Asian-fit models of three new Cartier sunglasses. Even before the partnership with Cartier, Kering Eyewear saw its proximity to the market and the needs of the local consumer as among the factors that contributed to its success in China. Kering is present in the country, with a design and supply chain team based in Hong Kong that manages the development of models for the Asian market and adapts products already in the collection with Asian fits; an e-commerce team in Shanghai that takes care of the flagship stores on Tmall and Jd.com; and a marketing team, also in Shanghai, that locally declines international campaigns and events. Kering Eyewear has commercial branches in both Shanghai and Hong Kong. In China, Kering Eyewear also has 5% of total production, essentially the creation of models for the Puma brand, in addition to the procurement of some components, such as molds for injected products.

As for the production and procurement of raw materials, for luxury companies the aim of internationalization is not economic arbitrage, but to satisfy objectives connected to the presence of local specializations (Indian embroidery is known for its extraordinary workmanship; flowers from Grasse, in France, are used in luxury perfumes) or proximity to the local market. The Italian furniture brand Cassina, for instance, pursued this strategy when it expanded into the US market in the 1970s; today, globalization makes shipping from its Italian factories easier, yet the company maintains warehouses in the United States and China to ensure quick shipping of its best sellers.

Several studies (e.g., the McKinsey's 2019 MGI report) confirm some main trends in the supply chain: delocalization based purely on labor-cost arbitrage is declining in some value chains; value chains are becoming more regional, i.e., production takes place within the region to serve the region;[6] and global value chains are becoming more knowledge intensive rather than goods intensive.

To reinforce the key message that luxury localization choices are primarily motivated by the search for particular specializations rather than economic arbitrage, we will conclude this subsection with two concrete cases, cosmetics and footwear, where international brands have decided to localize their production in Italy despite the lack of an evident cost advantage.

Case 1: Offshoring to Italy: The Case of Cosmetics

In the world of make-up, international brands have decided to entrust the production of their products to Italian companies.[7] It is not uncommon that, even when a brand relies on a cosmetics multinational to manage its product line, the latter in turn relies on specialized Italian suppliers for production. The Lombardy region has the highest density of cosmetics companies in Italy (more than 54% of all Italian companies are located there, and 50% of all Italian cosmetic employees work in the region) and is responsible for 65% of turnover in the Italian cosmetics industry. The Lombard companies are concentrated in the so-called cosmetic valley, a geographical area between Crema and Cremona. In this industrial cluster, there are companies specialized in various cosmetic products (from make-up to fragrances), as well as in cosmetics packaging and machines for the cosmetics industry.

The concentration of cosmetics companies in Lombardy is due in large part to their origins as subcontractors. In Italy, subcontracting generates a total turnover of more than €1.5 billion, 80.6% of which is concentrated in Lombardy.[8] In the 1970s, international cosmetics brands provided contract manufacturers with their own formulations, and the latter worked from these recipes rather than developing their own. Contract manufacturers were little more than simple transformers of raw materials into finished products. Today, many of these companies have become active in the innovation process, researching and creating new formulas themselves and starting to sell their ideas to brands, not just their production capacity. This acquired ability of Italian cosmetics companies has given Italy a sustainable competitive advantage in cosmetics production, making the country a primary destination for both established brands and emerging and independent ones. Indeed, it was precisely the presence of this production base that lowered barriers to entry in the cosmetics industry by removing from companies' entry calculations the huge investments necessary to start research and development and production activities.

For an entrepreneur with a creative or marketing idea in the world of beauty, entrusting development, production, and packaging to third parties is the fastest and easiest way to turn that idea into reality. Whether or not the entrepreneur is new to the beauty industry, setting up production with volumes that are sustainable economically is an impossible challenge, especially when multiple items rely on different technologies. In make-up, for example, the need to create batches that differ in terms of number of pieces, colors, and type of packaging requires machinery with different degrees of automation and mechanization. In addition, an experienced contract manufacturer can provide access to research and development, support commercial expansion activities, intermediate the purchase of packaging in a more convenient way by virtue of larger purchase volumes, and produce, pack, and distribute a product more efficiently. In a nutshell, in the beauty world, a well-chosen supplier can provide the following specific benefits:

- Knowledge of international cosmetic legislation
- Specialization in industrialization and production with versatile machinery for all customer needs
- A high level of quality control

This allows customer companies to focus on marketing and distribution activities as well as having access to a very large group of producers. Internationalization enters the picture because of the role that geographic proximity has played in concentrating high-level suppliers in Italy: for companies that place a high premium on quality, such as those in the world of luxury, outsourcing cosmetics production to an Italian supplier brings significant advantages.

Case 2: Offshoring to Italy: The Case of Footwear

Similar to the cosmetics/beauty industry, Italy has developed a reputation has a center for third-party production of high-end footwear: 32% of companies are located in the Marche region and 23% in Tuscany. Why do international brands increasingly rely on Italian factories for production in this industry? Here, the forces at play are slightly different from those that have drawn international cosmetics companies to the country:

- Italy has always had very strong craftsmanship skills and knowledge; several international companies have historically produced in Italy, attracted by a level of quality that they were not able to find elsewhere.
- Many local companies market products under their own brand and are therefore aware of market dynamics and commercial strategies.
- Local brands are increasingly putting their production capacity at the service of other Italian companies and international brands.
- Some international brands, including high-end brands, that left Italy to produce in Asia encountered production problems, leading to an increase in returns and complaints. Many of these have returned production to Italy.

It is also true that there is a growing awareness on the part of luxury companies of the importance that the supply chain plays in defining and communicating a brand's founding values. Suppliers play a decisive role in innovation processes, and therefore in differentiation policies, in achieving adequate service levels, and in the pursuit of a genuine philosophy of social responsibility. This makes it all the more important that companies use rigorous criteria to select partners, making decisions based on a common value system and not the benefits of individual stakeholders. This supply-chain logic can also facilitate the adoption of advanced technologies from upstream to downstream for the purpose of creating value for the customer in terms, for example, of customizing the experience and not just the product. The supply chain becomes part of a holistic view of product development, much as the factory becomes a part of a brand's narrative.

If it is indeed true, as seen in Chapter 1, that customer purchasing behavior for luxury goods is emotional and aspirational, it is not true that it is irrational. Customers are also interested in quality, durability, style, and comfort. Choosing the right producer affects a company's ability to meet customer needs. In the case of footwear, Italian producers have not only the skill to execute creative designs, but also the experience to know how to adapt them to actual wear, ensuring a maximum of comfort.

International brands have not only entered into supply agreements with Italian companies, they have also purchased Italian plants, interested in the extraordinary production capacities that characterize the workforce. Finally, the Italian footwear industry is diverse in its expertise, and there are companies that specialize in particular market segments, such as sports shoes. No production landscape in the world offers so much in terms of the variety of technologies it employs and its approach to the market. As both international brands and their suppliers look to the future, a 2020 study by the National Association of Italian Shoe Manufacturers (ANCI) identified the following trends, all of which bode well for the continued localization of foreign footwear production in Italy:

– The extinction of the mid-range of the market alongside upward or downward polarization – Italy is well-positioned to supervise the production of high-end products
– The ability of Italian production companies to achieve the low volumes needed for niche products
– The expansion of fashion toward streetwear, and therefore sports shoes, to the detriment of more classic and elegant footwear
– The digitization of production processes, such as modeling through digital tools instead of manual, which is pushing companies to keep up with new technologies to reduce time to market and delivery times

According to the ANCI's research, many companies are gearing up to provide services, such as rapid prototyping, and not just products. In light of this new trend, it is even more necessary for companies to innovate and work on the services surrounding the product. The challenge is no longer to be the best at making a certain type of product, but to provide a suite of services to potential clients. This is especially the case for companies that work with the world of luxury. For example, a client may arrive with a design in the morning and request a prototype ready for the afternoon. Fast prototyping is not a flashy service, but at the right moment, it makes a difference.

The qualities that define the Italian footwear industry – quality, expertise, market-awareness, and a forward-looking orientation that encourages specialization, innovation, and service development – make Italian production companies a valid choice for clients at the high end of the market, with low quantities but high margins. At the same time, relocation to low-cost countries is a viable strategy only for the production of large volumes and particular specialized components. This seems to be the reason why Balenciaga, for example, has decided to move the production of the Triple S sneaker, originally produced in Italy, to China. As the shoe has become a staple, production volumes have increased and the production process has standardized, making for a better fit with the expertise of a Chinese production company than an Italian one. This change has not affected the shoe's retail price; Balenciaga is adjusting its supply chain, but it is not altering the status of the Triple S as a luxury product. As reported by *The Fashion Law* in 2018, the company already produced the soles of its shoes in Eastern European countries prior to its move to China, suggesting that for this product at least, country of origin is incidental. Nor is Balenciaga an isolated case; rather, it's in good company – Gucci, Prada, Burberry, Armani, Dolce & Gabbana, and Miu Miu all have products made outside the brand's country of origin (Fashion Law, 2018).

Interviews and data analysis conducted by Bocconi University show that, in the footwear industry, companies tend to resort to offshoring according to a short-term strategy, regardless of what may happen in the future. However, various footwear companies that previously moved production to low-cost countries overseas are considering returning production to Europe, creating what has been called a "reshoring" phenomenon. This is because, in the long run, the cost advantages of current high-volume production centers may increase. For example, costs of production in China have risen over the past six to eight years, particularly compared to Vietnam, which as we have seen has grown exponentially as a destination for companies interested in offshoring their production. Problems related to quality can also arise, which in turn negatively impact the reputation of the brand. Consequently, when a company decides to move activities off shore, it is essential for it to evaluate the advantages of doing so according to a long-term time horizon, rather than a short one.

Reshoring is one of the main effects of the rethinking of supply chains that began before the Covid-19 pandemic. By consulting the European Reshoring Monitor database, we can see how, out of 41 Italian companies that returned to Italy between 2014 and 2018, three belong to the premium and luxury world: Azimut Benetti (from Turkey in 2012), Safilo (from China in 2016), and Prada (from China in 2015). These companies' official reasons for reshoring – those declared to the press – include the "Made in" effect, delivery time problems, stronger know-how in the home country, the need for greater organizational flexibility, offshored activities' control complexity, business strategy and global reorganization, increased home-country manufacturing productivity (e.g., in the US), and untapped production capacity.

Takeaways

- Luxury companies are engaged in internationalization both downstream (expansion into new markets) and upstream (offshoring, among other activities) in their supply chain.
- Downstream internationalization brings both potential advantages and potential obstacles to success. Companies therefore benefit from investing time and resources in evaluating market attractiveness.
- The relationship between the distance separating a company's home market from a new target market (CAGE difference) and the market's potential for growth and learning may suggest adjustments to the company's entry style, beyond the decision to enter or not enter.
- Beyond the production-cost reductions associated with offshoring to low-cost countries, upstream internationalization can have important strategic benefits. These include:
  - Securing crucial materials for production
  - Tailoring research and development to new markets
  - Benefiting from local expertise
  - Closing the distance between production facilities and important markets outside the home country
- Long-term trends for luxury indicate that expertise and control of the supply-chain will be of utmost importance to international companies. In addition to offshoring, some companies are beginning to bring production activities back to their home countries. This phenomenon is called "reshoring" and is related to the issues discussed in Chapters 2 and 4.

Notes

1 For an academic classification of motives to go abroad, see Gupta, A.K. and Govindarajan V., 2004, Global Strategy and Organization, NJ: John Wiley and Sons.

2 Discussions of the footwear industry included in this chapter are based on "Strategie di reshoring e punti di forza del tessuto industriale calzaturiero italiano", a research report carried out by SDA Bocconi School of Management for the Associazione Italiana Calzaturifici Italiani (ANCI) and presented at MICAM X, September 2020.

3 This example is based on presentations by the company in Bocconi classes, though the actual values of Illy's market share in various countries have been replaced with dummy values for the sake of confidentiality.

4 Our discussion of Shiseido's activities in France is an elaboration based on corporate information and *From Global to Metanational: How Companies Win in the Knowledge Economy*, by Yves L. Doz, José Santos, Peter J. Williamson, and Tanna Schulich.

5 As far as Ferrari is concerned, the product mix is highly differentiated by country. Ferrari's focus remains on exclusivity, with only 10k vehicles annually built-to-order. As a result, country-specific turnover is not published.

6 As an example, note that in Asia trade relations between China and Japan have increasingly intensified. China is the second destination for Japanese exports and Japan the third destination for Chinese exports (UNComtrade, 2020).

7 Just as there are areas (see Grasse in France) and companies (see Puig) that are considered destinations and preferred partners for the production of fragrances.

8 All these data come from Beauty Report 2019, Ermeneia-Cosmetica Italia.

6 Innovation, Creativity and Management of Luxury Product Portfolios: What's New and What is Not

In periods of strong economic and social turbulence, strategic decisions become especially complicated for companies. Uncertainty can obscure long-term risks, and missteps are hard to reverse. Emergencies can induce companies to focus on managing urgent problems, losing sight of the actions and investments that are necessary to prepare for the new era that will emerge once the crisis is over. External shocks can reorient the entire business environment, adjusting balances and setting new rules of the game. Companies facing times of crisis must therefore have both the clarity necessary to deal with the present and the perspective to set a new path for the future. Ambidexterity, which we have referred to extensively in this book, once again emerges as a precious source of resilience.

During the current period of transformation, luxury companies must consider their past as a driver of uniqueness and brand equity and valorize their heritage in all of their decision making for the future. Having said that, it is not easy to look into the future, especially in turbulent times. Thus, companies need to be aware of the importance of scenario planning, a strategic-planning method that organizations use to hedge their risks against possible failures. Scenario planning acts as a contingency to safeguard a company's most vulnerable industry and prevent catastrophic failures in the long term. While scenario planning requires foresight, companies do not need to forecast unforeseeable risks – doing so would be impossible. Rather, it is a way to delineate and describe multiple alternative scenarios in situations of true ambiguity and complexity. Scenario planning helps companies become more agile and better prepared to face an uncertain future while taking action to promote change in a specific, desirable direction. Figure 6.1 outlines the logical flow that connects strategic planning with scenario planning.

The first step of Scenario Planning is to gather key personnel in the organization to brainstorm and identify major potential issues. Next, the organization should sort through a selection of the most important issues and rank them by their potential impacts, using the evolution of the external context to guide their ranking.

In 2020, luxury companies around the world encountered a number of unforeseen events, including the Covid-19 pandemic, political unrest in Hong Kong, bushfires in Australia, and social protest around the world. Of these, the pandemic had the largest consequences for the world of luxury, as many companies had failed to plan for the possibility of store closures, nationwide lockdowns, and travel bans, all of which impacted the purchasing habits and methods of their consumers. The forced closure of non-essential businesses led to economic uncertainty and lower spending. Travel bans shifted the consumer base in countries that rely on tourism, such as France, Italy, the United Kingdom, and Singapore, from foreign visitors to local residents. Luxury companies have no excuse for failing to plan for these

https://doi.org/10.1515/9783110723519-006

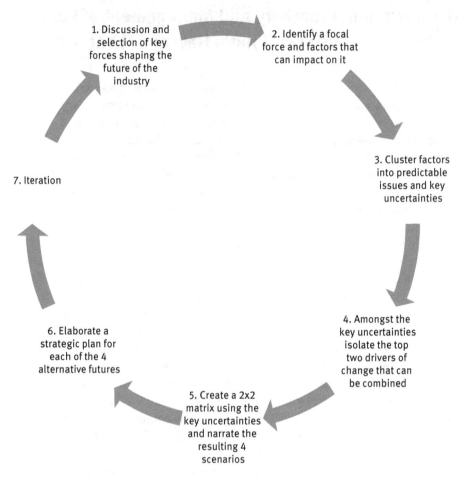

Figure 6.1: From Scenario Planning to Strategic Planning: Seven Key Steps.
Source: Compiled by authors.

scenarios, as they have encountered countless distressing situations. The SARS outbreak in 2002 prompted travel warnings and quarantines, the yellow vest movement in Paris caused disruptions throughout France, and, more recently, Hong Kong protests saw Asia Pacific's most lucrative luxury market plummet over 30%. These situations can occur in any city, at any point in time.

As we have experienced in 2020, a company's business model has a profound influence on how it will react to a given scenario. This makes scenario planning in the world of luxury very difficult. While other industries are process driven and continuous, the world of luxury is dynamic, especially in apparel and retail. A fashion collection lasts no more than six months, and the world of luxury's response horizon for crisis scenarios is likely to be just as short.

Scenarios developed in planning are not pure invention; they are part of a pro-active approach involving research and measurement. This includes regular inter-views with all the key players in the value chain as well as industry experts to identify forces that can shape the future. To this end, it is necessary to investigate key aspects and trends that have to do with the social, cultural, economic, technological, and reg-ulatory spheres. The outcome of this research should lead to a list of factors that can outline the evolution of the external context. A company can then identify which of these forces represent "key uncertainties" that have a lower degree of predictability and a greater potential impact on the future of the external context. The two most influential and informative uncertainties become the basis for an analysis of four pos-sible future scenarios using a 2x2 matrix (the two uncertainties are reported on two axes with the polar cases at each extreme). The identified scenarios should be accom-panied by an exhaustive narrative (Shoemaker, 1991; Swartz 1996; Garvin and Lev-esque, 2006).

For example, in early 2021, many senior managers questioned the impact of dig-ital commercial channel growth on the world of luxury and their businesses.[1] Obvi-ously this question led to a number of scenarios, depending on the geographical context of application (e.g., Asia vs. Europe), the business model (e.g., brick-and-mortar, pure digital player, marketplace, multichannel, and omnichannel), and the type of product (cosmetics are different from leather accessories). By identifying the forces driving digital growth and its possible impact on a specific brand, companies could develop strategies to cope with a changed context, a different relationship with customers, and the reorganization of some activities (e.g., communication, customer care, logistics, assortment management, etc.). A list of the forces driving digital growth could include the following factors:

1) Structural change in the customer's attitude toward online shopping
2) Innovation that allows digital players to better satisfy customers
3) The experience created by online brands
4) The degree of integration of physical and digital channels achieved by brands
5) The persistence of a travel ban
6) New local lockdowns
7) The strategies pursued by physical stores to attract customer attention
8) The resolution of logistical problems
9) The level of satisfaction with online vs. offline customer service
10) The management of returns online vs. offline
11) Online vs. offline pricing policies
12) The transparency of online communication policies
13) The information available about products online
14) Concerns about how a product could affect health
15) Economic uncertainty
16) Social media support for digital channels through ad hoc partnerships

This list obviously does not identify all possible factors behind digital growth; however, it can be used as a starting point to aggregate diverse factors into macro-categories. For example, travel bans and lockdowns both have to do with controlling the spread of Covid-19 until entire populations can be vaccinated, which is unlikely before the end of 2021. Aggregating factors into macro-categories can help a company's management team rank them by importance and degree of uncertainty in order to select the two critical, related uncertainties that will be used to create the 2x2 matrix and narrate the four possible scenarios. Assuming an analysis made by a luxury clothing brand with reference to European markets, Figure 6.2 shows an example of a matrix used to analyze the related dimensions of investments needed to be online (factors like 3, 4, and 15) and perception of the online experience (1 and 9).

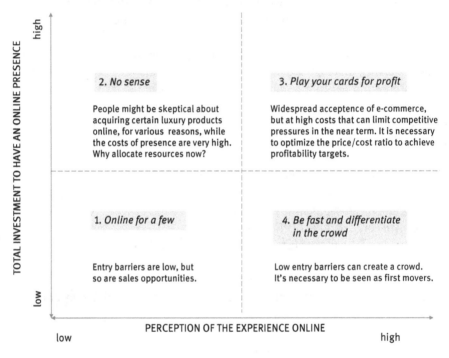

Figure 6.2: Scenario Planning: The Increase of Digital Sales.
Source: Compiled by authors.

Outlining the possible scenarios that could arise from the interaction of two important uncertainties provides us with more precise inputs for the strategic planning process. For example, the spread of digitization combined with the crisis triggered by Covid-19 raised some important questions for luxury companies: Should we review the organization of the supply chain? In which technology should we invest if we want to create customer engagement? How should we review our retail strategy? Does it make sense to change the pace and modality of product development and launch? Answering these questions requires companies to imagine alternative future situations with respect to the evolution of the external context.

It is clear how practicing imagining possible futures has an impact on the allocation of resources and on the identification of areas of focus, from a geographical as well as from a strategic perspective. Scenario planning should not be seen as a way to identify threats on the horizon but as a means of mapping the opportunities that could open up if companies are adequately prepared to catch them.

To stress the important link between scenario planning and decision making, we must frequently carry out exercises like the one above in executive board meetings. In spring 2020, we invited a group of luxury executives to raise some key issues facing hospitality due to the health and economic emergency triggered by Covid-19. The question we posed was: How can we compete today in an industry that has been highly and negatively impacted by the pandemic? The group adopted the perspective of a chain of around forty small and exclusive resorts in remote islands, one that also offered private jets at customers' disposal to curate a bespoke experience facilitated by a dedicated staff. Out of a long list of driving forces, the executives identified the following key uncertainties:
1) Whether people feel safe to travel
2) Whether people are willing to spend travel to isolated destinations

In addition to these forces shaping the industry, the executives also found consensus on some predetermined outcomes: a worldwide economic crisis and subsequent decline in consumption within the luxury market, government support for the tourism industry, the intensification of an ongoing trend toward sustainability, a preference for goods over experiences, the growing importance of health and security, and the increasing importance of digital technologies. Figure 6.3 shows the four possible scenarios the team came up with in response to their two key uncertainties.

All four scenarios were accompanied by some elements of attention. For example, for scenario 3, the team considered the opening of borders between countries, the resumption of air traffic and of work in the tourism industry, and recovering demand for isolated, high-end luxury destinations.

What is the link between scenario planning and product development? Products anchor brand identity for these companies, and product choices must respond to the external environment if they are to resonate with customers. Especially in times of change, decisions related to how to present new items – how frequently, how many, what approach to take (e.g., more design-driven or marketing-driven), how to adapt a design to specific geographies, how to set up the pricing strategy, what partnership to activate, etc. – also need to account for situations the brand may face in the future. In this chapter, we will discuss how luxury companies conceive of, develop, and launch new products. In doing so, we will adopt a process logic, favoring the activities carried out rather than the functions involved. This will allow us to best understand a world in which roles and their scope of action vary

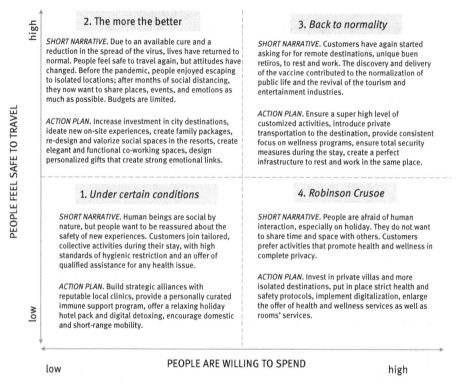

Figure 6.3: Scenario Planning: The Future of Luxury Hospitality.
Source: Compiled by authors based on team-based work done during the EMiLUX Program,
SDA Bocconi.

considerably from company to company and from industry to industry. In retracing the management decisions that determine a company's product portfolio, we will also highlight the key forces that could lead to a rethinking of those activities, including major changes that are under discussion in the world of luxury today.

A Holistic Perspective on Product Ideation, Development, and Launch (PIDL)

This section will present and discuss the key activities related to product ideation, development, and launch (PIDL). It will focus on personal goods (like beauty, apparel, and jewels) and furniture in order to be more specific and topical. Hospitality, automotive, food, and yachting are triggered by different factors and follow peculiar logics.

Luxury companies operate in industries in which the product mix can be highly complex, e.g., apparel, bags, shoes, jewels, watches. The main purpose of PIDL is to arrive at collections that:

– Have an internally coherent structure
– Perfectly integrate with permanent items (carryover)
– Appeal to different customer segments
– Contribute to the development of the brand
– Are appropriately priced
– Can be sourced and produced efficiently
– Can be distributed effectively through different channels
– Are ultimately profitable

The product is an important element of brand architecture and therefore has the power to affect customer perception. It is the beating heart of the company, and all other activities must be conceived in a way that is consistent with and in support of the product. As can be seen from this list of objectives, there is a link between the upstream part of the supply chain (i.e., production feasibility) and the downstream part (i.e., salability in different channels). Implementing multichannel strategies increases the complexity of the process. In the apparel industry, it is not uncommon to see parts of a collection destined solely for a brand's digital channel or pop-up stores. It is also necessary not to underestimate the importance of product pricing, which must not be guided by its industrial cost alone, but also by a sensitivity to the customer's aspirations and emotions. The analysis of the gross margin and therefore of the difference between the retail price and the cost of the product must be considered from the very beginning, that is, from the moment the product is conceived.

Figure 6.4 depicts key activities related to PIDL, including commercialization as a test of a collection's success and an important source of data for activating the new process. As far as apparel is concerned, fashion shows are part of the sales campaign – the moment when buyers draw up purchasing plans for boutiques and department stores.[2]

The eight activities shown in Figure 6.4 can be grouped into four main processes: collection preparation, collection development, sales campaign, and sales period. Figure 6.5 shows a more granular presentation of the PIDL process in apparel and accessories. There are activities such as manufacturing that can intervene both in the development phase of the collection, in support of prototyping and sampling, and after the store purchase plan. Indeed, the complete sourcing/manufacturing of a product rarely takes place until after the buying campaign, as everyone wants to be as flexible and "customer centric" as possible. Waiting on some aspects of production allows a brand to incorporate feedback and order numbers from the buying campaign into the process. While luxury companies do blind order fabric, zips, and hardware before a collection's presentation, these orders are based on estimates of what will be needed across the entire line, not specific items and quantities related

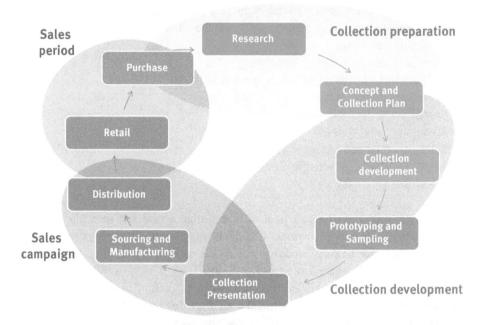

Figure 6.4: The Process of PIDL: An Overview.
Source: Compiled by authors.

to a single product. Only after the collection presentation/sales campaign does the production/manufacturing team know exactly how many pieces to launch.

If the uncertainty in demand and the instability of the production base we have seen throughout the Covid-19 pandemic persist, we could witness the emergence of a new organization of the supply chain, with production that is carried out only in the case of orders and for quantities strictly related to what has been ordered (this is the *pre-order model* that we have already described in other chapters). Online and brick-and-mortar stores will therefore have the task of both presenting the collection and acting as collectors of orders. The planning of the collection and the activities of sales management have already become much more complex following the need to operate and integrate not only different channels (retail and wholesale), but also different environments (online and offline).

In the fashion industry, the pace of the first part of the product development process has historically been dictated by the fashion show calendar, which focuses on two main-season collections: spring/summer (SS) and fall/winter (FW). This has forced companies to shape all processes and internal organization to meet the deadlines imposed by these seasonal events. Let's take the example of womenswear (WW), for which seasonal collections must be presented during the main fashion weeks in Milan, Paris, London, and New York in February (SS) and September (FW) (Figure 6.6).[3] However, with some exceptions, what we see on the runway is not

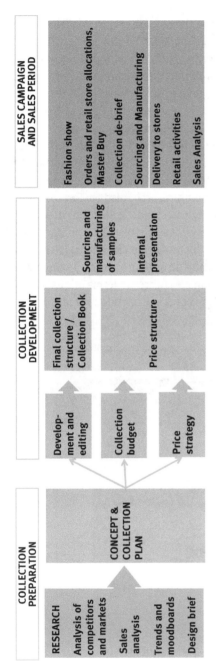

Figure 6.5: The Process of PIDL: Key Activities in Apparel and Accessories.
Source: Compiled by authors.

what ends up in the store. The show presents the theme of the collection in an "extreme" way to create an impression – as we saw in Chapter 2, fashion shows are a key venue for brands to interact with their customers. The garments and accessories therefore have a communication purpose rather than a direct connection with sales and margins. The selection, negotiation, and purchasing activities that determine what products will make their way to customers take place at other times of the same week, in dedicated showrooms where buyers have a direct impact on the offer.

Menswear collections (MW) are presented before WW, in January and June, and follow similar logics. The complexity of the process increases if, in addition to these two canonical collections, the brand introduces small product drops and inter-seasonal collections, the most common being resort/cruise (before SS) and pre-fall (before FW). Shows for these increasingly common collections typically happen four months before the main-season shows: resort/cruise 2022 in May 2021, pre-fall 2022 in November 2021. They are usually more commercial and help shorten the customer's wait for new-season clothes. They also tend to reach higher sell-through rates (ST), which can tell us about a product's success in terms of **quantities** and **prices.** Below, the formula to calculate ST, average price, and gross margin are illustrated.

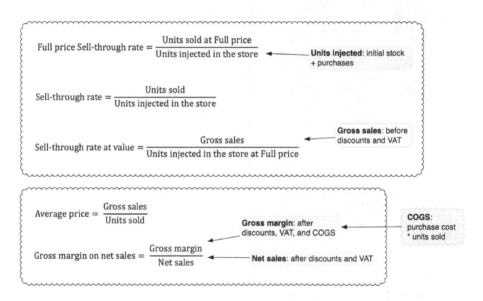

The fact that the product launch and the entire creative process follow specific exogenous cadences is true not only in the world of fashion, but also that of cosmetics, furniture, or watchmaking. These are all industries in which the leading, most innovative companies regularly put their research and creativity on display in the form of collections of products. Furniture companies often spend years preparing the pieces they launch at the annual Salone Internazionale del Mobile di Milano

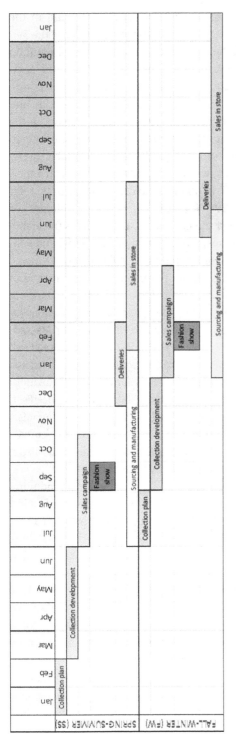

Figure 6.6: Traditional Womenswear Organization of Collections.
Source: Compiled by authors.

(Milan Furniture Fair), the largest and most prestigious event of its kind in the world. Rather than presenting an overview of the offer, these companies use the Salone to experiment and communicate with their audience through a special portfolio of products. They collect important feedback on prototypes, later refining the engineering to solve technical problems or reduce costs (so-called value engineering). Then there are products that represent experiments in economic, technical, and commercial feasibility and market response. For example, a company may use the event to explore a new production process or new materials that could contribute to the long-term expansion of its skills. Many of these products aim to shake up the collective imagination in a scenographic way, without considering immediate repercussions from a commercial point of view. Two other segments of the portfolio refer to products with strong commercial objectives (i.e., the generation of volumes) or profit goals (i.e., a strong contribution to margins). These four objectives (receiving feedback, experimenting with new approaches, pushing design standards, and generating sales) are usually combined and not considered in an isolated way.

In fashion, the pandemic has stimulated a further rethinking of calendars and of ways of presenting collections. In several April 2020 interviews, Toni Belloni, managing director of LVMH Group, expressed a desire to simplify the rhythm of the collections for the sake of production and inventory reduction. Gucci, where creative director Alessandro Michele has repeatedly declared that he wants to abandon the ritual of seasonal shows to connect the presentation of collections, probably two a year, to his artistic inspiration, is emblematic of this shift away from traditional formats and schedules. The first tangible sign of this new approach, destined to leave its mark, was GucciFest, seven short films co-directed by Gus Van Sant and Michele in which the protagonists (including the musicians Billie Eilish and Harry Styles) wear pieces from the brand's latest collection. This is not only a new format for presenting a collection, but also a special combination of fashion, music, and cinematography (Blanks, 2020).

For now, these new ways of presenting a collection have not led to abandoning the "in attendance" mode entirely, but to a hybrid form, with a closed-door fashion show and live-streaming connection. On this front, companies have not been caught totally unprepared, given that live streaming and the production of fashion show videos have been part of the industry since February 2010, when all London Fashion Week shows were for the first time available live on the official website for the event and subsequently uploaded to the Independent.co.uk. In September 2011, the *New York Times* reported that several fashion sites and individual designers would offer live streaming on their sites of that month's New York Fashion Week (Rosenbloom, 2011). What is different now, after the pandemic? A more intensive use of digital channels has forced companies to redefine the format of the show itself, as a mere replica of what was physical in a digital environment was certainly not very effective from a communication standpoint. In the future, this mix of limited attendance and livestreaming, outdoor events, and digital fashion shows will likely be maintained, and it is unlikely that in-person events will be abandoned entirely. Consider that in October 2020, the ten-day

Shanghai Fashion Week proceeded regularly, after an initial postponement, with ninety brands showing their collections – despite participating in a fully virtual showcase on Tmall, Alibaba's e-commerce platform, during the event's original dates in March of that year.

If, on the one hand, the disappearance of large parterres of people close to each other has reduced the element of spectacle for those who were present at fashion shows in 2020, on the other hand the exploitation of digital platforms has vastly expanded the reference audience, making the fashion world much more accessible. The connection between digital presentation and social media only amplifies this connection. TikTok has joined Instagram, which for years was the primary platform for fashion content, in helping brands reach ever-expanding audiences. The social platform, owned by the Chinese internet company ByteDance and launched in 2016, hosted its first fashion month in September 2020, featuring content from the New York, London, Milan, and Paris fashion shows. Hashtags, live videos, and two livestreamed shows a week featuring dedicated capsule collections by brands such as Louis Vuitton and Saint Laurent allowed users to participate in the month's events virtually. There are also those who have chosen, like JW Anderson with its womenswear SS 2021 collection, to use TikTok for important launches (Holland, 2020; Elan, 2020).

E-commerce sites are also well suited for hosting live presentations of collections. This is the path that Dolce & Gabbana chose after canceling its January 2021 menswear show. Instead, the brand decided to rely on Farfetch and its website to debut the new collection. On February 1, 2021, #DGTogether was livestreamed on Farfetch, followed by the sale of 20 looks from the new collection on the site. Elsewhere, plans for the 2021 Salone del Mobile in Milan include a digital exhibition in the spring followed by a physical edition planned for September.

All of these changes have consequences for a company's PIDL activities and for the various individuals and teams involved in them. The organizational structure of each company is different, depending on the complexity of the products, the degree of innovation, commercial vs. creative orientation, the degree of upstream and downstream vertical integration, and the availability of talent, which can allow a company to integrate multiple roles.

Designers, the design team, and the product team are in charge of identifying trends, preserving the heritage of the company,[4] providing inspiration, and designing products. Designers represent the *creative dimension* of the process. They are the custodians of the brand's archives and responsible for preserving its DNA. The product team is in charge of developing creative ideas. Working closely with designers and technical teams, they take new products from the design-concept stage through to prototypes, connecting with factories, sourcing samples of fabrics, and ordering materials. The manager in charge of the product team should be familiar with material specifications and able to analyze a product's cost structure, while also attending fairs and consulting specialized sources to track emerging trends. Frequent contact with marketing and retail departments, which can provide insights about competitors and historical sales performance by period, category, segment of consumers, retail channel, retail location, etc., helps these teams ensure that their ideas will find an audience.

The **merchandiser** is in charge of connecting all the activities related to product ideation and launch to each other, as well as coordinating related departments. This includes helping to develop collections and continuously monitoring and improving results, making sure that a collection "catches" all the opportunities in the market in terms of weight, price point, occasion of use, and seasonal celebration (e.g., Lunar New Year or Valentine's Day capsules), among others. He/she represents the *performance dimension* of the process. Whereas the product and design teams focus on more qualitative aspects of product development (i.e., *what* do we have to develop and launch), merchandisers focus on quantitative issues (i.e., *how much* do we have to develop and launch) such as sales analysis, pricing, quantities, allocation to stores (retail merchandising), in-season re-orders and re-assortments, and markdowns. Merchandisers need a strong understanding of performance drivers. Coordination between merchandiser, product team, and the designer/design team is essential and may vary in terms of power (merchandisers may work for designers or have equal standing) and integration (participation of product manager in the research and concept processes).

Marketing and retail are in charge of communicating to customers, collecting information (through CRM systems), analyzing competitors, managing distribution channels (online and offline, wholesale and retail), defining visual displays and windows, and providing customer service in-store and after sale. They represent the *commercial dimension* of the process.

Sourcing and manufacturing departments should ensure that collections are made efficiently, with the desired level of quality and the right materials, and are delivered according to schedules, in the necessary amount, and with some degree of flexibility. This is the *product dimension* of the process. These two activities have been increasingly affected by digitization, which allows for greater efficiency in prototyping through digital rendering, speeds up cost analysis, and lets companies create digital archives of patterns.

While the **finance department** functions largely behind the scenes, it is responsible for the flow of money inside the company. Merchandising and finance share information and collaborate every day in preparing budgets related to collection development (e.g., prototypes cost, materials cost, orders forecast).

In retail, there are two critical roles involved in the launch and marketing of products: merchandiser and buyer. Although they work together, their roles are distinct. The *retail merchandiser* decides how much to buy to create the appropriate assortment for their store in terms of customer satisfaction as well as the store's turnover and margins objectives. The merchandiser also handles sales plans and the sales forecast, creating the open to buy (OTB) plan (i.e., the amount of inventory that the retail store needs to purchase to meet customer demand while limiting mark downs and risk of stock out). The *buyer* has a role similar to that of the product manager and therefore must have a particular aesthetic sensitivity as well as an understanding of current trends and of other brands' offers. The buyer is involved in product selection and buying, making decisions based on numbers provided by merchandising, with a strong aesthetic sensitivity.

In the case of a wide and diversified product assortment, there are buyers/merchandisers for specific product categories. Often in the world of luxury, the term "merchandiser" designates the headquarters figure, who works with the product team to conceive of the collection and launch bulk orders, while the "buyer" is the merchandiser's counterpart within a specific region. The buyer has contact with the store/clients/local market and the competition and gives feedback to the merchandiser, who transmits information to the designers and product managers. Meanwhile, the merchandiser is in charge of "guiding" the buyer to follow the company's central buying strategy and implement it according to the specificities of the buyer's local market. Finally, in luxury, the numerical retail activities are the responsibility of the planning department. In terms of organizational structure, luxury companies usually have planning and merchandising departments at headquarters as well as separate regional planning and buying/merchandising departments in their market regions.

Detecting Trends and Creating New Products

A company might show a variable intensity of innovation for different products or periods. It's possible, then, to identify true creative leadership vs. progressive innovation. Creative leadership happens when companies introduce a breakthrough by detecting, initiating, and popularizing trends. Innovation leaders conduct research on society in general. The outcome is often a mega-trend destined to last for years, not a season (e.g., streetwear, inclusivity, genderless design, or feminism). A mega-trend influences the future while shaping business and society today, and it's rooted in demographic and social change. It may not be associated with a single theme, type of fabric, color palate, or shape; if it is, then it will be declined in different collections with a different concept.

Maria Grazia Chiuri, the first female creative director in Dior's 70-year history, has made a passionate feminist message integral to her vision for the brand since her first show in September 2016. There, a t-shirt with the words "We Should All Be Feminists", the title of Nigerian writer Chimamanda Ngozi Adichie's 2014 book, went viral on social media. Yet while Chiuri has become the poster child for feminist fashion design, this is not a new trend. Karl Lagerfeld recreated a feminist protest in the Grand Palais in Paris for Chanel's September 2014 fashion show. There, catwalk models carried signs with emancipatory slogans such as "Ladies First", "History is her Story", and "Women's rights are more than all right". Also, in 2014, many cosmetics brands began work on multi-tasking products (for the woman who works, has little time, and must adapt to different occasions during the day) and sculpting for a stronger look, anticipating that a feminist ethos would influence style and consumer behavior for years to come. As a cultural mega-trend, feminism's influence is not limited to fashion and cosmetics, but was already present in the worlds of music and cinema before these two areas began to shape themselves around it. What Chiuri did was develop a progressive innovation; she rode the trend.

Progressive innovation does not mean copying; it involves interpreting a trend in a way that is consistent with a brand's DNA, and it can lead to important new elements. For instance, Asian beauty ideals favor smaller lips, unlike in the West, where big, luscious lips are preferred. Women in Asia often apply gradient lip color to achieve a "porcelain doll" effect. There are many ways to achieve this look – for example, applying a layer of concealer before applying a small dab of color in the center of the lips – but some cosmetics brands identified this regional trend and created a dual lipstick to make the look easier to achieve.

The conception and design phase triggers the process of launching new products. This can be guided by different approaches. While we will present these approaches separately, they can also be combined in various ways depending on the situation at the company. Indeed, it is rare to find the source of innovation in a single approach. For example, a purely marketing-driven approach – looking at what competitors are doing and asking consumers what they would like to improve their experience – is unlikely to lead to a breakthrough because it may not take into due consideration commercial feasibility, differentiation from competitors, etc. if it does not also incorporate market, industry, and/or technical analysis. By defining them individually, we can better understand the strategic purpose of each approach and how they interact with the business model of a given company.

A **marketing-driven** approach focuses on the activities of the marketing department, which realizes a structured brief based on the outcome of focus groups, customer surveys, analyses of competitors, sales data, industry reports, etc. This results in market pull and commercially oriented design: the objective is to increase sales, at the expense of originality.

Competitor analysis plays a key role in a marketing-driven approach, allowing a brand to identify relative strengths and weaknesses in the offer as well as gaps that can be filled by the brand. It can also provide suggestions for new collections. It is important for competitor analysis to be carried out rigorously, starting with the correct identification of the cluster of competitors to be considered. The logical flow of analysis is depicted briefly in Figure 6.7.

The first step is to select the category that is being investigated – bags, for example. The category can then be segmented into typologies: shoulder bags, backpacks, belt bags, clutch bags, travel bags, mini bags, tote bags, cross-body bags, beach bags, bucket bags, laptop bags, etc. For each typology, it's necessary to identify main models (or lines or styles). For example, Bottega Veneta's offer of

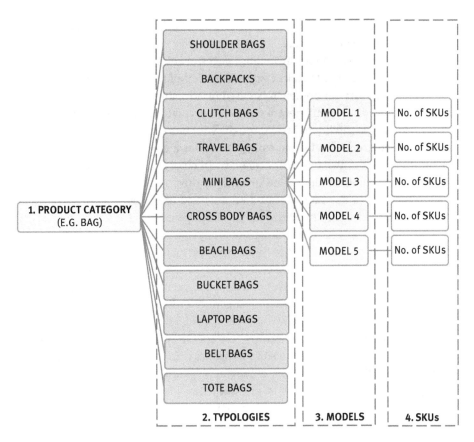

Figure 6.7: Logical Flow of Competitor Analysis.
Source: Compiled by authors.

mini bags includes five models: Mini Pouch, Mini Arco, Double Knot, Mini Bulb, and Mini Twist.

The same bag model (e.g., Mini Pouch) can have many variations. Each particular combination of material, color, size, details (e.g., type of strap), etc. is associated with a stock-keeping unit (SKU). The analyst must therefore create a database that includes the following dimensions for each SKU: price, country of origin, channel of distribution, availability (e.g., limited edition, on pre-order, sold out for now, carry over). Other qualitative information, like the main trends in the typology (e.g., increasing use of logos, adoption of new materials like raffia, etc.), can be collected to supplement the dataset. This work is replicated for all competitors in a cluster.

The SKU analysis is also accompanied by product images and descriptions. Traditionally, since this is information not from the brand doing the analysis but from competitors, it was not readily available. Analysts therefore relied on the results of surveys made in-store (retail safari, mystery shopping) and interviews with consumers and operators in the industry to compile details. However, the growth of digital channels and their greater use by companies for communication and sales activities has made vast quantities of information, including images, available online, and today it is much easier for companies to make complete dossiers of their competitors' products.

A **technology-driven** approach is based on investment in research and development aimed at discovering new materials, new combinations, and new artifacts. There is a higher possibility of breakthroughs with this approach, and therefore the possibility of creating an advantageous position for a company that will last for a long time. The Italian B2B cosmetics company Intercos, for example, has been able to skillfully combine marketing- and technology-driven approaches to generate innovation that serves its clients (beauty brands) and erects entry barriers for their competitors. Likewise, in Chapter 5, we saw how Intercos has created commercial and marketing offices and research and development centers around the world to capture trends in various countries and enhance local research skills in certain product categories. Intercos also uses marketing-driven techniques to test new formulas that originate in its research and development centers. Big data and advanced analytics methodologies can also help companies foresee opportunities, adding sophistication to their PIDL process.

A **human-driven** approach borrows concepts from design thinking (Lojacono and Zaccai, 2004). The driving force of innovation is in this case the skillful exploitation of information deduced from ethnographic studies. The structured observation of people's behavior in their usual context can highlight problems and needs that open up incredible opportunities for innovation. These opportunities are amplified if the analysis is carried out by a multi-disciplinary research team that is able to see the same phenomenon through different lenses. As in the previous two cases, focusing on behavior with respect to a specific theme does not exclude the use of secondary sources, such as the analysis of competitors or the creation of surveys, nor of technological interventions in the quest for innovation.

Finally, a **designer-driven** approach is based on the ability of creatives (or the creative team) to read the social context, interpret the needs of the company, and define the innovative scope of the creative project. Creatives carry out their own research in different areas, using technology to facilitate innovation that has more to do with a product's semiotics than its functionality (Verganti, 2009). In small and medium-sized enterprises (SMEs), sometimes the innovative momentum comes not so much from the designers as from the entrepreneurs themselves, especially if they have a strong aesthetic sensitivity for the product and understanding of social trends.

Creatives are not always internal to the company. Furniture companies typically collaborate with external designers, enlisting different ones for different projects. This has the advantage of differentiating product lines and allowing a company to draw on innovations from other industries. A creative director ensures coherence with the corporate image. External designers, who are usually remunerated with royalties from the product they conceive, receive a brief that articulates the company's needs and the reason for the request. The brief also provides information that can help the designer to better understand the request and respond effectively – for example, the analysis of competitors, the company's sales performance by category, model, channel, and geographic market, etc. A brief may be longer and more detailed if the designer has never before collaborated with the company, or short, unstructured, and even unnecessary if the designer is a frequent collaborator.

When a brief is unstructured, as in the case of very open commissions, a designer will often begin with a general concept or a kind of inspiration. The lighting company Flos has encouraged this approach in a series of highly successful models. For example, Philippe Stark's design, the Miss K, takes its form from a skirt his daughter, K., wore on her birthday. An internal diffusor gives the light emitted grace and elegance. Patricia Urquiola's Chasen reproduces the shape of the bamboo whisk used for the preparation of matcha tea. The final object is made of chemically photo-etched stainless steel and borosilicate. Marcel Wanders's Skygarden replicates the decorated ceiling typical of a Venetian house, allowing it to be transported to every other house in the world. This project required a great deal of materials research (i.e., chalk). The fact that the brief may be unstructured and the innovation more on an emotional and symbolic level than a functional one does not mean that the process is random. There are several gates and internal committees that rigorously assess whether the next step in the product development process can be taken.

The designer-driven approach is crucial in the world of fashion because the creation phase (and the success) of the collection depends on creatives who, with the support of the product and marketing office, carry out careful research aimed at defining the concept behind the collection. As we will see, this concept then helps to define the structure of the collection, which forms the basis of the merchandising plan. To arrive at the definition of the concept, designers rely on multiple internal and external sources. Among the internal sources are corporate museums and archives. Company archives preserve elements of previous collections that, despite being rooted in the past, have an enduring creative influence due to their timeless appeal. Internal sources also include quantitative data such as sales statistics, company reports, retail feedback, etc.

External sources are the most varied, and some of these are industry-specific. In fashion, the following can be mentioned:
- Fashion weeks (catwalk and showroom presentations)
- Trade shows (Première Vision, Tissu Premier, Pitti Immagine Filati) [5]
- "What's now" in retail, the design field, society (e.g., social purposes and causes, influential people and their messages), culture (e.g., foreign habits), technology, entertainment
- The internet and social media
- Information on fashion trends supplied by trend agencies (WGSN, Peclers) and trend setters (Pantone's "Color of the Year")
- Magazines (*Vogue, Business of Fashion, Women's Wear Daily*)

- World trends in global sourcing, finance, and economy
- Cultural and arts exhibitions

Inspiration can come not only from other industries and disciplines, but also from what is happening in different geographic markets. We have already dealt with China's role as a leader in digital experimentation. Likewise, Japan and South Korea are often the first to introduce what become the main trends in the cosmetic world (J-Beauty and K-Beauty).

Designers use *moodboards* to digest these inputs and find a personal interpretation. A moodboard is a visual summary of the inspiration and theme behind the collection and lays the groundwork for the design, product, and merchandising teams. If well-conceived from a visual standpoint, it is a powerful tool to share ideas with internal and external audiences. An effective moodboard catches your attention with a well-chosen title and contains visual references like fabric swatches, pictures, etc. linked by a common thread. A board could also represent a "mood" with a collection of inspirations or muses.

Making a good board to present a mood, trend, or style is anything but simple. It requires the ability to find multiple representations of the same concept without being too explicit and without being messy. It's necessary to be focused, and to capture the mood in a nutshell. An observer should be able to bring all the pieces of the mosaic back to the theme, reading behind the images. You can also put keywords on the board to organize the images and guide the observer. A good practice is to start with a holistic board that explores various ideas and sources of inspiration and then create a second one that extracts the essence of the theme.

The *design brief* is the first attempt to sort the collection into one or more themes. All the ideas coming from the design team are consolidated by the product team so that trends, silhouettes, colors, and prints are agreed on for each category/typology (e.g., bags, belts, shoes, blazers, skirts, etc.). The brief is a written explanation outlining the aims, objectives, and milestones of the design project that will result in a collection, and it is generally shared by the product team with designers and merchandisers. It helps develop understanding between all parties and serves as an essential point of reference for them. Above all, the design brief ensures that important design issues are considered and questioned before the designer starts working on sketches. The goal is to make it as complete and useful as possible. The design brief does not only include stylistic elements, it also outlines the guidelines for creating the detailed merchandising plan, as visible in Figure 6.8.

As depicted in Figure 6.8, in passing to the brief, it is necessary to combine the new (e.g., classic, special, etc.) with the continuative (i.e., carryover including iconic products). The brief is the step of the process that allows the team to move to defining the structure of the collection, i.e., the merchandising plan. The brief and the merchandising plan are the two key documents for the effective development of the collection, a process that involves many players: designers to create sketches,

1. MODELS
The range of jackets must be balanced between carryover and new styles. This is the SKU count.

Carryover	5
New	5
Total	10

2. CARRYOVER
We offer all bestselling models in seasonal colors to integrate with the FW collection.

3. NEW MODELS
We offer:
- 3 classical models in wool and silk, peaked lapel, double-breasted blazer within the price range €2,200–€2,500
- 1 new model in lambskin leather, fitted silhouette to offer a more sporty, but refined style, price should be in between €2,500 and €3,000
- 1 new stretch-wool fitted military jacket with a stand-up collar, a front button fastening, long sleeves, button cuffs, price of around €1,500 to attract a younger target

4. NEW SPECIAL MODELS
2–3 new seasonal and special jackets with new buttons and fabrics in line with the rest of RTW collection and main materials to better negotiate purchaising costs and delivery time

Figure 6.8: An Example of Guidelines provided in the Design Brief for Womenswear Jackets. Source: Compiled by authors.

merchandising to verify the objectives of the collection plan, the product team to translate the sketches into easily identifiable stylistic elements and proceed with the development phase, specialists to create prototypes and carry out tests to verify the fulfillment of functional requirements, and sourcing and manufacturing to start the procurement of raw materials for the production of samples. Regional buyers may also be involved in the process to represent the needs of specific local geographies.

The development of the project brief unites all the industries that we deal with in this book, from fashion and furniture to automobiles and jewelry. What changes is the relative weight of the different functions involved (e.g., marketing, research and development, style/product team, retail). For instance, at Cartier, briefs are generally created by marketing teams based on market insight and analysis of the existing product offer. Briefs are shared with "Creative Studios" (i.e., creative teams), organized according to métier (i.e., macro and micro product lines), that report directly to Cartier's president. Creative Studios work hand in hand with marketing teams organized by category (jewelry, watches, accessories, leather goods, fragrance). In some cases, Creative Studios undertake exploratory activities with no marketing brief, instead exchanging ideas and brainstorming directly with the president. Ideas and sketches are immediately transformed into prototypes that are shared with local markets to get feedback and allow different regions to anticipate their communications and commercial planning.

The differing needs of local markets mean that regional buyers often co-construct the collection by sharing local specificities:

> We should be close to the markets to put in place well-thought products that are in sound with markets. Shops are raising the hands for local product development; but we need a "relevant approach", not to be dependent on local exclusivity, avoiding too many adjustments and special editions that can have a negative impact on our image. We need to be more relevant, as [a] brand, also because regions become polarized, more diverging. We should find the right way to interact with local markets in terms of number of novelties and timing of launch.
>
> (Arnaud Carrez, International Marketing and Communications
> Director, Cartier, personal communication)

Time to market (TTM) for Cartier's jewelry and watches has been reduced to less than twelve months due to increased speed in the development process. The TTM for high jewelry, on the other hand, remains more or less three years.

Merchandising Plan and Collection Development

The Merchandising Plan represents the plan and structure of the collection. It starts with the analysis of the current portfolio, which is combined with sales data from past collections, competition and trend analysis, and the brief provided by the product and style team. The merchandising plan should include the structure of the collection in terms of:
- Number of lines/models/SKUs
- Carryover vs. new products
- Functionality (e.g., denim jacket, leather jacket/biker, trench coat, blazer, poncho, parka, military, wrap coat, zip-up hoodie, etc.)
- Typology/occasion (day, evening, etc.)
- Price range (low, medium, high).

Take as an example a company that has:
- Two haute couture women's collections
- Three main RTW women's collections: spring/summer (presented between late January and mid-February), winter (late July), and permanent collection (with all carryovers)
- Two pre-collections: cruise or resort (that anticipates SS) and pre-fall (end of May).[6] Cruise is presented in May, usually with a show, and arrives in stores in mid-October; pre-fall is presented between December and January, both with the sending of look-books and with events dedicated to press and buyers, and arrives in stores in early summer, usually in mid-May.

The company is involved in the development of a new FW line that will have a special focus on women's jackets and accessories. In order to consolidate and increase the performance of jackets, and assuming iconic and continuative models do not have any variation, key departments will start with the following guidelines:

- Every line should include **different materials, shapes, details** (e.g., buttons, pockets) following the new theme expressed in moodboards and the design brief
- It's important to develop the theme to allow **3–4 seasonal rotations** within stores and complement the classic color palette
- It's recommended to research **new fabrics and materials**, as well as design variants
- **Share the main theme** with other product categories (skirts, pants, bags; in our example, jackets are the focus that structures the collection)

Once these guidelines have been established, the design brief delivered by merchandisers becomes fundamental, as it will articulate the stylistic and quantitative aspects of the collection. Returning to the concept behind the collection, the team lays out how core stylistic details will carry the theme through the models and variants indicated by the guidelines. On the quantitative side, a first indication of the sell-out price range may be included in the brief at this stage. The design team can then compare the brief to previous analyses of the brand's competitors by the marketing and product teams to assess how innovative the collection is. Only then will designers begin sketching the collection, as well as sourcing materials and estimating manufacturing and industrial costs – luxury fashion generally retails at 60% above the wholesale price. The final merchandising plan includes models, number of variants, product descriptions, wholesale price targets, retail price targets, and sketches (or even pictures) of all items.

A distinction can be made between items that are conceived for commercial purposes, at the request of the buyers, and items created based on input from the style (or product) office. A successful collection balances these inputs in a particular way. Not all product categories are the same, and whether it's marketing or creative that has control over new designs depends on the purpose of the category. If jackets are supposed to be big sellers, then most jackets will be based on what the market wants. Meanwhile, the designer will be freer to take risks with, for example, dresses, though they can still add some dynamism to the collection as a whole. Let's say the brand in our example plans to include 16 jackets in its new collection: 4 new styles and 11 from a past offer. Of the 4 new jackets, only one may be the result of the creative process, meaning the other three will be developed based on market pull. Product categories that have a greater commercial purpose will include more market-pull designs than those for which the emphasis is less on sales than on showcasing creativity.

Once the initial designs for the collection have been completed, the merchandising team reviews the segmentation of the offer by price range, comparing it to the previous collection. In the lowest price range should be items that can contribute in terms of volumes of sales, for example jackets under €2,000. In the intermediate range, for example between €2,000 and €3,000, should be items that will both generate substantial sales volumes and contribute to the brand image. Finally, a small number of high-priced items, more than €3,000, should be well-positioned to "make their mark" from a communication point of view rather than to generate large volumes of sales.

This finalized collection plan will determine the ultimate structure of the collection, with color cards and materials. Some models may be added or deleted at this stage, with sketches of new products prepared by the design team. A collection book is assembled for use in presentations and training, outlining the collection inspiration and themes, its structure and product offer, models and details, materials explanation, and technical information related to product manufacture, all supported by images.

At this point, the collection plan becomes a *collection budget* that forecasts expected costs and revenues. This budget is used to prepare pre-orders to suppliers or in-house factories, which will be finalized when the collection is sold. Pre-orders allow suppliers and factories to order materials and plan deliveries. Production managers prepare a "cut ticket" that specifies the individual pieces of fabric that should be cut for each item. A second document, the "tech pack", includes the complete information for each item: the meters of fabric for different sizes in each cut, numbers of buttons, etc. These two documents quantify the material needs of the collection and allow manufacturers to place their orders with suppliers. Purchasing agents often act as intermediaries in these situations, ensuring clear communication between brands and their suppliers or manufacturers (Sherman, 2014).

Finally, the price of each item is set, accounting for all the information that the brand has assembled up to this point: industrial costs, product positioning in the portfolio and vs. competitors, price range within the collection, purpose assigned to each category (e.g., profitability, customers' attraction, cross-selling, etc.), special requests from local markets, exchange rates, and feedback from the commercial and marketing department. Pricing is a crucial activity to assure the collection's success.

It's now time to do the initial allocation of the collection to retail stores – the *master buy* – which is carried out before presenting the collection to external audiences. Product-assortment guidelines from the master buy will support retail buyers in their final selection. Allocation begins with the consideration of the different retail formats, both online and offline, as presented in Chapter 1: flagship, mono-brand stores, pop-ups, concessions, travel retail stores, and Brand.com. Within the different formats, stores are classified based on criteria such as generated sales volumes, geographical position, type of customers, etc. While a core offer will be displayed in all stores, only a few will feature the full assortment. What items a store receives depends on store capacity and on the financial targets that can be achieved in a certain location, which constrain inventory. A store's assortment selection (or *assortment edit*) will be "store-friendly" for a specific store format, size, or even location while also being representative of the brand values and the themes of the collection. Editing must make sure that the assortment in each store:

- Is coherent with the brand identity
- Includes iconic products ("must buy" items)

- Is properly balanced in terms of price range
- Includes different degrees of risk
- Includes the best seller, which may be different from the iconic products
- Includes NOOS, i.e., *Never Out of Stock* items (like black pumps, blue blazers, etc.)
- Is consistent with advertising and promotion

Editing is also used in wholesale, since this channel rarely buys the full assortment.

In defining the core collection for each type of store, the brand should achieve a good balance of product margins, prices, categories (e.g., jackets, trousers, dresses, etc.), degree of risk (e.g., logo vs. no-logo, the first being less risky), possible best sellers, and core vs. high fashion. The level of risk is then correlated with the open to buy (higher the risk, lower the OTB) and mark-down strategy. A golden rule in retail is the 80:20 ratio: 80% of sales usually come from 20% of the range.

Sales Campaign and Sales Period

Everything is now ready to be presented, both internally and externally. The internal presentation foresees that the merchandiser meets all the various functions, illustrating in detail the theme and structure of the collection. The collection book is part of the brand's internal presentation, which may include a real show. Externally, as discussed at the beginning of this chapter, the presentation takes place both at fashion shows and in the showrooms where buyers meet.

In other industries like jewelry, launch strategy does not depend on specific external events but satisfies internal strategic purposes. For instance, Cartier's launch strategy varies according to the specific collection and is not always simultaneous across all regions. The new version of Cartier's Pasha, a cult watch since its debut in 1985, launched first in China in early July 2020, then in Korea later that month, and finally in all other countries in September. Limited-edition jewelry collections can be also presented in a narrow selection of places. For example, Les Galaxies de Cartier launched in 2019 in less ten top boutiques around the globe, achieving an incredible success. As Cartier's international marketing and communication director Arnaud Carrez has noted, "Finding the right distribution for the new products is key. Right means the network of stores with consistent client targets" (personal communication).

In this crucial moment of the sales campaign, it is the merchandiser who must schedule meetings with buyers and store managers, not only to share the key messages of the collection, but also to receive feedback. Many brands also organize official collection debriefs between buyers and merchandisers so that they can compare the actual selection of retail buyers with the proposed master buy. This is essential if the merchandiser is to understand how the collection is perceived in different geographic markets.

Once all the orders have been collected, the delivery plan is triggered, starting sourcing and production at one end of the supply chain and the planning of all retail activities (e.g., different delivery windows for different groups of products, visual merchandising, in-store presentations, CRM actions, etc.) at the other. Ad hoc communication projects launch before and during the sales season to create awareness, push specific products, and react to retail and wholesale feedback. Crucial for the distribution success of the collection is how it is presented to clients. Sales associates must be able to provide all the information to customers and increase their desire for and attraction to the products in the collection. This is why brands provide immersive training plans for all retail employees: the collection should be properly explained to the sales force, not only to buyers.

When the collection is available for purchase, activities are carried out simultaneously both in the store (physical and virtual) and in the company. In-store, CRM actions are put on track to entice the customer to learn about and buy the new items. At the same time, data concerning new customers is fed into the CRM system. Expressions of interest and feedback received from customers are also tracked. The role of CRM in the sales period is the subject of the next section.

At both retail and HQ levels, extreme care must be taken with product management: optimizing the performance of various products through re-orders (to avoid stock-out), re-assortments (for permanent products), stock balancing (among areas and stores), and markdowns (to reduce remaining stock at the end of the period, as well as organizing pre-sales). At the HQs level, the merchandiser constantly monitors the performance of products during the sales period. Sales information is collected and analyzed as follows:

- By area, country, stores
- By product typology, seasonality, functionality
- By price range
- Full-price vs. markdown
- Year-to-date (YTD), season-to-date (STD), and month-to-date (MTD) performance
- Best and worst sellers in terms of product, materials, colors, models
- Stock levels

The collection is assessed according to three types of performance: economic (is the collection generating adequate gross margins), financial (is it generating adequate cash flows considering inventory, rents, salaries, etc.), and commercial (how are different regions, products, colors, store formats, price ranges performing).

These evaluation areas are then translated into a series of indicators and specific evaluations. The first quantity of analysis is the *mark-up*, which assumes sales at full price and indicates the potential profit to be realized through actual sales. This is determined by the ratio between full price and purchase cost – or alternatively by gross margin divided by per-purchase cost.

$$\text{Mark-up} = \frac{\text{Full price}}{\text{Purchase cost}}$$

$$\text{Gross margin} = \text{Full price} - \text{Purchase cost}$$

$$\text{\% Gross margin} = \frac{\text{Gross margin}}{\text{Full price}} \longleftarrow \text{Or "Intake margin"}$$

$$\text{Mark-up*} = \frac{\text{Gross margin}}{\text{Purchase cost}} \longleftarrow \text{Alternative version of Mark-up}$$

Sell-out performance relies on an analysis of full price ST, ST rate, ST rate at value, average price, and gross margin on net sales as described in this section.

Lastly, the monitoring of volumes and leftovers is carried out by the open to buy (OTB). OTB is a widely used method to optimize deliveries of products to stores based on sales and stock. It is calculated based on the relationship between stock in hand and planned sales. OTB allows companies to keep stock under control, minimizing both markdowns and store stock-outs. The formula to calculate the OTB is (Planned Sale + Planned Markdowns)-(Planned Beginning of Month Inventory-Planned End-of-Month Inventory). Consider that, in practice, stores will count on replenishments, capsule, and in-season collections to refresh their stock. In such a case, the following formula is applied.

(+) Planned Full price sales
(+) Planned Markdown sales
(+) Planned final left-overs

(=) **Inventory requirement**

(-) Initial inventory

(=) **Open to buy**

(-) Available replenishment
(-) Capsule or other in-season collections

(=) **Initial Open to buy**

OTB is usually based on purchase cost. Therefore, when planned sales are included, they are evaluated at cost, not at expected full price. OTB is projected over periods (months, weeks) to keep inventory under control. In directly operated stores, the OTB is "pushed" by headquarters, while in the wholesale channel, OTB is decided at the beginning of the season by store owners. However, it is becoming common for brands to have a high degree of control over wholesale OTB.

A complete economic performance analysis at the store level is usually delivered weekly through the weekly sales, stock, and intake (WSSI) report, which includes an analysis of weekly performance at the store level: sales (actual/forecast), markdowns, margins, stock, OTB, cover (current stock/average weekly sales),[7] comparisons to budget, and previous year. The cover is a widely used indicator of whether a store has enough stock of a given product to sell through the end of the sales period. For example, if cover is 4 weeks and there are 7 weeks to go, a re-order is necessary to avoid stock-out. If cover is 12 weeks and there are 7 weeks to go, then markdowns are probably necessary.

The WSSI report measures performance in the relevant categories, supports OTB decisions, and allows the merchandiser to adjust forecasting during the season to minimize markdowns and maximize margins. The retail network is under continuous monitoring and evaluation to check not only sales data and marginality, but also how stores are performing daily in terms of traffic, number of tickets, and average transactions. This is fundamental if a brand is to implement corrective actions promptly.

Customer Relationship Management (CRM)

Customer Relationship Management (CRM) strategies, systems, and software allow the brand to develop a direct knowledge of customers, their preferences, and their motivations to purchase. This information is essential to differentiate communication, services, and sales approaches to target specific client clusters or even individual clients. The goal of CRM is to build long-lasting relationships with customers (especially the most profitable and high spending ones), increase their loyalty to the brand and their purchasing value in a period and per single order, and attract potential new customers. Other benefits can be summarized as:

- Collecting information to support new product development to optimize the product mix
- Favor through cross-selling and up-selling actions
- Efficiency in warehouse management thanks to a better understanding of customers' tastes and more accurate predictions about what they will actually buy
- Reduction of the sales cycle, as the sales staff know customers' tastes and preferences

Information about current and potential clients is collected both on physical and digital channels, possibly in an integrated way, as suggested in the explanations of omnichannel strategies in Chapters 1 and 2.

Another interesting point to mention is brands' motivation to acquire a global vision of the customer that is not only transversal to their channels, but also to the geographic markets in which they operate. Customers travel the world and expect superior treatment any time they enter a boutique. By having a single database, an international brand can track customer behavior and purchases across regions and even individual stores, building a much more relevant and effective relationship. This can mean not contacting the client several times from different countries, and recognizing him/her as a VIP when he/she steps into an unfamiliar store location for a repair.

The use of CRM is not new. Luxury brands have relied on various systems to keep track of customer purchases and preferences throughout their history. However, today's CRM databases offer new possibilities for managing the brand/client relationship and developing tailored services that promote trust and loyalty on the part of luxury consumers. An important part of CRM is *lead nurturing*, the process by which continuous communication is established with a potential customer by providing relevant content and information aimed at maturing the customer's decision to purchase. Today, CRM activities can also attract new customers by generating leads and retargeting social media communications. An increasingly popular strategy is that of co-optation between brands, i.e., collaborating with other brands that are not direct competitors on exclusive joint events in the hope of recruiting new customers. For example, a watch brand that allies itself with car manufacturers, yachts, prestigious banks, etc. to share non-competitive access to customers with certain tastes, preferences, or spending habits.

Once a database of information has been built, it is necessary to create a single customer view, combining information from different data sources. This is usually achieved through *identity resolution*, which leverages predictive analytics to bring together personally identifiable information (PII) like first and last names, email addresses, and mailing addresses and connect it to transactional data, preferences, and behavioral data at the individual level to form known-customer profiles.

Within the CRM, companies analyze available customer and behavioral data to deliver insights aimed at supporting optimum and timely business decisions. Business intelligence (BI) and customer analytics (CA) applications approach this challenge by creating custom queries, dashboards, and reports to visualize purchasing behavior, retention rates, and recurring behavioral dynamics.

In addition, predictive analytics models and artificial intelligence (AI) are used to augment human judgment (seller feedback) and ongoing model retraining, calculating near real-time opportunity win/loss prediction and providing powerful analytics-based recommendations. Leveraging CRM data and predictive analytics/AI can support store associates in real time with info about a customer's past behavior and suggestions on the next best action (NBA). For example, Niemann Marcus developed an app that is only accessible to store associates and provides customer profiles. This gives associates a better understanding of customer preferences, purchase cycle, and browsing behavior, allowing them to better serve their clients. In addition to simply reporting on customer behavior, it's possible to leverage predictive analytics and machine learning to provide recommendations to store associates on what may interest a particular customer as well as the best strategies to nurture that customer and increase their lifetime value (LTV).

In addition to analytics and AI, companies have recently begun to rely on a customer data platform (CDP) that is used to coordinate marketing strategies across different channels and vendors. This new platform combines CRM with MarTech (i.e., marketing technology). It leverages customer data collected in a company's CRM system to create a centralized customer profile and enriches it with third-party data collected throughout the entire ecosystem (i.e., Facebook, agency, personalization vendors, etc.). For example, journeys can be built within the platform to enact a specific strategy for a customer segment and maintain a consistent message across all touchpoints. For companies using different marketing partners, this level of coordination is not be possible without a CDP synchronizing strategies and messages.

There are two types of CRM, which are usually combined. A first type is *one-to-many CRM*, which requires powerful IT platforms and exploits predictive analysis to segment customers into small groups, addressing individual customers based on actual behaviors. It also tracks customers and how they move among different segments over time (i.e., dynamic segmentation), including customer lifecycle context and cohort analysis. AI helps to accurately predict customers' future behaviors (i.e., convert, churn, etc.) and determine their lifetime value. The goal of one-to-many CRM is to inform the decision process and maximize long-term value by delivering the right message, at the right time, to the right person.

A second form is *one-to-one CRM*, also known as *clienteling*. Information is collected to create very detailed individual profiles rich in information on preferences and behaviors. A brand uses these to organize initiatives and communications targeted to an individual client by content and channel. More and more CRM campaigns mix these two forms to be more effective, even if one can prevail over the other. The two types are detailed in the next two parts of this section.

One-to-Many CRM

The goal of one-to-many CRM is to create segments and profiles that allow the brand to obtain information about where and when certain customers buy, or even which products they prefer. This should lead to a segmentation of a brand's offer and communications based on empirical evidence, with the aim of meeting the needs of consumers in the best possible way, maximizing their satisfaction and their loyalty. Typical segments of customers in a CRM system can be mapped as in the Figure 6.9.

The vertical axis shows the monetary value of customers' spending. Depending on the type of business, these values can be adjusted by mapping spending for the

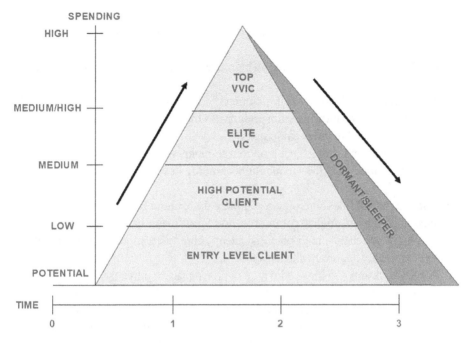

Figure 6.9: CRM Pyramid.
Source: Compiled by authors.

brand's existing client base onto the figure. The horizontal axis shows the frequency and recency of spending over time for various client segments. These three measures describe key aspects of customers' purchasing behavior:

- *Recency* refers to the last purchase made by a customer. Someone who made a large purchase (high spending) two years ago but nothing since (low recency) has the potential to drop to a lower customer tier according to the arrow on the right.
- *Frequency* indicates how often a customer purchases something from the company, expressed by the number of tickets over a specified period of time (i.e., number tickets/time).
- *Monetary Value* is the amount a customer has spent in the store or with the brand over time (following the arrow on the left), within a specific period. E.g., customer X spends €200 ten times within a year for an annual monetary value of €2,000.

By incorporating these three levers into a recency, frequency, monetary (RFM) analysis, brands can determine the behavior of their customers and answer questions like the following:

- Are they weekend clients?
- Are they seasonal clients or tourist clients (big purchases one or a few times a year)?
- Are they clients who follow the fashion calendar (do they only come in for the new collection)?
- Do they prefer fall/winter, spring/summer, cruise, or pre-season collections (this can help the merchandising team understand the preferences of their customers)?
- Are they attracted by sales campaigns?
- Are they occasional clients (e.g., random shoppers who pop in with no motives)?
- Are they frequent, but low- to medium-spending (loyal) customers?

CRM plays a critical role in helping a company understand its customers, its brands, and how to better personalize communication for different tiers of clients: potential clients, entry-level clients, high-potential clients, elite "very important clients" (VICs), and top "very, very important clients" (VVICs).

Potential clients are those who may not have made a purchase, but have a high chance of conversion if the brand follows up with them. It is assumed that everyone who walks into a store intends to make a purchase, so connecting with potential new clients is an important aspect of customer acquisition for CRM. These clients are also key to growing a customer base by converting them to loyal customers. CRM can be used to analyze the reasons a potential client did not make a purchase on their first visit to one of the company's stores. Was it because the desired item was not available? Did the item not meet their expectations? Was the client lost to a competitor? How could the company have converted the client?

Entry-level clients are those who have made purchases that are of low monetary value or one-offs. These have the potential to ascend to the second tier of the pyramid, depending on a number of variables: price point, product mix, and communication (e.g., activities such as pop-ups that remove the pressure of entering the store and making purchases).

High-potential clients are previously acquired clients (they are part of the company's database) with a purchase history. With the right tools (e.g., benefits such as events or free gifts), a brand could convince them to spend more, elevating their spending value over time.

Elite clients can be divided into two categories: (1) those who make frequent purchases of medium- to high-value items and (2) those who make high- to very high-value purchases one or few times within the specified time frame.

Top clients – VICs and VVICs – are usually loyal clients who have made high- to very high-value purchases consistently over many periods. These clients also enjoy benefits offered by the brand, such as invitations to fashion shows, discounts, access to pre-sales, etc.

Dormant/sleeper clients are those who have stopped making purchases after a certain period of time. It is important for brands to understand why these clients have stopped returning. An in-depth study of dormant/sleeper clients is extremely important as it could yield important information about the factors that have deterred the client from coming back:

- Is the client bored of the merchandise?
- Is the client in a period of economic difficulty?
- Is the client no longer interested in the brand value or brand meaning?
- Has the client out grown the brand/changed their taste?
- Did the client have a negative experience with the brand?
- Has the client allocated their budget to other types of spending?

The VIC and VVIC segments of the customer portfolio are the focus of CRM for many companies. The strategies they devise are intended to lead customers to increase their spending on the brand through targeted activities based on customer segment, with the aim of bringing the largest possible number of customers to the top of the pyramid. Brands achieve this by offering incentives, giving customers access to special benefits (discounts, invitations to events, product previews, exclusive products, pamper packages, gifts, etc.) as they move up the pyramid. In the 2020 lockdown, some brands sent flowers or fragrances accompanied by handwritten letters to their most important customers, offering them unique experiences to help them recover from a stressful period, such as a massage in an exclusive spa, a lunch in a sophisticated bistro, or a personalized tour to discover hidden corners of their city.

One-to-One CRM

One-to-one CRM or clienteling plays an ever more important role in luxury due to the customers' willingness to have increasingly direct and personalized relationships with a brand and its references (e.g., sales associates, store managers, fashion concierges). It is one of the most-used CRM tools at an operational level and involves using customers' information to create and manage a more direct relationship with them. Thanks to the information at their disposal, the sales staff can know a customer's tastes and preferences, exploiting them to create a personalized and intimate customer experience and develop a more meaningful, lasting relationship. Clienteling therefore concerns all the initiatives implemented by store staff to build and strengthen the relationship between a brand and its current client base. In a situation such as that generated by the uncontrolled spread of Covid-19, with lockdowns differentiated by country and consumers fearful of closed environments such as retail stores, a tool such as clienteling offers a precious opportunity to keep relationships with a brand's most loyal customers alive even far from the physical store. This is especially true given the acceleration of digital technologies in support of CRM that we discussed in Chapter 2. Today, all luxury brands offer their customers the possibility of organizing one-to-one virtual meetings to experience new collections or video calls on various platforms with sales associates to see the products in the store (Ell, 2020). In a period of profound change on the demand side, CRM is even more important as a fundamental tool to monitor the behaviors and preferences of brands' customers.

Takeaways
- Scenario planning is an important tool that companies can use to plan for uncertain futures, develop agility, and become more resilient.
- Products are central to brand identity, and effective PIDL is fundamental to success.
- Brands use a combination of approaches to develop products that are innovative, well-designed, and meet the needs of customers and markets.
- The design brief plays a crucial role in setting the tone for a new product or collection; the merchandising plan ensures its successful execution.
- Well-managed distribution at the level of regions, channels, stores, and even individual customers can ensure that a collection performs well both commercially and in terms of its contribution to a brand's reputation.

Notes

1 Business of Fashion and McKinsey's "State of Fashion 2021" survey and McKinsey Fashion Scenarios 2021 report that 71% of fashion executives expect their online business to grow by 20% or more in 2021.

2 For a detailed description of principles and practice in fashion, see J. Clark (2015) and Varacca and Misani (2017).

3 A season is a period of time during which a type of merchandise will sell as a result of demand and an offer's availability.

4 Product development activities and the style department are often united under the same umbrella. For the stake of simplicity, here we'll refer generically to the "Product Team".

5 Often, an important source of inspiration comes from actors and events that concern the upstream part of the supply chain (materials, fabrics, yarns, prints, etc.) around the world. Suppliers, with their innovation processes and their manufacturing skills, also make a valuable contribution to brands' design and product development processes. It is not uncommon for the entire collection to revolve around a particular and exclusive yarn or print that catches the attention of the public and triggers imitative processes in the industry.

6 These pre-collections, now very popular in the luxury world, are a recent phenomenon; the first cruise shows by Chanel and Dior date to the beginning of 2000. In addition to these "extra" collections, there are also capsules dedicated to special events. This multiplication of launches, with excessive organizational frenzy and an extravagant number of products offered to the market, has been much criticized in recent times and has led several brands to seek some rationalization of the portfolio and deadlines in the fashion calendar.

7 Cover can also be determined based on the previous week's sales rather than average sales.

7 Sustainability in the Luxury Context

Sustainability from a Global Perspective

Sustainability poses a paradox in the world of luxury, not only because of its focus on moderate and responsible consumption, but also its mission to close the gap between wealth disparities. Luxury has for many years been an exclusive ecosystem constructed to cater to a very selective and affluent clientele. Its customers seek rarity: rare animals, rare objects, rare experiences, all of which are symbols of elitism. In literature, luxury has been defined as "A lifestyle of excess, indulgence and waste" (Hennigs et. al, 2013, p. 25), which is why the concept of sustainability in luxury is an oxymoron.

The idea of sustainability has been ignored by the world of luxury since its inception. Many luxury companies saw sustainability only in terms of the longevity and legacy of a business, in the sense of having a steady stream of loyal customers and a family lineage to shepherd the company from one generation to another. While some companies have historically taken a wider view, going so far as to embrace a more responsible consumption of resources to avoid depleting the raw materials, which rely on to continue producing their their products. This is still far from reaching the true goal of sustainability from an ethical and environmental stand point.

In 2015, the United Nations General Assembly established the Sustainable Development Goals (SDGs) or Global Goals, highlighting seventeen interconnected objectives to create a "blueprint to achieve a better and more sustainable future for all". The intention is to achieve these goals by 2030, with actionable targets that are meant to be achieved between 2020 and 2030. Around the same time, external pressures from the consumer brought sustainability into the forefront of conversations within the world of luxury. The mid-2000s saw a number of economic and political crises that made social inequalities obvious to everyone, and sustainability moved from the agendas of activist groups like PETA and Greenpeace into the political mainstream. Consumers became more aware of ethical and environmental sustainability issues such as fair pay for workers, ethical sourcing of raw materials, and anti-slavery acts. The United Nations Sustainable Development Goals also provided companies with no prior experience in embracing sustainability practices with a roadmap they could use to develop their own sustainability goals.

Since then, many companies, especially those listed on the stock exchange, have started to publish their sustainability goals as part of their financial reporting. One example is Tiffany & Co., which has been issuing a sustainability report since 2017. In these reports the company dedicates an entire section to elaborate how the company contributes to the progress of the UN's seventeen SDGs. Other companies in different industries, such as Ferrari, are also using the UN's SDGs as a measure of their sustainability activities.

https://doi.org/10.1515/9783110723519-007

These changes in how luxury companies operate are occurring in response to shifting customer expectations. Millennials and Gen Zs are more concerned about the uncertainty of their future. They have been bombarded by scientific information about climate change, are now experiencing environmental disasters and the threat of extinction first hand. As a result, these younger generations are much more inclined to make ethically and environmentally driven choices than their predecessors. If luxury companies refuse to change, they too could find themselves facing extinction.

Sustainability and Luxury

The Affluent and their Consumption

While there are pressures from the consumer side to encourage luxury companies to put a higher emphasis on ethical and sustainable practices, it is also true that affluent luxury consumers are themselves implicated in unsustainable behaviors. A report on Confronting Carbon Inequality by Oxfam, published in September 2020, indicated that the richest 10% of the world's population is responsible for almost 50% of the world's total lifestyle production of carbon dioxide emissions; the poorest 50% of the world's population is responsible for only around 10% (Gore, 2020). The majority of this affluent population overlaps geographically with the world's largest luxury consuming populations, which are North America, Europe, and China.

One could argue that the outsize carbon footprint of certain population segments is due to aspects of an urban lifestyle such as the use of vehicles, energy, and manufactured goods (EPA, n.d.). However, it is the wealthy and upper middle class who take this lifestyle to extremes. This includes air travel, favoring imported goods and overconsumption. Celebrity culture provides numerous examples of these types of behaviors: Texas socialite Theresa Roemer, became famous for her three-story closet filled with thousands of luxury shoes and a collection of exotic handbags; Jamie Chua, a Singaporean digital influencer, often boasts about having one of largest collections of rare and exclusive Hermès bags in Asia. We often think of individuals as exceptions, but in reality, Roemer and Chua are merely exceptional in how openly they broadcast their consumption habits – they represent a much wider group of ultra-wealthy luxury consumers around the world. By scrolling through your Instagram feed, you will surely find thousands of digital influencers and celebrities who parade their million-dollar wardrobes for the world to see.

The luxury business thrived for many years on excessive consumption. As we discussed in Chapter 6, the way that luxury companies have structured their CRM pyramid makes it clear that they prioritize consumers who spend more on high-value goods and make these purchases more often. Just like airline points reward schemes, loyalty to a luxury brand comes with access to better customer service and further rewards. Often times, luxury consumers are encouraged by sales associates to make impulse purchases. However, in reality these customers often have no intension of ever using these luxury goods. They sit in boxes or on a shelf, untouched for years and years.

Why Luxury Should Care About Sustainability

Climate Change is Real

An increasing number of natural disasters brought on by a changing climate have made clear the urgency of issues related to sustainability. Especially significant were the 2019 wildfires in Australia, said to be the world's second largest of the twenty-first century, 2 million hectares short of those that spread through Russia in 2003. The first signs of fire were discovered in September 2019 in New South Wales, and wildfires eventually spread across the entire land mass of Australia, burning for a total of 79 days. More than 18 million hectares were affected, destroying habitats that were home to indigenous Australian flora and fauna and displacing human communities. This had huge environmental impacts, including in the supply chain of luxury goods.

Australia is the world leader in wool production, supplying around 25% of the total global wool market (Australian Government, n.d.). The most luxurious merino wool comes from Australia, supplying fabric makers such as Loro Piana, Ermenegildo Zegna, and Piacenza Cashmere. While the fires did not affect livestock directly, they destroyed large amounts of important grazing land. The Woolmark Company, an international secretariat representing Australia's wool industry, indicated that the disaster would have a significant effect the wool industry in the near future, impacting the supply chains of textile companies (Celeste, 2020).

It would be naïve to assume that the fires only affected the luxury supply chain, but the devastation tip the world's biodiversity on its head. Images of the destruction of ecosystems and communities – scorched landscapes, incinerated homes, and injured and dying wildlife – painted a vivid picture of the real scope of the tragedy. Even if wildfires are a seasonal occurrence in Australia, what happened between 2019 and 2020 has shaken a lot of people to the core. With climate change progressing, many of the protocols and fire prevention actions put in place by the Australian Government are unlikely to prevent future bushfires. The Earth's temperature could very well rise to a point of no return. On February 14, 2020, Antarctica recorded a record high temperature of 18.3 degrees Celsius. Climate change is a damaging reality to those across the southern hemisphere, especially in Polynesia, where many are being displaced from their historical islands and atolls due to the rising sea level. Scientists have said that if the Earth's temperature rises by 2 degrees Celsius, over 70% of the Earth's coastline will see sea levels rise by more than 0.2 meters, enough to have a serious impact on ecological systems (Buis, 2020).

The irreversible effects of climate change are not only a problem for poorer populations in the Global South; they also have devastating implications for wealthier countries such as Italy. In 2019, Venice – a location visited by over 5 million tourists a year (Statista, 2021), many of whom are luxury consumers – witnessed some of the worst flooding in its history. Images on the internet showed tourists using makeshift walkways to battle flood waters in St. Mark's square, with their luxury purchases held high. Dams built to divert seawater from the lagoons following catastrophic flooding in 1966 have helped Venice better manage the high tides and sinking seabed that have threatened the city throughout its history. However, in the last decade, scientists have indicated that rising sea levels, land erosion, and cruise ships are the main causes of recent flooding. As more tourists arrive on cruise ships and navigate the city's canals in their Riva yachts, further erosion could eventually destabilize Venice beyond a point of no return.

In addition to rising sea levels, the effects of climate change on biodiversity can also have enormous consequences for the environment and for humans. In late January 2020, a new virus strain (Sars-CoV-2) began to emerge, with cases appearing in Wuhan, China, and other parts of South East Asia. The World Health Organization labelled this virus Covid-19 in March, shortly before confirming its status as a pandemic. Scientists and medical practitioners working on understanding the virus, suspect that it is a mutation of one that existed in wild animals, an origin similar to that of SARS, which appeared in 2002. Over the last two decades, studies have shown that SARS-like viruses are likely to cross over into human populations from wild animals that have been removed from their natural habitat, either through poaching or deforestation (Tollefson, 2020).

One of the greatest fears throughout the 2020 pandemic was that the virus could mutate to a strain that would be resistant to the vaccines in production. This frightening possibility became reality when mink farmers in Denmark noticed flu-like symptoms in their animals and themselves, and tests revealed the virus to be a new strain of Covid-19. In November 2020, the Danish government ordered the culling of over 17 million mink from farms that supply luxury brand manufacturers, a decision that could eradicate an entire species of mink. While the Danish government argued that the culling is necessary to ensure that the potential mutation does not compromise studies into the virus and the race to manufacture a vaccine (BBC News, 2020), events such as this raise ethical questions about the fur industry more generally. Is the use of mink fur ethical in the first place? Should luxury brands ban the use of animal furs in their products? Will luxury consumers care if brands no longer use mink as a raw material? Raising questions like these is an important part of initiating change throughout luxury industries. For industries that are more familiar with sustainability and environmental practices, decisions about best practices are often made through a simple analysis of what British author and corporate social responsibility (CSR) expert John Elkington has called "the triple bottom line".

How to "Theoretically" Achieve Sustainability

Elkington first proposed the idea of a triple bottom line (TBL) in 1994. He argued that businesses should make decisions based on three separate bottom lines to account for the full cost involved in doing business. Traditionally, companies have only measured their corporate profit and loss as the "bottom line". However, research showed that measuring the effects of a company's decisions over time based on financial performance alone was not only insufficient but bound to fail. To gain an accurate picture of its successes and failures, a company should also consider the social and environmental aspects of its decisions. Identifying a "people account", which measures a company's social responsibility to its employees and those affected by the day-to-day operations of the business, and a "planet account", which measures the environmental impacts in the business's value chain, in addition to the traditional financial account, the triple bottom line proposes a way to balance the scorecard by taking other factors into consideration. Often referred to as Profit, People and Planet, it is illustrated in Figure 7.1.

The triple bottom line was created to help companies take a multifaceted approach to business decisions and avoid the imbalances of a traditional approach focused on one measure alone. For example, a company too focused on cost and profits may find itself engaged in:
- Child labor practices in poorer countries to manufacture goods for significantly lower costs
- Deforestation in the rain forest without considering conservation or responsible logging
- Polluting natural aquafers leading to the poisoning of a community's water resources

The examples above are actual events that have happened many times across many different countries and communities. In the past, companies were not held accountable for their actions, but in the last decade, these issues have become increasingly important and transparent.

Luxury companies have been as negligent as those in other industries. In 2018, Burberry made headlines when it admitted to burning merchandise such as apparel, accessories, and perfumes in order to uphold brand equity. Similarly, in 2010, the Environmental Transport Association declared the Lamborghini Murcielago to be the least environmentally friendly car on the market (Roberts, 2010). The study showed that driving the car for a year had the same CO_2 impact as felling a forest as big as a football pitch. Often, luxury brands have the "luxury" of ignoring environmental issues because the pool of customers they draw on, and therefore the number of products they produce, is limited. However, as the affluent population continues to grow, so will the rate at which they consume luxury goods. This kind of mentality is destined

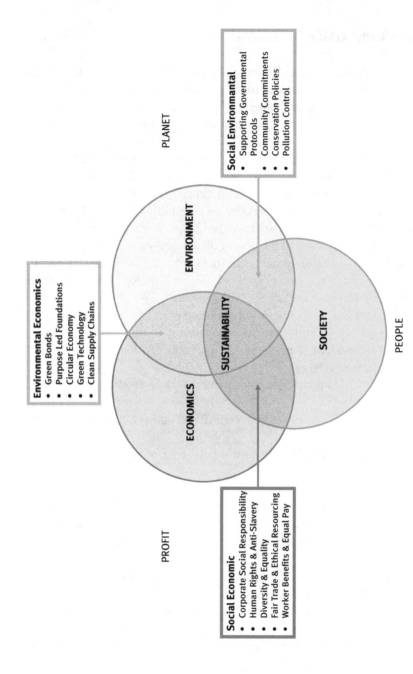

Figure 7.1: Triple Bottom Line Diagram.
Source: Compiled by authors.

to lead to very unsustainable behaviors. As such, luxury companies should be positioned to take responsibility for their actions.

Applying the Triple Bottom Line: An Example

How exactly can luxury companies incorporate a sustainable mindset into what they do? Adopting a triple bottom line is one of the simplest methods, as it allows key stakeholders in the company to raise important questions relating to the three key factors of profit, people, and planet. Alternatively, the activity of applying the triple bottom line can also trigger important discussions that could help a company grow into a more sustainable business. To better explain how a triple bottom line can be applied, consider the following scenario:

- A luxury company wishes to vertically integrate its manufacturing by bringing the production of leather goods in-house. In the past, the company relied on subcontractors in a particular region with whom it had worked for 40 years. The company has therefore decided to locate their new factory in the same region where their subcontractors are located. What questions should the company raise to evaluate its decision?

Questions from an Economic perspective:
- What is the overall cost of constructing our own manufacturing facility, and what is the ROI over time?
- Should we purchase the land and construct the factory? Or should we rent an existing factory?
- If we decide to build a factory, should we choose to buy an existing factory and rebuild it (brownfield) or to clear an uninhabited piece of land to build the factory from scratch (greenfield)?
- What kinds of materials should we use, and how much will they cost?

Questions from a Social perspective:
- Will the district we wish to build in allow us to purchase the land?
- Will the construction of our factory affect the society through traffic, roadblocks, transportation of building materials, noise, and dust?
- If we no longer use our sub-contractors, will this affect their employees?
- Can we hire employees from our sub-contractors to avoid job losses?
- Are we going to allocate a percentage of human resources to residents of the district to elevate their social welfare?

Questions from an Environmental perspective:
- Are we able to clear the land or build in this area? Are there any endangered species in the area?
- Would this construction have environmental impacts such as soil toxicity, ground erosion, groundwater poisoning, air pollution, etc.?
- How many trees will be taken down, and will we replant these trees elsewhere?
- Could we choose more environmentally friendly materials that are less likely to increase climate change?
- Should we apply for LEED certification for our new factory in order to be regulated throughout the construction process?

These questions are just a few examples of the issues that can be considered during an assessment of a company's triple bottom line. It should not come as a surprise that many of these questions are interlinked with one another. For example, the materials used to construct the factory was raised both in the economic perspective and in the environmental perspective. This is because the triple bottom line contains interlinked values. In Figures 7.2 to 7.4, we show the interlinkages between (1) economic and environmental actions (Figure 7.2), (2) environmental and social actions (Figure 7.3), and (3) social and economic actions (Figure 7.4) commonly found in organizations.

Figure 7.2: Economic and Environmental Actions.
Source: Compiled by authors.

Figure 7.3: Environmental and Social Actions.
Source: Compiled by authors.

SOCIO-ECONOMIC ACTIONS

Corporate Social Responsibility

Diversity & Equality

Fair Trade & Ethical Resourcing

Workers Benefits & Equal Pay

Human Rights & Anti Slavery Acts

Training & Development

Figure 7.4: Socio-Economic Actions.
Source: Compiled by authors.

As indicated in Figure 7.1, sustainability is achieved when all three factors – profit, people and planet – intersect with one another. However, it is inevitable that companies will find themselves struggling to achieve a perfect balance between the three factors. More often than not, companies try to formulate multiple goals which come close to achieving "total sustainability". This can be achieved by setting a combination of sustainability goals drawn from all three intersections. A leader in developing sustainability in luxury industries is Kering Group, as elaborated by the case study below.

Kering Group: Transforming into a Sustainable Centric Organization

In the last ten years, François Henri-Pinault, chairman and CEO of the Kering Group, has invested heavily in transforming his company into a beacon of sustainability for the world of luxury. He did this by first hiring competent people to be the driving force of his agenda. In 2012, he appointed Marie-Claire Daveu as Head Sustainability Officer. Daveu had previously occupied the post of principal private secretary for France's Ministry of Ecology and Sustainable Development. Her extensive experience both in sustainability and public administration enabled her to have a deeper understanding of how Kering could tackle issues relating to sustainability.

Upon Daveu's arrival at Kering, the company began to adopt various measurable sustainability goals, which were acknowledged for accountability purposes. One of the most significant projects was the introduction of the Kering EP&L – Environmental Profit and Losses – in 2018. Used to measure and quantify the environmental impact of Kering's activities and connect them to the group's financial performance, EP&L measures seven factors within the group's supply chain: carbon emissions, water consumption, air and water pollution, land use, and waste production. Kering is able to use this information to make its environmental impacts visible, quantifiable, and comparable, thereby converting them into monetary values that allow the group to work out the cost involved in its use of natural resources.

In August 2019, Henri-Pinault led the creation of "The Fashion Pact", a mission handed to him by French President Emmanuel Macron at the G7 Summit. The Fashion Pact is a global coalition of companies in fashion and textiles, as well as their suppliers and distributors. The aim is to formulate common goals to stop climate change, restore biodiversity, and protect the oceans. As of 2020, a total of 61 companies are signatories of the pact, including historic luxury houses such as Hermès, Chanel, and Armani Group. The Fashion Pact identifies seven tangible strategic targets related to its three areas of focus, with timelines ranging from five to ten years. Signatories will implement an operational structure to meet these targets and develop a digital dashboard of key performance indicators (KPIs) to measure each other's performance. The Fashion Pact is an example of companies *supporting governmental environmental protocols*. Since luxury companies are known to generate high profits, this is one way they can reciprocate and contribute to society and their governments.

One result of Kering's establishment of the EP&L and their involvement in The Fashion Pact is the creation and development of industry-wide standards for raw materials and manufacturing processes. The world of luxury has little to no regulation in terms of how and where it sources its raw materials or manufacture products. In 2019, the German state-owned broadcaster Deutsche Welle produced a documentary titled *Behind Fashion's Shiny Façade*, an investigative piece tracing the sources of leather and fur used by fashion companies. It exposed that a leather tannery in Italy was exploiting immigrants in a form of modern-day slavery, forcing them to work with harsh chemicals without providing proper personal protective equipment (PPE). While the brands mentioned in the documentary were not harmed by the exposure, consumers are increasingly aware of unethical practices and interested in using tactics including boycotts to force brands to change their ways. Kering and its team of sustainability practitioners are well aware of their responsibility for *fair trade and ethical resourcing* and have created standards to educate the group's partners and suppliers, implying that unethical practices will not be tolerated.

The case study above shows how Kering has established multiple simultaneous actions to address the three intersecting factors of sustainability: its triple bottom line. Sustainability cannot be achieved by applying one simple solution; it requires multifaceted approaches.

Reassessing Luxury's Environmental Footprint

Do Luxury Consumers Know Where their Goods Come From?

Most luxury consumers are unaware of the true origins of their luxury goods. While luxury brands are excellent storytellers – producing videos of leather artisans putting together a Lady Dior bag or engineers designing the aerodynamics of the latest model of Ferrari – the sources of their raw materials – yarn factories, tanneries, and iron smelters – are almost never shared. This has created a kind of blind spot for many luxury consumers; they are only able to trace their environmental footprint as far back as the factory that does the final assembly before products are shipped out to retail stores or showrooms. The key to developing a more sustainable business is to trace a product's footprint all the way to the source of its raw materials. We explore this topic in more detail further on in this chapter, when we look at the complexity companies face in their supply chain.

Lifecycle Assessment (LCA)

Lifecycle assessment or analysis has been in existence since the 1960s and was first used to regulate the rationing of raw materials and energy resources. Scientists at the time believed that the Earth's rising population would eventually deplete its natural resources, and that it was critical to understand the cost and environmental implications of future consumption. The first lifecycle assessment study was carried out by the Coca-Cola Company, which compared different beverage containers to determine which had the lowest impact on the environment as well as the footprint of each for its complete lifecycle. The study was able to quantify and measure raw materials and energy inputs to construct a clear picture of the resources, waste, and emissions involved in the production of a product. From the late 1960s through early 2000s, a number of studies gradually improved the methodology for lifecycle assessments due to the accessibility to environmental data driven by the mandate for its collection in certain industries (e.g., CO_2 emissions, water consumption, energy consumption, and waste generated). Despite this, lifecycle assessment is predominantly used by the fast-moving consumer goods (FMCG) and mass-manufacturing industries but rarely applied to the manufacture of luxury goods.

Lifecycle assessment is a circular model that generally follows a five-stage lifespan: raw materials, manufacturing and processing, transportation, usage, and retail and waste disposal. A company may perform various measures of impact at any of these five stages, and examining how they fit together allows us to categorize the lifecycle of a product. In the context of LCA, the typical lifecycle models are:

1) Cradle to Cradle (circular lifecycle)
2) Cradle to Grave (linear lifecycle)
3) Cradle to Gate (partial linear lifecycle)

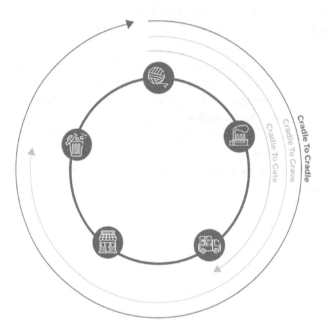

Figure 7.5: Lifecycle Assessment.
Source: Compiled by authors.

Cradle to Cradle. A cradle-to-cradle lifespan suggests that a product can be broken down into individual components that become the raw materials for a secondary product. The simplest example would be a diamond ring with a gold band. The diamond can be re-set into another piece of jewelry and the gold can be melted and formed into something else.

   Cradle to Grave. The majority of products have a linear lifecycle: They are manufactured, used, then disposed of at the end of their life. Occasionally, the timeline from cradle to grave can be extended through recycling, reuse, or repurpose. However, eventually the product will no longer be able to serve its purpose and will end up as waste.

   Cradle to Gate. Cradle to Gate is not a complete product lifecycle. The lifespan of a product starts with its creation and ends at the point where it is sold to a third party (the gate). This is commonly seen in certain industries where elements of the supply chain are detached from one another. More often than not, manufacturers lose control over the complete lifecycle of a product. A good example of this process is the extraction of metals. While we know that iron and aluminum are heavily used in the automotive industry, these metals are also commodities. Smelters melt the metals into blocks or flatten them into sheets to be sold to a third party. The third party may distribute these raw materials to various industries, to make various different products. In the luxury automotive industry, companies are predominantly assemblers, putting different parts together to form a final product. This means they have thousands of suppliers, and their suppliers have thousand more suppliers. Because they are connected to a large number of other actors, many of these suppliers can only regulate the lifecycle of their product from cradle to gate.

Stages of a Lifecycle Assessment

Over the past few years, luxury companies have begun to embrace lifecycle assessment because it allows brands to have a complete view of a product's lifecycle. The assessment should begin at the very first stages of life, whether this is the extraction of precious metals or the farming of livestock or plant materials. Every step involved in creating a luxury product should be reviewed to further understand its provenance and ethical practices. Figure 7.6 illustrates the lifecycle assessment of a cotton t-shirt.

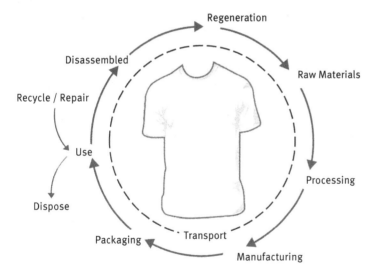

Figure 7.6: Lifecycle of a Cotton T-shirt.
Source: Compiled by authors.

Raw Materials. The process begins with the shirt's raw materials: land for farming, fertilizer and pesticides used in cotton plantations, and farmers, as well as the energy, water, and time input to grow cotton.

Processing. Once the cotton is ready for harvest, farmers pick the cotton and send it to a processing plant where the fibers are cleaned and turned into yarn. On average, it takes 1000 L of water to produce 1 kg of cotton, which will become four cotton t-shirts.

Manufacturing. The yarns produced move into the next step, where some are dyed with natural or artificial dyes before being knit into the fabric that will become t-shirts. The dyeing process is one of the most polluting steps in cotton manufacturing, as it discharges heavy metals and toxic chemicals into the environment. The manufacturing process also requires high amounts of energy, water, and human capital. Often times, this step raises concerns regarding ethical labor and workers' safety.

Packaging. Once the t-shirts have been completed, they are packaged, either in a bundle or individually, in single-use plastic and packed to be shipped.

Use. Often times, consumers are led to believe that the processing and manufacturing stages of a t-shirt are what contribute to its high environmental impact. However, it is also critical to understand that the use phase can be a highly polluting stage in a t-shirt's lifecycle. How often the t-shirt is used or worn, how long it lasts, and how often it is washed all affect the impact of its lifecycle.

Recycle/Repurpose/Repair/Dispose. The decision a consumer makes at the end of a product's life impacts how circular or linear its lifecycle is. In most cases, cotton t-shirts are disposed of rather than recycled or repurposed. In 2017, the US Environmental Protection Agency estimated that over 80% of textile waste – just over 11 million tons – ended up in landfills (EPA, 2020a).

Transportation. Transportation takes place throughout the entire lifecycle of a product, and shortening the supply chain is preferable when trying to reduce impact – the further goods have to travel, the higher their carbon footprint. The Stockholm Environmental Institute reported that imported goods from maritime shipping generated close to 1 billion tons of greenhouse gases per year (Trimmer and Godar, 2019). It is a major source of pollution, and often overlooked even when cities close to shipping routes suffer from smog.

The lifecycle assessment of a cotton t-shirt shows how every stage of its life contributes to its environmental footprint. It also illustrates how this type of assessment enables luxury brands to trace both the footprint and the cost of a product's production cycle. Lifecycle assessment is most effective when there is sufficient data available to provide a thorough inventory of the energy, water, and materials used, as well as the carbon and other pollutants emitted, throughout the value chain. By performing a lifecycle assessment, a brand can measure the cumulative potential of environmental impact as well as the lifespan of its products. Additionally, the LCA can assist brands in better educating their consumers on how they should use the products in ways that are more environmentally conscious.

Conscious Consumption

Consciousness plays a critical role in changing the mindset of luxury consumers. Earlier in this chapter, we discussed how luxury consumers engage in excessive consumption. This behavior is fueled both by a need to signal wealth and by the increasing accessibility of luxury goods. Sales promotions and incentive programs contribute to these habits. Included in the techniques that brands use to encourage consumption is the misuse of the term "sustainable" to lead consumers to believe that their extravagant purchases can be offset by more responsible options. For example, if choosing organic cotton over conventional cotton will have half the impact on the environment, this information can be used to justify purchasing double the amount of organic cotton apparel. Sustainability is not a zero-sum game; the goal is to continually decrease everyone's overall environmental footprint.

We have all heard the aphorism, "The most sustainable item is the one that is . . . " For apparel, it's the one in your wardrobe; for automotive, it's the one sitting in your driveway. No matter what type of luxury good you are seeking to purchase, the conscious choice is to consider the lifecycle of the product you wish to replace, or plan to acquire. After all, luxury goods are not necessities, making "conscious consumption", in this case, a relatively meaningless phrase. However, this does not mean that alternative options for both the luxury consumer and luxury brand do not exist, nor that different business models could not lead the world of luxury toward a more sustainable future.

Re-thinking the Way We Consume

When we think about the sustainability of a product, we often refer to the upstream process: the processing, manufacture, and transportation of goods. However, the downstream process can be equally damaging to the environment. According to a study conducted by the Trancik Lab at MIT, manufacturing the Tesla Model S P100D produces just over 12,000 kg/CO_2, while driving the car in the United States at an average of 270,000 km over its lifetime generated 48,600 kg/CO_2 (Wiedemann et al., 2020). This means that downstream emissions for the Tesla are four times its upstream emissions. While it's difficult to compare a car with apparel, not many consumers are aware of their usage habits and how their behaviors can impact the total lifecycle of a product.

Recent studies have shown that the method of care (i.e., how you wash your clothes) could also contribute to the CO_2 emissions associated with apparel. The article "What's the carbon footprint of . . . a load of laundry?" by Mike Berners-Lee, published in the *Guardian* in 2010, identified that washing and drying a load every two days could create about 440 kg of carbon dioxide each year. According to Berners Lee, the typical carbon footprint of a standard load of laundry in the UK is said to be:

- 0.6 kg CO_2 washed at 30°C, dried on the clothing line
- 0.7 kg CO_2 washed at 40°C, dried on the clothing line
- 2.4 kg CO_2 washed at 40°C, tumbled-dried in a vented dryer
- 3.3 kg CO_2 washed at 60°C, dried in a combination washer-dryer

This doesn't account for the type of laundry detergent used, nor the amount of micro-fiber released into the sewage system in each wash load. Water pollution through caustic chemicals and microfibers are environmental impacts that are not accounted for in the lifecycle of the apparel industry. According to a study conducted by Napper and Thompson in 2016, upwards of 700,000 fibers could be released from a standard 6 kg wash load of acrylic fabrics. The Ellen MacArthur Foundation, a registered charity based in the UK that invests heavily in circular economy research, has estimated that clothing care introduces around half a million tonnes of microplastic a year to water systems, significantly harming marine life.

In 2020, a new movement began to take shape, led by a number of fashion start-ups encouraging the redevelopment of care labels in clothing. Rather than sending clothes to the dry cleaner, or subjecting them to frequent washings, they recommended taking alternative steps, such as spraying down clothes with 50% to 70% alcohol solution or hanging clothes out in the sun and relying on UV rays to sanitize them. Clevercare Info, which is part of Ginetex, the international association for textile care and labelling, is also working toward promoting more sustainable ways to care for clothes. Luxury fashion companies should take initiatives like these as a model and play a bigger role in advocating for sustainable ways to care of their goods.

Second-Hand Market

The second-hand market is a common channel in many industries within the world of luxury. It is especially important for luxury cars, watches, and fine jewelry, and more recently luxury handbags. Cars and hard luxury items such as watches and fine jewelry are more likely to appreciate in value over time than soft luxury goods like apparel. The rarer they are, the more valuable they become. For example, the Rolex Submariner Stainless Steel Green Dial, often referred to as the "Rolex Hulk" was released to the market at about US$9,000. Even though it is not the rarest of the watches in Rolex's Submariner's collection, the current market price sits between US$18,500 and US$25,000, an appreciation of over 200%.

The second-hand market is an attractive avenue to sell or acquire vintage and rare pieces. The birth of this industry was not born out of sustainable behaviour; rather, it originally existed as a platform for trade and barter. Rare watches and fine jewelry were treated as art pieces or collector's items. This mentality aligned with that of first-hand luxury consumers, who aspire to be among the few who can afford the full collection. However, the concept of second-hand has evolved quite a bit in the last few decades. The second-hand market became a way to own a pre-loved luxury good at a more affordable price. As discussed previously, many luxury consumers purchase luxury goods they never use, if they continue to make purchases, they need to make room by constantly evaluating their collections. More often than not, this results in luxury goods entering pre-loved resell channels such as Vestiare Collective and The Real Real.

This new avenue has allowed consumers to extend the lifecycle of luxury goods, given second-hand consumers the option to make responsible choices and preventing the perpetuation of sales demand. Simple microeconomics dictates that an increase in demand leads to an increase of supply. In the past, luxury has been defined as something exclusive and rare, but the democratization of luxury has greatly affected its value chain; supply and demand have increased together, leading to a loss of value and an increase in the environmental impact of luxury consumption. The second-hand industry has the ability to change this, not only by reducing the amount of goods made, but by increasing the value of luxury goods over time. Less supply requires fewer resources, reducing the environmental impact of luxury overall.

Circular Economy

In a circular economy, the cycle of a product is continuous, with no waste and no introduction of new resources. Earlier in the chapter, we explored the three lifecycles of a product, touching on linear and circular models, with the differences between them illustrated in Figure 7.7. In a circular economy, the principals of the product lifecycle models become the basis for a systematic shift in how companies

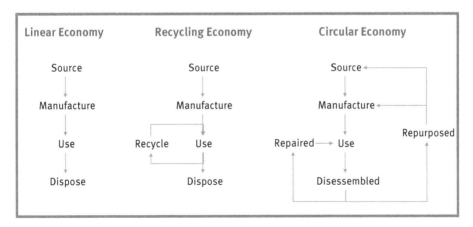

Figure 7.7: Linear Economy, Recycling Economy, and Circular Economy.
Source: Compiled by authors.

and consumers think about production and design as ways to create long-term resilience from an economic, environmental, and social perspective.

The idea of the circular economy first gained momentum in the 1970s, but its methods have been practiced in the fine jewelry business for centuries. Precious metals can be melted down to form other objects, and precious stones can be removed from their original settings to become elements of new pieces. One of the most recognizable diamonds in history, the Hope diamond, has been reset numerous times over the course of its history. According to the Smithsonian Institute, a French merchant acquired a 112-carat blue diamond from a mine in India in the mid-seventeenth century. The merchant sold the diamond to King Louis XIV in fifteen cut pieces, the largest of which would eventually be renamed the Hope Diamond. Recut and reset multiple times by King Louis XIV and his successors to form ornate ceremonial jewelry, it was stolen in 1791, following the downfall of the French monarchy. Shaved down, it passed through multiple owners, including the Hope family, who gave it the name it bears today, before finally landing in the hands of Pierre Cartier in 1909.

Mrs. Evalyn Walsh McLean, the last person to own the Hope diamond, acquired it from Cartier, who reset it in a headpiece on a three-tiered circlet of white diamonds when an earlier setting failed to attract her attention. Later, McLean had it reset again as part of a diamond necklace. Finally acquired by Harry Winston Inc. in 1949, two years after McLean's death, the Hope diamond now resides as a permanent exhibit at the Smithsonian Institute in the United States. Its most recent setting, a Harry Winston design, made a temporary appearance in 2010 as part of the museum's 100th anniversary celebrations.

The cyclical nature of the economy surrounding precious gems and metals arose because of their rarity and value; applying a similar model to industries or items that rely on raw materials of lesser value did not make sense. However, value, as many of us are beginning to realize, is subjective. Since our future wellbeing is wholly dependent on the health of our environment, it is in our interest to reassess the value of our resources in terms of their impact on our environment.

The world of luxury thrived for centuries on rare materials such as silks, wools, furs, and skins. However, the development of plastics and polymers around the turn of the nineteenth century brought new material possibilities to products and processes across all industries, luxury included. In the 1980s, Prada became one of the first luxury fashion houses to introduce the use of nylon in its products. Not many would consider this a luxurious raw material, but the possibilities were endless; Miuccia Prada's experiments in accessories and apparel transformed nylon into a luxury material (Prada, n.d.). In 2011, engineers at Aquafil, the Italian company whose chairman and CEO Giulio Bonazzi was an early proponent of the material, discovered a way to chemically transform pre- and post-consumer nylon waste back into virgin yarns. This means that nylon has a potentially infinite lifespan and could continuously feed the cyclical lifecycle of a product. Nylon is neither rare nor inherently valuable, but its ability to support a circular economy in luxury apparel increases its worth exponentially from a sustainability perspective.

A circular lifecycle is most effective when products are made of singular or modular materials. This means that homogeneous materials can be taken apart and recycled or repurposed. In the case of nylon, if a product is composed of 100% nylon – from the lining to the base and the stitching – it can be disassembled and chemically regenerated it into virgin nylon yarns by a company like Aquafil. To achieve a fully circular economy, this approach must be extended to all areas of a company's activity. In November 2020, the Ellen MacArthur foundation released a book on packaging solutions. The chapter on material circulation explicitly states that a material's ability to be broken down and reworked into future products is a crucial point to consider in choosing the materials used for any packaging (Ellen MacArthur Foundation, 2020).

For the time being, we are limited by the number of raw materials that are truly circular. This is not because we lack the technology; rather, there aren't enough people who are as brave as Bonazzi and would consider chemically breaking down polymers (plastics). As of today, most plastic recycling processes are done mechanically, this means plastics are broken down into either strips or chips and are bonded together or melted down to form other materials. Most industries opt for mechanical recycling because it is cheaper and faster – and usually carries much less risk. When Bonazzi established Aquafil, he had to start from the very beginning. He and his engineers had to create machines from scratch as they never existed before. Even though his Econyl brand is the most widely used eco-friendly nylon yarn in the automotive apparel and accessories industries, it took almost 10 years to get where it is today. Circular economy is the most efficient and effective way to reduce waste, but it also comes with a significant price tag. To invest in machinery such as Bonazzi has created for Aquafil would require significant funds and a forward-thinking mentality. But at the end of the day, all the invested capital would generate returns, not only economically but also socially and environmentally.

Sustainability in Practice: What Luxury Companies are Doing

Sustainability Governance in Luxury Companies

Sustainability governance is a new concept that only emerged in the mid-2010s. In Chapter 1, we described how luxury companies evolved from small, family-owned businesses to large conglomerates. This altered the way luxury companies viewed sustainability. In small, family-run businesses, values aligned with a company's social responsibility to its people and stakeholders. Private enterprises have no obligation to commit to sustainability goals, nor do they have to address demands from shareholders to meet a status quo. However, the opposite is true for conglomerates. In the last few decades, luxury companies have undergone mass-consolidation, moving from independent players to groups of companies from the same industry. Some examples are: Richemont, which is the world's largest player in high jewelry and watches; LVMH, which is the world's largest player in fashion apparel and accessories; Volkswagen Group, which owns Bentley, Bugatti, Lamborghini, and Porsche; and Lifestyle Design Group, which owns most of the world's luxury furniture businesses.

The aforementioned conglomerates are all publicly traded companies, which makes them more vulnerable to the demands of the public. This has been a great benefit in the drive for sustainability, since they are more vulnerable to shocks in the share market. Over the last few years, luxury companies that have long avoided the subject of sustainability have begun taking strides toward setting sustainability goals. Depending on the structure of these companies and which stock market they are listed on, the requirements for sustainability performance may differ. Some might take the initiative to declare their commitment through sustainability reporting, and others might be required to meet sustainability milestones to remain part of a stock index.

Sustainability Indexes

Sustainability indexes are a relatively new concept. Instruments to measure the responsibility of a company toward social and environmental issues, they are designed to communicate a company's commitment to sustainability and similar goals to its institutional and retail investors, ensuring accountability through a concise and measurable method. In turn, utilizing the parameters set by the indexes, a company is able to adopt a structure that allows its performance to be measured. As of 2019, the three sustainability indexes with the largest impact and representation were: the Domini 400 Social Index in the United States and the Dow Jones Sustainability Indexes and the FTSE4Good Indices in Europe. The latter two are the most commonly used in apparel and other luxury industries.

FTSE4Good Index. In 2001, the FTSE Group, a British provider of stock market indices owned by the London Stock Exchange, launched the FTSE4Good Indices, a series of ethical investment stock market indices available to UK, US, Japanese, and European markets. The indices are based on a range of corporate social responsibility criteria supported by the Ethical Investment Research Services (EIRIS), and exclude companies that are likely to be involved with unethical industries, such as tobacco, weaponry, nuclear- and coal-power industry, etc. The FTSE4Good Index Series utilizes the Environmental Social Governance (ESG) Ratings which includes over 7,200 securities in 46 developed and emerging markets. The overall rating can be broken down into three pillars and fourteen themes, exposures, and scores. The three pillars are similar to those of the triple bottom line – Environmental, Social, and Governance – while the fourteen themes are subcategories with individual indicators to assess each company's risk exposures. The themes include but are not limited to environmental sustainability, relationships with stakeholders, attitudes toward human rights, supply chain labor standards, and opposing bribery. Luxury companies that are listed in the UK FTSE4Good index include Burberry Group and Diageo.

Dow Jones Sustainability Index. The Dow Jones Sustainability Index (DJSI) was launched in 1999 and predominantly caters to the European market. The index evaluates the sustainability performance of companies that are publicly traded; it is operated under a strategic partnership between S&P Dow Jones Indices and Robeco-SAM (Sustainable Asset Management). The DJSI is the longest-running set of global sustainability benchmarks and has become the key reference point for sustainability investing. Similar to the FTSE4Good Index, the DJSI is based the analysis of the triple bottom line: corporate economic (33%), environmental (33%), and social (33%) performance. Its parameters include corporate governance, risk management, climate change mitigation, ethical supply chain standards, and labor practices. Each of the three criteria is broken down into a total of 24 parameters, and companies are assessed according to each dimension's assessment weight. In 2010, there were over 2,700 companies that had been accepted into the DJSI. Luxury companies that have been invited to join the DJSI include: Kering Group, Moncler, Richemont Cie Financière A Br, Hermès Intl, Tiffany & Co., Christian Dior SE, and Shinsegae International Co. Ltd.

Sustainability Reporting

Sustainability reporting began with individual companies' efforts to comply with various international standards. It is also one of the most important ways an organization can demonstrate its commitments and accountability to its internal and external stakeholders. The goal of a sustainability report is to identify the priorities the company has established to improve its triple bottom line. By setting periodic targets that can be measured based on performance indicators, as well as reporting progress annually, a sustainability report allows its readers to assess a company's sustainability performance the same way they would assess its financial performance.

Sustainability reporting is more common in large industrial companies, since their stakeholders often require it as a pre-requisite. However, more and more luxury companies are adopting sustainability reporting as a way to set goals that are transparent and measurable, helping to assure their final customers that they are dedicated to protecting everyone's wellbeing. In the last decade, many companies have begun issuing sustainability reports as part of their annual financial data, namely: Ferrari, Tiffany & Co., Richemont SA, LVMH, and Kering Group.

Sustainability as a Financial Indicator

As mentioned before, companies are increasingly linking their commitment to sustainability with their financial performance. Companies have often relied on their economic growth as an indicator of success, and the triple bottom line acknowledges that sustainability can only be achieved when the three indicators, Economic, Social, and Environmental, are in balance, suggesting that sustainability cannot be achieved without addressing all three interconnected indicators.

Environmental Profit and Loss. Kering Group is considered a pioneer in the field of sustainability, especially when it introduced the concept of environmental profit and loss (EP&L). The goal was to facilitate a better way of thinking, not only internally but also among the group's vendors and suppliers. Environmental profit and loss traces the entire value chain and helps companies make innovative and well-thought-out decisions to ensure that environmental sustainability is top of mind. The goal is to understand where the impacts are, develop a knowledgeable decision-making process, be transparent with stakeholders, steer the business strategy toward responsibility, strengthen the business, and manage risks for the future. Working with environmental specialists and engineers, Kering has developed a calculation to translate its environmental impact into monetary value. The data they collect is used to measure and understand the cost of their activities. By doing so, they can incorporate negative and positive environmental impact into their overall profit and losses, leading to better decisions overall.

Sustainability-Linked Bonds and Loans. While Kering Group turns environmental impact into losses on their balance sheet, smaller luxury houses are not able to indulge in such financial freedom. Reconfiguring an age-old company around sustainable practices is costly. It requires funding to introduce initiatives and seek alternative solutions, and more often than not, companies find themselves unable to fund sustainability projects. This is where sustainability-linked bonds come into the picture. Sustainability-linked bonds are a forward-looking, performance-based instrument that helps companies raise money and fund sustainability projects, regulated by agreed-upon targets. Holding these bonds signals to a company's shareholders this it is financially committed to meeting its sustainability goals. The terms of the bonds mean that the company can be held accountable, including necessitating restructuring and the disclosure of the details of a company's performance through reporting. The bonds' financial or structural characteristics (e.g., coupon rate) can be adjusted, so a company's failure to reach its goals would increase its coupon rate, while its success would decrease its coupon rate.

Sustainability linked bonds first emerged in 2019, when they were introduced by the Italian multinational energy company Enel. Since then, many luxury companies have followed suit, namely Chanel and Burberry. In September 2020, Chanel announced that it would work with BNP Paribas to lead the issuance of its first sustainability-linked bonds. The inaugural transaction involved around €600 million to fund the ambitious Mission 1.5° climate strategy and set the following targets:

- Decreasing Chanel's own (scope 1 and 2) emissions by 50% by 2030
- Decreasing Chanel's supply chain (scope 3) absolute greenhouse gas emissions by 10% by 2030
- Shifting to 100% renewable electricity in Chanel operations by 2025

The announcement of this sustainability-linked bond piqued observers' interest, as Chanel is the first unrated issuer to place public bonds linked to its sustainability objectives. Even though Chanel is privately held by the Wertheimer family, its strong performance over the years has inspired public confidence, and the bond was oversubscribed on the day of issue.

Prada took a similar approach with its sustainability-linked loan. In November 2019, the Italian fashion house announced that it had taken a five-year loan with interest rates dependent on the company meeting its sustainable targets. Just as sustainability-linked bonds encourage a company to adjust its financial and structural characteristics, these loans create financial consequences that incentivize the company to make real changes. Prada's initial loan of €50 million from Credit Agricole Group is based on the promise of meeting the following targets:

- Achieving LEED Gold or Platinum Certification for a set number of stores
- Providing employees with a set number of training hours
- Using Prada Re-Nylon (regenerated nylon) for the production of goods

In June 2020, Prada signed a new ESG loan with Japanese bank Mizuho to facilitate a €75 million, five-year-term loan to monitor the achievement of the same targets. In February 2021, Prada signed a further €90 million, five-year term loan with pan-European Commercial Bank Unicredit. (Zargani, 2021)

Sustainability in the Luxury Supply Chain

Having shared all the various tools luxury companies can use to regulate and measure their environmental and social impacts, we can conclude that the supply chain plays a very important role in the overall sustainability of an organization. This is because companies are well positioned to have better control over their upstream processes. By implementing better management controls throughout their supply chains, luxury companies can mitigate their environmental impacts in each of the three ESG aspects. However, this is not always as simple as we may think. For companies to achieve sustainability in their supply chains, they must first unravel their complexities.

Supply Chain Complexity

Luxury supply chains have always been clouded in ambiguity, since very few companies are truly vertically integrated or transparent. One of the very few companies that is known for its vertically integrated supply chain is Loro Piana, which has teams dedicated to sourcing raw materials in Mongolia, Australia, Peru, and Argentina. However, even a company like this can experience certain complexities when purchasing raw materials and other components for their end product. For example, the leathers used Loro Piana's apparel and shoes, the metallic hardware for its accessories, and the fur linings used in its Icery parka can all be challenging to source. Usually when it comes to family-run companies such as Loro Piana, before its acquisition by LVMH in 2015, suppliers are handpicked by the owners based on trust and credibility. However, as these companies grow, they will eventually outgrow their existing suppliers. At this point they will need to mitigate their risks by bringing multiple new suppliers on board.

Generally speaking, most companies have very stringent vendor review and onboarding processes whereby vendors must supply supporting documentation to guarantee their safety, quality, and ethical practices before being approved as trustworthy suppliers. More often than not, these review processes stop short, assessing only the supplier and its practices, rather than tracing back as far as the source of its raw materials. For example, when Ferrari sources brakes from Brembo, it review Brembo's quality, safety, and ethical practices. However, Ferrari does not inquire into whether Brembo is sourcing iron and aluminum from ethical smelters, nor does the automaker dive deeper into where these mines are located and whether or not ethical labor is involved. This leaves a blind spot for Ferrari in its ethical resourcing of the iron and aluminum ores used in its final product. These kinds of complexities are common across all industries and not exclusive to the world of luxury. Even the oil and gas industry has only in the last ten years begun to dive deeper into its supply chain.

One of the more recent incidents to reveal how complex our supply chain was the 2013 discovery of horse DNA in frozen meat products across Irish and UK supermarkets. An article by Felicity Lawrence from the *Guardian* (2013) stated that the Irish Agricultural department identified that "The factory that supplied Tesco with it's (sic) 29% horse 'beef burgers', for example was using 'multiple ingredients from some 40 different suppliers in its production batches, and the mixture could vary every half hour'". This kind of contamination is scary to think about, but it happens more often than we think. A documentary produced by German state-owned media outlet Deutsche Welle titled *Luxury: Behind the mirror of high-end fashion* tried to expose the leather and fur industry. The documentarians went all the way to China to discover that rabbit fur that was said to supply Italian fashion brand Max Mara came from diseased rabbits raised in unsanitary and inhumane farms. Like every other fashion company, Max Mara goes through a network of suppliers, which could explain why the sourcing manager located in Italy might not be aware that their fur suppliers are using unethical channels.

In the past five years, luxury companies have become more susceptible to the judgements of their customers. As a new wave of younger and more ethic-seeking consumers grow into luxury clients, they are beginning to question not only the source of their products, but also the socio-ethical practices behind them (e.g., who made my clothes). If luxury companies want to progress further in becoming more sustainable, it is inevitable that they will need to start decoding their supply chain and investing in the responsible sourcing of raw materials.

Responsibility and Traceability

Luxury goods companies across all industries are proud of their expertise in selecting the best materials and components. From cars and furniture to high values gems and fashion apparel, raw materials are a crucial ingredient in the construction of luxury goods. As such, the value chain in raw-material sourcing can be a huge source of risk for luxury companies. At every step, a company is exposed to the possibilities of unethical resourcing (e.g., in the mining industry), severe environmental impacts (e.g., cotton farming), and the disappearance of their main source of raw materials (e.g., extinction of animals). Due to this, many luxury companies are likely to hedge their risks by either bringing their suppliers in house or creating stringent sourcing policies.

Luxury companies, especially those that have extensive histories, are disadvantaged because of their long-term relationships with suppliers and partners. It is not easy to seek alternative sources of materials if you rely heavily on credibility, skills, and experience. Changing a supplier could lead to a severe disruption in the supply chain, which doesn't only affect a company's overall costs, but also its brand value. Companies with a high propensity for investments are likely to acquire their suppliers and initiate change from within, or to establish their own industry standard. Below are a few examples of companies in the world of luxury that are leading the way in the management of their upstream supply chains.

Cartier. In 2005, Cartier stood up for responsible practices in the gold industry. The company's director of corporate social responsibility at the time, Pamela Caillens, led Cartier, together with thirteen other companies, to become the founding members of the Responsible Jewellery Council (RJC). Cartier pledged to only buy gold from ethical sources such as the Eurocantera mine in Honduras, which is owned by an Italian company. Eurocantera uses environmentally friendly processes, for example, using water in the mining process instead of the industry standard cyanide and mercury, which could enter the ground water. It also recycles 100% of its waste and operates on a zero-water discharge management system, treating waste water before releasing it into the environment. Under the RJC, members of the council will be required to undergo a biannual certification process. The goal is to ensure transparency, professionalism, and responsibility. The RJC has established strict codes of practices and standards and also provides auditing and assurance services. Today, the RJC has over 1,250 members.

Loro Piana is an Italian company most famous for its precious fibers, namely vicuña, wool from the animal of the same name, a member of the camel family native to South America. In 1974, the vicuña was declared endangered, with less than 6,000 existing in the world, prohibiting the trade of its wool. Since vicuña is one of Loro Piana's "Excellences", the Loro Piana family felt that it was part of their responsibility to safeguard the animals and work toward reintroducing the "fiber of gods" into the market. In 2008, the company established the Reserva Dr. Franco Loro Piana, Peru's first private nature reserve. Five years after the construction of the reserve, the population of vicuña doubled. The company's efforts are not limited to Peru; in 2013, they expanded their venture into Argentina, where they purchased the majority share in a company that shears wild vicuña in a safe and ethical manner that prevents the death of the animals.

Apart from vicuña, Loro Piana is known for its use of other fine materials (Excellences) such as merino wool and cashmere. The company works directly with farmers in Mongolia and China for cashmere, and Australia and New Zealand for merino wool. Loro Piana employs its own people to organize sourcing and education for farmers to ensure that the management of these raw materials is of the highest caliber. By eliminating the middlemen, Loro Piana is not only able to vertically integrate, but also to have full transparency in their supply chain.

Moncler. In 2014, Moncler was the target of a scandal when the Italian state television network Rai alleged that the company had engaged with suppliers that were using inhumane methods to pluck geese. Moncler denied the accusations and started an inquest to audit its suppliers. A year later, Moncler introduced its Down Integrity System and Traceability (DIST) protocol, a strict program focused on traceability and animal welfare. The company has since required its suppliers to comply with its stringent requirements and undergo pre-verification before being integrated into the Moncler supply chain. The DIST protocol regulates farming standards, respect for animals, traceability of down, and technical quality. The key requirements are that down must be derived exclusively from farmed geese and be a by-product of the food industry. No form of live-plucking or force feeding is allowed.

As part of this protocol, Moncler is actively working to make its supply chain transparent, focusing on raw materials and manufacturing. Every element of its supply chain is subjected to regular audits and must be approved by experienced and accredited independent bodies, a process that must also be followed by its suppliers. Since 2017, all Moncler down jackets have possessed a DIST certification label.

Kering. Another company that has invested heavily in the establishment of supply chain standards is Kering Group. Unlike other manufacturing industries such as food, pharmaceuticals, and oil and gas, luxury industries do not possess international standards that govern their ethics or safety. In the food and pharmaceutical industries, companies are regulated by HACCP and Good Manufacturing Practices, which provide strict protocols for supply-chain management. Kering Group decided to be a pioneer in the world of luxury by creating one of the first sets of Standards for Raw Materials and Manufacturing Processes. These standards are guidelines for how suppliers can meet Kering's sustainability standards. They cover various raw materials used by the group, ranging from leather, silks, and animal skins to gold and gems. They also provide guidance on processing methods such as leather tanning and textile processing. Kering has made its standards public to encourage other luxury companies to join forces and set standards that will be applicable for all industries.

Tiffany & Co. The diamond industry is very complex. Despite the countless protocols put in place by governing bodies, assurances of conflict-free diamonds are still highly debated. At the start of 2019, Tiffany & Co. announced that it would be a pioneer in incorporating provenance into its designs by engraving place of origin onto its diamonds. However, this was just the start of a much larger project. In late August 2020, Tiffany & Co. announced that every diamond above 0.18 carats would now be accompanied by a certificate detailing its "Diamond Craft Journey". This document will identify the diamond's source, explain the selection process, identify the craftsperson who cut and polished the diamond, and finally indicate when the diamond was set. The purpose of the Diamond Craft Journey is to ensure traceability, ethics, and quality in each step of a Tiffany diamond's lifecycle.

Blockchain: A New Frontier?

Having seen how complex the supply chain can be in the world of luxury, it is clear that there needs to be a better way to regulate provenance and provide transparency to both companies and customers. Some companies have the financial capability or a narrow enough business model to vertically integrate. Yet even then it is nearly impossible to fully control a company's supply chain. With the emergence of new technology, many companies are seeking the assistance of artificial intelligence (AI), blockchain technology, or a combination of both. But how does it work?

Blockchain, as the name implies, is a chain of blocks of information in which each block is secured through cryptography. Essentially, it is an unchangeable ledger in which stored information is marked with a timestamp and "cryptographic hash", securing each block by encoding it with sequential information from the previous and following blocks. This means that any movement or change in the data can immediately be identified, making blockchain a tamper-proof method of record keeping. Blockchain can be applied in two formats, public or private; the most well-known public blockchain is Bitcoin, in which the public has complete access to the blockchain. This allows for more security because the public acts as surveillance agents. Alternatively, private blockchains are those used within organizations or consortiums. These are self-governing systems: members of a private blockchain have access to the data, and if one party misbehaves, their wrongdoing is fully visible to the other members. Private blockchains are commonly used in supply chains and by companies interested in experimenting with the technology.

Blockchain technology is quite technical, and this book does not aim to explain it in detail. However, it is a tool that a handful of luxury industries have experimented with to ensure that each step of a value chain can be traced and tracked. It is commonly used to mitigate counterfeiting and has also served as a digital provenance certificate. Below are some examples of where blockchain is used.

Diamonds. In 2006, Leonardo DiCaprio starred in a political thriller *Blood Diamond*, which exposed the world to the devastating truth behind the diamond industry and how it funds war crimes. While Hollywood has a way of dramatizing the details, the film is not too far from reality: In 2000, the United Nations came together to form the Kimberley Process to eliminate the legal trade of conflict diamonds. The Kimberley Process Certification Scheme supports the trade of rough diamonds, and any country that wishes to participate must ensure that its diamonds do not finance rebel groups or entities that wish to overthrow UN-recognized governments. Each diamond must be certified by the local government, and countries that wish to import diamonds must also be part of the scheme. However, many organizations still debate the credibility of the Kimberley Process, and since it only certifies rough diamonds, many polished diamonds can still slip through the cracks.

Many companies are trying to find the best possible process to ensure that the diamonds they source are not conflict diamonds, that they have not slipped through the cracks. While companies like Tiffany & Co. are applying a more hands-on approach, many others are seeking technological alternatives. De Beers, one of the world's largest suppliers of diamonds, which operates both upstream (mining) and downstream (retail), has decided to experiment with blockchain technology. Founded in January 2018, Tracr is focused on distribution traceability and the ability to securely track a diamond across the value chain. It is a consortium led by De Beers, but includes members from all stages of the diamond trade, from mining companies and diamond cutters to retail players such as Chow Tai Fook.

Fashion and Accessories. In April 2019, Consensys, an Ethereum-based blockchain consulting firm, issued a press release stating that it would be working with LVMH Group to launch the blockchain track-and-trace project AURA. AURA brings together three companies that are the largest in their respective fields: Consensys in blockchain, LVMH Group in luxury, and Microsoft Azure in cloud computing. The platform is aimed at serving the entire world of luxury, enabling consumers to access product history and proof of authenticity from a product's raw materials to its point of sale, even following it through the second-hand market.

As of May 2019, LVMH flagship brands Louis Vuitton and Parfum Christian Dior were involved in the project; the group will bring other brands within its portfolio on board further down the line. The development of AURA is the culmination of

LVMH's traceability program, which it launched more than three years before the announcement. LVMH plans to involve as many of its stakeholders as possible, including designers, suppliers of raw materials, manufacturers, and distributors. AURA will provide the company with tools to better control its supply chain, as well as a way to tell the story of a product's origin and savior-faire. Its ambition is to strengthen the group's commitment to sustainability while also providing customers with the peace of mind that comes from knowing a product's environmental and ethical impacts. Two years after the announcement of AURA Blockchain, Richemont's Cartier and Prada Group proudly announced their membership of the consortium.

Exotic Animal Skins and Furs. Exotic animal skins and furs are synonymous with luxury; their rarity and exquisite quality have made them some of the most sought-after raw materials. In the past, there was little to no regulation of the hunting and trading of these materials, which led to unethical practices and subsequently the near extinction of many precious animals. In 1963, the International Union for Conservation of Nature (IUCN) drafted the Convention of International Trade in Endangered Species of Wild Fauna and Flora (CITES) in Washington, D.C. A multilateral treaty created to protect endangered plants and animals, CITES went into effect in 1975.

Under CITES, any product consisting of wild fauna and flora must be accompanied by a specialized certificate when entering and exiting participating countries. While well intended, the process is cumbersome and archaic. For example, when a foreign traveler purchases a Himalayan Crocodile Hermès Birkin – one of the most expensive Hermès Birkins ever made – in Paris, with plans to bring the handbag back to their home country, the store must submit a CITES application to the Ministry of Foreign Trade or equivalent authority. In this application, the store must indicate that a purchase of exotic skins has been made and that the product will cross borders. The form must also include details about the purchaser and the bag's destination. Usually the submission of the form is completed after the purchase has been made. This could be done a day or a week after the sale. The heavy paper work and age old approach to the process can lead to a number of human error or mismanagement of information. Therefore, in December 2017, CITES launched a blockchain challenge (CITES, 2017), asking the public to produce a white paper underlying how blockchain could potentially replace its current processes. While this challenge has yet to be awarded, it shows the potential of blockchain in the world of luxury.

Raw Materials. When we discussed the complexity of luxury supply chains, we uncovered a network of loop holes that have led to poor regulation of ethical resourcing. One company that has invested in helping companies have more visibility and transparency over their supply chain is IBM. What started out as the IBM Food Trust has slowly evolved into a dedicated platform called the IBM Blockchain Transparent Supply. This platform uses blockchain to trace the entire spectrum of a product's lifecycle. In 2019, the Ministry of Economic Development in Italy launched a project in collaboration with IBM Blockchain to help protect the value of "Made in

Italy" (Ministero dello sviluppo economic, 2019). In late 2020, the initiative kicked off with a pilot project with Piacenza Cashmere.

IBM built its platform to support the tracing of the entire value chain, from the receipt of raw materials (either directly from farms or from wool auction houses), through cleaning, spinning, weaving, quality assurance, distribution, and sales. IBM was able to establish a shared, temper-proof ledger that records the entire process of fabric manufacture, from source to sales, including who, what, where, when, and under what conditions. All the information registered is linked to previous and subsequent blocks, ensuring that no alterations can be made after the fact. This helps both the company and their partners have better visibility over the quality and ethical practices within the supply chain. Not only do end customers gain peace of mind in terms of the environmental and social footprint of their purchases, the brands they purchase from are able to build credibility.

While blockchain has the ability to mitigate many of the supply chain's complexities and convoluted networks, it is still a relatively difficult technology to implement. If the supply chain extends to countries with low technology adoption or poor internet connectivity, this could limit the dissemination of blockchain and similar technologies.

Where Do We Go from Here?

According to researchers from the University of New South Wales in Sydney, Australia, "we cannot rely on technology alone to solve existential environmental problems – like climate change, biodiversity loss and pollution – but that we also have to change our affluent lifestyles and reduce overconsumption in a combination with structural change" (Wiedemann et al., 2020) Throughout this chapter, we have covered the themes of affluent lifestyle, overconsumption, and the hopes for technology to change the world in order to understand how luxury companies can address sustainability in their business practices. While luxury is not the primary cause of environmental and social instability, it has become an easy target because of the behaviors and mentality with which it is associated.

In Chapter 1, we highlighted how luxury companies in the past were structured to meet the needs of a specialized group of consumers. However, with the emergence of new business structures that turned family companies into portfolios for investment firms and conglomerates, bankers and entrepreneurs have transformed luxury brands into profit-centric assets. This led to a shift of focus from retaining a legacy to maximizing sales and growth. This has in turn led luxury companies to adopt different business models to ensure sustainability as part of their long-term goals.

Sustainability from a financial perspective means steady growth, both for the company and its revenues. However, we have now begun to understand that no level of growth is sustainable; luxury companies have to take the perspective of a post-growth future. But what exactly does this look like? The goal is to change the way brands and consumers think about growth.

Changing the Consumer's Perception

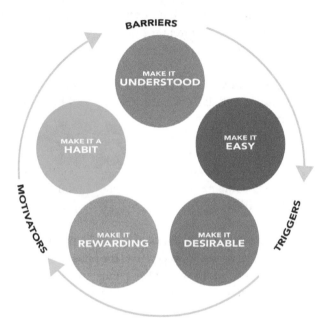

Figure 7.8: Five Levers of Change.
Source: Compiled by authors.

In 2012, Keith Weed, Unilever's Chief Marketing and Communications Officer (CMCO), formulated what are now known as the "Five Levers of Change" (see Figure 7.8) to help educate consumers about how they could make their consumption of fast-moving consumer goods (FMCGs) more sustainable. The concept is based on the following principals:

1. **Make it understood**: Consumers must be informed about their behaviors in order to understand what they are doing. This will allow them to make decisions based on issues or concerns that are relevant to them rather than simply following the herd. This lever is about raising awareness and encouraging consumers to accept the reality of climate change.

2. **Make it easy**: One of the most difficult situations with sustainability is that there is too much information, much of which is incredibly misleading. Consumers who try to make their behaviors more sustainable face complex and

difficult choices. This has benefitted "green washing" activities that offer simple and straightforward messaging. If sustainable activities are convenient and simple, consumers are more likely to have confidence that they are making the right decisions.

3. **Make it desirable**: Luxury plays on aspiration and a perceived lifestyle. Consumers do not buy a €5,000 Chanel handbag because of its functionality or necessity; they buy it because it represents something desirable. Sustainability needs to be equally desirable and aspirational from the perspective of the customer. It has to fit with how they relate to others and align with the lifestyle and habits of people they respect.

4. **Make it rewarding**: Donating to charity or paying a fee to offset your carbon footprint has the same effect as good will. It allows consumers to feel that they have contributed to something important, which can be rewarding. People are more likely to adhere to an activity if there is a pay-off in the end.

5. **Make it a habit**: Once consumers have taken their first few steps toward a change, it is important to support this behavior through reinforcement that reminds them of their journey. By encouraging consumers to follow through with their actions, a habit becomes unconscious.

Luxury consumers are often bombarded by information, making it difficult for them to have a clear understanding of right and wrong. In some ways, the onus is on Luxury companies to inform and educate their consumers. While scientists and activists play a big role in communicating information about sustainability, consumers have a special faith in the brands they purchase from. Kering Group has been working actively with scientists to achieve its sustainability goals. But they have also found a way to communicate these messages through influential characters such as the CEOs and creative directors of each of their brands.

Brands should create meaning and desirability in the products that they produce. The famous slogan from Patek Philippe, "You never truly own a Patek Philippe. You merely look after it for the next generation", signifies that the company's watches are heirlooms that are more valuable when they are passed down. Unlike other brands that market their products as collectibles, Patek Phillipe focuses on the longevity of its products and that owning one in a family is more than sufficient. After all, the company only produces a little over 60,000 watches a year (Millenary Watches, 2020), as compared to Rolex which manufactures over a million a year. Less really can be more.

De-consumption

Ezra Markowitz and Tom Bowerman, researchers at the University of Oregon and the authors of the paper "The attitude – Action Gap: Towards a better understanding of 'How much is enough'" (2016), have defined de-consumption as simply making do with less. The idea is to be materially poor and minimize your necessities. This is increasingly important as the world's population is getting increasingly wealthy. With more disposable income comes a greater propensity to spend. But whose responsibility is it to decrease overall consumption? Should companies produce less, or should consumers lower their demands? The responsibility lies with both parties. Luxury brands must look for alternative ways to grow financially and engage with their consumers in a way that allows them to both appreciate their purchases and adopt a more sustainable mentality. Likewise, consumers should change how they consume.

Realistically, luxury companies can only chart a path of growth for so long before ultimately reaching a plateau. As such, it is ever more important for them to consider their post-growth future. Just as we have described throughout this chapter, there are pressures coming both upstream (from investors and boards of directors) and downstream (the end consumer) for companies to constantly reinvent themselves – to be bigger and better. However, this type of growth will not only incur a huge cost over time, but also be detrimental to the environment. According to an article by Rachel Arthur in *Vogue Business*, the world currently manufactures between 80 and 150 billion items of clothing annually, a number that is projected to rise over 80% in the next 10 years. The estimated environmental impact of such growth is said to be an increase in the production of CO_2 gas by 50% and a global temperature rise of 1.5 degrees Celsius.

Consumers should be educated to truly understand the meaning of conscious consumption. We do not need a pair of shoes in every single color, nor a brand-new car every year. If the environmental cost of goods were reflected in monetary value, and accrued over time, maybe it could shift consumers' mindsets. De-consumption is not a strategy to deprive the consumer of luxury; rather, it is a way to restructure how luxury goods should be perceived: one luxury at a time, just as a lover of opera can only enjoy *Don Giovanni* at La Scala one performance at a time.

Prioritizing Margins

Compared to fast fashion, luxury is a margin-heavy business. The margins of luxury companies tend to exceed 30%. This is because consumer behavior toward price is inelastic. In the past, luxury companies took advantage of the democratization of their industries by introducing luxury goods at a price point that would attract the middle class. This has led to a complex business strategy, since luxury brands are constantly seeking to capture a larger audience while also balancing the risks of brand dilution. True luxury brands tend to fare better, since they cater to a niche and have full control over their markets.

Between 2011 and 2018, Lamborghini produced only three models of its cars. Each model was produced in limited numbers and priced so as to be exclusively available to some of the world's wealthiest people, and even they must apply through a waiting list. In 2018, the company released the Lamborghini Urus, an SUV super car, which took the market by storm. The sales volume more than doubled in just two years, growing from 3,400 to over 8,200. Despite the growth, Lamborghini has no wish to increase its production volume, instead choosing to sell additional services to increase its margins. For Lamborghini, the manufacturing of a vehicle follows a standard cost structure. While they have the freedom to set their own prices, they are not able to increase the margin from one client to another. However, by introducing other product offers and services as add-ons that allow its customers to express their creativity and ostentatiousness, the company creates a situation in which the margins are potentially limitless. Custom seats made by a specialty company or a custom paint color created for a specific client come with extravagant price tags – ones that incorporates margins as high as 90% of the company's costs.

Luxury companies have the autonomy to prioritize their margins because luxury goods are not a daily necessity, but an extension of oneself. Thus, when exploring sustainability strategies, luxury companies should consider selling less without sacrificing financial growth.

Reinventing the Customer Experience

If luxury companies want to champion the shift toward a more sustainable mindset, the onus of educating the luxury consumer falls on the companies themselves. With the rise in brands promoting their sustainable efforts, a lot of such messages fall on deaf ears. After all, how much does the average luxury consumer know about being sustainable? For companies to educate their consumers, they must start with quantifiable actions.

In June 2020, Farfetch, which owns the second-hand platform Second Life, launched a sustainability calculator in collaboration with the London Waste and Recycling Board that aims to encourage customers to quantify their fashion footprint. The calculator, which is currently available only to Farfetch customers in the UK, US, and China, informs the customer of a product's environmental impact. It then presents them with the option to compare that impact with that of the same product from its second-hand website. The report published by the London Waste and Recycling Board showed that on average, pre-loved goods could save 1 kg of waste, 3,000 L of water and 22 kg of CO_2. Not only is this a way to offer a more economical option for the consumer, but it prompts the customer to consider their commitment to the environment.

While companies such as Kering and Farfetch are taking a more measurable approach, Hermès is pursuing a more lighthearted strategy by up-cycling waste materials. Launched in 2010, Hermès's Petit H was established to engage with its customers through temporary installations in Hermès flagships around the world. Customers can book a session on the website to participate in the Petit H workshop. The activity bringing artisans and artists together to create unique objects with materials that Hermès *métiers* have no further use for, including leather, silk, and porcelain. The idea was based on the concept of "works in reverse" (Morris, 2019), creating unique crafts such as shoelaces, bookmarks, and key chains out of materials that were often scrapped and discarded. Those who participate in the activities have the chance to bring their works of art home to commemorate a once-in-a-lifetime experience. Some of these creations also end up in Hermès stores as merchandise. Such activities show consumers that even by-products of their exquisite goods can be turned into valuable pieces of art.

Takeaways

- Luxury customers seek rarity: rare animals, rare objects, rare experiences, all of which are symbols of elitism. As such, the concept of sustainable luxury is an oxymoron. The luxury business has, in recent years, thrived on excessive consumption. This is especially clear in how they have structured their CRM pyramid, reserving priority and access for those who spend more on high-value goods and make purchases more often. What will be the implications for luxury companies if they have to embrace a more environmentally ethical approach?
- Climate change has irreversible effects across the world; in the southern hemisphere, especially in Polynesia, many people are being displaced from their historical islands and atolls due to rising levels. This environmental phenomenon is also evident in Venice, where tourists hold their luxury purchases high above their heads, balancing on makeshift walkways to navigate increasingly frequent floods. An overall 2-degree Celsius increase in our atmospheric temperature could led to a 0.2-meter rise in sea levels.
- The triple bottom line was created to help companies take a multifaceted approach to business decisions and avoid the imbalances of a traditional approach focused on one measure alone. The triple bottom line is composed of interlinked principals, which combined can help companies achieve sustainability.
  - Economic and environmental impacts
  - Environmental and social impacts
  - Social and economic impacts
- Lifecycle assessment is a circular model that generally follows a five-stage lifespan: raw materials, manufacturing and processing, transportation, usage, and retail and waste disposal. Despite being infrequently studied, this model has shown high promise in the measurement of a company's environmental impact throughout a product's lifecycle. It can assist companies in making better environmental and ethical decisions, as well as considering a more circular approach in product development.
- Luxury industries should encourage their customers to be more conscious in their consumption, either by educating them about their environmental footprint or about the way they care for their products. There are a number of possibilities, such as embracing the secondhand market, choosing products manufactured through a circular approach, or even championing changes to care labels.

- Luxury companies are under pressure to implement better management controls throughout their supply chains as a way to mitigate their environmental impacts in each of the three ESG aspects. However, this is not always as simple as we may think. It is important to consider the complexities of the supply chain, and the many degrees of separation between the brand and its raw materials.
- Research has shown that no level of growth is sustainable, and luxury companies must therefore take the perspective of a post-growth future. This involves shifting the way brands and consumers think about growth – from rethinking the luxury value chain to restructuring a company's pricing strategies. A progressive slowdown is inevitable.

8 New Business Models of the 21st Century

From Innovation to Agility

Most strategy and marketing textbooks state that a lack of innovation will kill your business. This is especially true for luxury companies, as the business thrives on innovation. Consumers do not buy luxury goods to replace something they already have, they buy them because they want to have something newer or better. A Ferrari collector may have a few models in the garage, but what entices him or her to acquire another one is something new or improved – whether that is in terms of design or technical scope. Competition and technological advances also challenge car manufacturers like Ferrari to constantly innovate. These improvements may include up-to-date safety features, engine power, the evolution from combustion to fully electric, or even aerodynamic design. By constantly innovating, Ferrari has been able to remain as one of the most respected car manufacturers in the world.

However, success is not correlated to innovation alone, and this creates a dilemma for companies. Despite heavy investments in research and development, great, innovative ideas are frequently discarded in favor of focusing on what is important at the time. Examples of missed opportunities have long been favorite business-school case studies, from Kodak's digital-driven downfall to Disney firing the future founder of Pixar Studios.

In the case of Kodak, the photography giant's decades-long decline was due to its management team's inability to see digital photography as a disruptive technology. Despite being the first to invent the digital camera in 1975, the executives at Kodak could not recognise its potential. The first prototype was bulky and slow, and the company decided against investing in the technology for fear of hurting its successful film business. Kodak spent the next 10 years focusing almost exclusively on film and never prepared for the inevitable digital transformation of the photocamera industry. In reality, there would have been no risk for Kodak had it ventured into new technology. With a more agile and ambidextrous approach, it could have potentially conquered the digital photo market.

Similarly, in the early 1980s, John Lasseter, a cartoon artist and animator at Disney, pitched the idea of using computer animation for the company's animated films. When he tried to convince Disney executives of the value of this new innovation, Lasseter was told that computer animation was pointless unless it could reduce the company's overall production costs. He was later fired. This, however, turned out to be a good thing for computer animation. Spurned by Disney, Lasseter joined Lucasfilm Computer Graphics alongside co-founders Alvy Ray Smith and Ed Catmull. Under its new name, Pixar, the studio's early features *Toy Story*, *A Bugs Life*, and *Cars* challenged Disney's dominance of the animated film market; like Kodak, Disney lost a significant market share to a competitor that focused on an innovation

https://doi.org/10.1515/9783110723519-008

it had let pass by. Fortunately for Disney, its multiple business streams lessened the effects of this missed opportunity – it had the financial means to bring Pixar in-house through an acquisition by then CEO Robert Iger in 2006 for US$ 7.4 billion– passing on computer animation was one of the costliest lessons Disney has had to learn.

While innovation is important if a business is to adapt to the times and its surroundings, it is not the only thing that helps a business withstand crises. For a company to remain resilient, it has to be agile. But what does it mean "to be agile"? Simply put, it is the ability to sense, to anticipate, and to respond efficiently and effectively to changes that are occurring or are likely to occur in the future. The aforementioned case studies suggest that companies need to be ready to embrace innovation and be prepared for the future. This is ever more important during times of change, when an organization's natural reaction is to cling to old habits and practices, distracting it from more important work. In the face of budget reductions and the possibility of financial failure, it is understandable that companies would concentrate on investments in existing industries, which are likely to recover their revenues, rather than investing in innovative projects. Yet as we will discover in this chapter, the route to resilience is through intrepid investment in innovation. In troubled times, companies must lead with a pro-active mindset, rather than a reactive one. Even with great innovation in their hands, neither Kodak nor Disney had the courage or foresight to embrace inevitable change. Their inability to act cost both companies severely.

These lessons are crucial if we are to gain a deeper understanding of why agility is important in successful companies. Just like Kodak and Disney, luxury companies are not immune to constant changes both in their surroundings and their end customers. Over the last few years, the world of luxury has experienced tremendous transformations, and today's fast-paced environment driven by digital, social, and global changes is uncharted territory for luxury companies. The quick reflexes, nimble approach, and accuracy in execution that define athletic agility will benefit these companies as they prepare for the future. There is no such thing as a "one-size fits all" solution. Now more than ever, luxury companies must look at their consumers as individuals, consider the unique culture and heritage of every country in which they operate, and be ready with business models that can adapt to fit the changing demands of the market.

Luxury companies do not have the privilege of time to warm up to new technologies or business models. Their consumers are becoming more intelligent and more demanding than ever, and they are not afraid to put luxury companies on the spot. Chanel has endured never-ending criticism from industry media outlets about its restraint toward ecommerce, earning comparisons to Hermès, which is notorious for a highly selective offering made available on its ecommerce platform. Alternatively, Richemont has been actively investing in ecommerce capabilities, acquiring Yoox Net-a-Porter in 2018, and in 2020 beginning a joint collaboration with Farfetch and Alibaba to develop "Luxury New Retail". All of this is to combat potential cannibalization from competitors and wholesalers with well-developed ecommerce capabilities.

To have an agile business means to build a flexible organization that is capable of reacting to fast and unpredictable changes. Agile businesses can support themselves during disruptions, evolve, adapt, and eventually self-correct. An agile company follows three guiding principles:

1) To instil a growth mindset in each individual in the organization to allow flexibility and to continually focus on improving the organization
2) To encourage stronger communication between teams and groups within the organization so that they can adjust and adapt rapidly
3) To have people within the organization who are willing and open to the idea of change and who respond positively to disruption

In earlier chapters, we have discussed how luxury companies tend to operate in a very traditional way, prioritizing heritage and hierarchy over contemporaneity and agility. The world of luxury has one of the most top-down organizational structures in the business world, whereby the CEO and creative director govern the strategic and artistic directions of a company, respectively. As such, most luxury companies experience drastic strategic or artistic changes every time a new person is appointed. Burberry experienced upheaval in 2016 when Marco Gobbetti replaced Christopher Bailey as CEO, and again in 2017, when the company brought in Riccardo Tisci. The pivot within Burberry's top management has yet to show any benefit; indeed, the company's global revenue shrunk by an average of −1.5% per year in the period from 2017 to 2020. Similarly, Gucci underwent tremendous change after the sudden departure of Frida Giannini and Patrizio Di Marco in 2015. However, things turned out very differently for Gucci.

Agile Business Models in Luxury Companies: A Gucci Case Study

In 2015, Kering Group Chairman François-Henri Pinault shifted Marco Bizzarri from another position within the group to act as Gucci's CEO. The first item on Bizzarri's agenda was to recruit a suitable replacement for Giannini. Despite having the freedom to choose a big-name designer, Gucci's new CEO decided to look internally to rediscover the essence of the brand. He asked the company's HR department to arrange a meeting with the longest-serving employee on Gucci's design team. HR identified Alessandro Michele, who had spent over a decade at Gucci, starting out as an accessories designer when Tom Ford was at the helm, as a good candidate. Michele had been Giannini's right hand, climbing the ranks quickly after she took over. If there was anyone who truly understood Gucci, it was Michele. After their first meeting, Bizzarri instantly knew that he had found his ideal candidate. Michele was steeped in Gucci's rich history and filled with fresh ideas, a new vision for Gucci that had yet to be explored. Working in the shadows of Tom Ford and Frida Giannini, nobody had realized what Michele was capable of. When Bizzarri met

Michele at the latter's apartment, the designer was wearing the fur-lined Princetown slippers that would go on to become one of Gucci's best sellers and Michele's first iconic contribution as creative director.

Michele had precisely the kind of creativity and enthusiasm that Bizzarri had envisioned for Gucci. This was the start of a disruption, a long overdue shake-up of a static industry focused on consistency and heritage over agility and growth. During Bizzarri's first year as Gucci's CEO, he discovered the inefficiencies that had held the company back, and quickly eliminated them. "At the beginning when I started at Gucci", he recounted, during a 2017 lecture presentation to fashion students at Polimoda in Florence, "the mantra was 'no democracy', in the sense where if I wanted to be quick, I couldn't look for consensus from everyone as it would have taken too long". Bizzarri's distaste for red tape was not a sign of rebelliousness but of a desire to eradicate the politics that slowed down most fashion companies. He understood the speed at which the market was moving, and if Gucci was not agile, the company would lose out to its competitors and miss out on great opportunities.

The goal was to break the mold and establish a learning organization, one that did not need to rely on Marco Bizzarri's management decisions or Alessandro Michele's outstanding creativity to survive. Instead, Gucci would become an organization with a renewed culture that could drive itself forward. In the years of transformation, both Bizzarri and Michele embraced this agile business approach by inspiring and empowering everyone at Gucci to be responsible for the company's future.

To instill a growth mindset. The disruption at Gucci was a way to reprogram the organization. The fashion house's two previous eras had caused a slump – even Michele had considered leaving. Bizzarri knew that an injection of new values was important, but even more so, Gucci had to reawaken the confidence of its people. Bizzarri empowered employees to take risks and not expect repercussions for their failures. This mindset gave birth to some of the company's most innovative business strategies. One of these is Gucci 9, a series of call centers in cities around the world, decorated by Michele and filled with the icons and codes of Gucci's classic store interiors. In ambience and approach – the centers offer a personalized customer support experience that relies on trained staff – Gucci 9 has reinvented the traditional role of a luxury sales associate. By embracing a growth mindset, Gucci has allowed creativity to not only flow upwards, but also be disseminated across the organization.

Encouraging stronger communication. For as long as Gucci has been manufacturing shoes and bags, these departments have remained separate entities. In the wake of Bizzarri's assumption of the role of CEO, they have been brought together in one innovative and creative space with the intention of strengthening communication between the two teams. The integration was initially met with significant resistance, since craftspeople from each entity believed they were extremely specialized and had nothing in common with each other. However, as time passed, those who worked on shoes would cross paths in breakout rooms or at company events with those who worked on bags, and vice versa. This led to friendly banter and kinship amongst peers, and eventually the sharing of best practices. What started out as an uncomfortable situation became a strength for Gucci. Not only did the merging of shoes and bags help encourage innovation and creativity in the company's products, it led to stronger communication between the teams of people that make them.

Openness to the idea of change. In his 2017 lecture, Marco Bizzarri explained the meaning of the "Poetic Reactivation" of a brand:

> By instilling a common culture of creativity throughout the business, we should keep our growth sustainable. But a culture of creativity also means a culture that is not risk- averse. Not scared to be brave. Not afraid to take risks (but as I have explained, always be informed of the risks). In order to reinvent Gucci, there had to be a change in culture. We identified that people in the company who are willing to accept change and re-educate those that found it difficult. We needed to bring in new people to bring about change, too. All these people – Alessandro and myself included – had to embrace change and risks all the time. Because that is the only way in which, if I or Alessandro leave the company tomorrow, the organization will survive and outlive us all.

For Bizzarri, the only way for Gucci to move forward is to keep people in the company who are willing to accept change. And, as the company's leather-goods craftspeople learned, there are benefits to embracing evolution.

Ambidexterity in Luxury Companies

Looking back at the case study on Kodak, the root cause of the photo company's failure was its inability to accept change and embrace innovation. Organizational rigidity and a lack of vision in Kodak's management team contributed significantly to the missed opportunity. Had the company invested in even the incremental development of the digital camera, it could have exploited the market when the opportunity presented itself. This conclusion raises an important lesson for organizations, which is to avoid having a singular vision. Rather, it is important to be ambidextrous. Ambidexterity, according to its basic meaning, is the ability to use both the left and right hands equally well. When applied to the context of a business, it suggests that companies are able to keep two entities running equally well. In Chapter 1, we briefly explained ambidexterity from the perspective of O'Reilly and Tushman's research, in which they suggested that ambidextrous organizations have the ability to balance exploration and exploitation.

In this chapter, we will analyze the concept of ambidexterity on two fronts. The first will focus on the business structure that separates two entities to balance profitability and innovation. From this perspective, we will look at organizations that have created an emerging business entity to complement an existing business. Additionally, we will examine how a "bottom-up" approach can be used to generate new ideas in service-based industries in which companies are prioritizing the voices of the younger generation as a method of research and development.

The second will focus on product portfolio, where icons play an important role in balancing the commercial and creative efforts involved in product development. The concepts shared in this chapter should provide a deeper understanding of ambidexterity when thinking about the business model for the twenty-first century.

Research and Development's role in Luxury Companies

According to O'Reilly and Tushman (2004, 2008), exploration means seeking new ideas, while exploitation means using these new ideas when the opportunity arises. Unlike those in other businesses, luxury companies are constantly challenged to explore new avenues. Luxury moves at a rapid speed to keep up with the needs and wants of its consumers. Thus, luxury companies are less likely to follow in the footsteps of Kodak. To put it into context, Ferrari as a luxury automotive manufacturer is often compared to Lamborghini. However, Ferrari's ability to innovate is also challenged by the entire automotive industry, where its main competitors include Mercedes, Porsche, McLaren, Aston Martin, Pagani, and Maserati, as well as Tesla. In 2018, Ferrari announced that it would enter the super-SUV market with the "Puro Sangue" (Kozak, 2018). If Enzo Ferrari were alive today, he would never imagine the company he built for the sake of racing would enter category such as this. However, as times change so does the market. Consumers no longer dream of a two-seater supercar they can flaunt on the weekend, but of a functional supercar that can be driven daily. This lucrative super-SUV market has already been captured by most of Ferrari's competitors, namely Aston Martin, Porsche, Lamborghini, Bentley, and Maserati. If you consider that Lamborghini's entry in the category, the Urus, was responsible for over 50% of its sales in 2019 (Frank, 2020), it is obvious that not capitalizing on this segment would be a significant loss for Ferrari.

While many are still on the fence about Ferrari's decision to launch a super SUV, the decision is strategic and perfectly demonstrates how Ferrari is an ambidextrous organization. To start, the core of Ferrari's business model is built around its racing arm, Scuderia Ferrari, and its Gran Tourismo or GT division, which is responsible for the sale of road cars. Scuderia Ferrari is a high-capital business that requires a steady stream of investment to actively compete in Formula One competitions. Even Enzo Ferrari himself admitted that the sole purpose of establishing the GT division was to fund his love for racing. The two divisions are separated to serve different functions, but ultimately to strengthen the brand overall. Scuderia Ferrari is a platform for engineers and mechanics to experiment and discover ways to enhance the performance of a car. Having explored innovative techniques to identify cleaner design, aerodynamics, and horsepower, their discoveries are often shared with the team of engineers and mechanics in the GT division. In this way, racing innovations can be exploited to develop high-powered road cars. Over the years, Ferrari has incorporated many of the lessons of its Formula One program into its GT division. The Ferrari F50, manufactured between 1995 and 1997, used the same engine design as the Formula One car driven by Alain Prost and Nigel Mansell in 1990 (Lynton, 2013). The cycle as shown in Figure 8.1 explains how Ferrari has created an ecosystem within its organization to symbiotically enrich each division. The racing team builds up the dream for its wealthy fans, who purchases supercars within its GT portfolio, which in turn funds the racing team to explore breakthrough innovations in the automotive industry.

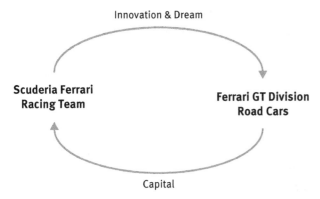

Figure 8.1: Ambidexterity in Ferrari's Business Model.
Source: Compiled by authors.

Ferrari's ambidextrous ecosystem has enabled a sustainable strategy that has proven its resilience even through the toughest times. Nonetheless, the approach is not unique to Ferrari. The LVHM-owned cosmetics retailer Sephora has also created a unique ambidextrous ecosystem.

Sephora was founded in 1970 in Paris but did not see much success until it was acquired by Dominique Mandonnaud in 1993. Mandonnaud grew Sephora mainly as a perfume retailer, subsequently moving into the cosmetic industry after its acquisition by LVMH in 1997. Sephora's footprint at the time was relatively local, but it expanded across Europe and around the world after its acquisition. Around the turn of the millennium, cosmetics and beauty was a relatively niche market, with industry heavyweights such as Estée Lauder, L'Oréal, and Coty as the main manufacturers. However, in 2010 influential creators and fashion brands started to extend their product categories to include beauty and cosmetics. David Suliteanu, who at the time was CEO of Sephora Americas, started Kendo Brands as an incubator for new beauty brands. Meanwhile, Sephora had already seen success as a retailer and was actively seeking to bring in up-and-coming brands. Kendo became the perfect space to explore opportunities, working with creators Sephora believed had appeal and potential to create brands that would then be sold exclusively through Sephora retail.

In 2011, Kendo Brands acquired Ole Henriksen skincare, which was then sold exclusively at Sephora and through the Ole Henriksen website. Kendo did not launch its own cosmetics brand until 2013, when Marc Jacobs Beauty was created. The birth of this brand was serendipitous as Marc Jacobs was also part of the LVMH's fashion and leather goods portfolio. Marc Jacobs Beauty became the first beauty brand created in-house by Kendo and marketed as a brand sold exclusively at Sephora. This strategy enabled LVMH to explore opportunities within beauty and skincare without seeking external input, at the same time controlling its distribution exclusively within its own channels. In 2014, Kendo Brands was separated from Sephora and joined the Perfumes and Cosmetics group of LVMH (Crunchbase, n.d.). In the years following the successful launch of Marc Jacobs Beauty, Kendo Brand has gone on to launch Kat Von D Beauty, Fenty Beauty, Fenty Skin, and Lip Lab (Kendo Brands, 2021). All of which are sold exclusively through its own channels or through Sephora.

Voices of the Younger Generation

Companies in an industry that is affected by constant change are under immense pressure to keep up with the latest trends. If a company's research and development does not keep pace with its core business, it risks falling behind not only to its competitors but its customers. But what about an industry that relies more on services than on products? As we have seen, research and development play a very important role in the exploration of new products, but luxury industries also rely heavily on elevating experiences and services. In the world of fast-moving consumer goods (FMCG), manufacturing conglomerates often turn to market research agencies such as Nielsen's, Kantar, and Ipsos, which use panels of everyday consumers to provide feedback about their purchasing journey and experiences. Alternatively, in politics and economics, government agencies use think tanks that perform research and advocacy related to topics around social policy, economic performance, technology, and culture to develop future strategies. Here, we will look at how luxury companies have applied similar strategies to further develop and improve their level of services.

The downfall of many luxury companies has been their inability to attract newer and younger consumers. Dunhill and Cerruti saw exemplary financial results pre-1990s but experienced a sharp decrease toward the 2000s and are almost nonexistent as top-of-mind brands for today's younger generation. One way for brands that have fallen behind to catch up is to engage with younger talent, for example by creating a young talent committee. A handful of companies have already taken this kind of bottom-up approach, disrupting their organizational structure by empowering its junior members.

At Gucci, the "Shadow Committee", a group of employees below the age of 30, discusses the same topics as the executive committee but provides ideas and feedback from a different perspective. Marco Bizzarri believes that this is a way to bridge the gap between the generations and to better serve customers who are the committee's peers. Similarly, Valentino also has a committee of millennials, composed of employees from every region, that meets regularly to discuss upcoming trends and perspectives. Creative director Pierpaolo Piccioli has said that the design of the "VLTN" logo the brand introduced in 2017 came from the young designers in his team, whom he referred to as "kids" (Bowles, 2019). There are only so many ways you can re-interpret apparel or fashion – clothes and accessories are far removed from the kind of technological advancement that drives the automotive and tech industries. Major breakthrough innovations are few and far between, and in the meantime brands that wish to stay fresh must reimagine their product or the way consumers experience it.

This is especially true in the hospitality industry. Aside from location, hotel design, or over-the-top concierge service, there isn't much room for innovation. The only way to remain current is to have a deeper understanding of what drives future customers to luxury hotels. While some historical hotel chains rely on tradition as part of their identity and cachet; Rosewood Hotel Group has a different approach. Sonia Cheng, joined New World Group and became Chief Executive Officer of Rosewood Hotel Group in 2018, overseeing three distinct hotel brands, including Rosewood Hotels & Resorts® an ultra-luxury collection of hotels around the world acquired in 2011. According to an interview with CNBC, Cheng planned to expand Rosewood by reinventing the brand to attract the younger generation (Handley, 2019). Herself being part of the millennial age group, wanted to break away from traditional hospitality practices and attract like-minded individuals who travel for experiences, digital presence, and food. For example, Rosewood Hong Kong features the Butterfly Room, one of the city's most coveted high tea rooms, with a month-long waiting list and Instagram-able tea settings. Or Rosewood Phuket, which re-created a street food stall inside the hotel and brought back the owners of the original street food store as the chefs, to honor its heritage and love for local food.

True to her desire to engage with a younger clientele, Cheng is also an avid believer of the engaging with the future leaders of the committee. In 2020, she launched a young talent program NextGen@Rosewood. This group of talent from various departments work closely with Cheng and the executive committee on innovation-related projects and co-create the future of the company. They receive mentorship from executives and cross-exposure opportunities. This ensures the group stays relevant and forward-thinking in a fast-changing world. As of early 2021, the Rosewood Hotel Group combined portfolio consists more than 40 hotels in 19 countries, with further expansions planned for the next few years, all-encompassing new ideas and innovation from the combination of traditional and innovative hospitality experiences for the luxury consumers of the future.

As we have seen, the world of luxury is extremely complex, and a one-size-fits-all strategy does not exist. To keep up with the times, companies must emphasize their ambidexterity, balancing day-to-day business operations and continual innovation. The innovations they pursue are not exclusive to products but extend to services, and depending on who the end customers are, it is important to understand from where these ideas should come. We saw how Ferrari finds innovation in both the automotive industry and race competitions, while in luxury fashion, brands seek to connect with future customers.

The Role of Icons in Luxury Houses

Just as Ferrari is challenged by the automotive industry, jewelry houses also face tough competition, many of them from each other. In the past, heritage jewelry brands had the upper hand, as they produced specialized pieces and were recognized for their craftmanship and design. Bulgari is known for its use of colorful gems in its distinctive cabochon cut – a smooth, convex shape – while Cartier stands out because of its affinity for art deco architectural designs. Customers of these brands returned because each house had its own unique feature. However, in the current market, the taste for jewelry has evolved, relying less on custom-designed item from the collection and more on iconic ones that carry a story of a maison's heritage. Today, a single piece can drive customer demand, encouraging more direct forms of competition. For example, one of Cartier's top selling products is the Love Bracelet. It was designed in 1969 by Aldo Cipullo, with a unique locking mechanism hidden by screws that match the pattern on its exterior. The Love Bracelet's popularity grew throughout the 2000s and 2010s, making it one of the most iconic products in Cartier's portfolio. Due to its popularity, other jewelry houses have adopted similar designs. Brands such as Van Cleef & Arpels, Bulgari, and Tiffany have introduced variations of the love bracelet.

In these kinds of competitive landscapes, it is important for a brand to stand out and be recognized as the originator of a popular product. Otherwise it will be drowned out by the noise created by its imitators. How do brands do this? By reinforcing their icons of course. Chanel is recognized for its black-tipped ballet flats, diamond-quilted flap bags, and tweed jackets. Hermès is known for its famous bags, The Kelly and The Birkin, and its silk scarfs decorated with equestrian themes, Burberry for its trench coats and tricolor tartan. Icons are long lasting and resistant to times of change. They are identifiable symbols that transmit a brand's message without loud logos or clear labels. As such, icons are essential to luxury companies; they are extensions of the brand that can outlive the brand itself.

Many luxury consumers, especially those who are purchasing luxury for the first time, consider luxury icons an investment: they are likely to appreciate in value over time and are easily recognizable. This belief has helped push luxury icons to be some of the best-selling products within a brand's product portfolio: Cartier's Love Bracelet, Chanel's classic flap bag, and Burberry's trench coat are all good examples. For most brands, icons are commercially successful products that act as consistent revenue generators. Since they tend to sell themselves, less effort is required in marketing and sales. When brands have strong, successful icons, they are better positioned structurally and financially, and they can shift their efforts and investment to new designs that requires more resources, time, and creativity. Luxury companies that possess icons are more likely to benefit from an ambidextrous product strategy than those that do not.

To delve further into ambidextrous product strategy, we can look at the example of Chanel, which has continually invested in the creation of new icons, including a few recent ones. Chanel's most iconic handbag is the 2.55, which was first created in February 1955, hence the name. It was the first women's bag to sit on the shoulder, rather than be clutched in the hand. It was a symbol of rebellion, something Gabrielle (Coco) Chanel was known for. The bag was designed with a secret zipped pocked inside, in which Chanel was said to store love letters from her illicit affairs. In the 1980s, Karl Lagerfeld reimagined the 2.55 flap bag, creating the Chanel Classic Flap Bag. Lagerfeld changed the 2.55's lock, replacing it with Chanel's double C logo, and wove leather into the bag's iconic chain. The next Chanel icon, the Chanel Boy Bag, was introduced in 2011. Another Lagerfeld iteration of the 2.55, it paid homage to Gabrielle Chanel's first love, Boy Capel. Its boxy shape and leather-and-chain strap spoke to the modern-day woman who sought a more androgynous, edgier style that was not too feminine.

In 2017, when the backpack trend was on the rise, Lagerfeld introduced the Gabrielle Bag. A completely new design, it featured a hard leather base and a lightweight body, usually in the same quilted leather as the classic flap bag, but occasionally in fabric or tweed to match the brand's seasonal colors. The bag was unique as it was worn as a crossbody shoulder bag, a re-interpretation of a backpack worn on the side. It was unlike anything any other brand had ever created, and it became instantly iconic. Two years later, Chanel introduced the Chanel 19. Another iteration of the 2.55, but adapted to the times, it was much larger and functions as an everyday bag. It has a double chain – a long one that sits on the shoulder and a shorter one that acts as a handle, allowing the wearer to create more versatile ways of carrying the bag.

The timeline of Chanel's iconic bags shows that icons do not require years to develop. Karl Lagerfeld and his collaborator and successor Virginie Viard have repeatedly adapted the 2.55 to suit contemporary tastes and trends. The double C logo was a status symbol in the 1980s, while androgyny and functionality defined 2010s. The evolution of a classic icon validates the concept that while icons are an important aspect of a business, innovation and design are equally as important if a brand is to stay current. Moreover, the significance of an icon as an appreciating asset allows brands to continually stretch the price point without any effects on price elasticity. In Figure 8.2, we see how Chanel has incrementally increased the price of its Classic Flap Bag year after year since 2008. In 30 years, from 1990 to 2020, the Chanel Classic Flap has appreciated in value by over 465%. Yet it remains one of Chanel's most stable products within its portfolio.

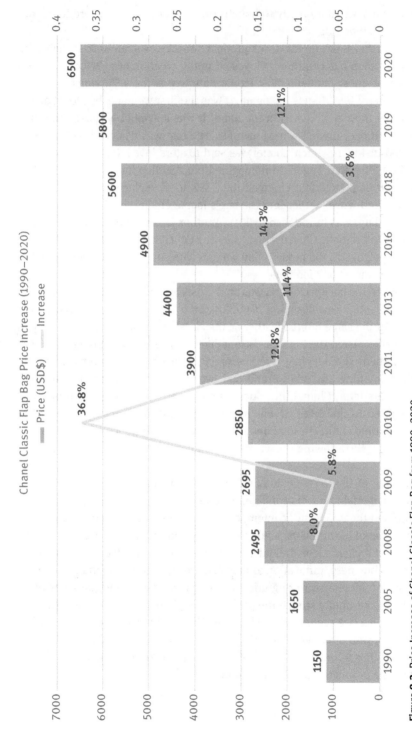

Figure 8.2: Price Increase of Chanel Classic Flap Bag from 1990–2020.
Source: Compiled by authors.

In Chapter 2, the second paradox, "How to be Timeless and Contemporary", explored how Sergio Rossi generated 100% of its turnover during the Covid-19 pandemic with shoes from its archives. Similarly, Cartier CEO Cyrille Vigneron recently acknowledged that the most resilient luxury houses throughout the crisis were those with clear and distinctive identities, pointing out that Cartier's simple icons were the most important categories within its portfolios (Vigneron, 2021). Likewise, Chanel, Hermès, and Louis Vuitton saw exponential growth at the end of the global lockdown in 2020. Hermès generated a revenue of US$2.7 million from a single day's transactions in a single store in Beijing. Similarly, when retail stores finally re-opened in China at the end of April, Louis Vuitton and Chanel were the first to announce price increases, mainly on their iconic bags – upwards of 14% and 17%, respectively (Reuters, 2020a). This led to long lines of eager consumers across China, who hoped to get their hands on these luxury goods before the price increase came into effect. Surprisingly, even after the price increase, clients remained undeterred and continued the shopping frenzy. Figure 8.2 shows that even after the great financial crisis of 2008, Chanel continued to raise its prices by 8% and 5.8% in 2008 and 2009, respectively.

New Business Models of the 21st Century

For luxury companies, agility and ambidexterity are crucial aspects of a successful business model. Companies must be flexible and well prepared to maintain a stable business strategy through times of change, sustaining a commercially strong business stream while at the same time exploring avenues for improvement. The last decade challenged companies to adapt to the acceleration of technology, a rise in the importance of social ethics, and new urgency to address climate change. As business models evolve, these core themes will continue to play an important role in the decisions luxury companies make about strategy and about the structure of their business.

As the Covid-19 pandemic reached peaked in 2020, three themes – digitization, social ethics, and sustainability – were at the forefront of discussions led by leaders in the world of luxury. The pandemic served as a wake-up call for many organizations that had been taking their time in transforming their businesses to meet the needs of the twenty-first century. A popular meme circulated on the internet showing a chief information officer (CIO) asking what accelerated the company's digital strategy, and the answer was Covid-19. While many laughed, they could also identify this as true. The year 2020 has become a pivotal turning point in the history of luxury, exposing many cracks within it. Conversely, it has also encouraged companies to become less risk adverse and experiment with new business ideas. For example, when retail stores were forced to close, luxury brands had to come up with inventive ways to interact with their customers. The following subsections will explore the different types of business models luxury companies should consider moving forward.

Shifting the Product Focus to Experiential Enticement

Earlier in this chapter, we discussed ambidexterity as companies' ability to balance the continuous generation of new products and services with the exploitation of existing lines. This is challenging even when companies have the means to predict their customers' needs and desires – and direct their exploratory energy accordingly. However, in these changing times, consumers' attention is becoming more scattered and difficult to predict. We can see the consequences of this fractured attention in recent developments in the long-running rivalry between French and Italian luxury brands. Both countries have highly developed luxury industries, but in the past 10 years, the competition has skewed toward the French. This is not because they produce higher quality goods; in fact, the majority of French luxury brands manufacture their goods in Italy. Rather, the French have gained an advantage because of the approach by which French brands positions themselves. Italian luxury brands are notorious for focusing on the quality of their products, and why wouldn't they? Italy is known for its leather makers, craftspeople, and artisans. Yet while the French brands Cartier, Louis Vuitton, Dior, Chanel, and Hermès all have shown spectacular financial results consistently since 2010, their Italian counterparts, including Gucci, Valentino, Prada, and Dolce & Gabbana have, in the same period, seen ups and downs. Why is this? There seems to be a clear distinction, where Italians have focused on why their luxury goods are better, the French have instead focused on the philosophy of owning something belonging to the brand.

This book is not an in-depth study of the differences between French and Italian brands. But the differences in approach between the two can tell us something about ongoing changes affecting the world luxury. While products play a vital role in enticing the luxury consumer, the philosophy of living a luxurious lifestyle is increasingly important. Consumers are no longer satisfied with their immediate purchases or the ownership of something luxurious. They seek excitement and adventure *through* their purchases. The modern luxury consumer cares less about the extrinsic value of a product, such as its country of origin, quality of manufacture, or raw materials. Instead, they care about its intrinsic value. What do people think when they see me with this brand? What does this brand say about my social class?

French luxury brands have always focused on cultivating intrinsic value, so much so that the most exclusive seem to exist in a separate class. Recently, the Chinese cult TV series *Nothing But Thirty* featured a scene in which a group of housewives excluded the protagonist from a group photo because she was not carrying a Hermès Birkin or Kelly bag but a limited-edition Chanel 2.55. The message conveyed by this scene was clear: If you do not own a Hermès handbag, you are not a part of our social circle. Even sourcing a Hermès from a pre-loved or secondhand merchant (as one of the women was later revealed to have done) is better than not having one at all. That the offending bag was also French only makes the French/Italian opposition clearer. Today, it is difficult to find an Italian brand that is held in as high a regard as the French brands.

In 2015, when Alessandro Michele took over as creative director of Gucci, he and Marco Bizzarri transformed the Italian brand into a state-of-mind rather than a luxury company that produces luxury goods. Gucci rarely advertises its products as "Made in Italy", nor does it focus on its connections to artisans and craftspeople. Instead, messaging focuses on making Gucci synonymous with feeling good or being part of the in crowd alluded to in American rapper Lil Pump's "Gucci Gang", This strategy has helped propel Gucci to become the brand with the highest engagement rate on Instagram, outpacing Louis Vuitton.

Luxury goods possess a different meaning now than in the past. After the democratization of luxury, the ownership of luxury goods does not hold the same prestige as it once did. If you have €8,000 to spare and the relentless dedication to pester your sales associate at Hermès, or are willing to pay one-and-a-half times the premium at a secondhand store such as Vestiaire Collective, a Hermès Birkin is within your reach. As luxury products have become more accessible, experience has become a valuable way to maintain exclusivity. In Paris, for example, VIP luxury clients might be invited up to Hermès's secret garden on the rooftop of their Rue de Faubourg Saint Honoré flagship store or offered a private tour of Gabrielle Chanel's apartment at 31 Rue Cambon. These experiences also extend to front-row seats at the haute couture fashion shows and endless pampering. As we saw in Chapter 2, today, top luxury clients are offered one-to-one services such as private shopping, concierge services, and an extension of experiences outside of the retail space. Only those who have the means to sustain a luxury lifestyle beyond a few select purchases can access these experiences; VIP customers typically spend hundreds of thousands of euros on their preferred brands on a regular basis.

Charm them through Retail Experiences

While top clients are important to luxury brands, the acquisition of newer and younger consumers is equally, if not more, important. Previously, we discussed how brands such as Cerutti and Dunhill have declined due to their inability to attract the new generation of luxury consumers. To tap into this lucrative market, brands must focus on establishing enticing experiences that align with their values.

When iPhones were first introduced in 2007, Apple founder Steve Jobs promised the potential of a smartphone. But nobody predicted how it would eventually change the way people consumed information and goods. While we have certainly benefited from the smartphone's convenience and its role in technological innovation, our dependence on it has also desensitized us to traditional means of excitement. Why does this matter? Excitement is controlled by dopamine, a neurotransmitter, which helps humans strive, focus and triggers interests. When a person's dopamine levels are elevated, they tend to feel a sense of excitement and contentment (Parker-Pope, 2005). Research has shown that luxury purchases can trigger the release of dopamine (Kershaw, 2009). Shopping has the ability to activate key areas of the brain, boosting a person's mood and making them feel better. This includes window shopping or obtaining something that is hard to find, like a limited-edition item.

The way smartphones and social media have changed the way humans react to dopamine releases poses both a risk and an opportunity for luxury brands. Luxury companies may risk losing the attention of their consumers, if their approach remains unchanged. A 1955 study by researchers at the University of Kentucky looked at how rats behaved when exploring unfamiliar compartment in their cages as a way to simulate how people behave when discovering new stores. Results showed that the rats' dopamine levels surged whenever they encountered an unexplored compartment, indicating that newness has the ability to drive excitement. The traditional luxury retail format has become stale and repetitive: stores such as Loewe and Yves Saint Laurent are decorated the same way, with the same aesthetics. What was once a way to standardize the same formats and interiors in the early 2000s, – no matter where they are in the world, retail stores are furnished the same, just as McDonalds and Starbucks around the world, as a way to create familiar surroundings for the consumers; have become stale and uninteresting.

Cartier CEO Cyrille Vigneron was one of the first to publicly declare that the uniformity of his brand's retail network was out of date. In an interview with *Fashion Network*, he stated, "If New Bond Street looks like Montenapoleone, which looks like Faubourg St-Honoré that looks like Ginza, then why travel?" (Deeny, 2019). According to Vigneron, modern consumers, more well-travelled than previous generations, are seeking uniqueness in their luxury experience. This includes the stores they visit while on holiday or a business trip. In 2019, Cartier embarked on an ambitious project to revamp 65 retail stores worldwide. Each store will include a local touch, such as a cocktail bar in their New Bond Street location or a revolving theme that sees the brand's Cannes store transformed from a nautical-inspired boutique by day to a swank, loungey villa by night. Cartier has also acknowledged that its stores can be intimidating to people who aren't accustomed to luxury. The brand has therefore begun hosting welcoming, experience-driven pop-up events designed to make Cartier more approachable to a wider clientele. The first event, Un Cartier de Paris, took place in St. Germain, Paris, in December 2017. Held just before Christmas, the event included gastronomic experiences, free gifts, and a space to try on Cartier jewelry. It opened doors to customers who would never consider walking into a boutique, creating a different experience, something they could share on social media without facing the daunting stares of sales associates.

Cartier has continued to create experiential pop-ups, such as the Cartier Konbini in Tokyo in September 2018. *Konbini* are convenience stores such as Seven-Eleven or Family Mart – quintessential emblems of everyday Japanese culture. Cartier Konbini was a pop-up featuring one of the brand's iconic lines, Juste un Clou. The store, set up like a typical *konbini*, offered fridges filled with Cartier-branded champagne and cakes and shelves stocked with energy bars and cup noodles, as well as the chance to try on the jewelry on display (William, 2018). In 2019, Cartier's Singapore pop-up for the collection

Clash de Cartier played on the concept of duality – soft and bold. Visitors were invited to discover their alter egos through a quiz on an iPad. They could then proceed to "The Bookstore" for a personalized haiku poem or to "The Record Store" to listen to music curated by Michel Gaubert, the French music director renowned for his work on fashion shows. Pieces from the collection were available to view and try on, and the tour ended with complementary food and drinks in the pop-up's café (Dejiki, 2019).

Shifting from Transactional to Aspirational

In the previous chapter, we discussed the fallout from Dolce & Gabbana's 2018 marketing campaign in the lead up to their cancelled Shanghai fashion show "DG Loves China". Stereotypical images of Chinese culture and a series of unflattering videos showing a Chinese model struggling to eat typical Italian dishes with chopsticks were met with outrage from Chinese audiences. At the time of the scandal, Dolce & Gabbana was a raging success in China. Between 2016 and 2018, the brand had incorporated an increasing number of Chinese models on its runway and in editorials, as well as engaging China's sweetheart, actress Dilraba Dilmurat, as its spokesperson. Dolce & Gabbana had believed that the Shanghai show would expand its brand awareness throughout the country and exponentially grow the market. Instead, customers argued that the brand's slogan should be changed from "DG Loves China" to "DG Loves Chinese Renminbi" (the currency of China). As consumers become more informed, they are more aware of the tactics luxury brands deploy. As such, brands that act purely transactionally will be called out for treating their customers as cash cows. This has been especially true among Chinese consumers.

China has been a driving force in the twenty-first-century expansion of the world of luxury. Fueled by both an industrial revolution and wide-spread corruption, Chinese wealth drove the luxury market to grow by about 46% in the period from 2010 to 2014 (D'Arpizio and Levato, 2019). This growth allowed luxury brands to raise their price points, as Figure 8.2 shows Chanel did between 2010 and 2011. The same trend can be observed in Figure 8.3, which shows how Cartier increased the price of its iconic Love Bracelet by 23% in 2010 and 2011. This period, also known as the "drugged market", left many luxury companies in a comfortable position. With little effort required to sell luxury goods – especially iconic pieces like Chanel's handbags and Cartier's Love Bracelet – companies changed their attitudes from service centric to fulfilment centric. Sales associates no longer needed to engage customers in conversation or make recommendations, and the relationship between the sales associate and the client became purely transactional. However, when Chinese President Xi Jing Ping set out to curb corruption in early 2013 (Cendrowski, 2015), the luxury consumption in Asia started to dip. The full effects of the crackdown didn't materialize until late 2014, when the jewelry and apparel industries saw significant decreases in sales from the previous year – 10% and 12%,

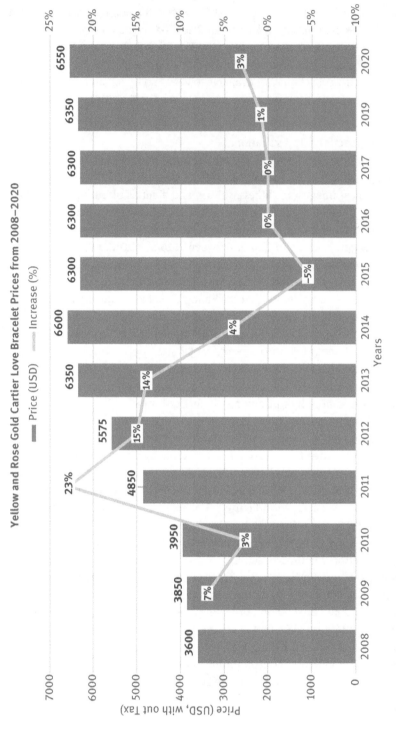

Figure 8.3: Yellow and Rose Gold Cartier Love Bracelet Prices from 2008–2020.
Source: Compiled by authors.

respectively (Holcz, 2016). In 2015, Cartier decreased the price of its Love Bracelet by 5%, the first time the brand had done so.

Thanks to the drugged market, in 2015, luxury goods were priced 50% above what they had been in 2010. This caused many iconic products to be perceived as overvalued. Luxury brands were now in a difficult situation, as they needed to replicate their growth in previous years with a significantly smaller Chinese market driving demand. Thankfully, this period also coincided with another phenomenon, which was the rise of aspirational luxury (not to be confused with aspirational brands).

When American hip-hop artist Kanye West released his coveted Yeezy shoe collection, a collaboration with sportwear brand Adidas, in February 2015, a potential, un-tapped market revealed itself. The collection was released in limited supply and worn by Hollywood A-listers and social media mega-influencers. On resale sites, customers were soon paying up to ten times the shoes' retail price to secure a pair. Though originally less expensive than a typical pair of high-end shoes (Yeezys retailed at US$399 while a pair of entry-price Christian Louboutin pumps were around €550 – a little over US$600 – in the same year), Yeezys effectively *became* a luxury item. With resale prices exceeding US$4000, a pair of the shoes could cost as much as a Chanel Classic Flap bag in 2015. This brought a new meaning to luxury, and a whole new way to experience it. Consumers were no longer purchasing a luxury good because it made them feel good; they wanted something because it gave them an identity, a way to signal their place in (rarified, celebrity) society.

The success of Yeezys initiated a new trend for "hyped" luxury goods. Online publications such as *Hypebeast* and *Highsnoberity* were now key opinion leaders, dictating trends and informing readers about new releases and drops. The growth of aspirational luxury was fueled by the lifestyles and purchasing behavior of tastemakers with expansive collections of limited-edition sneakers, Cartier jewelry, Audemars Piguet watches, and Chanel or Hermès handbags. The phenomenon has transformed the value of luxury goods, which is no longer based on whether or not one can afford a particular product, but whether or not one has access to it. Even though the question of access is not a new concept – it has long been at the core of Ferrari's and Hermès's sales strategies – the sales context that surrounds it has shifted. Rather than selling as much as possible, as they did during the period from 2010 to 2014, brands are now withholding their iconic goods, selling certain items only to loyal customers.

By picking and choosing who has access to their goods, luxury brands have removed the emphasis on their high price point, focusing instead on creating the desire for ownership. Examples of this include Chanel's Classic Flap in black caviar leather and the Balenciaga Triple S. Chanel does not display the black Chanel Classic Flap on its shelves – the bag is shown only upon request. Depending on the store you visit and the relationship you have with the sales associate, you may be told it is unavailable even if there are some in the store's inventory. Meanwhile, the Balenciaga Triple S was an overnight success, something neither Balenciaga nor

Kering had anticipated. The highly coveted "dad shoes" were so in demand that lines were forming outside retailers across Europe so that customers could have a chance to purchase a pair in their size. This also brought about controversy in 2018, when a Chinese mother and son duo were accused by security at Printemps Paris of cutting the line, when in reality it was a group of French shoppers who disrespected the queue. This caused immediate outrage by Chinese netizens, who went on to blame Printemps and Balenciaga for racial profiling, leading to a temporary boycott of the brand. This strategy has also given rise to successful limited-edition drops, such as Louis Vuitton's collaboration with Supreme, Christian Dior's with Nike Air Jordan sneakers, and Rimowa's luggage collaboration with Off-White.

While scarcity is one way to drive aspirational luxury, pop-culture and the legitimization of influencers also play crucial roles. Despite its losses between 2014 and 2015, Richemont (Cartier's parent company) was quick to bounce back at the tail end of 2015 with sales growing by 15%, mostly driven by its jewelry segment. Digital creators and fashion influencers drove this upturn by showing off their stacks of Cartier Love Bracelets on social media. With the likes of Kylie Jenner, Chiara Ferragni, and Alec Monopoly proudly displaying their "arm candies", the demand for the bracelet grew fervently. Its popularity continued to grow as YouTubers began rewarding themselves with the Cartier Love Bracelet as soon as they received their first paycheck, seeing it as something that legitimized their career as well as a symbol of success. Unlike in the past, when success could seem out of reach for all but a few, the accomplishments of digital creators and fashion influencers exist in a world where anyone can attain a life of luxury if they find their niche.

Connecting the Dots with Omnichannel

Omnichannel is a concept that has been, in some ways, over-discussed in the world of luxury. It is, fundamentally, a sales and marketing ecosystem where every touchpoint and point of communication is fully connected, with the customer at its center. Rather than engaging new customers, it serves to provide existing customers, who are already interacting with the brand, a seamless and consistent experience, regardless of which channel they are using. In the past two decades, the entire world of luxury has undergone a massive digital transformation, with the goal of bringing online into brands' omnichannel strategies. Almost every luxury fashion brand is either supported by an ecommerce wholesaler or has its own ecommerce capability. Likewise, each and every luxury company, from high-end jewelry to 5-star hotels, has a strong presence on social media with at least 10,000 followers.

Luxury companies no longer have the option to remain silent or exclusive. Instead, they are expected to communicate and deliver exceptional experiences to signal their luxury status. This includes their digital marketing strategy and their sensitivity to cultural events and celebrations, as well as their voices on social issues. Luxury brands have a tough juggling act, as they must balance their own heritage with the demands of the public. A fully connected omnichannel strategy is no longer simply advantageous, but mandatory. Figure 8.4 provides a snapshot of what a true omnichannel ecosystem should look like, where a client can access a brand through any of their various touchpoints, and at the same time experience the same level of attention.

A client of a brand such as Fendi, which has physical retail, ecommerce capabilities, and a strong presence on social media, should expect to have a seamless and consistent experience throughout these touchpoints. Nowadays, consumers are ubiquitous, and they will approach brands through as many platforms as are available. Chatbots or customer service representatives, for example, should be ready for a client who spends most of his or her time on Instagram. Any shift to a customer representative in the client's home country should be conducted seamlessly, including asking if the client wishes to be contacted by phone, by email, or to meet with a sales associate in-store. Whichever option the client chooses, the associate who will manage the issue should be fully informed of the situation, so as to be prepared to offer the best solution possible. A true omnichannel experience ensures that no matter where or how a customer approaches the brand, they will be met with full cooperation and assistance, as well as a consistent level of service.

Figure 8.4: A True Omnichannel Ecosystem.
Source: Compiled by authors.

One company that has embraced a total omnichannel strategy is Gucci. When Marco Bizzarri took over as CEO, he identified that each and every one of Gucci's touchpoints had to be connected. Bizzarri therefore introduced a number of initiatives, both physical and digital, to ensure that the brand would meet this goal. The first thing he did was to transform Gucci's stores to match the stories the brand was telling through the dreamy, colorful, and maximalist approach of designer Alessandro Michele. From the brand's location on Rodeo Drive in Beverly Hills to its outlet in Serravalle, to the Gucci Museum in Florence, its offices in Rome, and the Gucci 9 call centers in cities around the world, all of the brand's spaces got the Michele treatment to bring them in line with its new ethos. The Gucci 9 call centers, briefly discussed earlier in this chapter, have been key to Bizzarri's expanded omnichannel strategy for the brand. A category of consumers located far from Gucci's boutiques can now expect the same kind of interaction with sales associates over the phone as they would in-store, something that sets Gucci apart from every other luxury brand.

This seamless experience has also been applied to Gucci's digital channels. Since the appointment of Bizzarri and Michele, Gucci has grown into a mammoth business. It is no longer a fashion brand, but a lifestyle brand, with retail stores, a museum, restaurants, and a beauty line as well as a charity organization. With so many diverse businesses, it would be impossible to create a truly omnichannel ecosystem. Instead Gucci's smartphone app, originally a platform for augmented reality experiences and digital try-ons, has become a control center, connecting all of Gucci's business streams under a single umbrella. Today, the app offers product information, the latest brand news, access to the beauty collection, links to events, and the reservation page for Osteria Gucci (both Florence and California locations), as well as access to some of the brand's latest projects. The story remains the same, the level of service will always be exceptional, but Gucci allows you, as the app user, to define your own path.

Alternatively, brands may also try to connect online consumers to offline channels. According to Bain and Company's 2019 Luxury Report, 75% of luxury purchases were influenced by online channels, while only 20–25% of luxury purchases were made online. This means that the majority of consumers are still researching online and purchasing offline (ROPO). Digitally inclined companies can leverage this statistic to offer a complete omnichannel experience. Moncler offers an example of how to do this successfully. Visitors to the Moncler website are able to browse the latest collection. Once they have selected a product, they have the option of either purchasing it online or setting up an appointment with an associate to try on the product in-store. Moncler has blurred the lines between online and offline, creating a frictionless experience for customers for whom purely digital or in-store shopping may not be convenient or desirable. Unfortunately, this is not the norm for luxury companies. More often than not, ecommerce platforms are operated separately from boutiques.

As technological innovation continues, and social media platforms begin to introduce more in-app shopping capabilities, luxury brands need to keep connecting the dots between platforms. Not only linking shoppable items on their Instagram page to their ecommerce website, or WeChat announcements to mini programs, but also ensuring that conversations between client and brand are attended to and allowing clients to move seamlessly through a brand's ecosystem.

Engaging through Online Games and Digital Realms

Livestreamed fashion shows, augmented reality applications, and virtual reality experiences are old news. They were becoming the norm in the world of luxury even before the lockdowns that accompanied the Covid-19 pandemic. Luxury fashion brands give their Instagram followers full access to their seasonal fashion shows, even exclusive events like Chanel's private haute couture shows. Brands such as Balmain and Christian Dior have also experimented with Oculus to recreate their fashion shows through virtual reality experiences. While exciting at the time, these experiments did not lead to fundamental changes in how customers interacted with these brands; the Oculus devices used to create them now lie dormant in storage, collecting dust. However, a new breakthrough in brand engagement is on the horizon – gaming.

Most people alive today have played on or owned a game console at some point in their lives. From the launch of the first Atari consoles in the 1970s to the Nintendo 65 and the PlayStation 5, from Apple's Macintosh to custom-built gaming PCs, electronic games have become ubiquitous. However, despite consistent growth, the gaming industry was until recently ignored by businesses and brands in other industries because of stigma. Gamers were perceived as social outsiders, people who lived in their parent's basements and did not have real jobs. This changed in the 2000s, when online gaming went from pastime to lucrative business.

Esports first emerged in 1972, with the Intergalactic Spacewar Olympics, a small tournament organized by Stanford students (Good, 2012). They have evolved to become some of the largest sporting events in history. Teams battle one another in huge stadiums filled with tens of thousands of spectators, competing for prizes of over US$10 million. As of 2019, the prize money for The International, an esports tournament held in Shanghai, was worth around US$34.3 million. In the same year, Riot Games' *Fortnite* was handing out a total of US$15.3 million in prize money in its final round, split between three players. To put this into context, the winner of the 2019 US Open Singles division, the largest purse awarded to an individual in a traditional sporting event, took home US$3.7 million. Collectively, the two largest esports tournaments in 2019 gave out close to US$50 million (Statista, 2020c). According to Newzoo, a gaming marketing insights company, esports generated US$1.1 billion in revenues in 2019, which was a year-on-year increase of 26.7% (Pickell, 2019).

Luxury and Esports

It was Louis Vuitton that pioneered luxury's entry into esports. The brand had been involved with sports in the past – since 2010 it has designed the trophy case for the FIFA World Cup – so its 2019 announcement that it would be creating the case for that year's League of Legends World Championship in Paris should have come as no surprise. After all, Louis Vuitton was known for its unexpected collaborations, teaming up with cult streetwear brand Supreme in 2017. This time, it worked with Riot Games (the developer of *League of Legends*) to dress hip-hop group True Damage in Louis Vuitton skins (digital clothing for in-game characters) for their opening ceremony performance at the championship. Following the success of this alliance, Louis Vuitton created a League of Legends capsule collection of 40 pieces designed by womenswear creative director Nicolas Ghesquière (Phelps, 2019).

League of Legends is one of the most-played multiplayer games, with around 115 million monthly players worldwide (Spezzy, 2021). It is also the most-played game in esports worldwide. The esports industry is worth US$950 million as of 2020, and is predicted to reach US$1.6 billion by 2023 (Statista, 2020a). This is a huge opportunity for luxury brands, considering the vast exposure it provides. Unlike any other platform, the esports stage has a dedicated and concentrated viewership composed of people of all ages and various financial backgrounds. More recently, we are seeing a rise in newfound wealth among gamers and live streamers. Current estimates suggest that top streamers earn upwards of US$500,000 a month, potentially outpacing high earners in traditional career paths. In April 2020, in the middle of the global pandemic lockdown, Travis Scott, an American rapper, drew a crowd of 27 million players to a digital live show on *Fortnite*'s platform. The replay of the concert hit a record of 120 million views on YouTube. Had Scott been dressed by a luxury brand, just as True Damage was the League of Legends World Championship, this would have meant astronomical exposure.

Online Games as an Outlet for Luxury Fashion
Online games have become an extension of entertainment that cannot be ignored. They exist across all genres and platforms and cater to a wide range of different consumers. While *League of Legends* and *Fortnite* are marketed mainly toward male audiences, Nintendo's *Animal Crossing* is designed to be more appealing to females. In May 2020, luxury fashion brands Marc Jacobs and Valentino transformed designs from their current collection into outfits which could be worn by the player's avatar (Craddock, 2020), in Valentino's case, working with Kara Chung of the popular Instagram handles @animalcrossingfashionarchive and @crossingtherunway. While this collaboration did not necessarily translate into revenues, it created a new way for consumers to engage with the brand.

Gaming has a particularly large footprint in China, where over 620 million mobile games generate US$36.5 billion in yearly revenue, just US$300 million short of what the industry earns in the United States. China is also home to one of the world's largest game developers, Tencent, which also owns the social media platform WeChat. Tencent generated US$18.4 billion in revenue in the third quarter of 2020, 45% of which was generated by its online games industry. In China, gaming culture emerged in parallel to the country's digital transformation. Gamification is imbedded into every aspect of digital transactions in China, from paying for a meal to making a purchase through a mobile device. In 2017, Chinese online marketplace Alibaba gamified the shopping experience for a Singles Day event, creating a mobile game featuring the Tmall cat and daily slot machines. Players had to catch different version of the cat the same way as you would catch Pokemon in the mobile augmented reality game *Pokemon Go*, except instead of "being" anywhere in the world, the augmented reality cats can be found in stores and shopping malls. Shoppers were able to win cash vouchers and discount codes by playing the game.

Some luxury brands have likewise tried to capitalize on the gamification of digital interactions by using proprietary games to engage with customers. In 2019, Fendi launched a WeChat mini program that allowed subscribers to play the *Fendi Ways to Rome* game. Similar to *Super Mario*, players of *Fendi Ways to Rome* jump over gaps and avoid blockages while riding a Vespa around Rome. While there are no prizes at the end, users can compare high scores with their friends. Fendi was the first luxury brand to create this kind of experience and it was well received, the idea being to raise brand awareness rather than to convert game play into revenues (T. Zhang, 2019). A few months later, Burberry created its first mobile game, *B Bounce,* using the brand's deer mascot as a character. Players bounce the deer upwards on a series of platforms, with the possibility of speeding up as the deer collects TB logo coins. The objective is to reach the moon as quickly as possible. In addition to offering the game as an app, customers were able to play *B Bounce* on the big screen at Burberry's Regent Street location. Prizes for high scores included the puffer jackets the game was created to advertise (Alexander, 2019).

Online and mobile games have immense potential for the world of luxury, especially since a large majority of those who play them are between the ages of 15 and 54. This segment gained even more momentum in 2020, when the global pandemic forced many countries into lockdown.

Beyond Gaming and Digital Realms

Demna Gvasalia, the current creative director of Balenciaga, belongs to a new wave of creative directors that includes Kim Jones at Christian Dior, Matthew Williams at Givenchy, and Virgil Abloh at Louis Vuitton, all of them hand-picked by the leaders of luxury conglomerates to bring new life to heritage brands. Gvasalia, the founder of the cult streetwear brand Vetements, has always been very forward thinking. It was no surprise to most when Balenciaga announced that it would showcase its fall/winter 2021 collection on the game-streaming platform Twitch. Gvasalia and his team at Balenciaga created an online role-playing game (RPG) titled *Afterworld: The Age of Tomorrow* in which players take a journey into a dystopic world set in 2032. Following illuminated arrows through a series of zones, they encounter non-playable characters (NPC) – models wearing the latest collection. This digital realm mimics game play, where you move from one level to the next, with each level designed according to a different theme. What Balenciaga created was out of this world. It resonated deeply with its target audience because they now believed the brand truly understood what was relatable to them. Luxury fashion has always been about pushing the limits of creativity and finding newer ways to engage with the end customer, but Gvasalia found a revolutionary format to showcase that creativity while connecting with Balenciaga's target audience.

The dystopia Balenciaga created for *Afterworld* demonstrated how digital realms can offer a kind of escape. The year 2020 was a time of great distress; many faced new feelings of constraint and isolation. Games like Nintendo's *Animal Crossing* transported players away from their mundane zoom meetings and daunting housework to another world. More than a distraction, *Animal Crossing* allowed people to travel vicariously to different islands and socialize with friends from all over the world. It also gave players the opportunity to dress up in designer clothing as a way to express themselves freely.

The example of social games like *Animal Crossing* has opened a world of possibilities for luxury brands, which are beginning to create their own digital realms where people can socialize and conduct activities as they would in person. In 2018, Valentino partnered with Alibaba to launch a virtual store as part of the latter's newly created TMall Luxury Pavilion. Luxury Pavilion members could now shop virtually, browsing Valentino's digital store as they would a real-world boutique. While many other brands have experimented with similar concepts, virtual shopping took center stage during the global pandemic. Luxury brands that had never considered virtual shopping quickly adapted and soon introduced these services. Cartier offered its clients virtual tours of its boutiques with the assistance of a sales associate. Clients could point out pieces for a closer look, and the sales associate would zoom in and provide a narrative. This approach is still in its testing phases – it had a very limited launch and has not been advertised – and many assume that once lockdowns and travel bans are lifted, physical retail will return to normal. However, this type of technology should not be ignored, as it can provide further opportunities that have yet to be realized.

Avatars and Alter Egos

One thing that the gaming industry offers is the ability to become someone else by adopting an alter ego. In almost every RPG, players are able to select and customize characters, making decisions about what they look like and what unique traits they possess. One of the most successful avatar-based games of the past decade is Maxim's *The Sims*, in which players have the ability to create facial features and body shapes that correspond almost exactly to their own – or to those of the person they wish to be. In addition, players can define the unique social and emotional traits of their avatars. In previous versions of the game, players could even create their own clothing through a Developer Studio expansion pack. The possibilities were endless. More recently, luxury companies such as Moschino and Gucci have collaborated with Maxim (now owned by EA Games) to use *The Sims* to further develop their presence in gaming. Moschino released an expansion pack consisting of fashion-studio furniture (e.g., studio lights, a backdrop stand, and cameras on tripods) and a Moschino signature-collection supplement to the existing in-game wardrobe. The game play allowed players to create their own storyline, portraying themselves as a fashion model, a fashion photographer, or a fashion designer.

Creating alter egos and avatars can be a form of escapism, but it can also allow people to discover their creative side. In many ways, an avatar allows us to be more openly expressive because it removes the pressure of being completely ourselves. This became even more apparent in 2020, when most social interactions moved online. The social media platform Snapchat introduced the avatar-builder Bitmoji after it acquired Bitstrip, a comic-creation app, in 2016. Bitmoji started out as a storytelling platform but soon became a tool for users to communicate digitally with emotion and gestures, which were otherwise only possible face to face. A 2016 article in *Forbes* indicated that avatars have become a person's digital identity (Krueger, 2016). As we move into the future and detach ourselves from face-to-face interactions, avatars are merging our real-world identities with our digital identities. In 2020, Ralph Lauren, Levi's, and Jordan Brand released digital versions of their products on the Bitmoji app, letting users isolated at home incorporate them into their avatars' outfits (Parisi, 2020). Avatars may not be us, but that doesn't mean they can't help us create the best versions of ourselves.

A newcomer to the avatar game is Gucci, which in 2018 worked with avatar-creation company Genies to launch this functionality on its app. Gucci Genies, as they are now called, allow users to interact with friends on chatroom platforms (e.g., iMessage, Facebook Messenger, and WhatsApp) using stickers and avatars of themselves reacting to conversation. In earlier magazine publications, Gucci proposed to use Gucci Genies as a way to transform its future shopping experience. However, this lacked potential since Genies have large heads and comparatively smaller bodies rather than realistic human proportions. So, in February 2021, Gucci announced that it would collaborate with *Zepeto*, a mobile game, to create lifelike avatars that could be dressed proportionately in Gucci's latest collection. *Zepeto*, developed by South Korean tech giant Naver, which has been gaining popularity in Asia, allows users to create a 3D animated version of themselves by taking a picture or uploading one from their library. The initial *Zepeto* avatar can be further edited to adjust the likeness. The game geo-localizes players to allow their avatars to meet on the street, where they can interact and play games. Gucci's collaboration with *Zepeto* aims to create a community where users can experiment with virtual clothing and spark communication around the brand's latest collection. Will this be the future of earned media?

Data, Privacy and Artificial Intelligence

In this day and age, data has become a company's most valuable asset – the largest companies in the world are the data giants Amazon, Alphabet, and Facebook. According to Facebook's 2020 financial reports, 99% of its revenue came from advertising, which relies on the platform's access to data from 2.45 billion users (as of the third quarter of 2019). Companies that advertise on Facebook set parameters to target a particular audience; for example, a color-cosmetics brand could choose to target a predominantly female audience between the ages of 16 and 35, living in English-speaking countries, and currently following brands such as MAC Cosmetics and Laura Mercier.

Despite increasing concern about its practices – Facebook has long had its critics, and CEO Mark Zuckerberg faced questioning by the US Senate Judiciary Committee in November 2020 – brands continue to use Facebook as a source of targeted advertising because it has the best insights on customer preferences and behaviors. Similarly, Alphabet, Google's parent company, has unprecedented access to the trends and conversations of the general public through its ubiquitous search engine, which geolocates its users and tracks the terms they search for. Someone whose Google search history includes "black tote bags", "luxury goods", and "medusa" is extremely likely to be directed to the Versace website set to the region where they reside.

Data as a Way to Elevate Customer Experience

Of course, data is not limited to search engines and social media platforms. Since the start of the digital transformation, brands have been collecting data and storing it for future use. Ecommerce platforms have benefitted the most from the sudden ease of obtaining customer information, as they have been fully digital from the beginning, while luxury retail was for a long time limited to their customer relations (CRM) forms, which customers fill out at the end of a purchase and were only mandatory for those who wished to join a mailing list or make a tax claim. However, the role of CRM shifted when brands began to realize the power of understanding their clients. Most brands today possess a robust CRM system that tracks each client's purchase history, spending behavior, and preferred sizes. Luxury companies use this information to identify top-spending and loyal customers, who then receive special treatment and rewards. However, brands have yet to maximize the full potential of their databases.

One of the most forward-thinking companies in this area is Mytheresa, an ecommerce platform operated out of Germany and partially owned by American luxury department store Neiman Marcus. When a person makes a purchase from Mytheresa.com, they are required to enter their details and contact information at checkout. Once registered, they are part of a system that tracks the journey through the Mytheresa site, collecting information on which designers they search, which types of products they look at, and what products they place in their shopping cart. Armed with this information, Mytheresa is able to send each of its customers a personalized newsletter that highlights new products from the designers that the customer has recently viewed, as well as recommending other products calculated to be most appealing to them. This type of personalized marketing is especially important not only because it can increase the conversion rate, but because it indicates to the customer that recommendations have been curated specifically to their preferences.

In the boutique, this type of engagement is most likely to occur only when the sales assistant has a close relationship with the client. But what if a loyal Louis

Vuitton customer based in Singapore walks into the brand's Champs-Élysées store on holiday? Unless the sales associate assigned to this customer asks for their details (something that normally happens at the end of a transaction), there is no way to know their purchase history or preferences. To solve this problem, since the 2010s, luxury brands have encouraged their clients to make an appointment ahead of their visits. This is most commonly practiced in Paris, as a way for loyal clients to avoid lining up outside the store. While making an appointment leaves no room for impulse visits and purchases, proactive sales associates could encourage their clients to inform them of travel plans, allowing a team in another city to have crucial information on hand for a more spontaneous visit. For example, if a client informs their sales associate at the Montenapoleone store that they will be travelling to Hong Kong next week, the sales team in Hong Kong can send an email to the client with the contact information of a sales associate who can assist them during their stay. The problem with this type of solution is that it is managed manually and leaves quite a bit of room for error. It relies on two teams of sales associates, not to mention the client they're working with, to essentially predict the future.

However, with the technological tools at their disposal with smartphones and apps, brands could expand their ability to accommodate customers, regardless of location. The ability to opt in to geolocation would let customers passively share their locations with their preferred brands, which could then notify local stores and potentially assign sales associates to clients visiting from elsewhere. Allowing those clients to accept or deny an assignation would give them some control over when and where to share details like their purchase history and size preferences while helping to ensure that when a client enters a store in a new city, that store has sufficient information to provide an exceptional experience. Luxury brands could also use geolocation and other in-app data to share pop-ups, events, and other experiences that are exclusive to a particular market. The luxury clients of today are not stationary and are willing to spend money not just on products, but on experiences. If a client is known to have a purchase history in London, Paris, Milan, Hong Kong, New York, and Tokyo all throughout the year, brands can be informed of that client's travel frequency and extend invitations to events held in their most frequented cities. Not only does this build a close relationship between the brand and the client, but also it allows the brand to constantly adapt to changing consumer behavior.

Luxury and Artificial Intelligence

Artificial Intelligence, or AI, is playing an ever more important role in how companies operate. In the world of luxury, AI can help brands predict trends, using machine learning – an AI system that adapts as it absorbs and "learns" ever-increasing quantities of data – to better understand the market. Older methods, such as relying on trend forecasting and trend spotters, are no longer effective because consumer taste may differ depending on various factors such as culture, country of origin, and skin tones. AI has the ability to process and analyze millions of conversations people are having about brands, current affairs, social change, and other topics across social networks. Some companies have even begun experimenting with incorporating data from machine learning into the design process. In 2019, the Chinese telecommunications company Huawei collaborated with Chinese designer Anna Yang to create an AI-driven fashion collection. Huawei trained its Fashion Flair app on tens of thousands of iconic fashion images from the past 100 years. The app's AI then created a mood board based on filters Yang had set and proposed a number of outfits. The designs were quite futuristic, featuring ultraviolet light reflective fabrics and ethereal themes (Huawei, 2019). Yang believes that this is the future of fashion, as the AI was able to predict trends and help with the creative process. Similar technology has been developed and tested within IBM's Watson AI division. In 2016, IBM worked with Australian couture designer Jason Gretch to create a new fashion line with data driven insights (Cameron, 2016).

Apart from its ability to forecast trends, AI has other functions within the world of luxury. With the rise of ecommerce and online presence, luxury brands are challenged to be more responsive to the needs of their clients. The following five tools have helped these brands bring immediacy to their online interactions with clients.

1) **Chatbots**

    Chatbots have become an essential tool for companies with an online presence. Ecommerce and social media platforms are constantly inundated with questions and feedback, and more often than not, brands do not have sufficient staff to respond directly to each one in a timely fashion, especially at odd hours. For example, the Louis Vuitton website is available at all hours of the day; if a person is awake at 3 am in Frankfurt, they can browse the site with the intention of purchasing a bag. Louis Vuitton, however, is not expected to have a customer service representative online in the middle of the night. To avoid losing the sale, the brand can deploy chatbots to attend to immediate and frequently asked questions, guiding the customer through their purchasing journey. Versatile chatbots that can recognize millions of combinations of questions allow brands to be available 24 hours a day. If the AI fails to answer a customer's queries, it will connect the customer with a human customer service representative during working hours.

2) **Targeted Product Advertising**

    As previously elaborated in the case of Mytheresa and its personalized product suggestions, machine learning is used by ecommerce platforms to track a user's shopping behavior. This behavior can then be translated into personalized notifications about products, sales, etc., which are relayed through a curated collection displayed on the landing page (the page you see when you enter the website or an app), or in a weekly newsletter.

3) **Image Recognition**

    In 2005, four years after Google introduced Google images, it added another function to its repertoire – Google Image Search. Just as a search engine matches search terms with keywords, image search and image recognition match search terms to points within an image. Much of this relies on AI technology that is able to process huge amounts of data at high speed. Companies such as Browns Fashion, Neiman Marcus, and Zara have included this technology in their search functions to help consumers quickly find a product based on its features as presented in images from the brand's website (e.g., color, sleeve length, type of garment, material, fit). However, this technology has even greater potential. Imagine you were walking down the street and you saw someone wearing a coat or a pair of shoes in the exact style or color you had always wanted. Approaching someone to ask where they bought a piece of clothing can be awkward, but there are apps that can assist you in tracking down the item by simply taking a picture of it. The AI can "look" and the images captured and identify similar or like for like items that match the parameters (e.g., color scheme, embellishments, logo, design, or dimensions) the items in the picture you took. The South East Asian fashion start-up GOXIP was created to utilize this technology. It re-directs users to a shoppable page with items closely related to things they've photographed and uploaded or searched elsewhere. Image recognition goes beyond keyword search and allows consumers to approach online product research differently.

4) **Digital Try-Ons**

The breakthrough innovation that propelled Snapchat to become one of most popular social media platforms in 2015 was its face detection lenses. Face-detection technology pinpoints facial markers, allowing users to apply "masks" and play with different features in real time. What began as a fun way to add dog ears and fairy make-up to a short video has evolved into a useful tool on ecommerce platforms, specifically those selling cosmetics and eyewear. L'Oréal was one of the first companies to implement this technology, allowing consumers to use their smartphone's front camera as a mirror to virtually try out different shades of lipstick before making an online purchase. Similarly, Chanel has collaborated with Farfetch this division has been renamed to "Farfetch Platform Solutions" to introduce a platform within its application that allows consumers to try on sunglasses from its collection. The technology recognizes face shape and digitally "fits" the sunglasses. The user can scroll through the collection and select the model they wish to purchase.

While face detection technology does not require AI – it is built to recognize facial markers – AI technology can be applied to make the process smarter by analyzing consumer data and offering recommendations. For example, cosmetics companies can offer color suggestions based on a user's skin tone, ethnicity, or current trends. Likewise, eyewear companies can use measurements based on facial data to determine the most suitable frame. This not only reduces the number of returns, it allows users to better understand what styles are most appropriate for their face shape. AI has huge potential to help consumers in their purchasing journey. Just as a sales associate at the boutique provides feedback, recommendations, and styling tips, AI has the potential to fulfil this role online.

5) **Predictive Merchandising**

In Chapter 6, we explored the complexity of Merchandising and the dependency on processing data to better understand seasonal trends and consumer preferences. In the luxury fashion industry, merchandisers are limited by the information accessible to them, as well as by their capability for data processing. With AI, it is possible to comb through years' worth of sell-in, sell-through, and sell-out rates. It can also account for other sources of data, such as purchase intention and click-through rates. AI has the ability to make sense of this data and identify the best merchandising strategy to reduce over manufacturing or incorrect pricing.

Is Our Privacy at Stake?

Data can be extremely useful, as the previous examples show. Brands have access to a customer's purchase history, travel habits, and location. However, this access comes with a trade-off in terms of personal privacy, which has recently become a heated topic for debate. Surveys conducted by market research institutions such as Ipsos, Pew, and Microsoft, have shown that almost 99% of respondents across all demographics believe that data privacy is extremely important (Luxury Institute, 2020). Facebook and Cambridge Analytica's involvement in the 2016 Presidential Election and in the UK prior to Brexit show what can happen when access to data isn't regulated. Concerns have only increased since the Covid-19 pandemic. The popular Netflix documentary *The Social Dilemma* highlighted the spread of misinformation on social media, showing how people can be brainwashed through personalized advertising. The documentary and other reporting in the media have made people more aware of the dangers of their data being used against them. Luxury brands that rely heavily on user data must walk a fine line between using it to encourage their clients to consume more and providing an exceptional shopping experience – clients are increasingly aware, and wary, of data misuse.

As of now, luxury companies are in the same boat as any other company. Their privacy policies are caught in a push and pull between legislators and IT experts. In Europe, the government has adopted the GDPR – General Data Protection Regulation – which aims to give EU residents more control over their data by putting strict limits on how companies can use it. All companies operating in the EU are required to inform their clients of how they collect, use, share, secure, and process personal data. EU residents have the option to opt out of as many data collection options as they choose, and companies are required to adhere to their wishes – or face fines of upwards of €20 million or 4% of their annual revenue. While EU citizen are protected by such laws, many countries have yet to implement privacy protection policies. And as technology continues to advance, the risk for data mismanagement will only increase.

Fortunately, luxury companies have long operated their businesses with the utmost discretion. After all, the wealthiest people in the world are also those who value their privacy the most. Luxury brands have yet to be ousted for mishandling client information or accidentally leaking personal data. To maintain their track record, luxury companies must demonstrate their due diligence in the protection of their customers' data by creating and enforcing privacy policies and investing in robust IT systems.

Rethinking the Supply Chain

Luxury companies, particularly those in luxury fashion, are facing increased scrutiny over production, extensive markdowns, and waste. In the past decade, brands such as Burberry and Stefano Ricci have come under fire for destroying unsold stock season after season. While many brands that practice the burning of inventory may feel it is a necessary evil, today's consumers, who are very concerned about the environment, don't feel the same way. Alternatively, brands who choose not to destroy their inventory move unsold stock to a secondary channel: off-price or off-season retail. This channel, spearheaded by companies such as McArthur Glen Group, Outnet. com, and Yoox.com, has grown significantly in the past 30 years. The idea was to move off-season collections to a secondary retail platform to be sold at a markdown, recouping losses at a lower margin. However, for luxury brands, sales and markdowns are not seen as positive signs, and the can dilute a brand's equity.

For years, luxury brands have chosen to hold off on discounting for as long as possible, or to select a very limited number of pieces for sales. However, when luxury companies encounter financial downturns and the drops in consumption that follow, discounts can be a last resort. This was the case when UK department store Harrods was forced to close its doors in early 2020. The lockdown ordinance forced a three-month shut-down of operations – three *critical* months, as they fell between the sales period and the arrival of the new spring/summer collection. Harrod's solution to this problem was to establish an 80,000 square foot pop-up outlet store in Westfields, London, to quickly get rid of its inventory (De Klerk, 2020). Many industry insiders challenged this idea, believing it would dilute the value of the products displayed at the outlet, as well as Harrod's prestige.

Unfortunately, in hard times, companies such as Harrods must consider their best interests, both for the sake of their employees and the business. Still, luxury brands that oppose to putting their goods on sale may draw up an agreement with their wholesale partners to buy back goods at the end of the season. This has been particularly favored by Richemont Group, which spent hundreds of millions of euros buying back unsold watches during the drop in demand from Chinese consumers in the 2010s (Dalton, 2018). Fortunately for Richemont, it was working with materials that could be disassembled and melted down to form new products. Alternatively, luxury brands might establish new agreements with wholesale partners to exclude the brand from discounts. One of the first brands to pursue this strategy was Gucci, when Marco Bizzarri boldly announced in 2015 that Alessandro Michele's Gucci would not go on sale (Milligan, 2015). The news was a shock to many consumers who had become accustomed to Black Friday and end-of-season sales. Bizzarri wanted Gucci to control its own off-season inventory, which would be sent to its chain of outlet stores to be sold six to twelve months after it was first showcased. Since then, many other brands have followed suit.

The problem luxury fashion companies are facing in dealing with their inventory is two-fold: first, they are over producing and second, they have shifted from timeless luxury to contemporary fashion. As described earlier in this chapter, luxury goods have become more accessible and aspirational to the general public, thus increasing demand. Luxury brands have seized the opportunity to grow both in width (producing more product lines) and depth (offering more choices per product line). However, this short-term vision for growth has resulted in a long-term inventory problem. As such, many luxury companies have started to adopt new business models based on rethinking their supply chains.

Pre-Order

When the South East Asia luxury bubble burst following China's crackdown on corruption spending, Hong Kong was one of the markets that suffered the most. A city that houses more luxury retail stores than Milan or Paris combined became more cautious, no longer counting on a flood of customers blindly picking out the most expensive goods. As a way to avoid over-budgeting their open to buy (OTB), luxury brands such as Chanel and Christian Dior have adapted to a pre-order strategy, organizing trunk shows a few months after their Paris shows to present the collection that will be made available to Hong Kong. Sales associates sit with their clients and fill their orderbooks based on their clients' selections. At the end of the trunk show, the clients pre-pay to guarantee their items will be made available to them as soon as the collection is ready. Not only does this help balance the store's profit and losses, it keeps its clients satisfied by providing them a unique experience, as well as the chance to have first access and to secure exactly what they want from the collection. This is especially important for brands such as Chanel or Christian Dior, which manage brand equity and desirability by distributing goods in limited quantities. And even though a customer may enter the store on the day an item is released, they can leave empty handed and disappointed.

Similarly, ecommerce platforms that work closely with their partners have implemented this strategy. Luisaviaroma.com and Modaoperandi.com were some of the first to introduce pre-order option for incoming collections. Since brands showcase their collections on the catwalk some six months before they go to market, many luxury consumers are well aware of what's coming, and some have even bookmarked their favorite pieces on social media. Pre-order therefore has the opposite effect of discounts and mark downs. It allows customers to have first access to products, often in fixed quantities. Price is also less likely to be a deciding factor for pre-order customers, for whom the value of being first outweighs the financial implications of a purchase.

What about collections that are not showcased on the runway? In Chapter 6 on Merchandising, we noted that in luxury fashion, pre-season collections (curated by the merchandising team) are released in parallel to actual season collections (curated by the design team). The pre-season collection is usually a "filler" collection that supplements the season collection; it's often not featured on the runway, and can include carry-over accessories in new seasonal colors. In February 2020, Bottega Veneta gifted social influencers carryover shoes and bags in the colors of the upcoming pre-season collection. While they were under no obligation to wear these items during the Milan and Paris fashion weeks, however, Bottega Veneta bags and shoes were the most photographed accessories throughout both events, effectively advertising the pre-season collection. But when people went to Bottega Veneta's website, they discovered that these shoes and bags were visible but could only be pre-ordered. A week after Milan Fashion Week, the Italian government requested a total shut down of the country, and factories were asked to close, with the exception of those in essential businesses, halting the production process for the country's luxury industries. This led to those, who had placed a pre-order on the shoes they saw at Milan Fashion Week, not receiving their items until late May, when factories were allowed to resume operations. The fact that they had pre-paid meant that Bottega Veneta was the only brand within the Kering Group portfolio that saw a positive financial result during the first wave of the European lockdown. What Bottega Veneta had done, was to anticipate the standard sales campaign period, and selling their collection a couple months in advance. Unbeknownst to Bottega Veneta, it had been one of the best decision, as the March 2020 lockdown in Italy caught the entire luxury industry by surprise. Its sister brand Gucci, which released their collection under their standard buying and merchandising calendar was caught in the middle of the daunting lockdowns and a shift in consumer behaviour. Since Bottega Veneta had intended to shorten its supply chain, they also benefited from the timing of everything.

Flexible Supply Chain

In Chapter 4, we looked at the significance of country of origin in the world of luxury. While in some cases, the country of origin is equally as important as the product (e.g., Ferrari and Hermès's Birkin), most luxury consumers now disregard the place of manufacture since they trust that a reputable luxury brand will make the right decisions. Louis Vuitton, for example, has for many years exploited offshore manufacturing to keep up with demand from various markets. It has manufacturing plants in the United States (two in California and one Texas), Spain, Portugal, Italy, and Romania (White and

Denis, 2018). The reason for Louis Vuitton's vast footprint is to shorten the supply chain and subsequently its lead time to better cater to different markets. Fortunately for Louis Vuitton, its product structure is relatively robust, and the majority of its sales come from its iconic and timeless leather goods, while a minority is derived from its fashion-forward apparel collection. This means that Louis Vuitton can establish fulfilment centers around the world to replenish its inventory of season-less goods.

What about other fashion-forward companies, ones without timeless collections to rely on? Is there a way to regulate their inventory without over production? The answer is yes, but it requires heavy investments and a very well-aggregated and connected market structure. This is a strategy that has been long adopted by ecommerce platforms such as Matchesfashion and Net-a-Porter, which serve relatively large markets of 176 and 180 countries, respectively. To create an effective supply chain, ecommerce platforms set up warehouses close to their global headquarters with a fixed allocation of stock. The countries they sell to are then aggregated by region, with each warehouse or fulfilment centre serving a specific market or collection of markets. For example, Matchesfashion established a warehouse in Hong Kong to serve the Asia Pacific and Australian markets. The choice of location was based on administrative and logistic convenience, since Hong Kong operates in a tax-free zone. Of course, many luxury companies possess similar structures; however, they lack the data-driven algorithms that would allow them to regulate the movement of inventory to best serve each store.

Ecommerce platforms differ from physical retail stores in that in ecommerce, each input and output can be digitally regulated – they have the algorithms that traditional retail lacks. In retail stores, most of inventory checks are still conducted manually. Due to this, companies in retail have often experienced mismanagement of stock, which leads to high inventory costs. To curb this, many retail companies outside the world of luxury have adopted new strategies and technologies to overcome this issue.

RFID Inventory Management and Process Acceleration

In 2016, French sportswear retailer Decathlon shared news of its investment in incorporating radio-frequency identification (RFID) tags into its products. The aim was to have better control over its massive inventory, as well as integrating their predominantly retail-focused strategy into an omnichannel ecosystem. Decathlon's RFID project was a huge undertaking. It collaborated with SML Group to work with their network of suppliers to adopt RFID stickers and labels that would be sewn into the clothing during the manufacturing process. Each RFID indicator is assigned an individual electronic product code (EPC), which identifies the unique product SKU. This allows for item-level tracking both in the supply chain as well as inventory checks (Tageos, 2016). Decathlon has reported that the new technology has vastly improved its inventory management, providing it with better visibility of what is available in-store or in the warehouse. Additionally, RFID has helped reduce stock out and improved customer service.

In 2019, Decathlon utilized its existing RFID tags as a way to accelerate its check-out process. The "scan and go" service was tested in the Netherlands. The concept was developed in response to changing customer behavior, as well as increased mobile payments. The service allows customers to drop a basket full of merchandise in a self-service check-out bay and have all the items automatically registered on the payment system. Customers pay for items on their smartphones, and the RFID tag is disabled as soon as an item exits the store (Halliday, 2019). Not only does this cut down on check-out time, it allowed Decathlon to automate its inventory recording. While the incorporation of RFID tags is not particularly new – H&M introduced them in 2014 and Zara in 2017 – this technology is on the rise. The latest company to adopt RFID is Japanese retail giant Uniqlo. Unlike Decathlon, Uniqlo has extended its capabilities to include the use of digital displays to help guide shoppers through customer reviews and product information. Uniqlo, whose stores are comparatively larger than regular retail, has also considered downsizing its stores and using RFID technology to help customers identify other color options without putting everything out on display.

It's clear that RFID tags have significantly improved the operations and supply chains of big-box retailers; however, this technology has yet to be picked up by luxury industries. RFID is not new, and a few luxury companies have adopted it. As early as 2010, Fendi incorporated RFID tags into its labels as a way to authenticate its products. Yet it has not developed the technology any further. Alternatively, Farfetch used RFID technology in their initial plans for their Store of the Future, a fully interactive store similar to Amazon Fresh. But like Fendi, Farfetch has not publicly shared any information about further developments of this technology. This is a shame, as RFID has a multifaceted potential for luxury brands, not only to help with their inventory problem, but to transfer their physical store data onto a database and create a flexible supply chain.

Luxury brands, unlike big-box retailers, often deal with significantly smaller numbers of products. However, this does not mean that each luxury item undergoes a less complicated supply chain. Quite the opposite. Due to a combination of scarcity and high demand, luxury goods often move through multiple stores in their lifecycle. For example, Fendi has twelve boutiques in Italy, but not all twelve boutiques hold the same products. A client in Venice who sees a dress on Fendi's Instagram may find that it is not available locally. A sales associate will then have to check the inventory on Fendi's internal system. If the database shows that the dress is available in Rome, a hold request can be made, but it must be approved by the store manager before the dress can be shipped to Venice. More often than not, inventory volumes are done periodically and not always updated in real-time, so just because it says the dress is in Rome, it may not be. Moreover, the store manager is often not sitting in front of a desktop to approve such requests. The entire process is as cumbersome as it sounds, and RFID tags have the potential to optimize and streamline it. RFID technology has the ability to transmit real-time data, create records, and conduct calculations, allowing luxury brands to automate processes and fully integrated them into internal enterprise resource planning (ERP) systems (e.g., SAP, Oracle, or Salesforce) that can be connected to sales associates' mobile devices. A transfer request for a dress that currently takes more than 24 hours to approve could be done in just a few seconds.

Agile Supply Chain

Agile supply chain is a relatively new concept and was first discovered by Spanish fast-fashion retailer Zara, which produces upwards for 40,000 unique pieces per cycle, to be distributed to a network of 2,250 stores worldwide. By making its supply chain more agile, it has allowed Zara to react quickly to market demands and avoid losses. In fast fashion, the season cycle can be as short as two weeks. Failure to catch trends can lead to losses including on the cost of materials, manufacturing, shipping, and inventory. Ever since the introduction of this new strategy, Zara has managed to reduce its volume of markdowns from the industry's average of 50% to just 15% (Sull and Turconi, 2008). In theory, an agile supply chain should answer some of fashion's biggest problems, yet Zara has been one of only a few companies to adopt this strategy. This is likely because Zara has a vertically integrated supply chain. While it still needs to procure raw materials from fabric makers, Zara is known to purchase plain fabric in bulk and dye it as needed.

This kind of business model is impossible for luxury companies, especially brands such as Gucci, Christian Dior, and Valentino that use various types of materials, patterns, and prints in each season cycle. Furthermore, these luxury houses have existing agreements with long-term suppliers and manufacturers that stipulate their minimum order volume per season. To break out of or amend these agreements could result in high penalties on fixed costs. As covered in the discussion of merchandising in Chapter 6, it is important for luxury fashion houses to be fully aware of their product strategy and to maximize their sell-out volume. Yet while the full application of an agile supply chain is difficult to achieve, luxury companies can adopt a few of Zara's innovative strategies.

As previously mentioned, the seasonal cycle for fast fashion is comparatively short. Companies such as Zara continuously release new collections to keep their consumers enticed. In many ways, luxury fashion houses have adopted a similar strategy. In the past, fashion houses would release two seasons per year: the spring/summer collection, which would reach stores between January and February, and the fall/winter collection, which would debut in July. In the past ten years, this structure has changed to include in-between collections such as pre-spring/summer, pre-fall/winter, cruise collection, and various capsule collections. Each of these is often as big as the main collections, as they create more variety and purchasing possibilities for clients. However, this approach is no longer sustainable.

One of the ways Zara has managed to reduce over-production while exploiting its mass assortment is by creating small drops of an initial collection and measuring the sell-through rate. If, for example, Zara releases 50 miniskirts in various styles, colors, and fabrics into the market, it will review the performance of all 50 miniskirts throughout their first weeks. If only 20 miniskirts sell out, while 10 other skirts perform poorly, Zara will remove the 10 skirts from its total collection of 50 and ramp up production of the 20 that sold out. Moreover, Zara can see how well certain products are doing in certain markets. If one type of product is performing significantly better in Asia than in Europe, Zara will shift the slow-moving stock from one region to another. By doing so, the company has the ability to satisfy demand without exceeding its supply.

The difference between Zara and luxury fashion is the mass of products involved and the speed at which those products move. Luxury brands produce significantly less and are priced much higher. However, in the summer of 2020, rolling lockdowns forced luxury fashion houses to adopt a strategy similar to Zara's agile supply chain. The Covid-19 pandemic, which severely affected Northern Italy, forced many luxury goods manufacturers to halt operations. This created a domino effect, as they were no longer able to satisfy their order schedule. When operations resumed in May, the volumes manufactured were much less than predicted, meaning that stores received a fraction of what they had purchased during the sales campaign six months prior. Since consumer demand was expected to slow down, many brands had decided to cut production volume and to hedge their risk of over-production. Surprisingly, the slump they predicted never materialized, and many brands, such as Christian Dior and Fendi, were stocked out across the board. So as to not disappoint their clients, these brands opted to offer the option of placing a a made-to-order request and have the product delivered directly to the customer from the warehouse.

While these 2020 changes to the supply chain were a result of an unusual situation, brands should consider the opportunities of shortening their supply chains and working closely with suppliers to reduce supply and efficiently meet the demands of the market. It is also worth considering earlier practices, including stretching out each seasonal cycle with quick replenishments of successful products and discontinuing goods that are slow moving. Just as Giorgio Armani shared in his open letter to the fashion industry (Zargani, 2020), luxury was built of scarcity and rarity. Today, collections no longer align with the weather or commercial season, instead answering a constant need to feed the attention of consumers who are accustomed to multiple collection drops each year. Luxury businesses must carefully and intelligently slow down their growth by re-introducing value so that their customers can enjoy the true value of luxury.

Putting Your Employees' Needs First

"The customer is always right" has been a retail and hospitality mantra for years. However, many fail to understand that "people" (i.e., employees) are the most important asset of any business. Sir Richard Branson, the founder of Virgin Group, has received endless praise since the 1990s for his disruptive philosophy toward how bosses should treat their employees. Since Virgin Group is heavily involved in the service industries, which encompass hotels, airlines, and restaurants, Branson attributes his success and impeccable customer service to his belief that *"[c]lients do not come first. Employees comes first. If you take care of your employees, they will take care of the clients"* (Tucker, 2019). Unlike many other CEOs, Branson wants his employees to feel appreciated, often putting himself in their shoes to understand the full extent of their day-to-day duties. This is in contrast to Amazon, the most successful company in the world, where the focus is wholly on the customer. Amazon is operated like a machine: it maximizes productivity to generate high turnover. However, this tactic has also led to high employee turnover. CNBC has reported that Amazon employees, while often very well paid, have high expectations placed on them and are measured by tough key performance indicators. This has led to a high-stress environment and often an unhappy one. In Chapter 1, we looked at how luxury companies have transformed from family businesses to global conglomerates, and, more so now than ever before, how each one is measured by its profitability. While economic growth is important, luxury companies should not focus on establishing a business model that resembles Amazon. Rather, they should find one that offers intangible values to the final customer.

What separates regular retail from luxury retail? If you were to respond with "the products" or "the brand", then you would unfortunately be mistaken. A consumer can purchase a plain white t-shirt from Uniqlo for €10, and they can purchase a plain white t-shirt from Prada for €150. Likewise, the same luxury consumers who frequently purchase Hermès Birkins and Chanel tweed jackets also appreciate emergent direct-to-consumer brands such as Pangaia and ByFar. What truly separates regular retail from luxury retail is the level of service a customer experiences throughout their purchasing journey. To put this into context, imagine you were to enter a Zara store and then a Fendi Boutique – would you have the same expectations from both stores? Would you experience the same level of service? We would assume not.

At Zara, you would most likely be left on your own to browse and source an item in your size. You might have to line up for the changing room, making sure to bring everything you wanted to try – in multiple sizes – to ensure you wouldn't have to return to the floor if something wasn't right. At Fendi however, you would first be welcomed by a doorman and immediately be greeted by a sales associate who would attend to your needs. As you browsed through the store, the sales associate would offer recommendations and interesting details behind the collection, noting your interest in different items and ready to assist if there were any issues with fit. The journey of exploration at the Fendi Boutique is carefully curated from accessories to ready-to-wear and unique fur pieces. Zara, meanwhile, is a maze of clothing racks and hangers that you must navigate alone, occasionally sighting of an employee who can assist you with a product you might have seen online. While luxury fashion plays a big part in the retail industry, it differs from other retail formats because it is hugely dependent on customer service.

The world of luxury has always served a demographic of clients that expects nothing but the best, which led to brands constantly striving to raise their level of service. This is because excellent customer service puts the customer at ease; an empathetic sales associate can help customers feel appreciated and understood throughout the purchasing journey. However, there is not always a one-size-fits-all approach, as customers from different regions may have different expectations. Imagine you are in a luxury shoe store, and you encounter two sales associates. The first tells you the shoes you are trying look beautiful on you, even if you are feeling unsure about the color or pattern. You then proceed to ask for another pair, and the sales associate continues to suggest the first pair is better. The second sales associate, however, sees your discomfort or uncertainty and brings out another pair of shoes that you might prefer. You then proceed to share your doubts about the sizing, and the sales associate replies with, "If you're not sure, it's better to not buy it rather than regret it later".

Which of the two sales associates would you feel more comfortable with? Some may prefer the first sales associate, the one who provides reassurance and confirmation. Others might prefer the second, who shows empathy and a more conservative approach. Luxury customer service is incredibly complex, and sales associates are required to know at a glance how to best manage a client's needs. Thus, it is important for managers within luxury companies to consider the perspective of both the company and the end consumer when making hiring decisions. From a financial targets point of view, the first sales associate seems like a better fit, while the second may seem to have pushed customers away. However, from the end consumer's perspective, the first sales associate's approach may feel like undue pressure to make a purchase, while the second might have made the client feel understood and developed trust.

Most luxury consumers are unaware of the amount of training and education each luxury brand provides to its sales team. Chanel, for example, is known to have the most stringent training program, something that resembles an army boot camp, where sales associates are required to learn the ways of Chanel, from how to speak to customers to the way to present the packaging at the end of each customer's purchase. Every sales associate is required to undergo six months of training and can only be accepted as a full-fledged employee once they have passed all their tests. Similarly, Valentino has invested in establishing the Valentino Academia, which serves to educate their sales associates on product history (e.g., when each lace style was developed, when the first silhouette of an iconic dresses was designed, what type of material or pattern is used for a particular collection, etc.), as well as current news (e.g., which Valentino item is most searched for on the internet, which award show a Valentino dress appear in, etc.). Grueling training programs like these prepare sales associates to engage with their customers and deliver an exceptional shopping experience. On top of this, sales associates are also required to show passion for the brand and occasionally tolerate difficult personalities.

If luxury companies demand such high expectations from their people, then their employees should expect their efforts to be reciprocated. French luxury brands such as Hermès and Chanel have leveraged their success on the relationships their sales associates build with their customers, so much so, that the unspoken rule for increasing your chance of obtaining a rare product is to establish a close relationship with your sales associate. If sales associates wield such power over customers, then it is only wise to ensure the working environment is created to protect them. This was put to the test in 2020, when the global pandemic created financial uncertainty for many businesses. On April 8, 2020, Chanel was the first fashion house to release a statement declaring that, as it faced the unprecedented health crisis, it would act responsibly by refusing to participate in the partial unemployment systems put in place by the French government. It also declared that it would, for a period of eight weeks, maintain the full salaries of its 8,500 employees in France (Crash, 2020).

Similarly, Hermès released a statement to its shareholders indicating that it would trim its 2020 dividend and use the funds to support the salaries of 15,500 employees worldwide without the help of the state financial aid available to the company in France or elsewhere (Reuters, 2020a). In March 2020, Dorchester Collection announced that hospitality was likely to suffer the most from Covid-19-related disruptions, while promising to guarantee the jobs of all its employees regardless of the duration of the pandemic. Dorchester Collection CEO Christopher Cowdray was quoted as saying, "As our employees are our greatest assets and we are grateful for their long-term loyalty, we have guaranteed all jobs and protected salaries at Dorchester Collection" (Zohar, 2020). In a time of uncertainty, when job security is under threat, companies must stand up to protect their people. These actions mean more than donations to an outside cause, which can be seen as setting a double standard if the company making the donation does not take the same care with those it deals with directly.

Managers and executives of luxury companies must structure their business models to provide a safe space for employees. Just as Cowdray of Dorchester Collection has stated, "*[their] employees are [their] greatest assets*". This is not exclusive to an employee's job security, but extends to social justice. Ferrari, an automotive business that has always been male dominated, was one of the first luxury companies to be awarded the Equal Salary Certification (Ferrari, 2020), which recognizes companies that compensate employees based on their qualifications and position, regardless of gender or physical capabilities. The issue of equal pay is not new; it traces back to a *New York Times* letter to the editor in 1869 (Alter, 2015). Surprisingly, after a century and a half, women are still paid less statistically than their male counterparts. As we move into the future, it is unrealistic for brands to believe that their customers are more important than their employees. Luxury companies must demonstrate their commitment to their employees, ensuring that they feel cared for and valued. This will in turn generate loyalty, passion, and trust between the employee and their employer so that, as Sir Richard Branson has said, "they will take care of your clients".

Takeaways
- Innovation is one of the key drivers of resilience in a company. However, the world of luxury is undergoing a shift from innovation to agility as managers and industry leaders look to invest in innovations that will strengthen their companies' foundations.
- There is no such thing as a "one-size-fits-all" solution. Nowadays, luxury companies must look at their consumers as individuals, consider the unique culture and heritage of every country in which they operate, and be ready with business models that can adapt to fit the changing demands of the market.
- An agile business is a flexible organization that is capable of reacting to fast-moving and unpredictable changes. Agile businesses can support themselves during disruptions, evolve, adapt, and eventually self-correct. They are governed by the following three principals:
  - A growth mindset
  - Strong communication
  - Openness to the idea of change
- Ambidexterity is the ability to use both the left and right hands equally well. When applied to the context of a business, it suggests that companies are able to keep two entities running equally well, balancing exploration and exploitation. There are, naturally, two sides to ambidexterity. It is, first of all, a business structure that separates two entities to balance profitability and innovation. It is also a way to approach the product portfolio, where icons play an important role in balancing the commercial and creative efforts involved in product development.
- Today's world of luxury is undergoing an important shift in focus from products to a philosophy of luxurious living. Owning luxury goods helps define who we are and where we belong in society. Luxury is about more than an appreciation for craftmanship and quality.
- Retail experience has evolved. Today's consumers, more well-travelled than previous generations, are seeking uniqueness in their luxury experience. Traditional luxury retail has become stale and repetitive, with brands deploying the same formats and interiors in all their locations, aiming to creating familiar surroundings for consumers rather than something extraordinary. Luxury companies must learn to entice their customers, offering unique experiences that differ from city to city.
- Luxury companies must think outside the box to relate to their future customers – the use of traditional media is outdated and often fails to intersect with their values. Companies must therefore learn to find a balance between heritage and adaptation if they are to continue to attract customers' attention in the years to come.
- The world of luxury must continue to innovate, applying new technologies such as AI to process data and information at a much faster rate. Not only can this improve data processing to determine customer preferences, it can minimize the complexities of inventory management. Luxury companies should look to fast-fashion retailing companies for examples of practices that can increase efficiency and cut costs in a responsible manner.
- A company's employee should be placed at the center of the business. Luxury companies, which use exceptional service to differentiate themselves, must invest in their people – through training, equitable pay, protection, and recognition for their work. This will in turn generate loyalty, passion, and trust between the employee and their employer, empowering employees to better care for clients.

References

Aaker, D. A. (2010). *Building Strong Brands*. Simon & Schuster.

Abnett, K., 2015. Michele Momentum Means No Markdowns at Gucci. [online] The Business of Fashion. Available at: [Accessed 29 November 2020]. <https://www.businessoffashion.com/articles/retail/michele-momentum-means-no-markdowns-at-gucci>

Achille A., & Zipser D. (2020, April 1). *A perspective for the luxury-goods industry during and after Coronavirus*. Retail Practice, McKinsey & Company. Retrieved March 8, 2021, from https://www.mckinsey.com/industries/retail/our-insights/a-perspective-for-the-luxury-goods-industry-during-and-after-coronavirus

Adams, C. (2019, October 18). *Louis Vuitton Opened a Factory in Texas, Y'all!*. American Manufacturing. Retrieved March 8, 2021, from https://www.americanmanufacturing.org/blog/louis-vuitton-opened-a-factory-in-texas-yall/

Agrawal, A., Gans, J. S., & Goldfarb, A. (2018). *Prediction machines: The simple economics of artificial intelligence*. Harvard Business School Press.

Agrawal, S., Gupta, K., Chan, J. H., Agrawal, J., Gupta, M. (Eds.) (2021). *Machine Intelligence and Smart Systems*, Proceedings of MISS 2020. Springer Singapore.

Aichner, T. (2014). Country-of-origin marketing: A list of typical strategies with examples. *Journal of Brand Management*, (21), 93. https://doi.org/10.1057/bm.2013.24.

Alcácer J. (2015). *Competing globally*. Harvard Business School Press.

Alcácer, J. (2014, March). Competing globally. *Harvard Business School Course Overview Note*, 1–38.

Alchin, L. (2017). *America the New World*. Land of the Brave. Retrieved March 8, 2021, from https://www.landofthebrave.info/america-the-new-world.htm

Alexander, E. (2019, October 21). Burberry launches its first fashion game and it's very addictive. *Harper's Bazaar*. Retrieved March 8, 2021, from https://www.harpersbazaar.com/uk/fashion/fashion-news/a29532461/burberry-launches-its-first-fashion-game/

Alter, C. (2015, April 14). Here's the history of the battle for equal pay for American women. Retrieved March 8, 2021, from *Time*. https://time.com/3774661/equal-pay-history/

Arora, N., Dřeze, X., Ghose, A., Hess, J. D., Iyengar, R., Jing, B., Joshi, Y., Kumar, V., Lurie, N., Neslin, S., Sajeesh, S., Su, M., Syam, N., Thomas, J., Zhang, Z. J. (2008, December). Putting one-to-one marketing to work: Personalization, customization, and choice, *Marketing Letters, 3/4* (19), Seventh Tri-Annual Choice Symposium, 305–321.

Atsmon, Y., Salsberg, B., & Yamanashi, H. (2009, May). *Luxury goods in Japan: Momentary sigh or long sayonara?* McKinsey Asia Consumer and Retail. Retrieved March 8, 2021, from http://www.mckinsey.com/clientservice/retail/pdf/Japan-Luxury-report.pdf

Atwal, G., & Bryson, D. (2017). *Luxury Brands in China and India*. Palgrave Macmillan.

Australian Government: Department of Agriculture, Water and Environment. (n.d.). *Wool – Department of Agriculture*. Retrieved March 8, 2021, from https://www.agriculture.gov.au/ag-farm-food/meat-wool-dairy/wool#statistics-and-information

Bain & Company. (2017, May 18). *The millennial state of mind*. Bain & Company.

Blanchard, T. (2010, October 22). *Prada's new range is made in heaven*. Retrieved from The Telegraph: http://fashion.telegraph.co.uk/news-features/TMG8081394/Pradas-new-range-is-made-in-heaven.html

BBC News. (2020, November 5). *Denmark to cull up to 17 million mink amid coronavirus fears*. BBC. Retrieved March 8, 2021, from https://www.bbc.com/news/world-europe-54818615

BBC News. (2019, October 17). *Dior apologises for using China map without Taiwan*. BBC. Retrieved March 8, 2021, from https://www.bbc.com/news/business-50078886

https://doi.org/10.1515/9783110723519-009

Berners-Lee, M., & Clark, D. (2020, September 23). What's the carbon footprint of . . . a load of laundry? *The Guardian*. Retrieved March 8, 2021, from https://www.theguardian.com/environment/green-living-blog/2010/nov/25/carbon-footprint-load-laundry

Binkley, C. (2019, December 19). Dolce & Gabbana has a new succession plan. *Vogue Business*. Retrieved March 8, 2021, from https://www.voguebusiness.com/companies/dolce-and-gabbana-designers-succession-plan

Bizzari, M. (2017, February 13). *The poetic reactivation of Gucci* [lecture transcript]. Polimoda. Retrieved March 8, 2021, from https://www.polimoda.com/the-poetic-reactivation-of-gucci

BOF Team, & McKinsey & Company. (2020, December 7). The year ahead: Fashion is set for a surge in M&A. BOF.

Bordieu, P. (1979). *Distinction: A social critique of the judgement of taste*. Harvard University Press.

Bourdieu, P. (1984). The forms of capital. In J. Richardson (Ed.), *Handbook of theory and research for the sociology of education* (pp. 241–258). Greenwood.

Borgomeo, V. (2020, March 11). The birth of the legend. *Ferrari Magazine*. Retrieved March 8, 2021, from https://magazine.ferrari.com/en/cars/2020/03/03/news/ferrari-the-birth-of-the-legend-76681/

Boston Consulting Group & Altagamma. (2020, June 23). *True luxury global consumer insight*. Boston Consulting Group & Altagamma. Retrieved March 8, 2021, from https://image-src.bcg.com/Images/True-Luxury-Global-Consumer-Insight-2020-PR_tcm9-252200.pdf

Bourne, F. (1957). Group influence in marketing and public relations. In R. Likert & D. P. Hayes (Eds), *Some applications of behavioral research* (pp. 2017–257). UNESCO.

Bowerman, T., & Markowitz, E. M. (2012). Author response to: The Attitude-Action Gap: Toward a better understanding of "How much is enough?" *Analyses of Social Issues and Public Policy*, *12* (1), 230–238. https://doi.org/10.1111/j.1530-2415.2012.01294.x

Bowles, H. (2019, March 11). Inside the private world of Valentino's Pierpaolo Piccioli. *Vogue*. https://www.vogue.com/article/pierpaolo-piccioli-valentino-interview

Blanks T. (2020, November 22). Is there a new Gucci brewing?. *Business of Fashion*. Retrieved March 8, 2021, from https://www.businessoffashion.com/reviews/fashion-week/is-there-a-new-gucci-brewing

Brand Finance. (2020, October 13). *Top 50 most valuable luxury & premium brands could lose up to $35bn of brand value from Covid-19*. Retrieved March 8, 2021, from https://brandirectory.com/rankings/luxury-and-premium/

Britannica, T. Editors of Encyclopedia. (2020, October 22). *Ming dynasty. The Encyclopedia Britannica*. Retrieved March 8, 2021, from https://www.britannica.com/topic/Ming-dynasty-Chinese-history

Buis, A. (2020, October 12). *A degree of concern: Why global temperatures matter*. NASA: Climate Change: Vital Signs of the Planet. Retrieved March 8, 2021, from https://climate.nasa.gov/news/2865/a-degree-of-concern-why-global-temperatures-matter

Burberry Shenzen China. (n.d.). Burberry Corporate Website. Retrieved March 5, 2021, from https://www.burberryplc.com/en/company/social-retail.html

Cabigiosu, A. (2020). An Overview of the Luxury Fashion Industry. In *Digitalization in the Luxury Fashion Industry* (pp. 9–31). Palgrave.

Cameron, N., 2016. IBM's Watson bring data-driven insight to Australian fashion couture. [online] Cmo.com.au. Available at: <https://www.cmo.com.au/article/606085/ibm-watson-bring-data-driven-insight-australian-fashion-couture/> [Accessed 26 November 2020].

Cartier-Brickell, F. (2020, April 21). *The Story of Tutti Frutti Jewels, As Told by a Cartier Descendant*. Sothebys. Retrieved March 8, 2021, from https://www.sothebys.com/en/articles/the-story-of-tutti-frutti-jewels-as-told-by-a-cartier-descendant.

Casey H. (2021, January 14). No magic bullet to tapping China's 750. *Business of Fashion*.

Celeste, S. (2020, January 11). How Australia fires will impact fashion. *NOWFASHION*. Retrieved March 8, 2021, from https://nowfashion.com/how-australia-fires-will-impact-fashion-29006

Cendrowski, S. (2015, December 7). The worst may be over for luxury goods in China. *Fortune*. Retrieved March 8, 2021, from https://fortune.com/2015/12/07/luxury-goods-china-corruption-probe/

Chada, R., & Husband, P. (2006). *The cult of the luxury brand: Inside Asia's love affair with luxury*. Nicholas Brealey Publishing.

CITES. (2017). *The CITES blockchain challenge*. Convention on International Trade in Endangered Species of Wild Fauna and Flora. Retrieved March 8, 2021, from https://cites.org/sites/default/files/eng/com/sc/69/inf/E-SC69-Inf-33.pdf

Chaganti, R., & Sambharya R. (1987). Strategic orientation and characteristics of upper management. *Strategic Management Journal*, (8), 393–403. http://www.jstor.org/stable/2486022

Chanel. (2019, November 08). Watch Wiki. https://www.watch-wiki.net/index.php?title=Chanel

China Daily. (2015, June 15). *German fashion brand under fire for racist slur on Chinese*. chinadaily.com.cn. Retrieved March 8, 2021, from https://www.chinadaily.com.cn/china/2015-06/15/content_21008937.htm

Chow, T. (2014, April 9). *Super 130s Super 150s – What does it mean?* Senszio. Retrieved March 8, 2021, from senszio.com/super-130s-super-150s-what-does-it-mean/

Clark, E. with contributions from Conti, S., & Ell., K. (2020, November 5). Mega partnership: Farfetch links with Alibaba, Richemont. Kering's Pinault family is also putting funds into the new luxury retail venture. *WWD*. Retrieved March 8, 2021, from https://wwd.com/business-news/financial/partnership-farfetch-alibaba-richemont-kering-luxury-1234653058/

Clark J. (2015). *Fashion Merchandising*. Palgrave.

Clé de Peau Beauté. (n.d.). *Our story: Clé de Peau Beauté*. Retrieved March 4, 2021, from https://www.cledepeaubeaute.ca/our-brand-story.html

Collins, M. (2015, May 6). The pros and cons of globalization. *Forbes*. Retrieved March 8, 2021, from https://www.forbes.com/sites/mikecollins/2015/05/06/the-pros-and-cons-of-globalization

Confraternita dei Legnaioli. (n.d.). *L'arte dei cuoiai o galigai – confraternità dei legnaioli*. Retrieved March 4, 2021, from http://www.confraternitadeilegnaioli.it/arti-minori/larte-dei-cuoiai-o-galigai/

Contractor F.J., Kumar V., Kundu S., Pedersen T. (2011). *Global outsourcing and offshoring* (pp. 3–47). Cambridge.

Corbetta G. (2020). Corporate strategy. In G. Corbetta & P. Morosetti, *Corporate strategy for a sustainable growth: Alignment, execution, and transformation* (pp. 1–14). Egea Spa Bocconi Univ.

Corbetta, G. & Morosetti, P. (2020). *Corporate strategy for a sustainable growth*. Bocconi University Press.

Corbetta, G., & Morosetti, P. (2020). *Corporate strategy for a sustainable growth: Alignment, execution, and transformation*. Egea Spa Bocconi Univ.

Corder, R. (2018, September 18). *Chanel buys stake in F.P. Journe parent company*. Watch Pro. Retrieved March 8, 2021, from https://www.watchpro.com/chanel-buys-stake-in-f-p-journe-parent-company/

Coumau, J.-B., Durand-Servoingt, B., Kim, A., & Yamakawa, N. (2017). *2017 Japan luxury report: Changing channels landscape to satisfy Japanese luxury consumers' appetite for novelty*. Tokyo: Mckinsey & Company.

Craddock, R. (2020, May 4). *Random: Fashion brand Valentino shares custom Animal Crossing: New Horizons clothing codes*. Nintendo Life. Retrieved March 8, 2021, from https://www.nintendolife.com/news/2020/05/random_fashion_brand_valentino_shares_custom_animal_crossing_new_horizons_clothing_codes

Crash. (2020, April 8). *Chanel issues a statement regarding Covid-19*. Crash Magazine. Retrieved March 8, 2021, from https://www.crash.fr/chanel-issues-a-statement-regarding-covid-19/

Cristoferi, C. (2019, August 27). Dolce & Gabbana sees sales slowdown in China after ad backlash. *Reuters*. Retrieved May 27, 2021, from https://www.reuters.com/article/us-dolce-gabbana-results-idUSKCN1VH1EV

Crunchbase. (n.d.). *Kendo Holdings – Crunchbase company profile & funding*. Retrieved March 4, 2021, from https://www.crunchbase.com/organization/kendo-holdings

Dabral, A. (2020, June 15). *Elizabeth Taylor & Bulgari*: A love affair set in stones. Lifestyle Asia India. Retrieved March 8, 2021, from https://www.lifestyleasia.com/ind/style/jewellery/eliza bethtaylor-bulgari-a-love-affair-set-in-stones/

Davis, D. S. (2010, October 11). *Prada's New Project Is All Over the Map*. Retrieved from Harpar's Bazaar: https://www.harpersbazaar.com/fashion/trends/a5979/prada-made-in-project-1010/

Dalton, M. (2018, September 6). Why luxury brands burn their own goods. *Wall Street Journal*. Retrieved March 8, 2021, from https://www.wsj.com/articles/burning-luxury-goods-goes-out-of-style-at-burberry-1536238351

Danforth, C. (2017). *Here's how the Balenciaga Tripple S sneaker got its name*. Highsnobiety. Retrieved March 8, 2021, from https://www.highsnobiety.com/p/balenciaga-triple-s-fw17

D'Arpizio C., & Levato F. (2019, November). *Bain-Altagamma 2019 worldwide luxury market monitor: The luxury customer is present*. Bain & Company.

D'Arpizio C., & Levato F. (2020, November). *Bain-Altagamma 2020 worldwide luxury market monitor: Slow motion but fast forward*. Bain & Company.

Datta, D. K., & Guthrie, J. P. (1994, September). Executive succession: Organizational antecedents of CEO characteristics. *Strategic Management Journal, Vol 15, No 7*, 569–577.

De Barnier, V., Falcy S., & Valette-Florence, P. (2012, May). Do consumers perceive three levels of luxury? A comparison of accessible, intermediate and inaccessible luxury brands. *Journal of Brand Management, 19*(7). https://doi.org/10.1057/bm.2012.11

De Bussière, Zoé. (Director) (2020). Luxury: *Behind the mirror of high-end fashion* [Film]. Deutsche Welle.

Deeny, G. (2019, April 30). Anne Grosfilley on Dior's revolutionary linkup with Uniwax and African printing. *Fashion Network*. Retrieved March 8, 2021, from https://uk.fashionnetwork.com/ news/Anne-grosfilley-on-dior-s-revolutionary-linkup-with-uniwax-and-african-printing,1094362.html

Dejiki. (2019, November 15). *Clash de Cartier Studio pop-up in Singapore*. Dejiki.Com. Retrieved March 8, 2021, from https://dejiki.com/2019/11/clash-de-cartier-studio-popup-singapore/

De Klerk, A. (2020, August 7). Everything you need to know about the Harrods outlet store. *Harper's Bazaar*. Retrieved March 8, 2021, from https://www.harpersbazaar.com/uk/fashion/fashion-news/a32707698/harrods-outlet-store/

Deloitte. (2020). *Global powers of luxury goods 2020: The new age of fashion and luxury*. Deloitte.

Elan, P. (2020, September 13). TikTok to host its own month-long digital fashion event. The *Guardian*.

Ell K. (2020, August 20). Clienteling Takes Fashion Retailers Directly to Shoppers. *WWD*.

Ellen MacArthur Foundation. (2020). *Upstream innovation: A guide to packaging solutions*. Ellen MacArthur Foundation.

Elsaid, E., Benson, B. W., & Worrell, D. L. (2016). Successor CEO functional and educational backgrounds: Influence of predecessor characteristics and performance antecedents. *Journal of Applied Business Research (JABR), 32*(4), 1179–1198. https://doi.org/10.19030/jabr.v32i4.9730

EPA. (2020a, November 12). *Textiles: Material-specific data*. US EPA. Retrieved March 8, 2021, from https://www.epa.gov/facts-and-figures-about-materials-waste-and-recycling/textiles-material-specific-data

EPA. (2020b, December 4). *Sources of greenhouse gas emissions*. US EPA. Retrieved March 8, 2021, from https://www.epa.gov/ghgemissions/sources-greenhouse-gas-emissions

Ermeneia-Cosmetica Italia. (2019). *Beauty Report 2019*. Ermeneia-Cosmetica Italia. Retrieved March 8, 2021, from https://www.cosmeticaitalia.it/centro-studi/Beauty-Report-2019/

Fasel, M., 2018. *Burton Didn't Propose to Elizabeth Taylor With A Ring*. [online] Theadventurine.com. Available at: <https://theadventurine.com/culture/elizabeth-taylor/burton-didnt-propose-to-elizabeth-taylor-with-a-ring/> [Accessed 14 November 2020].

The Fashion Law. (2018, February 14). *Are your "Made in China" luxury goods just as luxurious?*. The Fashion Law. Retrieved March 8, 2021, from https://www.thefashionlaw.com/are-your-made-in-china-luxury-goods-just-as-luxurious/

The Fashion Law. (2019, November 6). *Ferrari to cut its licensing deals in half as it looks to move its non-car offerings up the luxury ladder*. The Fashion Law. Retrieved March 8, 2021, from https://www.thefashionlaw.com/ferrari-to-cut-its-licensing-deals-in-half-as-it-looks-to-move-up-the-luxury-ladder/

Ferrari. (2018, October 2). *Ferrari Monza SP1 e SP2: capostipiti di "Icona", un nuovo concetto di vetture in serie limitata* [Press release]. Retrieved March 8, 2021, from https://corporate.fer rari.com/it/ferrari-monza-sp1-e-sp2-capostipiti-di-icona-un-nuovo-concetto-di-vetture-serie-limitata

Ferrarini, P. (2010, Septemer 29). *Prada Made in. . . Traditional craft and manterials star in Prada's new capsule collection*. Retrieved from Cool Hunting: https://coolhunting.com/style/prada-made-in/#:~:text=%E2%80%9CPrada%20Made%20in%20India%E2%80%9D%20is,woven%20sandals%20and%20artisinal%20handbags.

Ferrante, F. (2015, September 4). *Made in Japan by Ermenegildo Zegna Couture*. Retrieved from Vogue Italia: https://www.vogue.it/uomo-vogue/news/2015/09/zegna-made-in-japan

Ferrari. (2020, August 28). *Ferrari receives equal salary certification* [Press release]. Retrieved March 8, 2021, from https://corporate.ferrari.com/en/ferrari-receives-equal-salary-certification

Flora, L. (2016, July 4). *As tastes mature, Chinese crave native materials*. Business of Fashion. Retrieved March 8, 2021, from https://www.businessoffashion.com/articles/global-currents/chinese-consumers-seek-tradition-material-techniques-yak-wool-tea-silk

Frank, R. (2020, January 13). *Lamborghini's 2019 sales jump 43%, driven by its Urus SUV*. CNBC. Retrieved March 8, 2021, from https://www.cnbc.com/2020/01/13/lamborghinis-2019-sales-jump-43percent-driven-by-its-urus-suv

Franke, N., Keinz, P., & Steger, C. J. (2009, September). Testing the value of customization: When do customers really prefer products tailored to their preferences?. *Journal of Marketing*, 5(73), 103–121. https://doi.org/10.1509/jmkg.73.5.103

Friedman, S. D. (1991). Why hire from within? Causes and consequences of internal promotion systems. *Proceedings of the Academy of Management Meetings*, Miami, 272–276

Friedman, S. D., & Singh, H. (1989). CEO succession and stockholder reaction: the influence of organizational context and event content. *Academy of Management Journal*, 4(32),718–744. https://doi.org/10.5465/256566

Friedman, V., & Paton, E. (2020, October 30). Tiffany deal is a signature move by the Sun Tzu of luxury. *The New York Times*. Retrieved March 8, 2021, from https://www.nytimes.com/2020/10/30/business/bernard-arnault-lvmh-tiffany-battle.html

Fujioka, R., Li, Z., & Kaneko, Y. (2018). The Democratization of Luxury and the Expansion of the Japanese Market 1960–2010. In P.-Y. D. Fujioka, *Global Luxury: Organizational Change and Emerging Markets since the 1970s* (pp. 133–156). Palgrave Macmillan.

Garvin, D. A., & Levesque, L. C. (2006, July 31). *A note on scenario planning*. Harvard Business School.

George-Parkin, H. (2018, May 24). *Balenciaga's dad shoes could help the brand hit the billion-dollar sales mark*. Footwear News. Retrieved March 8, 2021, from https://footwearnews.com/2018/business/news/balenciaga-triple-s-sales-dad-shoes-ugly-sneakers-1202566492/

Ghemawat, P. (2001, September). Distance still matters: The hard reality of global expansion. *Harvard Business Review*. Retrieved March 8, 2021, from https://hbr.org/2001/09/distance-still-matters-the-hard-reality-of-global-expansion

Ghemawat, P. (2007). *Redefining global strategy*. Harvard Business School.

Gilbert, C., Eyring, M., & Foster, R. N. (2012 December). Two routes to resilience. *Harvard Business Review*. Retrieved March 8, 2021, from https://hbr.org/2012/12/two-routes-to-resilience

Glass blowing history – glassblowing art. (n.d.). History of Glass. Retrieved March 4, 2021, from http://www.historyofglass.com/glass-history/glass-blowing-history/

Good, O. (2013, June 19). *Today is the 40th anniversary of the world's first known video gaming tournament*. Kotaku. Retrieved March 8, 2021, from https://kotaku.com/today-is-the-40th-anniversary-of-the-worlds-first-known-5953371

Gosselin, V. (2019, February 8). *Sneakers: The new it bags for luxury brands*. Heuritech. Retrieved March 8, 2021, from https://www.heuritech.com/blog/articles/sportswear/sneakers-the-new-it-bag-of-luxury-brand

GPHG. (2019, November 11). *Watchonista – the winning watches of the 2019 Grand Prix D'hologerie de Genève (GPHG)*. Grand Prix Horlogerie Geneve. Retrieved March 8, 2021, from https://www.gphg.org/horlogerie/fr/revue-de-presse/2019/11/11/watchonista-winning-watches-2019-grand-prix-dhorlogerie-de-geneve-gphg.

Guilbault, L. (2020, October 22). Kering sales beat expectations, adding to luxury buoyancy. *Vogue Business*. https://www.voguebusiness.com/companies/kering-sales-beat-expectations-adding-to-luxury-buoyancy

Gupta, A. K. (1984). Contingency linkages between strategy and general manager characteristics: A conceptual examination. *Academy of Management Review, 9*, 399–412. https://doi.org/10.5465/amr.1984.4279658

Gupta, A. K., & Govindarajan, V. (1984). Business unit strategy, managerial characteristics and business unit effectiveness at strategy implementation. *Academy of Management Journal, 27*, 25–41. https://doi.org/10.5465/255955

Gupta, A.K. and Govindarajan, V. (2000). Knowledge Flows within Multinational Corporations. Strategic Management Journal, 21, 473–496. http://dx.doi.org/10.1002/(SICI)1097-0266 (200004)21:4<473::AID-SMJ84> http://3.0.CO;2-I

Gupta, A. K., & Govindarajan, V. (2004). *Global strategy and organization*. John Wiley and Sons.

Guthrie, J. P., & Olian, J. D. (1991). Does context affect staffing decisions? The case of general managers. *Personnel Psychology*, (44). https://doi.org/10.1111/j.1744-6570.1991.tb00959.x

Hall, C. (2020, November 9). *How Farfetch-Alibaba-Richemont alliance could change the game in the world's largest luxury market*. Business of Fashion. Retrieved March 8, 2021, from https://www.businessoffashion.com/articles/global-markets/how-the-farfetch-alibaba-richemont-alliance-could-change-the-game-in-the-worlds-largest-luxury-market

Halliday, S. (2019, September 19). *Case Study: Decathlon: getting smart with RFID tags*. Rain Alliance. Retrieved March 8, 2021, from https://rainrfid.org/case-study-decathlon-getting-smart-with-rfid-tags/

Hambrick, D. C., Black, S., & Fredrickson, J. W. (1992). Executive leadership of the high-technology firm: what is special about it?. In L. R. Gomez-Mejia & M. W. Lawless (Eds.), *Advances in Global High-technology Management* (pp. 3–18) (Vol.2). JAI Press.

Handley, L. (2019, July 5). *Sonia Cheng: The Hong Kong CEO on her billionaire family and luxury hotel group Rosewood*. CNBC. Retrieved March 8, 2021, from https://www.cnbc.com/sonia-cheng-the-rosewood-ceo-on-her-family-and-her-hong-kong-hotel/

Harrison, S. (1995, June). Four types of symbolic conflict. *Journal of the Royal Anthropological Institute, 2*(1), 255–272.

Haynes, T. (2021, February 4). *Dopamine, smartphones & you: A battle for your time*. Science in the News. Retrieved March 8, 2021, from https://sitn.hms.harvard.edu/flash/2018/dopamine-smartphones-battle-time/

Helmich, D. L. (1977). Executive succession in the corporate organization. A current investigation. *Academy of Management Review, 2*, 252–266. https://doi.org/10.5465/256123

Hennigs, N., Wiedmann, K., Klarmann, C., & Behrens, S. (2013). Sustainability as part of the luxury essence: Delivering value through social and environmental excellence. *The Journal of Corporate Citizenship*, (52), 25–35. http://www.jstor.org/stable/jcorpciti.52.25

History of Tiffany & Co.: FundingUniverse. (n.d.). Funding Universe. Retrieved March 6, 2021, from http://www.fundinguniverse.com/company-histories/tiffany-co-history/

Hitt, M. A., Ireland, R. D., & Palia, K. A. (1982). Industrial firm's grand strategy and functional importance: moderating effects of technology and uncertainty. *Academy of Management Journal, 2*(25), 265–298. https://doi.org/10.5465/255990

Hofer, C. W. (1980). Turnaround strategies. *Journal of Business Strategy, 1*, 19–31. https://doi.org/10.1108/eb038886

Holcz, A. (2016, June 11). *The economics of anti-corruption: The Chinese luxury goods market*. Curias. Retrieved March 8, 2021, from https://www.curias.net/politics/2016/6/11/the-economics-of-anti-corruption-has-chinas-luxury-goods-market-lost-its-shine

Holland, O. (2020, September 11). *TikTok to host its own digital fashion month*. CNN. Retrieved March 8, 2021, from https://www.cnn.com/style/article/tiktok-fashion-month/index.html

Home – Hofstede insights organisational culture consulting. (2021, March 5). Hofstede Insights. Retrieved March 8, 2021, from https://www.hofstede-insights.com/

Huawei. (2019, May 9). *Huawei presents Fashion Flair: The world's first fashion collection developed using AI* [Press release]. Retrieved March 8, 2021, from https://consumer.huawei.com/uk/press/news/2019/huawei-presents-fashion-flair/

Hymer, S. H. (1960). *The international operations of national firms, a study of direct foreign investment* (Thesis). MIT Department of Economics. Retrieved March 8, 2021, from http://hdl.handle.net/1721.1/27375

Hymer, S. H. (1976). *The international operations of national firms: A study of direct foreign investment*. MIT Press.

Il Messaggero. (2015, June 23). Philipp Plein in Cina risponde alle accuse di razzismo per una t-shirt del 2007. *Il Messaggero*. Retrieved March 8, 2021, from https://www.ilmessaggero.it/moda/stilisti/philipp_plein_cina_risponde_alle_accuse_di_razzismo_t_shirt_2007-1107554.html

International Council of Tanners. (2019). *Statistics & sources of information*. The Global Resource for Leather Industry. Retrieved March 8, 2021, from https://leathercouncil.org/information/statistics-sources-of-information/

Johanson, J., & Vahlne, J.-E. (1977). The internationalization process of the firm: A model of knowledge development and increasing foreign market commitments. *Journal of International Business Studies, 8*(1), 23–32. https://doi.org/10.1057/palgrave.jibs.8490676

Johanson, J., & Wiedersheim-Paul, F. (1975). The internationalization of the firm? Four Swedish cases. *Journal of Management Studies, 12*(3), 305–323. https://doi.org/10.1111/j.1467-6486.1975.tb00514.x

Jones, G. G. (2010). *Beauty imagined: A history of the global beauty industry*. Oxford University Press.

Jones, G., & Atzberger, A. (2015, September 3). *Hans Wilsdorf and Rolex*. Harvard Business School.

Kapferer, J. N. (1998). Why are we seduced by luxury brands?. *J Brand Management, 6*, 44–49. https://doi.org/10.1057/bm.1998.43

Katsikeas, C. S., & Leonidou, L. C. (1996). Export market expansion strategy: Differences between market concentration and market spreading. *Journal of Marketing Management, 1–3*(12), 113–134. https://doi.org/10.1080/0267257X.1996.9964404

Kawano, S., Lu, J., Tsang, R., & Liu, J. (2015, November). *The Asian consumer: The Chinese tourist boom*. The Goldman Sachs Group, Inc. Retrieved March 8, 2021, from https://www.goldman sachs.com/insights/pages/macroeconomic-insights-folder/chinese-tourist-boom/report.pdf

Keller, K. L. (2009). Building strong brands in a modern marketing communications environment. *Journal of Marketing Communications*, *15*(2), 139–155. https://doi.org/10.1080/13527260902757530

Kendo Brands. (2021, March 2). *About our beauty brands: Kendo Brands: Cosmetics*. Retrieved March 8, 2021, from https://kendobrands.com/about-us-2/

Kershaw, S., 2009. Consumed With Guilt. [online] Nytimes.com. Available at: [Accessed 17 November 2020]. <https://www.nytimes.com/2009/08/16/t-magazine/womens-fashion/16brain.html>

Khan, H., & Bamber, D. (2008). Country of origin effects, brand image, and social status in an emerging market. *Human factors and ergonomics in manufacturing*, *5*(18), 580–588. https://doi.org/10.1002/hfm.20126

Khordipour, B. (2019, August 5). *The complete history of cartier*. Estate Diamond Jewelry. Retrieved March 8, 2021, from https://www.estatediamondjewelry.com/the-complete-history-of-cartier/

Koetse, M. (2019, August 15). *Hong Kong protests: Brand 'witch hunt' takes over Chinese internet*. BBC. Retrieved March 8, 2021, from https://www.bbc.com/news/world-asia-china-49354017

Kozak, G. (2018, September 19). *The Ferrari Purosangue, the brand's first SUV, is coming in 2022 . . . and it will be a hybrid*. Autoweek. Retrieved March 8, 2021, from https://www.autoweek.com/news/luxury/a1707571/ferrari-purosangue-brands-first-suv-coming-2022-and-it-will-be-hybrid/

Krueger, A., 2016. *The Inside Story of Bitmojis: Why We Love Them, How They Make Money, Why They Are Here To Stay*. [online] Forbes. Available at: https://www.forbes.com/sites/alysonk rueger/2016/03/24/the-deeper-meaning-behind-bitmojis-why-we-all-love-them-so-much/?sh=3317a5e74a43 [Accessed 26 November 2020].

Landes, D. (2000). *Clocks and the making of the modern world* (revised and enlarged edition). Belknap Press.

Lawrence, F. (2018, August 18). Horsemeat scandal: Where did the 29% horse in your Tesco burger come from? *The Guardian*. Retrieved March 8, 2021, from https://www.theguardian.com/uk-news/2013/oct/22/horsemeat-scandal-guardian-investigation-public-secrecy

Lojacono, G. & Venzin, M. (2008). Da Export Manager a International Business Developer nelle PMI del sistema arredo. Economia & Management, 4, 54–55. http://hdl.handle.net/11565/2161391

Lojacono, G. (2018). The world wears Italian sunglasses. In L. Carcano & G. Lojacono, *Made in Italy industries, managerial issues and best practices*. Bocconi University Press.

Lojacono, G., & Carcano, L. (2018). *Made in Italy industries, managerial issues and best practices*. Bocconi University Press.

Lojacono, G., & Misani, N. (2017). *Davines: Internationalizing a niche*. The Case Center.

Lojacono, G., & Misani, N. (2019). *Farfetch: How to stay ahead of the curve in luxury e-commerce?*. SDA Bocconi Case Study Collection.

Lojacono, G., & Pan, L. (2020). *Ferrari: Exclusivity and resilience*. SDA Bocconi Case Collection.

Lojacono, G., & Zaccai, G. (2004, March). The evolution of the design-inspired enterprise. *MIT Sloan Management Review*. Retrieved March 8, 2021, from https://sloanreview.mit.edu/article/the-evolution-of-the-designinspired-enterprise/

Lim, A. (2019, August 26). *Sephora's HK return: LVMH-owned retailer to offer 'most extensive' beauty brand portfolio*. Cosmeticsdesign-Asia.Com. Retrieved March 8, 2021, from https://www.cosmeticsdesign-asia.com/Article/2019/08/26/Sephora-s-HK-return-LVMH-owned-retailer-to-offer-most-extensive-beauty-brand-portfolio

Luxury Institute. (2020, September 15). *Luxury Institute: Data privacy is a brand reputation issue, not a compliance issue* [Press release]. Retrieved March 8, 2021, from https://www.prnews wire.com/news-releases/luxury-institute-data-privacy-is-a-brand-reputation-issue-not-a-compliance-issue-301131266.html

LVHM. (2020, February 4). *Louis Vuitton celebrates unique ties with Japan with opening of new flagship in Osaka* [Press release]. Retrieved March 8, 2021, from https://www.lvmh.com/news-documents/news/louis-vuitton-celebrates-unique-ties-with-japan-with-opening-of-new-flagship-in-osaka/

Lynton, A. (2013, May 11). *Top 5 Ferrari concepts*. Carbuzz. Retrieved March 8, 2021, from https://carbuzz.com/news/top-5-ferrari-concepts

Made in Italy Accessories. (2014). *History of Leather*. Made in Italy Accessories. Retrieved March 8, 2021, from https://madeinitalyaccessories.com/history-of-leather

Madsen, A. C. (2020, December 6). 5 Things to know about Balenciaga's virtual reality AW21 show. *Vogue*. Retrieved March 8, 2021, from https://www.vogue.co.uk/news/gallery/balenciaga-autumn-winter-2020

Management Decisions. (2019). *There's a snake in my boot!: Kering and the exotic skin dilema*. Corporate Brand Management and Reputation: Master Case Series. Retrieved March 8, 2021, from https://lup.lub.lu.se/luur/download?func=downloadFile&recordOId=8988528&fileOId=8988532

Mandarin Oriental. (2020, October 19). *Mandarin Oriental Hyde Park, London launches "penthouse to penthouse" luxury experience by Harrods* [Press release]. Retrieved March 8, 2021, from https://www.mandarinoriental.com/media-centre/press-releases/corporate-london-penthouse-to-penthouse

Marketing China. 2016. T-Mall has sold 100 new Maserati SUVs. . . in 18 seconds! – Marketing China. [online] Available at: <https://marketingtochina.com/15003-2/> [Accessed 15 October 2020].

Marketing to China. (2018, February 27). *T-Mall has sold 100 new Maserati SUVs . . . in 18 seconds!* Retrieved March 8, 2021, from https://www.marketingtochina.com/15003-2/

Martin, I. M., & Eroglu, S. A. (1993). Measuring a multi-dimensional construct: Country image. *Journal of Business Research, 3* (28), 191–210. https://doi.org/10.1016/0148-2963(93)90047-S

Martuscello, J. (2019, February 26). *Premiumization: The key to brand growth*. Green Book. Retrieved March 8, 2021, from https://www.greenbook.org/mr/brand-impact/premiumization-the-key-to-brand-growth/

McGee, P. (2017, November 8). Electric cars' green image blackens beneath the bonnet. *Financial Times*. Retrieved March 8, 2021, from https://www.ft.com/content/a22ff86e-ba37-11e7-9bfb-4a9c83ffa852

McKinsey & Company. (2020, December). *The state of fashion 2021: In search of promise in perilous times*. Retrieved March 8, 2021, from https://www.mckinsey.com/industries/retail/our-insights/state-of-fashion#

Mellery-Pratt, R. (2015, April 19). *Chanel, the saviour of savoir-faire*. Business of Fashion. Retrieved March 8, 2021, from https://www.businessoffashion.com/community/voices/discussions/how-can-traditional-craftsmanship-survive-in-the-modern-world/chanel-saviour-savoir-faire

Mezias, J. M. (2002). Identifying liabilities of foreignness and strategies to minimize their effects: the case of labor lawsuit judgments in the United States. *Strategic Management Journal, 23*(3), 229–244. https://doi.org/10.1002/smj.220

Michaelis, M., Woisetschlager, D., Backhaus, C., & Ahlert, D. (2008). The effects of country of origin and corporate reputation on initial trust: An experimental evaluation of the perception of Polish consumers. *International Marketing Review, 25*(4), 404–422. https://doi.org/

Michel, G., & Willing, R. (2020). *The art of successful brand collaborations*. Routledge. https://doi.org/10.4324/9781351014472

Michel, J. G., & Hambrick, D. (1992). Diversification posture and top management team characteristics. *Academy of Management Journal, 35*(1), 9–37. https://doi.org/10.2307/256471

Millenary Watches. (2020, March 2). *How many watches does Patek Philippe make per year?* Retrieved March 8, 2021, from https://millenarywatches.com/many-patek-philippe-watches-per-year/

Milligan, L. (2019, August 15). Why Michele's Gucci will not go on sale. *British Vogue*. Retrieved March 8, 2021, from https://www.vogue.co.uk/article/no-gucci-sale-markdown-not-discounting-for-black-friday

Minichilli, A., & Quarato, F. (2020). Ownership and corporate governance. In G. Corbetta & P. Morosetti, *Corporate strategy for a sustainable growth* (pp. 159–174). Bocconi University Press.

Ministero dello sviluppo economico. (2019, November 14). *La blockchain per tutelare il Made in Italy*. Governo Italiano. Retrieved March 8, 2021, from https://www.mise.gov.it/index.php/it/198-notizie-stampa/2040469-le-blockchain-per-tutelare-il-made-in-italy

Morosetti, P. (2020a). The Choice of the Core Business. In G. Corbetta & P. Morosetti, *Corporate strategy for a sustainable growth* (pp. 55–62). Bocconi University Press.

Morosetti, P. (2020b). Chapter 6 "Scale and corporate scope" and Chapter 7 "Growth with a synergy approach". In G. Corbetta & P. Morosetti, *Corporate strategy for a sustainable growth* (pp. 63–88). Bocconi University Press.

Morris, L. G. (2019, December 12). How Hermès' Petit H highlights its creative process via temporary takeovers. *Frame*. Retrieved March 8, 2021, from https://www.frameweb.com/article/how-hermes-petit-h-highlights-its-creative-process-via-temporary-takeovers

Mosk, C. A. (2007). The role of tradition in Japan's industrialization: Another path to industrialization (review). *Journal of Japanese Studies*, *33*(2), 529–533. https://doi.org/10.1353/jjs.2007.0073

Nielsen. (2016). *Moving on up: Premium products are in high demand around the world*. Nielsen. Retrieved March 8, 2021 from https://www.nielsen.com/wp-content/uploads/sites/3/2019/04/EstudoGlobal_ProdutosPremium.pdf

Ohmae, K. (1986, March 1). Becoming a triad power: The new global corporation. *International Marketing Review*. https://doi.org/10.1108/eb008307

Ohmae, K. (1989, March-April). The global logic of strategic alliance. *Harvard Business Review*. Retrieved March 8, 2021, from https://hbr.org/1989/03/the-global-logic-of-strategic-alliances

O'Reilly, C. A., & Tushman, M. L. (2004, April). The ambidextrous organization. *Harvard Business Review*, *4*(82), 74–81. Retrieved March 8, 2021, from https://hbr.org/2004/04/the-ambidextrous-organization

O'Reilly, C. A., & Tushman, M. L. (2008, December). Ambidexterity as a dynamic capability: Resolving the innovator's dilemma. *Research in Organizational Behavior*, (28), 185–206. https://doi.org/10.1016/j.riob.2008.06.002

Ossola, G. (2020, August 6). The omnichannel playbook. *Vogue Business*. Retrieved March 8, 2021, from https://www.voguebusiness.com/consumers/insight-report-the-omnichannel-playbook

Ovans, A. (2020, November 17). What is a business model? *Harvard Business Review*. Retrieved March 8, 2021, from https://hbr.org/2015/01/what-is-a-business-model

Oxfam Media. (2020). *Confronting carbon inequality: Putting climate justice at the heart of the Covid-19 recovery*. Retrieved March 8, 2021, from https://www.oxfam.org/en/research/confronting-carbon-inequality

Passport, Euromonitor International (2020, December). Where and How Consumers Shop in Fashion and Luxury Goods. Euromonitor.

Pan, Y. (2019, January 7). *Bvlgari's Chinese New Year campaign isn't Kosher*. Jing Daily. Retrieved March 8, 2021, from https://jingdaily.com/bvlgari-china-jew/

Pangaia. (n.d.). *Pangaia*. Retrieved March 4, 2021, from https://thepangaia.com/

Parisi, D. (2020, December 3). *Why more fashion brands are investing in Snapchat's Bitmoji*. Glossy. Retrieved March 8, 2021, from https://www.glossy.co/fashion/bitmoji-attracting-ad-dollars-from-big-fashion-brands/

Parker-Pope, T. (2005, December 6). This is your brain at the mall: Why shopping makes you feel so good. *Wall Street Journal*. Retrieved March 8, 2021, from https://www.wsj.com/articles/SB113382650575214543

Paton, E. (2018, August 20). Farfetch, online retailer, plans to go public as luxury e-commerce grows. *The New York Times*. Retrieved March 8, 2021, from https://www.nytimes.com/2018/08/20/business/dealbook/farfetch-ipo.html

Pfeffer, J. & Salancik, G. R. (1978). *The external control of organizations: a resource dependence perspective*. Harper and Row.

Phelps, N. (2019, December 9). Louis Vuitton's new capsule with League of Legends brings French high fashion to online gaming – and vice versa. *Vogue*. Retrieved March 8, 2021, from https://www.vogue.com/article/louis-vuittons-new-capsule-with-league-of-legends

Pickell, D. (2019, August 20). *What is esports and how did it become a $1 billion industry?* Learning Hub. Retrieved March 8, 2021, from https://learn.g2.com/esports#:%7E:text=Esports%20traces%20its%20origins%20back,Invaders%20Championship%20yielded%2010%2C000%20participants.&text=As%20the%202000s%20rolled%20around,Gaming%20(MLG)%20in%202002.

Pieraccini, S. (2020, November 11). Nasce Fendi Factory, nel distretto della pelletteria di lusso impianto di 60 milioni. *Il Sole 24 Ore*. Retrieved March 8, 2021, from https://www.ilsole24ore.com/art/nasce-fendi-factory-distretto-pelletteria-lusso-impianto-60-milioni-ADJccj1?refresh_ce=1

Piron, F. (2000). Consumers' perceptions of the country-of-origin effect on purchasing intentions of (in)conspicuous products. *Journal of Consumer Marketing*, 4(17), 308–321. http://doi.org/10.1108/07363760010335330

Plażyk, K. (2014). *The democratization of luxury: A new form of luxury*. The 9th International Scientific Conference for PhD Students and Young Scientists, Bratislava, Slovakia.

Pott, H. F. L. (1928). *A short history of Shanghai: Being an account of the growth and development of the international settlement*. Kelly & Walsh.

Prada. (n.d.). *Prada nylon*. Prada Group. Retrieved March 4, 2021, from https://www.pradagroup.com/en/perspectives/stories/sezione-know-how/prada-nylon.html

Prahalad, C. K., & Hamel, G. (1990, May-June). The core competence of the corporation. *Harvard Business Review*. Retrieved March 8, 2021 from https://hbr.org/1990/05/the-core-competence-of-the-corporation

Rapp, J. (2017, March 13). *Luxury automakers in China are getting smart about e-commerce*. Jing Daily. Retrieved March 8, 2021, from https://jingdaily.com/luxury-automakers-china-getting-smart-e-commerce/

Ravasi D., & Rindova V. (2008, September). Creating symbolic value: A cultural perspective on production and exchange. *SDA Bocconi Research Paper*, 111(04). http://doi.org/10.2139/ssrn.1265021

Rees, C. (2018, March 20). Rosso Ferrari. *Ferrari Magazine*. Retrieved March 8, 2021, from https://magazine.ferrari.com/en/cars/2018/03/20/news/ferrari_colors_rosso_portofino_rosso_corsa_racing_red-38043

Reuters. (2020a, March 30). *UPDATE 1-French luxury group Hermes reduces proposed dividend over coronavirus*. Retrieved March 8, 2021, from https://www.reuters.com/article/hermes-dividend/update-1-french-luxury-group-hermes-reduces-proposed-dividend-over-coronavirus-idUSL8N2BN8TH

Reuters. (2020b, June 20). *Gucci hikes handbag prices to curb coronavirus hit*. Business of Fashion. Retrieved March 8, 2021, from https://www.businessoffashion.com/articles/luxury/gucci-hikes-handbag-prices-to-curb-coronavirus-hit

Rezvani, S., Shenyari, G., Dehkordi, G. J., Salehi, M., Nahid, N., & Soleimani, S. (2012). Country of origin: A study over perspective of intrinsic and extrinsic cues on consumers' purchase decision. *Business Management Dynamics, 11*(1), 68–75.

Rigby, C. (2020, November 13). *Farfetch reports strong sales growth as shoppers turn online to buy luxury goods – and narrowing pre-tax losses.* Internet Retailing. Retrieved March 8, 2021, from https://internetretailing.net/strategy-and-innovation/strategy-and-innovation/farfetch-re ports-strong-sales-growth-as-shoppers-turn-online-to-buy-luxury-goods–and-narrowing-pre-tax-losses

Roberts, L. (2010, June 16). Lamborghini is the least environmentally friendly car. *The Telegraph.* Retrieved March 8, 2021, from https://www.telegraph.co.uk/news/earth/environment/ 7831634/Lamborghini-is-the-least-environmentally-friendly-car.html

Rosenbloom, S. (2011, September 11). Way off the runway: Live streaming of fashion week. *The New York Times.* Retrieved March 8, 2021, from https://www.nytimes.com/2011/09/08/fashion/ live-streaming-of-runway-shows-new-york-fashion-week.html

Rynes, S. L., Orlitzky, R. D., & Bretz, Jr. (1997). Experienced hiring versus college recruiting: Practices and emerging trends. *Personnel Psychology, 50*(2), 309–339. https://doi.org/ 10.1111/j.1744-6570.1997.tb00910.x

Saaty, T. L. (2013). The modern science of multicriteria decision making and its practical applications: The AHP/ANP approach. *Operations Research, 61*(5), 1101–1118. https://doi.org/ 10.1287/opre.2013.1197

Salsberg, B. (2009, August). *Japan's luxury shoppers move on.* Mckinsey & Co.: Retrieved March 8, 2021, from https://www.mckinsey.com/~/media/McKinsey/Industries/Retail/Our%20In sights/Japans%20luxury%20shoppers%20move%20on/Japans%20luxury%20shoppers% 20move%20on.pdf?shouldIndex=false

Salter, S. (2019, May 1). *Meet the dior cruise collaborator who dressed nelson mandela.* I.D. Vice. Retrieved March 8, 2021, from https://i-d.vice.com/en_us/article/neanmz/meet-the-dior-cruise-collaborator-who-dressed-nelson-mandela

Sanders, E. (2020, November 11). *What do luxury brands' inflating prices mean for them & for the industry at large?.* The Fashion Law. Retrieved March 8, 2021, from https://www.thefashion law.com/what-do-luxury-brands-inflating-prices-mean-for-them-for-the-industry-at-large/

Schendel, D., Patton, G. R., & Riggs, J. (1976). Corporate turnaround strategies: A study of profit decline and recovery. *Journal of General Management, 3*(3), 3–11. https://doi.org/10.1177/ 030630707600300301

Schoemaker, P. J. H. (1991, November). When and how to use scenario planning: A heuristic approach with illustration. *Journal of Forecasting, 6*(10), 549–564. https://doi.org/10.1002/for. 3980100602

Schwartz, K. B., & Menon, K. (1985). Executive succession in failing firms. *Academy of Management Journal,* (28), 680–686. https://doi.org/10.5465/256123

Schwartz, P. (1996). *The art of the long view.* Currency Doubleday.

SDA Bocconi School of Management. (n.d.). *Strategie di reshoring e punti di forza del tessuto industriale calzaturiero italiano.* SDA Bocconi School of Management for ANCI (Associazione Italiana Calzaturifici Italiani).

Sherman, L. (2014, October 31). *The secret journey of a fashion piece. – Part 2: Manufacturing and production.* Business of Fashion. Retrieved March 8, 2021, from https://www.businessoffa shion.com/articles/news-analysis/secret-journey-fashion-piece-part-2-manufacturing-production

Sherman, L. (2020, November 15). *Richemont needs a transformational move,* Business of Fashion. Retrieved March 8, 2021, from https://www.businessoffashion.com/articles/luxury/richemont-needs-a-transformational-move

Shipilov, A. & Godart, F. (2015, June). Luxury's talent factories. *Harvard Business Review*. Retrieved March 8, 2021, from https://hbr.org/2015/06/luxurys-talent-factories

Shiseido Repositions Its Clé de Peau Beauté Brand for Global Luxury Market. (2010, November 15). Global Cosmetics Industry. Retrieved March 8, 2021, from https://www.gcimagazine.com/business/marketers/positioning/108169884.html

Shorrocks, A., Davies, J., & Lluberas, R. (2020, October). *Global wealth report 2020*. Credit Suisse Research Institute.

Silbert, J. (2018, January 23). *Balenciaga confirms Triple S is now made in China*. Hypebeast. Retrieved March 8, 2021, from https://hypebeast.com/2018/1/balenciaga-triple-s-made-in-china.

Silver, D. (2019, March 26). Charting the evolution of Gucci. *CR Fashion Book*. Retrieved March 8, 2021, from https://www.crfashionbook.com/fashion/a26934683/evolution-gucci-designer/#

Slater, S., & Umemura, M. (2017). Country of origin narratives of brand image for Japanese cosmetics through a consumer lens: An abstract. *Marketing at the Confluence between Entertainment and Analytics*, 645. Springer, Cham.

Snell, S. E., & Bigelow, T. (2019, November). *Chalhoub Group: Transforming the luxury retailer*. University of Virginia, Darden School Foundation, Charlottesville, VA.

Socha, M., & Esch, L. (2020, November 18). Coed design duos are proliferating in fashion. *WWD*. Retrieved March 8, 2021, from https://wwd.com/fashion-news/fashion-features/fashion-coed-design-duos-prada-raf-kim-jones-fendi-1234644011/

Spezzy (2021, March 4). *How many people play League of Legends? – UPDATED 2021*. LeagueFeed. Retrieved March 8, 2021, from https://leaguefeed.net/did-you-know-total-league-of-legends-player-count-updated/#:%7E:text=League%20of%20Legends%20has%20reached,become%20the%20King%20of%20Games

Starbuck, W. H., & Hedberg, B. L. T. (1977). Saving an organization from a stagnating environment. In H. B. Thorelli (Ed.), *Strategy + Structure = Performance* (pp. 249–258). Indiana University Press.

Statista. (2019, September 3). *Made-In index: Attributes associated with products made in Italy 2017*. Retrieved March 8, 2021, from https://www.statista.com/statistics/683810/made-in-index-attributes-associated-with-products-made-in-italy/

Statista. (2020a, October 13). *Revenue of the global eSports market 2018–2023*. Retrieved March 8, 2021, from https://www.statista.com/statistics/490522/global-esports-market-revenue/#:%7E:text=Revenue%20of%20the%20global%20eSports%20market%202018%2D2023&text=In%202020%2C%20the%20global%20eSports,rapidly%20in%20the%20coming%20years

Statista. (2020b, November 23). *Leading 10 footwear producers worldwide 2013–2019, by country*. Retrieved March 8, 2021, from https://www.statista.com/statistics/227256/leading-10-global-footwear-producers-by-country/

Statista. (2020c, November 27). *Leading eSports tournaments worldwide as of 2020, by prize pool*. Retrieved March 8, 2021, from https://www.statista.com/statistics/517940/leading-esports-tournamets-worldwide-by-prize-pool/

Statista. (2021a, March 1). *Leading personal luxury goods markets worldwide in 2020, by country*. Retrieved March 8, 2021, from https://www.statista.com/statistics/245645/leading-personal-luxury-goods-markets-by-country/

Statista. (2021b, March 3). *Number of tourist arrivals in Venice 2003–2020*. Retrieved March 8, 2021, from https://www.statista.com/statistics/732406/overnight-tourist-arrivals-in-venice-italy/

Sull, D. & Turconi, S. (2008). Fast fashion lessons. *Business Strategy Review*, *19*(2), 4–11. https://doi.org/10.1111/j.1467-8616.2008.00527.x

Tageos. (2016, April). *Decathlon: Leading sporting goods retailer uses RFID to identify millions of items worldwide*. Retrieved March 8, 2021, from http://www.tageos.com/assets/2016-04-25-Tageos-Case-Study-Decathlon.pdf

Tetsuji, O. (2015, February 9). *Lessons from the Japanese miracle: Building the foundations for a new growth paradigm*. Nippon.com. Retrieved March 8, 2021, from https://www.nippon.com/en/in-depth/a04003/#:~:text=Japan's%20Postwar%20Miracle&text=The%20devastated%20Japanese%20economy%20rose,era%20of%20rapid%20growth%20era

Thomsen, S. & Pedersen, T. (2000). Ownership structure and economic performance in the largest European companies. *Strategic Management Journal, 21*(6), 689–705. https://doi.org/10.1002/(SICI)1097-0266(200006)21:6%3C689::AID-SMJ115%3E3.0.CO;2-Y

Tollefson, J. (2020). Why deforestation and extinctions make pandemics more likely. *Nature, 584* (7820), 175–176. https://doi.org/10.1038/d41586-020-02341-1

Trimmer, C. & Godar, J. (2019). *Calculating maritime shipping Emissions per traded commodity* (SEI Brief). Stockholm Environment Institute. Retrieved March 8, 2021, from https://www.sei.org/publications/shipping-emissions-per-commodity/

Tucker, J. (2019, April 8). *Creative entrepreneurs: Employees come first for Sir Richard Branson*. Headspace. Retrieved March 8, 2021, from https://www.headspacegroup.co.uk/sir-richard-branson-employees-come-first/

Unknown. (2010, November 15). *Shiseido Repositions Its Clé de Peau Beauté Brand for Global Luxury Market*. Retrieved from Global Cosmetics Industry: https://www.gcimagazine.com/business/marketers/positioning/108169884.html

Urbonavičius, S., & Gineikienė, J. (2009). Importance of the product country-of-origin factor on purchasing process in the context of globalization. *Ekonomika, 85*, 37–44

Varacca P., & Misani N. (2017). *Fashion collections: Product development and merchandising*. Bocconi University Press.

Veale, R., & Quester, P. (2009). Do consumer expectations match experience? Predicting the influence of price and country of origin on perceptions of product quality. *International Business Review*, 2(18),134–144. https://doi.org/10.1016/j.ibusrev.2009.01.004

Velasquez, A., & Donaldson, T. (2018, August 15). Sourcing snapshot: Global footwear manufacturing and trade. *Sourcing Journal*. Retrieved March 8, 2021, from https://sourcingjournal.com/feature/global-footwear-manufacturing-snapshot-115380/

Verganti, R. (2009). *Design-driven innovation: changing the rules of competition by radically innovating what things mean*. Harvard Business School Press.

Vianelli, D., & Marzano, F. C. (2012). *L'effetto country of origin sull'intenzione d'acquisto del consumatore: una literature review*. EUT Edizione Universita di Trieste.

Vigneron, C. (2021, January). Post [Linkedin.com]. Retrieved March 8, 2021, from https://www.linkedin.com/in/cyrille-vigneron-b21b1512/?originalSubdomain=ch

Vishwanath, V., & Rigby, D. K. (2006, April). Localization: The revolution in consumer markets. *Harvard Business Review*. Retrieved March 8, 2021, from https://hbr.org/2006/04/localization-the-revolution-in-consumer-markets

Vogue. (2013, October 29). The Tank, one store that's always on sale. *Vogue India*. Retrieved March 8, 2021, from https://www.vogue.in/content/the-tank-mumbai-always-on-sale

Wattles, J. (2017, September 9). *Ferrari sells for record $10 million at charity auction*. CNN Business. Retrieved March 8, 2021, from https://money.cnn.com/2017/09/09/autos/ferrari-aperta-charity-auction/index.html

Westreich, S. (2020, October 15). *Camels, not unicorns, are the new darlings of Silicon Valley*. UX Collective. Retrieved March 8, 2021, from https://uxdesign.cc/camels-not-unicorns-are-the-new-darlings-of-silicon-valley

White, S., & Denis, P. (2018, March 27). *Louis Vuitton expands French manufacturing to meet handbag demand*. Reuters. Retrieved March 8, 2021, from https://www.reuters.com/article/us-lvmh-vuitton-manufacturing/louis-vuitton-expands-french-manufacturing-to-meet-handbag-demand-idUSKBN1H32X3

Wiedmann, T., Lenzen, M., Keyßer, L. T., & Steinberger, J. K. (2020). Scientists' warning on affluence. *Nature Communications*, *11* (1),n/a. https://doi.org/10.1038/s41467-020-16941-y

Wiersema, M. F., & Bantel, K. A. (1992). Top Management team demography and corporate strategic change. *Academy of Management Journal*, *1*(35), 91–121. https://doi.org/10.5465/256474

William. (2018, September 24). *Cartier opens luxury Juste un Clou convenience store in Omotesando, Tokyo*. Japan Trends. Retrieved March 8, 2021, from https://www.japantrends.com/cartier-luxury-juste-un-clou-convenience-store-omotesando-tokyo/

Wingard, J. (2019, August 2). Rihanna's 'Fenty Beauty': a leadership case for customer inclusivity. *Forbes*. Retrieved March 8, 2021, from https://www.forbes.com/sites/jasonwingard/2019/08/02/rihannas-fenty-beauty-a-leadership-case-for-customer-inclusivity/#6379fea93460

Worldometer. (n.d.). *United States population (2021): Worldometer*. Retrieved March 6, 2021, from https://www.worldometers.info/world-population/us-population/

Zaheer, S. (1995, April). Overcoming the liability of foreignness. *The Academy of Management Journal*, *2*(38), 341–363. https://doi.org/10.5465/256683

Zajac, E.J. (1990). CEO selection, succession, compensation and firm performance: A theoretical integration and empirical analysis. *Strategic Management Journal*, *11*(3), 217–230. https://doi.org/10.1002/smj.4250110304

Zargani, L., 2021. Prada Signs New Loan Linked to Sustainability Targets. [online] WWD. Available at: https://wwd.com/sustainability/business/prada-signs-new-loan-linked-to-sustainability-targets-1234726927/ [Accessed 15 February 2021].

Zhang, Q. (2008). What and how can we learn from ZARA. *IEEE International Conference on Service Operations and Logistics, and Informatics*, 2464–2468.

Zhang, T. (2019, June 26). Brands get creative with WeChat Mini-Programs. *WWD*. Retrieved March 8, 2021, from https://wwd.com/business-news/technology/brands-are-getting-creative-with-wechat-mini-programs-1203203729/

Zohar, E. W. (2020, March 25). Dorchester Collection protects jobs and salaries for all employees worldwide during coronavirus crisis. *Forbes*. Retrieved March 8, 2021, from https://www.forbes.com/sites/ericawertheimzohar/2020/03/24/dorchester-collection-protects-jobs-and-salaries-for-all-employees-worldwide-during-coronavirus-crisis/?sh=80475432430

Zook C., & Allen J. (2001). *Profit from the core*. Harvard Business School Press.

Zook, C. (2004). *Beyond the core: Expand your market without abandoning your roots*. Harvard Business School Press.

Zook, C. (2007, April). Finding next core business. *Harvard Business Review*. Retrieved March 8, 2021, from https://hbr.org/2007/04/finding-your-next-core-business

List of Figures

https://doi.org/10.1515/9783110723519-010

List of Tables

https://doi.org/10.1515/9783110723519-011

Index

Note: The abbreviation COO stands for Country of Origin. CRM is used for Customer Relationship Management; TBL for triple bottom line.

https://doi.org/10.1515/9783110723519-012

About the Authors

Gabriella Lojacono is Associate Professor at the Department of Management and Technology and Director of the Made in Italy Vertical, B4I, Bocconi University.

She is a senior researcher of the Gucci Lab, Bocconi University. From January 2017 to December 2020, she was Faculty Deputy of the Strategy and Entrepreneurship Knowledge Group. She has been the Director of the Executive Master EMiLux, SDA Bocconi since 2016. She has run several executive education open programs and custom initiatives with some of the leading companies in apparel and leather goods, design, jewelry, hospitality, F&B, automotive, eyewear, and cosmetics. Her research projects have focused on the international growth of the Made in Italy industries and companies as well as on luxury strategy and business models.

She is the author of numerous books and articles on her topics of interest. Her works have been published in Economia & Management, Sloan Management Review, Long Range Planning, and International Business Review, among others. She has authored numerous case studies, filed in international databases, about multinational companies such as Farfetch, Starbucks, Davines, Inditex, Ferrari, Illy, Gucci, and Valentino. Gabriella earned a degree in Business Administration from Università Bocconi with a specialization in Finance, then a Ph.D. in Economics and Management from SDA Bocconi and an ITP (International Teachers Programme) organized by ISBM at HEC in Paris. During her Ph.D., she was a Visiting Scholar at Copenhagen Business School.

Laura Ru Yun Pan is an SDA Lecturer in the Department of Strategy and Entrepreneurship at SDA Bocconi School of Management and an Academic Fellow at Bocconi University. She is also a junior researcher in the Gucci Lab and recently appointed as the coordinator of the Executive Master in Luxury Management (EMiLUX), SDA Bocconi.

Prior to entering the faculty, Laura spent most of her career as a process engineer in various industries such as manufacturing, wastewater treatment, automotive, and oil and gas. However, her area of expertise is in process optimization, operations, environmental management, and sustainability. Having spent a career working in various companies across different countries, she was able to gain a global perspective on the context of multinational companies.

Laura Pan has a double degree in Chemical Engineering and Food Manufacturing from RMIT University, Australia. In 2018, she graduated with a Master of Business Administration (MBA) from SDA Bocconi school of Management, with a specialization in Luxury Business Management. Upon the completion of her MBA, she worked in retail operation at Loro Piana and gained a deeper understanding of how a luxury company operates.

https://doi.org/10.1515/9783110723519-013

CPSIA information can be obtained
at www.ICGtesting.com
Printed in the USA
JSHW030959080921
18552JS00002B/66